SO-AIN-759

KF   Koh, Harold Hongju   26,284
4651
.K64 The national security
1990   constitution

DATE DUE

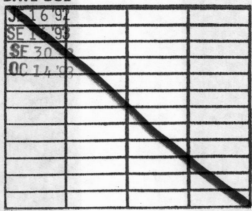

5-91
35.⁰⁰
B+T
VER

THE NATIONAL SECURITY CONSTITUTION

THE NATIONAL

SECURITY

CONSTITUTION

SHARING POWER AFTER
THE IRAN-CONTRA AFFAIR

HAROLD HONGJU KOH

YALE UNIVERSITY PRESS

NEW HAVEN AND LONDON

VERMONT REGIONAL
JUNIOR COLLEGE LIBRARY

Copyright © 1990 by Mary-Christy Fisher, Trustee. All rights
reserved. This book may not be reproduced, in whole or in
part, including illustrations, in any form (beyond that copying
permitted by Sections 107 and 108 of the U.S. Copyright Law
and except by reviewers for the public press), without written
permission from the publishers.

Set in Times Roman type by The Composing Room of
Michigan, Inc. Printed in the United States of America by
Vail-Ballou Press, Binghamton, New York.

Library of Congress Cataloging-in-Publication Data
Koh, Harold Hongju, 1954–
    The national security constitution : sharing power after the
    Iran-Contra Affair / Harold Hongju Koh.
        p.   cm.
    Includes bibliographical references.
    ISBN 0–300–04492–5 (alk. paper). —
    ISBN 0–300–04493–3 (pbk. : alk. paper)
1. United States—Foreign relations—Law and legislation.
2. Separation of powers—United States.   3. United States—
National security—Law and legislation.   4. Iran-Contra
Affair, 1985–   5. North, Oliver—Trials, litigation, etc.
I. Title.
KF4651.K64   1990
342.73′0412—dc20
[347.302412]   89-25042
                                                          CIP

The paper in this book meets the guidelines of permanence
and durability of the Committee on Production Guidelines for
Book Longevity of the Council on Library Resources.

10   9   8   7   6   5   4   3   2   1

To my parents,
my life teachers, and
to Mary-Christy and Emily,
my life companions

Contents

Acknowledgments

I began grappling with the constitutional issues surrounding the conduct of our foreign affairs nearly a decade ago while serving as a law clerk to two courageous judges who later became my heroes, Justice Harry A. Blackmun and Ambassador Malcolm Richard Wilkey. My sustained encounter with these questions commenced in 1983, when I spent two years as an attorney-adviser in the Office of Legal Counsel of the United States Department of Justice. Ted Olson and Larry Simms, two outstanding lawyers in that office, showed me that the struggle among the branches for control of foreign affairs was not simply an academic exercise, but a matter of pressing national concern, as well as the guts of a government lawyer's trade. After I came to Yale Law School in 1985, students in my course "Legal Constraints on the Foreign Affairs Power" stimulated my thinking on these questions and forced me to address them in the context of the Iran-contra affair. One of those students, Peter Bass, encouraged me to set forth my ideas in the article that culminated in this book, "Why the President (Almost) Always Wins in Foreign Affairs: Lessons of the Iran-Contra Affair" (97 *Yale Law Journal* 1255, 1988). While writing that article I presented portions of it at the April 1987 annual meeting of the American Society of International Law, the November 1987 Federalist Society Conference entitled "Foreign Affairs and the Constitution" (later published in 43 *U. Miami L. Rev.* 106, 1988, which holds copyright on that article and has granted permission to reprint portions of it here), the November 1987 Hofstra University Presidential Conference entitled "Richard Nixon: A Retrospective on his

Presidency" (conference proceedings forthcoming from Greenwood Press), and the Yale Law School Faculty Workshop.

My dean, Guido Calabresi, always said yes and by word and deed continually reaffirmed my hope that scholarship could be accomplished with humanity as well as excellence. Marian Ash, Otto Bohlmann, John Covell, Karen Gangel, and Stacey Mandelbaum of the Yale University Press provided welcome patience and support; Lorraine Alexson edited the manuscript magnificently. At Yale Law School, Kay Bradley, Gene Coakley, Russ Hentz, Joanne Kittredge, and Peter Paris have been special friends, supplying endless assistance without complaint. Five talented Yale Law students—Jack Goldsmith, David Hayes, Geoff Klineberg, Jeff Meyer, and Ron Slye—have offered crucial research assistance and friendship. My colleagues at Yale and elsewhere have pressed, provoked, and patted me on the back. I owe special thanks to Bruce Ackerman, Akhil Amar, Jules Coleman, Theodore Draper, Dan Freed, Bob Ellickson, Owen Fiss, Paul Kahn, Rob Kurz, Gerry Lynch, Jules Lobel, Marc Miller, Alice Miskimin, Gerry Neuman, Stephen F. Ross, Peter Schuck, Gaddis Smith, Kate Stith, Charles Tiefer, and Harry Wellington, all of whom made vital contributions to this manuscript.

My parents, Doctors Kwang Lim and Hesung Chun Koh, have supplied me with a lifetime of love and an ideal of scholarship that has sustained me for every moment of my professional career. My siblings (in flesh and in law) and their families have renewed me continually with their faith and spirit. William and Sally Fisher and Mary O'Hagan have acted as my second parents. And through it all, Mary-Christy Fisher and Emily Jennings Youngyon Koh, my wife and daughter, have made it all worthwhile. The last days of preparing this book have been the most difficult. Just before the manuscript saw print, my father, Dr. Kwang Lim Koh, suddenly passed away. Nothing will ever be the same. Yet in these pages my father lives. As my wife and daughter have been my dearest friends, my parents have been my wisest teachers. It is to our life together that I dedicate this book.

Introduction

As the nation settles into its post-Reagan years, the Iran-contra affair has begun to fade into the mists of time. Yet even as the affair itself recedes from public consciousness, its participants have assumed new and important positions in public life. Five months after Ronald Reagan relinquished office as the most popular president of modern times, a federal judge sentenced the affair's central protagonist, Lt. Col. Oliver North, to a suspended sentence, civil fines, and community service.[1] Shortly after former Vice President George Bush ascended to the White House as president, the affair's most celebrated investigators accepted leading roles in an executive branch and Congress that pledged new fealty to a bipartisan foreign policy. The new president appointed one of the three members of the Tower commission, Brent Scowcroft, as his national security assistant and named Dick Cheney, the ranking Republican on the House Iran-Contra Committee, as his secretary of defense. Even as these executive transitions occurred, the House and Senate elected two other prominent members of their Iran-contra committees, Thomas Foley and George Mitchell, to serve as Speaker of the House and Senate majority leader, respectively.[2]

As these veterans of the Iran-contra affair assume command of United States foreign policy for the 1990s, it is worth asking whether they—or any of us, for that matter—have properly learned the lessons of the affair. For that unhappy historical episode has left in its wake two competing conventional wisdoms, which now seem jointly to have adherents among most members of the American public. The first view, suggested by the reports of both the Tower commission and the majority members of the Iran-contra congressional committees, is that the Iran-contra affair resulted primarily from a failure of people and not of laws.[3] Holders of this view treat the affair as a lesson in executive hubris. Like Watergate, they argue, the Iran-contra affair shows that second-term presidencies riding high on landslide political victories overreach, at which point the checks and balances within our constitutional system bring them into line. Thus, Contragate, like Watergate, is ultimately a cause for celebration because in the end, the "system worked."[4] Congress need not now consider new national security legislation to prevent future Iran-contra affairs, both because those responsible have departed and because, as the majority members of the Iran-contra committees put it, "Congress cannot legislate good judgment, honesty, or fidelity to law."[5]

Those maintaining the second, contradictory conventional view—asserted by the Iran-contra committees' minority members (among others)—consider the affair an exercise in congressional folly. Having unearthed no smoking gun answer to the Watergate question—What did the president know and when did he know it?—proponents of this view conclude that the congressional hearings represented yet another effort by a Democratic Congress to "micromanage" a Republican president's foreign policy.[6] This perspective depicts the independent counsel Lawrence Walsh's prosecution of Oliver North, Vice Adm. John Poindexter, Maj. Gen. Richard Secord, and Albert Hakim as a congressional attempt "to criminalize policy differences between co-equal branches of government and the executive's conduct of foreign affairs."[7] Subscribers to this view thus deem new national security legislation to be not only unnecessary, but in the words of the minority members of the Iran-contra committees, "unconstitutional and unwise" and "unconscionably meddlesome."[8]

In my judgment, both views about the Iran-contra affair are dangerously incomplete. Neither fully recognizes the affair for what it was, a nearly successful assault upon the constitutional structures and norms that underlie our postwar national security system—what I will call our *National Security Constitution* (a concept that I define in chapter 3 and that I capitalize throughout). To treat the Iran-contra affair solely as an exercise in executive hubris or congressional folly is to ignore its broader historical significance: as an uncured constitutional crisis in national security decision making that waits to afflict us anew. I argue that we must learn a different lesson from the Iran-contra affair. In the end, that affair should be understood not as a case of bad people violating good laws (as the various investigators concluded), or of good people violating bad laws (as Oliver North's supporters maintained), but of seriously mis-guided people violating seriously ineffective national security laws. In the long run, simply throwing out one group of officials or renewing homage to a "bipartisan foreign policy" can offer only partial and tran-sient solutions to this grave, lingering national problem.

The chapters that follow are not meant to add yet another volume to the rapidly growing list of completed or pending Iran-contra autopsies and biographies.[9] Instead, I argue a deeper point—that history should re-member the Iran-contra affair not as an aberration, an error on the part of certain individuals within a particular administration, but as a fundamen-tal failure of the legal structure that regulates the relations among the president, Congress, and the courts in foreign affairs. Those who hold both conventional views of the Iran-contra affair have misjudged its import in three crucial respects. First, each faction has mistaken the relevant historical precedent for the Iran-contra affair, which was not Watergate but Vietnam. Second, each has misdiagnosed the underlying problem. The Iran-contra affair represents not simply the wayward acts of a few personalities, but deeper systemic flaws in our foreign policy-making process. Third, and inevitably, by misunderstanding both the precedent and the problem underlying the affair, proponents of both views have reached the wrong prescription. The first group rejects new laws as unnecessary, reasoning that our national security system is ulti-mately self-regulating; the second rejects new laws because it considers that system as currently overregulated. Yet what the Iran-contra affair actually reveals is that our national security system is *inadequately* regu-lated. To cure that inadequacy, our new president and Congress must work together to enact framework legislation—a new national security charter—that will modernize our National Security Constitution for the twenty-first century.

In this book I present a different view of the precedent, problem, and prescription for the Iran-contra affair. In the first part I unearth the histor-ical precedent for the affair. In chapter 1, I examine why each of the three principal investigators of the affair—the Iran-contra committees, the Tower commission, and the independent counsel—failed to grasp the broader import of the affair. After reviewing the reports of the committees and the commission and the prosecution of Oliver North and his associ-ates, I conclude that all three investigative bodies avoided the constitu-tional questions raised by the affair. Each focused narrowly upon what happened during the affair itself, ignoring the broader pattern of history into which that event fits. In chapter 2, I argue that the investigators should have reviewed not simply the history of presidential scandals, but also the recent string of congressional-executive conflicts that have swept the spectrum of United States foreign policy concerns. Had they done so, they would have seen that the affair was not quintessentially a presidential scandal, but a failure of the foreign policy process, the latest episode in a history of executive avoidance of legislative constraint in foreign affairs that goes back to Vietnam.

If the affair exposed systemic, not localized, defects in the American foreign policy process, why did the investigators overlook these problems? In part 2, I show that the Iran-contra investigators lacked a coherent constitutional vision regarding how national security decisions should be made. Yet in chapters 3 and 4 I explain that such a vision exists and has existed throughout our constitutional history. The text of the Constitution as construed by Supreme Court decision, subsequent legislative enactments, and historical practice, describes a National Security Constitution that facilitates and constrains the operation of our national security policy process. That National Security Constitution rests upon a simple notion: that the power to conduct American foreign policy is not exclusively presidential, but rather, *a power shared* by the president, the Congress, and the courts. The constitutional system of checks and balances is not suspended simply because foreign affairs are at issue. To the contrary, in foreign as well as domestic affairs, our Constitution requires that we be governed by separated institutions sharing policy powers.[10]

In chapter 3, I define the concept of a National Security Constitution and examine the four discrete historical eras in its evolution, dating to the beginning of the Republic: a precarious infancy that ended with the Civil War; a heady adolescence terminated by the dawn of the twentieth century; an adulthood that stretched to World War II; and a hegemonic era that is swiftly coming to a close. Through each of these eras, I argue, the nation has adhered to a foreign policy decision-making structure premised on the balanced institutional participation of all three governmental branches. Although the National Security Constitution has assigned the president the predominant role in making foreign policy decisions, it has granted him only limited *exclusive* powers. Thus, the Constitution directs most governmental decisions regarding foreign affairs into a sphere of concurrent authority, under presidential management, but bounded by the checks provided by congressional consultation and judicial review.

Viewed against this normative background, chapter 4 argues, the Iran-contra affair represented not simply a collection of unconnected indiscretions or statutory violations, but a fundamental assault upon the National Security Constitution that we have inherited. What makes the affair so remarkable is that many members of both Congress and the executive branch defend it still, by invoking a dramatically different vision of the National Security Constitution. That vision views virtually the entire field of foreign affairs as falling under the president's exclusive domain, without the meaningful participation of either Congress or the courts. The Iran-contra affair represented a more serious constitutional crisis than most commentators have conceded precisely because the president's men used the alternative vision of unchecked executive discretion to subvert the cardinal principle of shared power.

Upon closer inspection, the Iran-contra affair exposed not just a constitutional crisis, but also a pressing policy problem. In recent times, our national institutions have failed voluntarily to preserve the core notion of the National Security Constitution: shared foreign-affairs decision making. Thus, the most important question left by the affair is not one of individual responsibility—What did President Reagan (or for that matter, President Bush) know and when did he know it?—but rather, a more basic structural question: Why, despite the constitutional mandate of power sharing, does the president almost always seem to win in foreign affairs? The answer to that question, I assert in chapters 5 and 6, ultimately lies in three sets of institutional factors that currently characterize our branches of national government. First, and most obviously, the presidency has won because it has institutional incentives to take the initiative in foreign affairs and has often done so by construing laws that were enacted to constrain executive authority to authorize its actions. Second, the president has won because Congress as an institution has persistently acquiesced in what he has done. Third, as described in chapter 6, the president has won because the federal courts have tolerated his acts, particularly in recent years, either by refusing to hear congressional or private challenges to presidential action or by hearing those challenges on the merits and ruling in the president's favor. This three-part combination of executive initiative, congressional acquiescence, and judicial tolerance has broadly insulated the president from foreign affairs accountability. By so doing, these factors have jointly operated to undercut the Constitution's mandate of balanced institutional participation in national security decision making.

Given this statement of precedent and problem, what policy prescription would most likely prevent future Iran-contra affairs? Part 3 argues that the time is now right for a systematic reconsideration of our National Security Constitution. In other areas of pressing national concern, such as budget, tax, and trade reform, we have not relied upon periodic voluntary commitments to bipartisanship as long-term solutions to recurring problems. Instead, Congress has enacted "constitutional 'framework' legislation . . . [to] interpre[t] the Constitution by providing a legal framework for the governmental decision-making process."[11] More than forty years ago, Congress enacted the first such framework statute to govern national security decisions, the National Security Act of 1947.[12] The Iran-contra affair confirmed that statute's obsolescence as a mechanism to govern national security decision making into the twenty-first century.

Before memories of the Iran-contra affair dim, the administration and Congress should make a comprehensive effort to enact a new framework statute that would reassert the constitutional principles of shared power in foreign affairs. Like the omnibus tax, budget balancing, and trade reform acts that Congress has recently passed, this national security *reform* act would seek to redefine the role that all three branches play within our national security system. Admittedly, Congress cannot legislate executive self-restraint, legislative will, or judicial courage. But Congress can and should seek to alter recurrent patterns of wayward executive behavior by restructuring the institutional attributes that now create incentives for executive officials to act irresponsibly and for congressional and judicial officials to permit such actions. Thus, the new national security charter should focus not only upon restraining executive adventurism, but also upon attacking the institutional sources of both congressional acquiescence and judicial tolerance.

In chapter 7, I sketch a comprehensive legislative charter that would redesign the institutional incentives facing all three branches in accordance with the vision of shared institutional powers in the Constitution. In addition to making particular policy proposals, that chapter outlines the general principles that underlie a broader legislative strategy for attacking the deeper institutional causes of the Iran-contra affair. Those principles rest upon Justice Robert Jackson's axiom that the Constitution "enjoins upon its branches not separateness but interdependence, not autonomy but reciprocity."[13] To avert the recurring cycles of interbranch warfare that we have recently experienced, we must reject notions of either executive or congressional supremacy in foreign affairs in favor of more formal institutional procedures for power sharing, designed clearly to define constitutional responsibility and to locate institutional account-ability.[14] In addition, we must develop legal structures to promote the interbranch dialogue essential to any "'bipartisan foreign policy': [congressional] consultation on the formulation of policy, participation in its execution, and information about its operation."[15]

Even if only partially successful, a congressional attempt to consider omnibus national security legislation would properly focus national attention on the constitutional issues raised by the Iran-contra affair and redefine the way we think about national security law. After evaluating the legislative prospects for such a charter, in chapter 8 I suggest how, even without sweeping reform, Congress could apply the general principles enunciated in chapter 7 to improve particular key areas of foreign policy decision making—war powers, treaty making, emergency economic powers, intelligence oversight, and information control.

The ninth and concluding chapter anticipates likely critiques of the charter proposal and speculates more broadly about the future of the National Security Constitution after the Iran-contra affair. In his last major foreign-policy address, President Reagan declared: "Today we live in a world in which America no longer enjoys preponderant power, but must lead by example and persuasion; a world of pressing new challenges to our economic prosperity; a world of new opportunities for peace and of new dangers. In such a world, more than ever, America needs strong and consistent leadership, and the strength and resilience of the Presidency are vital."[16] In chapter 9, I accept President Reagan's diagnosis but conclude that his policy prescription is sadly incomplete. Today's world demands not simply a strong president, but one who operates within an institutionally balanced constitutional structure of decision making. In all national affairs, Justice Brandeis has told us, our constitutional system of checks and balances was designed "not to promote efficiency but to preclude the exercise of arbitrary power."[17] Whether or not a national decision-making structure ruled by an imperial and unencumbered executive suited an era of world history marked by American hegemony, it invites only crippling interbranch strife in a posthegemonic world.

In short, the Iran-contra affair was not an aberrant historical episode that we can now safely forgive or forget. The affair exposed a serious and growing constitutional imbalance in our national processes of foreign affairs decision making. The institutional problems that caused it still live. The challenge the affair poses is how to remake our National Security Constitution for the posthegemonic age. To prevent its recurrence, we must look for structural solutions aimed at promoting regularized interbranch communication, encouraging executive self-restraint, and revitalizing Congress and the courts as institutional counterweights to the president. Only such solutions can both restore balance to our national security decision making and reaffirm our constitutional conviction that America's foreign affairs power is a power shared.

PART ONE
THE PRECEDENT

1 How the Iran-Contra Investigators Failed: An Autopsy

For those who lived through the Watergate summer of 1974, the Contragate summer of 1987 painted eerie historical parallels. A congressional panel and special prosecutor convened to question the president's men about their activities, asking what the president knew and when he knew it. The congressional committees concluded that the president's men had been running an illegal secret operation out of the White House and placed ultimate blame upon the president himself.[1] While the president continued to deny responsibility, Washington rang with talk of pardons for the accused.

Striking analogies have been drawn between Watergate and Contragate. During Watergate, a team of White House "plumbers," formed to plug government leaks regarding the Vietnam War, was discovered illegally breaking into Democratic National Headquarters. During the Iran-contra affair, a team of White House staff members, charged with supporting the covert war in Central America, was discovered illegally selling arms to Iran and diverting the proceeds to the contras, the Nicaraguan resistance. In both cases, funds of unaccountable origin and private agents were used to conduct covert actions directly from the White House. During both episodes, high executive officials stretched or disregarded the rule of law. Both incidents ultimately stemmed from executive efforts to sustain a war in a Third World country by bypassing established channels of command.[2]

These parallels were not lost upon the select committees that the House and Senate created to investigate the Iran-contra affair.[3] Yet the two affairs differed in one crucial respect: unlike Watergate, the Iran-contra affair was implemented not simply by a covert operation, but by a covert foreign policy. That policy was apparently determined by a private cadre, upon whose decisions neither Congress nor the people had an opportunity to pass judgment. The cadre's members read the Constitution as giving the executive branch unfettered discretion to make national security decisions and denied that such decisions need be shared with Congress.[4] Thus, while the Watergate investigations revolved principally around a factual question—What happened?—the Contragate investigations also raised a knotty constitutional issue: In foreign affairs, who decides?

One might have expected the latter question to have been closely scrutinized by the Iran-contra committees or by the Tower commission and the independent counsel, the other two government entities specially created to investigate the affair.[5] Yet ultimately, none of these investigative bodies grappled with the heart of the constitutional crisis exposed by the Iran-contra affair.

Why did the Iran-contra investigators fail? At first blush, one might have expected these three entities to adopt a straightforward division of labor. As a special review board created by executive order, the Tower commission had a mandate from the president to recommend changes in *executive policy* regarding the future roles and procedures of the National Security Council staff. As select committees chosen by the House and Senate leadership, the Iran-contra committees were charged by congressional resolution not only to uncover the factual outlines of the affair, but also to recommend future *legislative action*. As a special prosecutor appointed by a three-judge court pursuant to a post-Watergate congressional enactment, the independent counsel had a *judicial directive* to investigate individual wrongdoing, bring indictments, and obtain convictions.[6]

In this chapter, I suggest that each of the Iran-contra investigators incompletely executed its assigned role. After missing numerous key facts, the Tower commission recommended few meaningful changes in executive policy. The House and Senate select committees misdefined their role as a search for individual responsibility rather than as a quest for legislative reform. In seeking to punish the guilty, the independent counsel encountered myriad roadblocks, many of them thrown into his path not by the defendants, but by the rest of the United States government.

None of the investigators squarely addressed the constitutional question of who decides. The Tower commission dodged the question because it viewed its function as one of reinforcing, not challenging, executive prerogative. The House and Senate select committees raised the issue but left it buried amid their single-minded search for facts. The independent counsel considered the question but was forced by his pursuit of convictions to put it to one side. In short, despite the extraordinary public resources and attention that these three investigative entities lavished upon the Iran-contra affair, their combined efforts have illuminated only dimly the deeper significance of the affair for the constitutional conduct of our foreign affairs.[7]

THE TOWER COMMISSION

Of the three investigative bodies, the presidentially appointed Tower commission convened first, met in haste, and issued a report that was long on facts and short on policy or legislative recommendations. Ordered by the president to produce a report in two months, the commission took nearly three, requesting repeated extensions of time.[8] Thinly staffed and lacking the power to subpoena witnesses, to take sworn testimony, or to grant witnesses immunity against prosecution, the commission could neither demand documents from nongovernmental agencies nor compel testimony from key figures in the affair. Consequently, both the Federal Bureau of Investigation (FBI) and the independent counsel rejected the commission's information requests and three of the affair's key protagonists—Poindexter, North, and Secord—simply refused to appear before it.[9]

As a result, factual gaps dot the commission's hastily drafted final report. The report failed to determine how much money from the arms sale had been diverted to the contras, leaving it "up to the committees in Congress and the special prosecutor to analyze new evidence."[10] Large amounts of information were left undigested because the commissioners simply lacked the time to untangle the web of foreign intermediaries and bank accounts that North and his compatriots had used to execute the affair. The unsworn testimony taken by the commission was fraught with disagreements among senior administration officials about the key details of critical meetings, leaving the final report both incomplete and vulnerable to the charge that it was skewed too heavily in favor of certain participants.[11]

Upon releasing its report, the Tower commission pointedly stressed the limits of its inquiry. Significantly, President Reagan had never formally ordered the commission to review the legal structure of the foreign policy-making process or even to study the affair itself. Instead, the president's executive order had simply directed that the commission review the National Security Council (NSC) staff's "proper role in operational activities" and study its "*future* role and procedures . . . in the development, coordination, oversight, and conduct of foreign and national security policy."[12] Accordingly, the commissioners offered no retrospective judgments regarding either criminal culpability or legal violations. Yet at the same time, they focused less upon President Reagan's written directive than upon answering his oral request that "all the facts come out," a decision that made their detail-laden report read like a first draft of the congressional committee report that was to come.[13]

Given this fact-specific focus, it is not surprising that the final Tower report chose to emphasize the affair's aberrant nature. Announcing the report's release, the commission's chair declared that "[t]he Iran-contra affair was clearly an aberration."[14] Brent Scowcroft, now George Bush's national security assistant, reiterated that "the problem, at the heart, was one of people, not of process."[15] Accordingly, the commission downplayed proposals to revise the decision-making structure in favor of its well-publicized critique of President Reagan's lax "management style."

That focus led the commissioners to reject the notion that the Iran-contra affair illustrated any need for legislative reform. Their report found existing congressional oversight of the intelligence community to be adequate and rejected proposals that the NSC be statutorily barred from implementing policy. Nor did the commission even "recommend barring limited use of private individuals to assist in United States diplomatic initiatives *or in covert activities*."[16] The commission would still permit such privatization so long as "implementation and policy oversight [are not] *dominated* by [private] intermediaries," a nebulous standard that the NSC arguably satisfied even during the Iran-contra affair.[17] Furthermore, the commission pointedly opposed suggestions that Congress either stiffen the National Security Act of 1947 or subject the national security assistant to congressional confirmation.[18]

Not surprisingly, the few structural reforms actually offered by the commission have yielded little effect. Its recommendation that the national security assistant should have greater access to legal counsel encouraged the president to create a new post of NSC legal adviser, but allowed him to ignore the Tower commission's more important policy suggestion that NSC actions be subjected to interagency legal review by the Justice Department or the legal adviser to the Department of State. The commission also proposed that Congress combine the existing House and Senate intelligence committees into a smaller joint committee. But that recommendation was later rejected by the majority of Congress's Iran-contra committees on the ground that it would not enhance, but rather, would "inevitably erode Congress' ability to perform its oversight function." [19]

Nor did the Tower report ultimately question either the wisdom or the constitutionality of unrestrained executive discretion in national security affairs. If anything, the report reaffirmed the view that the president, not Congress, should call more shots in foreign affairs than he currently does. Under the commission's view, President Reagan failed during the Iran-contra affair not by calling too many shots, but by personally calling too few (and then forgetting those that he did call). [20] Indeed, Michael Ledeen, one of the affair's most ardent defenders, praised the Tower commission precisely because it "resisted the temptation to recommend an overhaul of the national security system. . . . [i]n the face of the congressional power grab." [21]

Upon reflection, it appears that the presidential commission process virtually preordained this pro-status quo result. By their nature, presidential commissions are appointed to address explosive political problems, to insulate the president from criticism for inaction, and to reach high degrees of consensus about relatively restrained solutions. They aim less often at broad-ranging structural reform than, in Professor Falk's words, reaching "a consensus that earn[s] instant respect, being neither too apologetic to be dismissed as a whitewash nor too critical to shake any fundamental foundations of confidence by the citizenry in the capacities and integrity of the governing process." [22]

The Tower commission's composition reinforced this structural tendency. Although two of the commission's three members, Edmund Muskie and John Tower, had once been senators, the former had served as Jimmy Carter's secretary of state (and had run for president) and the latter had long favored executive prerogative (a predilection later acknowledged by his brief, ill-fated nomination as secretary of defense in the Bush administration). [23] It was therefore predictable that their report, coauthored with once and future National Security Assistant Brent Scow-

Scowcroft, should have generally favored the presidency, even while laying the blame for the affair at the door of a specific president.

Nor should it surprise, in retrospect, that the Tower report has inspired no subsequent diminution in the NSC's role in national security decision making in the Bush administration. To the contrary, the commission's most telling recommendation, little noticed at the time its report was issued, was that the national security assistant should chair the senior-level committees of the NSC system, assuming greater, not lesser, prominence in the national security decision-making structure. It was therefore foreseeable that one of President Bush's first major foreign policy directives should be to elevate the National Security Council to this central status in the decision-making apparatus and to place Brent Scowcroft at its head.[24]

THE IRAN-CONTRA COMMITTEES

I do not denigrate the crucial service that the congressional committees performed for the nation by quickly exposing the affair's details to public scrutiny. Working under severe time pressures, the committees and their staffs held hearings only five months after formation on a case that, by one estimate, would have occupied eighteen months of a prosecutor's time.[25] But if the Iran-contra committees had a unique mission among the three investigating bodies, it was to recommend legislative, not executive or judicial, action. In the end, however, the committees devoted nearly all of their 690-page report to recounting facts and legal violations, devoting only four and one-half pages of the majority report and three pages of the minority report to recommendations for legislative reform.[26]

Why did the committees virtually ignore the crucial legislative portion of their institutional mandate? A look back at the committee hearings suggests that they committed an error of role definition, which led them to focus too narrowly on particular events and retrospective questions of individual responsibility. By adopting a quasi-judicial tone for their report, the committees treated the affair as a morality play, in which the American public played the jury and Congress played both the judge and prosecutor. In taking this approach, the committees too narrowly defined their goal as a retrospective search for individual responsibility—a search far better suited to the independent counsel than to Congress—rather than as a prospective quest for legislative reform.

Once the congressional committees had so misdefined their task, institutional constraints inherent in every phase of the unwieldy legislative investigative process disabled them from completing it. At the outset, the predictable jurisdictional jealousy of the permanent committees denuded the committees of meaningful legislative clout. Ordinarily, members of Congress sort themselves through self-selection into standing committees, which then exercise "gatekeeping" powers to wield special influence regarding particular bills over which they exercise jurisdiction. Yet the multifaceted Iran-contra affair overlapped the legislative jurisdiction of several permanent committees, each of which refused to cede jurisdiction to one another or to any ad hoc entity. Congress's leadership therefore chose to constitute the Iran-contra committees as temporary select committees lacking continuing legislative jurisdiction. It thereby created a transient investigative entity, which lacked the institutional influence of its permanent committee counterparts.[27]

That decision having been made, the affair's highly public profile engendered two select committees of far larger than optimal size. The Iran-contra committees numbered twenty-six members and close to one hundred staff; the Senate Watergate committee, by comparison, included only seven members plus majority and minority counsel.[28] Agitation by members to share in the spotlight led the Speaker to appoint to the House select committee the chairs of five key committees. Not surprisingly, their other weighty assignments left them little time to prepare for the hearings, to attend planning sessions, or to formulate coherent questioning.[29]

Once constituted, the select committees conducted duplicative parallel investigations for about two months before deciding to merge their inquiries. Yet rather than create a joint investigating committee with a single staff, the separate committees agreed only to hold joint hearings, with each committee maintaining separate staffs and the House committee staff remaining divided between Democrats and Republicans. The committees then paid inefficient homage to protocol by rotating their forty days of public hearings between houses. The Senate committee's chair presided and applied Senate rules when hearings were held in the Senate caucus room and the House committee head applied House rules when hearings switched to the House side.[30]

As the hearings began, the use of trial lawyers and former prosecutors as committee counsel, rather than experts in administrative process or foreign-affairs law, greatly enhanced the flavor of the proceedings as a quasi-criminal prosecution, rather than a study of foreign-policy decision making. The House's failure to agree upon a single staff counsel and the absence of hierarchy among the questioners led to endless multiple questioning of the most important witnesses and to the disjointed questioning of logically related witnesses. Although the committees generally used a designated-hitter system, whereby one majority and one minority member from each committee bore chief responsibility for questioning each witness, at times all twenty-six members and three different sets of staff counsel questioned a single witness. Because each questioner was left to define his own role, some interrogators aggressively questioned witnesses in the style of a traditional courtroom lawyer, while others allowed the same witness to testify at length without discrediting or challenging the testimony.[31] The televising of the hearings greatly enhanced the opportunity for individual members to engage in grandstanding and "credit-claiming."[32] More subtly, members' awareness of the public effect of testimony served to diminish gradually even the marginal inquisitorial control exercised by the committee counsel as the hearings proceeded.[33] Finally, the absence of a judge to rule on the numerous objections made by the witnesses' attorneys created the curious spectacle of the chief investigator, the Senate committee chairman, repeatedly overruling objections to his own questions.[34]

That two congressional committees should not totally succeed in conducting a quasi-criminal prosecution should surprise us no more than a dog's failure to walk gracefully on two legs. Nor should it astonish us that a witness as well-prepared and represented as Oliver North should have exploited this incongruity so effectively. North's prepared statement struck a chord with the public simply by pointing out the manifest institutional awkwardness of Congress's role definition. North told the committees: "I believe that this is a strange process that you are putting me and others through. . . . It's sort of like a baseball game in which you are both the player and the umpire. It's a game in which you call the balls and strikes and where you determine who is out and who is safe. And in the end you determine the score and declare yourselves the winner."[35]

On reflection, the committees' errant role definition assured that North's celebrated congressional testimony would succeed. For prosecutors are trained at a minimum to cut off rambling answers, to probe inconsistencies in testimony, and to cast doubt on an adverse witness's credibility, all with an eye toward directing the jury's attention to a progressively narrower set of facts underlying specific claimed legal violations. Yet all of these tasks assume that the prosecutor will be guided by a specific indictment or information, heard by a neutral judge and jury, and headed by a single, controlling intelligence. The Iran-contra committees lacked all of these. Thus, North's success before the committees demonstrated less his superhuman qualities, or those of his attorneys, than the unremarkable fact that a competent witness can evade episodic cross-examination by a distracted, hydra-headed prosecutor, simply by appealing directly to a public that will catch his best moments on the nightly news.

In particular, the committees violated the first rule of cross-examination, that an examiner should "[k]no[w] what the witnes[s] probably will say . . . not only for deciding what to ask but also for deciding what not to ask."[36] Initially, North refused to be questioned in private before the public hearings, claiming that a private deposition was not a "proceeding" in which Congress could by statute compel him to testify.[37] Because North was an executive branch employee, the committees arguably lacked statutory authority to hold him in civil contempt had he flatly refused to testify.[38] Nor could any criminal contempt prosecution have been completed until long after the self-imposed August 1987 deadline set by the committees for completing hearings. Facing strong public pressure for North's testimony, the committees unwisely acceded to his demand to be heard in private in a single one and one-half hour session that was limited in subject matter and held only partially under oath.[39] Consequently, the committees simply did not know what North would later say during six days of public testimony. North, on the other hand, was both fully apprised of and fully prepared to answer the charges against him.

Despite their institutional disqualification from prosecuting the responsible individuals, the committees' initial role misdefinition led several members to fasten on the question asked endlessly about President Nixon during Watergate: What did he know and when did he know it?[40] Yet that question would have been central to the Contragate investigation only if the committees were considering whether or not to seek impeachment of those responsible. The Iran-contra committees' inability to find a smoking gun damning the president effectively mooted the impeachment question, leading several members to act as if their inquiry were exhausted.[41]

More egregiously, the superficial analogies between the Iran-contra

VERNON REGIONAL
JUNIOR COLLEGE LIBRARY

affair and Watergate misled some committee members—particularly those in the minority—to argue that the affair, like Watergate, represented an extreme case of politics as usual.[42] Yet the Watergate analogy implies that the defendants dispute only the facts and not the validity of the laws allegedly violated.[43] Under such circumstances, the appropriate remedy would be retrospective individual punishment rather than prospective structural reform.

But in the Iran-contra affair, unlike Watergate, the defendants admitted many of the facts but denied that they had violated valid laws. Excepting a few charges of unlawful personal enrichment, the defendants claimed that the criminal charges against them sought to punish their patriotic decisions to carry out the president's, rather than Congress's, foreign policy. Given this fundamental interbranch dispute over what the rules of law governing national security should be, the majority members of the committees simply begged the question when they claimed that the real issue was executive accountability to the "rule of law." For if the majority had truly believed that the Iran-contra affair represented more than just politics as usual, it should have gone on to demand clarification of precisely what those governing rules of law should be. One commentator has suggested that "[a] constitutional moment . . . begins when people realize that throwing the rascals out will not suffice; the problem is no longer perceived as solvable merely by replacing the people in authority. Rather, the structure of authority itself must be changed."[44] The committees never fully grasped either the constitutional moment or the legislative opportunity that the Iran-contra affair presented to them.

The Iran-contra report did not wholly ignore the constitutional question of who decides. At one point, the majority members of the committees declared that the Constitution mandates that "Congress shares with the President powers in the conduct of foreign policy" and that "[t]he sharing of power over foreign policy requires consultation, trust, and coordination." The minority responded to the majority's vision of shared power by denying that the affair had created a constitutional crisis. "The Constitution created the Presidency to be a separate branch of government whose occupant would have substantial discretionary power to act," the minority argued. "As long as any President has those powers, there will be mistakes" of the kind that led to the affair.[45]

Having opened this constitutional debate, however, the members of the committees never squarely joined it. For instead of buttressing its statements of constitutional principle with a comprehensive legislative program, the majority proffered only scattered recommendations for structural reform of the national security process. In particular, the majority recommended stiffening the so-called finding and reporting requirements in the intelligence oversight laws; modifying the laws governing the NSC; creating a CIA inspector general; mandating Senate confirmation of the CIA's general counsel and revitalization of the Intelligence Oversight Board; and calling for congressional review of numerous statutes at issue in the affair. But while many of the majority's policy and legislative recommendations were individually laudable, the committees presented them in a disjointed grab bag, offering no analysis of the relationship among them or any explanation of how they would systematically promote interbranch dialogue and power sharing. Nor did the majority ever suggest how those proposals constituted a coherent legislative strategy for attacking the affair's deeper institutional causes.[46]

Perhaps the most puzzling feature of the majority's report was its denial, in virtually the same breath as it presented its legislative proposals, that new framework legislation was needed to reinforce its constitutional vision of shared power. The national need, the majority concluded, is "not for new laws but for a renewal of the commitment to constitutional government and sound processes of decisionmaking."[47] Not surprisingly, the minority seized upon this concession to support its opposition to legislative reform and then countered with five recommendations of its own, all predictably designed to strengthen presidential discretion.[48] Given the majority's ambivalence about the need for structural reform, its policy recommendations, predictably, have had little impact. For example, although the majority recommended "that Presidents adopt as a matter of policy the principle that the National Security Adviser . . . should not be an active military officer," President Reagan promptly ignored that recommendation, appointing Army Lt. Gen. Colin Powell (now chair of the Joint Chiefs of Staff) as his last national security assistant.[49]

In defense of the committees, one could argue that the task of investigating was more than enough to occupy their time. Under this view, Congress did not so much misdefine its institutional task as leave it unfinished. On numerous occasions in the past, Congress has responded to national sensations by immediately forming select committees to hold hearings, dramatize abuses, and generate revelations, leaving longer term legislative reform to the cooler subsequent reflection of its standing committees.[50] It was not until four years after the Watergate hearings, for example, that Congress finally addressed the structural problems raised by that affair by enacting the independent counsel provisions of the Ethics in Government Act of 1978. But to the extent that congressional investigations represent means to legislative ends, Congress leaves its job half done when it investigates and then fails to legislate based upon the findings of its investigation. Thus far, this is precisely what Congress has done with regard to the Iran-contra affair. At this writing, not one of the committees' legislative recommendations has been enacted into law. Instead, the committees have disbanded and their members have moved on, with many participants now acting as if the scandal were over and the last word spoken.[51]

THE INDEPENDENT COUNSEL

Although the independent counsel, Lawrence Walsh, and his team have successfully tried and convicted Oliver North, all indications are that they will fare little better than their fellow investigators in exposing the affair's deeper causes. Three factors contribute to this situation. First, under the independent counsel provisions of the Ethics in Government Act (Independent Counsel Act), Walsh was appointed as a special prosecutor, not as a legislator. As a prosecutor, his assigned institutional task was to prove the defendants' criminal responsibility, not to expose underlying defects in the legal structure of our foreign-policy decision making. It was never Walsh's job to pursue the latter, legislative assignment simply because the congressional committees had improvidently chosen to pursue his.

Second, as originally conceived, Walsh's prosecution pursued a broad constitutional theory in a narrow criminal forum. As initially drafted, Walsh's indictment effectively charged that North, Poindexter, Hakim, and Secord had conspired to conduct a covert foreign policy in violation of federal laws. Thus, the trials initially appeared to offer, in the context of trying the Iran-contra defendants' culpability, a forum for a deeper public examination of what had gone wrong in the national security decision-making process. Yet as I elaborate below, Walsh was ultimately forced to dismiss those broad conspiracy charges during pretrial proceedings in the North, Poindexter, and Secord cases, thereby returning all three cases to a narrower focus on whether the individual defendants had committed particular crimes beyond a reasonable doubt. Consequently, none of the trials will likely provide an arena for examining the deeper constitutional issues underlying the affair.

Third, Walsh's prosecution was hampered by a curious fact. At some point before the jury was sworn, the case of *United States v. North, et al.* degenerated into the case of the United States versus itself. The road to trying the Iran-contra defendants proved tortuous, with the North case alone going to the Supreme Court three times even before the jury rendered its verdict.[52] Along that road, the case was subtly transformed from a straightforward contest between the independent counsel and the defendants into one that pitted the independent counsel against the rest of the United States government. For although Attorney General Edwin Meese had specifically requested appointment of an independent counsel and President Reagan had promised Walsh his "complete cooperation," the Justice Department, the congressional committees, the White House, and the intelligence agencies all subsequently threw major roadblocks into the independent counsel's path.[53]

Coupled with the aggressive tactics of the defendants' skilled counsel and the management of a determined judge, these intragovernmental obstacles cumulatively served to narrow the counsel's ambitious case into an ordinary criminal prosecution. In the end, rather than claiming that the defendants had conducted an unauthorized foreign policy with a secret treasury comprising millions of dollars in government funds, Walsh and his team were reduced to asking whether North had lied to Congress, altered documents, improperly received a $13,800 residential security fence, or converted less than $5,000 in job-related travelers' checks for his personal use. Systematically removed from the case were broader, unexplored public questions regarding the subversion and mismanagement of the foreign-policy process.

Constitutional Impediments to Prosecution

Almost as soon as the grand jury was impaneled in January 1987, it became apparent that Walsh would face serious constitutional problems in prosecuting his case. North sought to enjoin the grand jury proceedings, claiming that the Independent Counsel Act (under which Walsh had been appointed) violated constitutional principles of separation of powers. Although Attorney General Meese quickly reappointed Walsh, granting him executive authority virtually identical to that statutorily granted him by Congress, Meese refused to defend the constitutionality of the Independent Counsel Act itself. Instead, he contemporaneously filed briefs in another case echoing North's claim that the independent counsel statute should be invalidated.[54]

However well-meaning Meese's actions may have been, they placed a constitutional cloud over all of Walsh's ongoing investigative activities. On the one hand, Walsh's prosecutorial authority rested on a statute whose constitutionality was under challenge; on the other, it derived from an unprecedented parallel appointment that potentially compromised his prosecutorial independence. In time, the Supreme Court sustained the constitutionality of the independent counsel statute and the court of appeals upheld the parallel appointment in a case over which the Supreme Court declined review.[55] Nevertheless, the ongoing litigation placed the constitutional underpinnings of Walsh's prosecutorial power in doubt for some nineteen months after his initial appointment.

Even while these challenges proceeded, the immunity grants and extraordinary public awareness fostered by the congressional hearings vastly complicated Walsh's efforts to assemble his case and bring it to trial. Unlike the Watergate committees, which heard testimony from John Ehrlichmann, H. R. Haldeman, and John Mitchell without ever awarding them immunity against prosecution, the Iran-contra committees chose, over Walsh's opposition, to confer broad grants of testimonial immunity upon Poindexter, North, and Hakim.[56] For nearly two years before trial, those immunity grants obliged the counsel's office to adopt onerous prophylactic internal procedures to shield its attorneys from direct or indirect exposure to the nationally publicized congressional testimony.[57] Despite these measures, both the defendants and the American Civil Liberties Union (ACLU) made powerful pretrial arguments that the indictments should be dismissed, claiming that North's widely publicized immunized testimony would inevitably be used against him.[58]

Although Judge Gerhard Gesell, the able trial judge, rejected these claims as a bar to trial, the court of appeals sustained him on this point only provisionally.[59] Moreover, even Walsh's contingent victory was blunted by Judge Gesell's contemporaneous directive that each defendant be tried separately.[60] The judge properly reasoned that a joint trial would create constitutional problems. One codefendant might seek to exculpate himself before the common jury by using another's congressionally immunized testimony, thereby potentially incriminating that codefendant with his own immunized testimony in violation of the Fifth Amendment. But the severance of the trials gravely compounded Walsh's task. Not only did it force him to field four separate trial teams and to shield them artificially from one another, it also required him to try alleged co-conspirators before separate juries, a move that almost invariably causes a conspiracy prosecution to "lose its flavor and its punch."[61]

As North's own trial approached, the enormous pretrial publicity severely hampered Walsh's efforts to find an unbiased jury pool. During the jury selection process, North's attorneys moved to strike every prospective juror who had ever seen or heard of their client. That left Judge Gesell with a Hobson's choice—to deny North's motions and give him yet another basis for appeal or to grant them and significantly shrink the available jury pool.[62] While denying those motions, Judge Gesell wondered aloud whether the pretrial publicity surrounding the hearings had detrimentally affected "the triability of the case." He ultimately attributed that problem not to trial counsel, but to Congress's prior decision "to walk in and take over the functions of the grand jury."[63]

The Narrowing of the Charges

After the cases had been splintered and the lead prosecution of Oliver North took center stage, other Justice Department interventions dramatically narrowed the scope of the charges for which North would be tried. Although some have called the North trial a simple embezzlement case, it did not begin that way.[64] The wide-ranging indictment that Walsh originally filed against North and his compatriots in March of 1988 charged them with four discrete types of criminal offenses: conspiring to defraud the United States by obstructing lawful governmental functions; diverting public monies to "public" ends that the defendants themselves had designated (namely, diverting proceeds from the Iranian arms sales to the Nicaraguan contras); diverting public monies to the defendants' own, private ends; and lying to or withholding information from Congress and the attorney general to disguise their actions. Of these four types of charges—the conspiracy, the diversion, the theft, and the cover-up—only the third constituted an allegation of routine criminal activity. The other allegations essentially charged that the defendants had secretly conducted a private foreign policy, in violation of the substantive and procedural norms of national security decision making prescribed by our Constitution and statutes.

The guts of the original indictment lay in its first two counts, which examined the full sweep of the defendants' covert plan to sell arms to Iran and to divert the profits to the Nicaraguan contras. The first and broadest count stated a simple normative proposition: that the Constitution and laws of the United States require the *balanced participation* of all three institutional branches of government—Congress, the presidency, and the federal courts—in the making of foreign policy. When the government operates lawfully, the indictment charged, Congress's constitutional appropriations power gives it exclusive authority to establish and oversee the permissible uses of government funds. Executive branch officials should honestly and faithfully spend those publicly appropriated monies for officially established public purposes and conduct covert military actions consistently with existing legal arrangements for congressional and presidential supervision. The courts should criminally punish executive officials who violate these principles, the first count charged, because those officials conspire to defeat the lawful operation of government. To this broad allegation, the indictment's second count simply added the claim that the defendants had implemented their conspiracy by stealing government property.[65]

In contrast to these two core charges, the rest of the original twenty-three-count indictment focused upon epiphenomena, not the heart of the affair. Ten of the remaining counts addressed the cover-up, charging North or Poindexter with obstructing or testifying falsely to Congress. Three others accused North of obstructing the attorney general's investigation. Another count charged that North had conspired to defraud the Internal Revenue Service by using a tax-exempt organization to solicit money for contra weapons. The balance of the charges revolved around North's alleged private enrichment, as exemplified by his alleged receipt of a residential security system and conversion of government travelers' checks.[66]

Predictably, North and his supporters denied all of these allegations. But what made their theory of the case distinctive was their dramatically different characterization of what constitutes "lawful government operation" in the foreign-policy arena. Like the minority members of the Iran-contra committees, North rejected the notion of foreign-policy power as a power shared. Instead, he argued that the constitutional principle that guides foreign-policy decision making is not one of balanced institutional participation, but of unchecked executive discretion. Under North's reasoning, neither the courts nor Congress may restrain the president or his men in foreign affairs. Diversion of profits from the Iran arms sales to the contras did not constitute "theft of government property," North claimed, because his acts were all known and authorized by other executive officials.[67] Nor could the courts pass judgment upon those acts because they were immune from judicial review under the "political question" doctrine.[68] Executive circumvention of the Boland amendments, which had barred any "entity of the United States involved in intelligence activities" from spending available funds to assist the Nicaraguan resistance, could not constitute "conspiracy to defraud the United States" because Congress never intended those statutory provisions to apply to the NSC. Even if Congress did so intend, North argued, those laws constituted unconstitutional congressional attempts to use the appropriations power to usurp the president's foreign affairs authority.[69] Finally, North asserted that exigent political circumstances—what he had called in the congressional hearings "weigh[ing] in the balance the difference between lives and lies"—justified both his private conversions of property and his decisions to mislead and withhold information from Congress and the attorney general.[70]

In a variety of pretrial orders, Judge Gesell rejected North's theory of unchecked executive discretion and reaffirmed the principle of balanced institutional participation. Gesell denied that the political question doctrine barred the court from passing on the legality of North's conduct. Regardless of whether the Boland amendments were constitutional, the president had signed them and ordered the NSC to act in compliance with them. That suggested that both political branches had agreed as to how foreign policy should be made. Those amendments represented not congressional usurpation of presidential power, but interbranch accommodation: "The affected Branches have accommodated to each other's interest to establish the manner in which government will function."[71] The judge further found that North's alleged diversion of government funds, if proved, would constitute illegal conversion in violation of that interbranch accord.[72] Rejecting North's "constitutional argument . . . that the asserted primacy of the White House in foreign affairs precludes officials working for the executive from being prosecuted for false statements made to Congress," Gesell declared: "Congress surely has a role to play in aspects of foreign affairs, as the Constitution expressly recognizes and the Supreme Court of the United States has affirmed. . . .

Where, as here, *power is shared among the branches,* willful and deliberate deceit such as North allegedly espouses cannot be excused on constitutional grounds."[73]

One might have expected the attorney general, Dick Thornburgh, whose predecessor had been victimized by North's alleged deceit, to be sympathetic to Walsh and Gesell's theory of the case. But shortly before trial, the president's lawyers announced that they largely shared North's vision of the foreign policy decision-making process. After North moved to dismiss the initial three counts of Walsh's indictment, claiming that his actions had not obstructed any lawful governmental function, the Justice Department filed an extraordinary *amicus curiae* (friend of the court) memorandum attacking the constitutional underpinnings of the indictment's first count. Rejecting the independent counsel's vision of the foreign policy-making process as entailing the balanced participation of the president, the Congress, and the federal courts, the department echoed North's sentiments:

> The [independent counsel's] characterization of the institutional allocation of foreign affairs authority is incorrect. The President has plenary authority to represent the United States and to pursue its interests outside the borders of the country, subject only to the powers assigned Congress and the limitations specifically set forth in the Constitution itself. Moreover, it follows that Congress cannot through its appropriations or other powers invade any sphere of constitutional authority granted exclusively to the President. In particular, the President has plenary power which Congress cannot invade to conduct diplomacy, including covert diplomacy that seeks support (including financial contributions) for the foreign policy he articulates on behalf of the Nation.[74]

Having asserted this expansive view of presidential authority, the department claimed that Walsh had too "broadly characterize[d] Congress' constitutional authority with respect to foreign policy." The department asserted that, "[c]ontrary to the [independent counsel]'s suggestion, there is a sphere of presidential activity that could not constitutionally be limited by any congressional enactment." Moreover, the department charged that Walsh's theory of the case "potentially criminalizes any political dispute between Executive officials and Congress over foreign policy" and denied that courts have any significant role to play in examining executive conduct in foreign affairs. "'[P]olitical' behavior," the department argued, "is permitted by the Constitution, and the penalties for it should remain within the political process and not be brought to a court for prosecution."[75]

In response, the independent counsel simply reiterated his theory of balanced institutional participation. He asserted that North had employed a series of deceptive acts "to obstruct . . . the operation of a series of congressional enactments and rules promulgated by the executive branch." To conclude that such acts constitute a crime, Walsh suggested, one need not ascribe to Congress the dominant role in foreign affairs. Rather, "the 'only' proposition regarding the constitutional role of the National Legislature needed to support the indictment" is the notion "that the Congress has *a legitimate role* with respect to foreign affairs."[76] By challenging the indictment's core counts, North and the president asserted a vision of unchecked executive power that denied Congress even that limited role.

In hindsight, one might well question the breadth of Walsh's original indictment. A forum created to test whether an individual has committed a crime beyond a reasonable doubt is hardly ideal for investigating whether a foreign-policy decision-making process has gone constitutionally awry. As Professor Abraham Goldstein has pointed out, the concept of "conspiracy to defraud the United States" is inherently woolly.[77] Thus, most federal indictments avoid that count and limit themselves to charging conspiracies to violate particular criminal statutes. By broadly charging that the defendants had conspired to defraud the United States by violating both civil and criminal statutes, Walsh opened up the possibility that North would interpose broad intent defenses that would have been difficult to overcome at trial, particularly given the high beyond-a-reasonable-doubt standard of proof in a criminal case.

The broader point, however, is that the independent counsel's prosecution, like the Iran-contra report before it, exposed two competing constitutional visions of the foreign policy decision-making process: North's (and the attorney general's) vision of unchecked executive discretion versus Walsh's vision of balanced institutional participation. As I explore in chapters 3 and 4, the pretrial clash between those two visions in the North case merely replicated a much larger ongoing controversy about the meaning of the National Security Constitution, a controversy that lies at the heart of the Iran-contra affair.

Clashes over Classified and Privileged Information

Three events that transpired during the last months before North's trial starkly illustrated the continuing struggle between these competing images of the foreign-policy process: Walsh's reluctant decision to seek dismissal of the first two counts of North's indictment, the district court's decision permitting Presidents Reagan and Bush to resist North's testimonial subpoenas, and the battle between the independent counsel and the attorney general over disclosure of classified information.

It was widely anticipated that Walsh might encounter difficulties in bringing his entire indictment to trial. Defendants in national security cases—usually former government employees—have long sought to "graymail" the prosecution by threatening to disclose classified information in their defense unless the government drops its charges. Before 1980, intelligence agency refusals to disclose classified information had sometimes deterred the Justice Department from prosecuting former government employees with access to national security secrets. As one former government lawyer recalled, such refusals had "foster[ed] the perception that government officials and private persons with access to military . . . secrets have a broad *de facto* immunity from prosecution for a variety of crimes."[78]

It was precisely to remedy the government's "disclose or dismiss" dilemma that Congress enacted the Classified Information Procedures Act of 1980 (CIPA), the law that the North trial would thrust into national prominence.[79] This act sought to minimize both unnecessary disclosure and unnecessary dismissals by requiring the defendant to notify the government in advance of any classified information that he intended to use at trial. Once notified, the trial judge could hold pretrial *in camera* hearings on the use, relevancy, and admissibility of the classified information, and afford the prosecution alternative methods—such as substituted or redacted documents—for introducing relevant facts into evidence without exposing classified information.[80]

One of the principal purposes of CIPA was to rescue prosecutors from the pressures regularly exerted upon them by intelligence agencies to drop prosecutions rather than disclose national security information.[81] To assure executive officials that legitimate national security interests would be protected without being unduly indulged, CIPA authorized a judge to examine privately the classified information that the government sought to withhold at trial. It further empowered the judge to screen out classified information that would later be ruled inadmissible at trial and to "sanitize" relevant classified information through redactions. With these tools the judge could both minimize the extent of the likely disclosure and let the prosecutor know in advance what price in disclosure he or she would have to pay in order to obtain a conviction.

Thus CIPA assumed that judges, prosecutors, and defense counsel would work together to obtain fair trials with minimal disclosure. In many respects, the seven months before the North trial began constituted a model of judge-prosecutor accommodation in CIPA matters. During that period, Judge Gesell issued more than twenty CIPA orders formulating specific guidelines regarding the admissibility of classified evidence at trial, none of which the independent counsel Walsh challenged or appealed. But the North trial differed from prior CIPA cases in one crucial respect. Under the independent counsel provisions of the Ethics in Government Act, the special prosecutor seeking the conviction is formally independent of the rest of the executive branch. In the ordinary CIPA case, the attorney general (and ultimately, the president) controls decisions regarding both disclosure and dismissal and can therefore resolve most conflicts between the prosecutor and the intelligence agencies before indictment. But in the North case, such conflicts were not resolved and the intelligence agencies, the attorney general, and the president—and not the independent counsel—retained final power over what evidence could be disclosed. That authority enabled them to impose broad de facto limits on Walsh's freedom to prosecute, even though the independent counsel laws barred them from controlling his prosecution directly.

Exactly this scenario came to pass in December 1988, when Judge Gesell issued a detailed order delineating which parts of three hundred classified documents would be deemed relevant and admissible at trial.[82] Although Walsh apparently was ready to try the first two counts of the indictment based upon redacted documents that the administration had cleared, Judge Gesell concluded that a full and fair defense would require additional disclosure. An interagency panel of cabinet and intelligence officials refused to approve that disclosure. After negotiating unsuccessfully with the panel to drop its objections, Walsh was forced reluctantly to dismiss the two first and most important counts of his indictment. Within a year, Walsh had dropped the same counts in two other cases and had failed to block dismissal of a third.[83]

Although the independent counsel did not publicly dispute the panel's underlying basis for withholding the contested documents, the dismissal vividly illustrated the consequences of exclusive executive branch control of classified national security information. As described in chapters 7 and 8, decisions regarding the release of classified information currently rest almost exclusively in the hands of the executive branch, although all three branches of government participate in national security decision making. Thus, outsiders can never know whether the panel correctly exercised its discretion in refusing to disclose the information. The executive branch's information monopoly simply prevents neutral external examination of the way in which that discretion was exercised.

However, other classified information that later became public during the trial cast doubt on the validity of the government's sweeping claims of secrecy. The intelligence agencies initially demanded, for example, that Judge Gesell seal his entire final pretrial CIPA order as classified. But when Judge Gesell later ordered that order unsealed, only two words of the ten-page order had been redacted.[84] Similarly, a memorandum that the prosecution introduced into evidence in edited form was later discovered to have been made public in its entirety in a civil lawsuit the previous year, suggesting to the judge a troubling "looseness in Government dealings with this problem of classified information."[85] In a later written order, Judge Gesell declared that he was facing an "absurd situation where the press is accurately reporting information in the public domain while the court is confronted with representations that the same facts must never be officially acknowledged."[86]

Ironically, the forced dismissal of the two core counts illustrated the value of a neutral judge and independent prosecutor to a president who withholds classified information. Public suspicion that President Reagan had issued North a "pocket pardon" was dampened only by the fact that neither the judge nor the independent counsel had challenged publicly the legitimacy of the nondisclosure. Thus, despite the Reagan administration's questioning of both the fitness of the case for judicial examination and the constitutionality of independent counsels, only the independent participation of both Gesell and Walsh allayed public doubts about President Reagan's motives for withholding the information.[87]

The attorney general and the Senate select committee counsel sought to minimize the significance of the two dropped counts. They argued that the completeness of the foregoing congressional investigation of the affair had obviated the need for a wide-ranging criminal investigation.[88] Yet this argument simply inverted an earlier executive branch claim made at the time of the hearings themselves—that a sweeping congressional investigation was unnecessary because the truth would ultimately emerge through the criminal investigative process. Both arguments misunderstood the fundamental point that congressional investigations and criminal prosecutions complement rather than substitute for one another. The congressional committees institutionally could not answer one crucial question: Whether executive officials who maintain a privately controlled cache of government funds to conduct a foreign policy program prohibited by Congress are guilty not merely of overzealousness, but of crimes against the United States.[89] The deletion of the indictment's first two charges ensured that no court would answer that question either.

Shortly after the two main charges against North were dropped, the Justice Department once again championed executive discretion by moving to quash testimonial subpoenas that North had directed against both Presidents Bush and Reagan. Claiming that "[t]he spectacle of a former or sitting President being subjected to peremptory judicial process may chill foreign governments in the way they deal with the President now and in the future," the department urged the court to hold that a sitting or former president may never be subjected to oral testimony "in a courtroom or even at a deposition." Notwithstanding the historic occasions on which presidents and ex-presidents have been called as witnesses, the department claimed that even forcing an ex-president to decide whether or how to testify would create a "risk of harm to our foreign relations."[90] Judge Gesell refused to enforce the subpoenas. He later declined to compel Reagan's testimony during trial on the ground that North had not demonstrated sufficient need for the former president's testimony. At the same time, however, Gesell flatly rejected the department's far-reaching theory, as another judge would later do in Poindexter's case, finding "no doubt that the Court has power to enforce its compulsory process."[91] Yet once again, the episode revealed the department's expansive view of a president's foreign affairs duties, now invoked to justify granting even a departed president near-total immunity from judicial process.

The executive branch's final pretrial challenge to Walsh's authority came only one day before opening statements were scheduled in the North case. Although more than seven months had passed since the CIPA process commenced, the Justice Department appeared and for the first time moved to narrow Judge Gesell's pretrial disclosure orders. The department claimed that the judge's final CIPA order would allow North's lawyers to unveil state secrets in their opening statement and through their trial examination of witnesses.[92]

The department's last-minute intervention prompted the sharpest clash between an administration and an independent counsel since the 1974 "Saturday night massacre," when President Nixon fired the Watergate special prosecutor, Archibald Cox. Judge Gesell rejected the Justice Department's motion, holding that only Walsh, the prosecutor in the case, had standing to take an appeal from the CIPA order. After the department twice failed to win review of that ruling by the court of appeals, it won a stay from Chief Justice Rehnquist before the independent counsel and the department finally settled upon a disclosure procedure that allowed the case to proceed.[93]

The attorney general's Supreme Court papers asserted that only the president could determine when national security information may be exposed at trial. Thus, once again, the president claimed that a national security decision was for him alone to decide. Walsh and Judge Gesell countered that such disclosure decisions should be made through balanced institutional participation, by a judicially appointed independent counsel with statutory prosecution powers and a federal judge construing a congressionally enacted classified information disclosure act. Thus, this episode, too, manifested the unresolved battle between competing visions of executive supremacy and balanced institutional participation. By the time this last pretrial flurry reached the Court, the independent counsel had fittingly abandoned any pretense regarding his real adversary in this battle. Walsh's papers filed at the Supreme Court were captioned not *"United States v. Oliver North,"* but *"Dick Thornburgh, Attorney General v. Lawrence Walsh, Independent Counsel."*[94]

The Trials

Given this three-way pretrial sparring, the remarkable feature of the North case was not that it took so long to reach trial, but that it came to trial at all. As Judge Gesell noted early in the case, Congress "probably . . . never contemplated that classified information problems of this magnitude would be presented to a trial judge in a single case."[95] A less able trial judge could easily have been overwhelmed by the torrent of written and oral pretrial motions filed by North's attorneys. Judge Gesell crafted his numerous pretrial rulings most cleverly in a largely successful effort to shield them from trial-delaying interlocutory appeals.[96] By relentlessly narrowing the issues to triable criminal offenses, he dramatically limited the possibility that any broader foreign policy issues would undergo judicial examination. The resultant winnowing of the indictment converted the independent counsel's trial of North from a public debate over the prerogatives of Congress and the president in foreign affairs into a relatively straightforward case about North's private enrichment, lying, and cover-up to Congress.

Once the trial began, however, debates over the proper constitutional roles of Congress and the executive in foreign affairs resurfaced. North rested his defense less on denials of fact than upon claims of exclusive presidential power. During opening statements, his attorneys generally conceded that North had performed the acts alleged, but asserted that he lacked criminal intent because higher-ups, including the president, had authorized all of his acts. The defense further claimed that North was justified in keeping those acts secret because "the Congress of the United States leaked like a sieve." The chief prosecutor defended Congress's role in the foreign policy process, responding that North had indeed intended to lie to officials and to alter documents and that lying "to Congress because you mistrust it is a crime and not a defense."[97]

The prosecution then opened its case by calling a congressman, Lee Hamilton, who testified that executive officials had misled him in his capacity as chairman of the House Intelligence Committee. The defense responded by calling former President Reagan as North's lead witness. When the judge denied that request, North's attorney took the risk of allowing North himself to take the stand.[98] Not surprisingly, North fared far less well under cross-examination by a real prosecutor than he had under previous cross-examination before the Iran-contra committees.[99]

Like his congressional testimony, North's trial testimony marked a turning point in the proceedings, but this time to North's detriment. The prosecutor's aggressive assault on North's credibility during cross-examination stripped away much of the congressional-executive overlay that had hung over the trial to that point and returned the focus of the case to the pending criminal allegations regarding North's personal enrichment.[100] Yet the greatest public furor during the trial arose not from North's testimony, but from the introduction into evidence of seven previously undisclosed documents and a detailed stipulation of facts. These papers suggested that both President Reagan and then–Vice President Bush were far more deeply involved in circumventing the Boland amendments than either the Tower commission or the Iran-contra committees had previously suggested.[101] Predictably, the administration challenged the validity of the stipulation by blaming the independent counsel.[102] But whether true or not, these new factual revelations cast little light on the central legal issue in the case: whether anyone in the executive branch— be it the national security assistant, the vice-president, or the president himself—had legal authority to order North to lie to Congress. In his final instructions to the jury, Judge Gesell answered that question firmly in the negative. "Neither the President nor any of the defendant's superiors had the legal authority to order anyone to violate the law," he declared; "[o]ur country is governed by the rule of law."[103]

Judge Gesell's "superior orders" instruction cut to the heart of North's defense by reaffirming the notion that the foreign affairs power is a power shared. Even the highest executive officials, he suggested, must share vital foreign affairs information with Congress. An executive official's intentional distortion or concealment of such information from Congress, even under orders from the president himself, is therefore a crime punishable in a court of law.

After extensive deliberations, however, the jury apparently ignored that instruction. It voted to convict North on only three of the twelve counts charged: obstructing Congress by creating false and illegal chronologies; altering, destroying, and concealing documents; and receiving a residential security system as an illegal gratuity. As serious as those charges were, the jury simultaneously acquitted North of nine other counts, including seven counts of lying to or obstructing Congress and the attorney general.[104] In effect, the jury convicted North only for those acts that he had plainly performed of his own volition and on his own responsibility, acquitting him of those he claimed to have committed under superior orders. Judge Gesell's surprisingly lenient sentence, which spared North any prison term for crimes for which sentencing experts would have recommended twenty-one to fifty-seven months in prison, only compounded the impression that North's crimes were insubstantial.[105] Although North did not wholly escape punishment, the verdict and sentence sent a troubling message to both lower and higher executive officials, that lower officials will not be seriously punished for lying under orders about foreign affairs to Congress and that higher executive officials can escape accountability for ordering such acts so long as they carefully preserve their own "deniability."

As North's case moves through the appellate process, the Senate majority leader has ordered an investigation into the reasons underlying the independent counsel's decision to dismiss the indictment's first two counts. The majority leader may also propose new legislation modifying CIPA to require declassification in certain criminal cases and to address how CIPA should operate in independent counsel prosecutions. Meanwhile, the Watergate analogy continues to dominate the thinking of both Congress and the media, as they persist in demanding facts about what the president knew and when he knew it—but this time focusing on President Bush rather than President Reagan.[106] Meanwhile, the intragovernmental clashes that characterized the North case have recurred with increasing intensity during the trials of John Poindexter, Joseph Fernandez, and the other Iran-contra defendants.[107]

The statute creating the position of independent counsel does empower Walsh to make a final report to Congress after all prosecutions and convictions have been fully pursued.[108] At that time, the independent counsel may summarize the unclassified evidence upon which he based the dropped counts of his indictment of North, Poindexter, and Secord. Conceivably, he might even offer recommendations for legislative reform. But in the end, one can hardly fault the independent counsel if he fails to pursue this dimension of these cases. For as we have seen, his assigned task was to determine the defendants' criminal responsibility, not to expose defects in the legal structure of our foreign-policy decision making. Nor can Judge Gesell be criticized for failing to pursue the broader constitutional questions raised by North's case, for his office obliged him first and foremost to provide North with a fair trial. In Gesell's own words, "[t]his is not a trial of the national security system; this is not a political trial. It is a trial of Oliver North."[109]

Of the three principal investigators of the Iran-contra affair, only the congressional committees held responsibility for putting the national security system on trial. Once the committees had bypassed that quintessentially legislative task, the participants in the criminal case bore no obligation to assume it. Yet as we have seen, Congress retains an advantage that federal courts and ad hoc presidential commissions lack. Years after particular scandals or cases and controversies have faded from the headlines, Congress may, with the benefit of hindsight, finally undertake a sober consideration of the deeper institutional causes that led to a particular policy failure and constitutional crisis. In the heat of Contragate summer, the congressional committees ignored that task because they looked in the wrong places. But their error only raises the question that is addressed in the next chapter: If the investigators had only looked in the right places, what would they have seen?

2 Recognizing the Pattern of History

Congress's Iran-contra committees focused almost exclusively on what happened during the affair itself rather than on trying to understand the broader pattern of history into which that event fit. Yet to comprehend fully the origins of the affair, the committees should have reviewed not just the immediate history of presidential scandals, but also the congressional-executive conflicts that have recently spanned the United States foreign-policy horizon. Had the committees conducted a more comprehensive survey of war making, treaty affairs, emergency economic powers, arms sales, military aid, and covert operations, they would have recognized that the historical precedent for the affair was not Watergate, but Vietnam. Even a glimpse of recent history in each of those areas reveals a consistent pattern of executive circumvention of legislative constraint in foreign affairs that stretches back to the Vietnam War and persists after the Iran-contra affair.

WAR POWERS

This pattern of executive circumvention emerges most clearly in the realm of the war powers. In August 1964, American ships conducting covert operations were attacked by North Vietnamese torpedo boats in the Tonkin Gulf. America's response, allegedly in self-defense, was followed by another reported attack only days later, which inspired President Johnson to order the first aerial bombing of bases in North Vietnam. President Johnson then asked Congress for the Tonkin

Gulf Resolution, a joint resolution of support that he subsequently construed as broad congressional authorization to escalate the Vietnam War.[1] By 1973 that foreign policy nightmare had triggered the passage, over President Nixon's veto, of the War Powers Resolution, a statute imposing consultation and reporting requirements and a sixty-day time limit upon the president's commitment of troops overseas without express congressional authorization.[2]

Congress passed the War Powers Resolution to prevent future Vietnams, undeclared creeping wars that start and build before Congress or the public are fully aware. Yet Congress markedly undercut the resolution's effectiveness by failing to address two new types of military action that soon came to dominate the 1980s. First, the resolution did not address covert wars, in which intelligence operatives acting under civilian supervision conduct paramilitary activities against foreign governments. By its own terms, the resolution regulates only "United States Armed Forces" and did not reach the allegedly private activities of former Central Intelligence Agency (CIA) operatives such as Eugene Hasenfus, who later worked during the Iran-contra affair for the "Enterprise" supervised by Oliver North.[3] Second, Congress said nothing about short-term military strikes that could be completed well within the resolution's sixty-day time limit. Congress's silence has freed the executive branch to treat that statutory limit as de facto congressional permission to commit troops abroad for a time period of up to sixty days. Thus, in 1975 President Ford sent troops briefly to Vietnam to evacuate American citizens and to Cambodia to free the *Mayaguez,* an American merchant ship. President Carter attempted an abortive military rescue of American hostages in Iran in April 1980. President Reagan dispatched forces to Grenada in October 1983, authorized a "surgical" strike against Libya in April 1986, and ordered attacks upon Iranian oil platforms in the Persian Gulf in October 1987 and April 1988. During his first year as president, George Bush sent U.S. troops to El Salvador, the Philippines, and Panama, in each case avoiding full compliance with the resolution's consultation and reporting requirements.[4]

Ironically, the resolution has also demonstrably failed to prevent even the type of creeping escalation that it was expressly enacted to control. For example, President Reagan sent U.S. troops to Lebanon in August 1982 without prior consultation with Congress and kept them there until February 1984. When Congress finally sought to force the removal of those troops after more than two hundred combat fatalities, the president successfully bargained for a joint resolution extending the time deadlines of the War Powers Resolution from sixty days to eighteen months, without ever articulating what policy the United States military presence was meant to serve.[5]

Similarly, while the Iran-contra furor raged, American ships continued to patrol the Persian Gulf, convoying reflagged Kuwaiti tankers. Fearing Iranian attacks on United States ships, which might have prompted President Reagan to ask Congress for another joint resolution of support, the Senate passed a bill in the fall of 1987 that imposed a new sixty-day reporting requirement on the president and that contemplated a future resolution setting durational limits on the commitment of troops in the Persian Gulf without express congressional authorization.[6] The House took no action on this de facto proposal to reenact the War Powers Resolution because more than one hundred of its members had filed suit in federal court to force the president to acknowledge the applicability of the existing War Powers Resolution to his Persian Gulf activities. But as the 100th Congress concluded, no new law had been passed, the congressional suit had been dismissed as a nonjusticiable political question, and an American navy ship acting out of perceived self-defense had shot down an Iranian jetliner in the Gulf.[7] Thus, more than fifteen years after the War Powers Resolution first became law, scholars and legislators continued to debate whether Congress should reenact a variant of it in order to enforce the resolution's original purpose.[8] Years of congressional-executive struggle over the war powers had brought us from the Tonkin Gulf only so far as the Persian Gulf.

THE TREATY PROCESS

Had the investigators turned their gaze to the treaty process, they would have detected a similar historical pattern of executive circumvention of legislative constraint. In the years before the Vietnam War, the president asserted increasing control over one discrete phase of the treaty process, namely treaty making. But in the post-Vietnam years, he extended that control as well to treaty breaking and what might be thought of as treaty bending, a category that encompasses both treaty modification and reinterpretation.[9]

The Constitution speaks about international agreements only in sparing terms. In Article I, it bars the states from entering treaties or "Agreement[s] or Compact[s] with . . . foreign Power[s]"; in Article II, it authorizes the president to "make Treaties, provided two thirds of the Senators present concur"; and in Article VI, it declares that "all Treaties made . . . under the Authority of the United States" shall reign supreme over state law.[10] While vague, the historical record suggests that the Framers drafted these provisions with a twofold intent: to ensure that the federal treaty power would prevail over state actions and to require that within the federal government both the president and the Senate would participate before a treaty was concluded.[11] Although the Constitutional Convention considered at various points granting either the president or the Senate "the sole and exclusive power to . . . make treaties," Hamilton and Madison urged the adoption of Article II's current language, reasoning, in Hamilton's words, "that the joint possession of the [treaty] power, by the President and Senate, would afford a greater prospect of security than the separate possession of it by either of them."[12] Neither constitutional text nor constitutional history speaks specifically to treaty breaking or bending, but a close reading of Jay's Federalist No. 64 reveals that the Framers intended the constitutional design to reflect a prudential as well as a legal judgment, that a wise treaty process would give the president the lead in treaty matters but would require him to act in consultation with the Senate.[13]

During our Constitution's first century and a half, controversy swirled mainly around the supremacy of federal treaties and executive agreements over state law, questions the Supreme Court did not conclusively settle until the early 1940s.[14] Thereafter, battles for dominance over treaty making between the branches of the federal government took center stage. President Roosevelt quickly followed his famous 1940 destroyers-for-bases deal with Great Britain—a "transaction . . . sustained under statutes which hardly bear the construction placed upon them"—with two 1941 executive agreements that sent American troops to Greenland and Iceland without express congressional consent.[15] By the end of World War II, advocates of presidential power were urging broad use of the executive agreement instead of the treaty to pave the way for U.S. entry into the United Nations and Bretton Woods multilateral treaty systems.[16]

By the mid-1960s, the president had firmly asserted his prerogative to conclude international accords through means that avoided prior congressional consent. During the nineteenth century, the United States had entered approximately one executive agreement and three treaties per year, a number that had risen to twelve agreements and twelve treaties

annually by 1933. But even though the annual average of treaties thereafter remained at twelve, the number of agreements rose to nearly 183 per
year.[17] With few exceptions, however, Congress acquiesced in that
trend. It generally authorized the president's pre-Vietnam agreements,
whether by Senate ratification, prior or subsequent statutory approval or
by appropriating funds to implement United States participation in international organizations. Moreover, the Supreme Court largely validated
the president's use of the executive agreement, enabling postwar presidents to lead the United States into the brave new era of multilateralism.[18]

During the Vietnam War, however, fears that the president would
employ secret executive agreements to make binding commitments about
overseas bases and troop deployment multiplied congressional objections to solo presidential agreement making. In 1969, the Senate adopted
Senator Fulbright's National Commitments Resolution, which expressed
the sense of the Senate that promises to assist foreign states with American armed forces or financial resources could be made only by treaty or
act of Congress.[19] Soon thereafter Congress considered stringent legislation calling for the legislative review of all executive agreements.[20]
When the president opposed that legislation, Congress enacted a less
restrictive version, the Case-Zablocki Act, which required the president
to notify Congress of any recently concluded international agreement.[21]

Until recently, Case-Zablocki constituted the high-water mark in congressional efforts to reassert control over the agreement-making process.
In the years following Vietnam, the Nixon, Ford, Carter, and Reagan
administrations developed a host of subtle and innovative methods to
create or amend international obligations without congressional review.
Presidents Nixon and Reagan employed the technique of "nonagreement
agreements"—characterizing some executive agreements as "voluntary
export restraints"—to avoid notifying Congress of trade accords on steel,
automobiles, machine tools, and semiconductors.[22] To accept some, but
not all, provisions of unratified treaties, Presidents Carter and Reagan
selectively complied with those treaties by issuing "parallel unilateral
policy declarations." In 1977, President Carter unilaterally declared that
the United States would comply with the expired SALT I (strategic arms
limitation talks) treaty so long as the Soviet Union did the same.[23] The
Reagan administration similarly complied with the warhead limits in the
unratified SALT II treaty until it chose to "breach" them in December
1986.[24] President Reagan also refused to sign the United Nations Con-

vention on the Law of the Sea, but announced that the U.S. would comply with many of its provisions as a matter of customary international law.[25] This technique, again used by President Reagan with regard to Protocol II Additional to the 1949 Geneva Conventions, enabled the president to "get the international law we want without having to undergo the 'give' part of the 'give-and-take' of the [international] legislative process."[26]

The most creative post-Vietnam technique of executive treaty making has been the method of reinterpretation. Under this technique the president seeks to give an existing agreement a reading different from that accepted by the Senate when it gave its original advice and consent, thereby effectively amending the treaty without congressional approval. The best-known case of treaty reinterpretation transpired in October 1985 when the Reagan administration sought unilaterally to reinterpret the 1972 Anti-Ballistic Missile (ABM) Treaty, broadening its terms to accommodate executive planning for a Strategic Defense Initiative (SDI). The ABM reinterpretation controversy sparked the sharpest conflict between the two political branches over treaty matters since the Vietnam era. Congress issued a threefold response to the president's actions, declaring that no funds from the 1988–89 fiscal year defense appropriation could be used for new SDI tests; reporting a Senate resolution reaffirming its understanding of the so-called narrow interpretation of the treaty; and attaching to the Senate's resolution of ratification of the U.S.-USSR Intermediate-Range Nuclear Forces (INF) Treaty the "Byrd amendment," a condition that declared that the United States shall not adopt a treaty interpretation that differs from the common understanding of that treaty shared by the executive and the Senate at the time of Senate advice and consent.[27] The president responded by ratifying the INF Treaty and by challenging the Byrd amendment's constitutionality, stating that he could not "accept any diminution claimed to be effected by such a condition in the constitutional powers and responsibilities of the Presidency."[28]

During the years leading to Vietnam, presidents avoided securing Congress's prior consent in order to enhance international mechanisms of multilateral cooperation. The post-Vietnam years, by contrast, have witnessed the reverse trend, America's flight from international organizations and multilateral cooperation. If the early postwar years were America's era of treaty making, then the post-Vietnam years have just as surely been its era of treaty bending and breaking. Once again, the president has generally led the way, but now by unilaterally breaking or modifying preexisting international commitments, usually without consulting either Congress or our treaty partners.

The recent presidential efforts to bend and break existing treaties without Congress's prior consent have differed from the presidential agreement-making years that preceded Vietnam in another crucial respect. Although the Supreme Court generally validated expansion of the president's executive agreement-*making* authority in the pre-Vietnam years, it has not similarly endorsed the president's more recent techniques of treaty bending or breaking on the merits. In its 1979 decision in *Goldwater v. Carter*, the Court summarily dismissed Senator Goldwater's challenge to President Carter's decision unilaterally to terminate the U.S. Mutual Defense Treaty with Taiwan in accordance with its terms. Yet in *Goldwater*, only one Justice voted to uphold the president's treaty-termination decision on the merits. Even that vote rested on the fact that the case involved recognition of foreign governments, an issue over which the Constitution has been read to grant the president plenary power.[29] Nevertheless, executive branch lawyers have gone on to read *Goldwater* to authorize much more. After *Goldwater*, if the president has not liked an existing treaty, he has unilaterally terminated it without congressional consent, as President Reagan did, for example, when terminating the U.S. acceptance of the compulsory jurisdiction of the International Court of Justice, the bilateral Friendship, Commerce, and Navigation Treaty with Nicaragua, and U.S. membership in the United Nations Educational Scientific and Cultural Organization (UNESCO).[30] When a treaty's terms have required the United States to give six-months' notice before terminating it, the president has evaded that restraint by purporting to "modify" the treaty temporarily without congressional consent, as occurred, for example, when President Reagan modified for two years the United States' acceptance of the World Court's compulsory jurisdiction.[31] Whenever the president has proposed to ratify a multilateral treaty without fully subjecting U.S. conduct to international examination, he has used a line-item veto approach. Under this selective nullification technique—recently employed with regard to both the Genocide and Torture conventions—the president has attached so many conditions to his request for Senate advice and consent that those exceptions have significantly altered the terms of U.S. acceptance.[32]

The executive branch has even circumvented congressional efforts to enforce existing multilateral treaties by entering new executive agreements. For example, President Reagan's commerce secretary concluded a side agreement authorizing Japanese fishermen to evade the zero quota imposed by the International Whaling Commission against the killing of whales.[33] With some judicial support, the president has also asserted a sweeping power "to disregard [rules of customary] international law in service of domestic needs."[34] Finally, the executive branch has adapted its novel method of unilateral reinterpretation to break as well as modify preexisting commitments. In one recent case, less well-publicized than the ABM Treaty dispute, the Department of the Navy reinterpreted a United States-Iceland treaty to the detriment of a U.S.-flag shipper that sought to carry military cargo between the two nations. While enjoining the navy from implementing its reinterpretation, a federal judge announced that "[t]he arrogance of power has seldom been displayed in more telling fashion."[35] In short, just as the years leading up to Vietnam witnessed dramatic presidential domination of the process of agreement making, the years since Vietnam have marked a parallel era of executive aggrandizement of the coordinate phases of agreement bending and breaking.

EMERGENCY ECONOMIC POWERS

The vast majority of the foreign affairs powers the president exercises daily are not inherent constitutional powers, but rather, powers that Congress has expressly or implicitly delegated to him by statute. Yet closer examination of the areas of foreign affairs in which Congress has extensively legislated reveals a pattern of executive ascendancy in statutory realms even more striking than the president's continued domination of the constitutional realms of war making and treaty affairs.

In the early 1970s, the Vietnam debacle stimulated a powerful congressional reaction against executive dominance in foreign affairs. During those years, dramatic institutional changes substantially transformed the seniority system in the House and altered congressional rules to enhance the independence of subcommittee chairs and the influence of rank-and-file members. The Vietnam and Watergate-driven congressional election of 1974 brought to power an extraordinarily large number of reformist liberal Democrats. Congress made efforts to close the expertise gap between itself and the executive branch in foreign policy matters, augmenting its committee staffs with foreign policy specialists (the so-called S. Res. 4 staffers). At the same time, Congress for the first time developed an impressive in-house research capability in foreign affairs.[36]

During the immediate post-Vietnam years, a rare synergy between these internal institutional reforms and external circumstance drove Congress to enact statute after statute subjecting the president's delegated foreign affairs powers to stringent procedural constraints. The names of these curative statutes are familiar. In addition to the War Powers Resolution and the Case-Zablocki Act, the list included the 1977 International Emergency Economic Powers Act (IEEPA) and the National Emergencies Act to govern exercises of emergency economic power; the Arms Export Control Act of 1976 to regulate arms sales; the International Development and Food Assistance Act of 1975 and the 1974 Hughes-Ryan amendment to the Foreign Assistance Act to regulate foreign and military aid; the Trade Act of 1974 and the Export Administration Act of 1979 to manage import and export trade; and the Foreign Intelligence Surveillance Act of 1978 and the Intelligence Oversight Act of 1980 to oversee intelligence activities.[37]

These enactments typically conditioned presidential exercises of delegated authority upon adherence to elaborate statutory procedures, including factual findings, public declarations, committee oversight, prior reporting and subsequent consultation requirements, and the legislative veto, the congressional control technique of choice in the post-Vietnam era. With few exceptions, however, this generation of statutes created not only procedural constraints, but also substantial fresh delegations of foreign-affairs authority.[38] By the late 1980s, it had become clear that the executive branch had successfully tapped many of these broad new authorizations while paying only lip service to the accompanying procedural strictures.

The most glaring example of this trend has been the International Emergency Economic Powers Act.[39] Congress enacted IEEPA specifically to limit executive abuses of the national emergency powers that the Trading with the Enemy Act (TWEA) had conferred on the president sixty years earlier.[40] TWEA had authorized the president to wield an enormous store of delegated power in both wartime and nonwartime situations, simply by declaring the existence of a national emergency. But TWEA's subsequent history had demonstrated that presidents rarely terminated such emergencies once they had been declared. While Congress was considering IEEPA's enactment in 1977, for example, members were shocked to learn that both President Roosevelt's 1933 TWEA declaration of a national banking emergency and President Truman's 1950 declaration in response to the Korean conflict were still in force. As Justice Blackmun later recognized, "TWEA emergency authority operated as a one-way ratchet to enhance greatly the President's discretionary authority over foreign policy. . . . [T]he President retained broad authority of indefinite duration to respond to anything that logically could be related to the general threat of the spread of Communism."[41]

Stung by perceived presidential abuses of its delegated TWEA power, Congress drafted IEEPA specifically to narrow the president's authority in nonwartime situations. Although Congress sought to ensure that the president would have sufficient emergency powers to deal with unforeseen circumstances, it conditioned his exercise of emergency powers upon prior congressional consultation, subsequent review, and legislative-veto termination provisions. Yet three successive Supreme Court decisions quickly emasculated IEEPA's various congressional control devices.[42] In 1981, the Court generously construed the president's IEEPA authorities as authorizing him to settle the central aspects of the Iranian hostage crisis. Two years later, the Court's sweeping opinion in *INS v. Chadha* invalidated the legislative-veto provision that had authorized Congress to terminate presidentially declared IEEPA emergencies. And in a dubious opinion the following term, the Court weakened IEEPA's statutory requirement that the president declare a national emergency, by upholding the president's authority under TWEA's "grandfather clause" to exercise preexisting statutory emergency powers against Cuba without declaring a new national emergency.

Those rulings freed the president to use IEEPA to conduct widespread economic warfare merely by declaring a national emergency with respect to a particular country, as Presidents Carter and Reagan have subsequently done against Iran, Libya, Nicaragua, South Africa, and Panama.[43] Moreover, despite the insistence of the House of Representatives that "emergencies are by their nature rare and brief, and are not to be equated with normal, ongoing problems," the president has made and sustained such declarations virtually without regard to whether bona fide "emergencies" have existed.[44] Of the five nations against which the president has imposed IEEPA sanctions since 1979, only Iran's actions posed an "unusual and extraordinary threat" constituting a national "emergency" in the layperson's sense of those terms.[45] Nevertheless, the courts have regularly rebuffed challenges to the president's declarations of emergency under IEEPA on the ground that such determinations constitute nonjusticiable political questions.[46] Thus, like the TWEA national emergencies that preceded it, the Iranian emergency has now continued unterminated for more than a decade.

Perhaps most troubling, the president has recently begun to declare national emergencies under IEEPA not only in response to hostile foreign action, but also in response to Congress's failure or unwillingness to act in accordance with his will. In 1983 and 1984, the president twice triggered IEEPA to sustain the existing export control laws and foreign boycott restrictions after Congress had failed to reauthorize the Export Administration Act.[47] When the House of Representatives rejected covert aid for the Nicaraguan contras in the spring of 1985, the Reagan administration again declared a national emergency. In an action later sustained by the lower federal courts, the president applied IEEPA sanctions against the Sandinistas as a substitute for congressional action, even though the alleged emergency conditions had persisted for many months.[48] Later that year, President Reagan abruptly declared a national emergency and imposed IEEPA sanctions upon South Africa in an unsuccessful effort to preempt Congress's eventual enactment of comprehensive antiapartheid legislation.[49]

By the end of the Reagan administration, executive officials were branding as "draconian" even the statutory requirement that the president declare a national emergency before invoking his IEEPA powers.[50] With the help of the courts, the president had won broad discretion to decide how strictly to comply with IEEPA's procedural requisites. Although avowedly passed to limit the president's discretion, IEEPA, along with the plethora of statutory emergency powers enacted by Congress during the 1980s, unwittingly enhanced executive power by fostering the "routinization of crisis government."[51] In only one decade, the executive branch had succeeded in extracting from IEEPA the same sweeping delegation of emergency authorities that Congress had expressly sought to remove from it after Vietnam.

ARMS SALES, MILITARY AID, THE NSC, AND COVERT OPERATIONS: THE IRAN-CONTRA AFFAIR

Had the committees placed the Iran-contra affair against this broader historical background, they would have recognized that it represented not just a passing historical aberration, but merely the latest act in a foreign policy drama that has been playing out since the early 1970s. Indeed, far from being unprecedented, each of the four elements of the Iran-contra tableau—the covert sale of arms to Iran, the diversion of funds to the contras in apparent violation of the Boland amendments, the "operationalization" of National Security Council (NSC) staff, and the abuse of covert operations—repeated historical events that had first occurred during the Nixon era. Viewed in light of events of the early 1970s, the Iran-contra affair emerges as an extreme, but foreseeable, episode in the continuing post-Vietnam flow of foreign affairs power from Congress to the executive.

The Arms Sale

The Reagan administration was not the first to sell weapons systems secretly to Iran. In May 1972, President Nixon sold fighter aircraft and associated equipment to the Shah over the opposition of both the State and Defense departments. Because that sale was primarily for cash on commercial terms, it evaded the legislative controls built into the 1949 Mutual Defense Assistance Act, which authorized the president to sanction government-to-government cash sales to foreign countries without congressional approval.[52]

The 1972 Iranian transaction marked an important turning point in both the nature and direction of American arms sale policy. Although massive private American arms sales had occurred in World War I, the American government's modern role as an international arms supplier began with the Lend-Lease program of 1941. Before 1970, most American governmental arms supplies were directed toward developed nations, principally to North Atlantic Treaty Organization (NATO) allies, and included surplus or obsolete, as well as sophisticated military weapons. Although the Foreign Military Sales Act of 1968 created a formal procedure for cash and credit sales of large quantities of weaponry, it left executive discretion largely unconstrained, thereby freeing the president to use arms sales as an ad hoc tool of foreign policy.[53]

In the early 1970s, supplying modern arms to South Vietnam formed an important component of President Nixon's program to "Vietnamize" the war. The Nixon administration hoped to preempt the necessity for future direct American troop support to threatened Third World nations by supplying them with arms, expecting that those nations would then assume primary responsibility for their own defense.[54] As part of this global plan, in 1972 President Nixon promised the Shah of Iran open-ended access to state-of-the-art nonnuclear weapons in the American arsenal in exchange for the Shah's commitment to accept the lead role in protecting Western interests in the Persian Gulf. As former NSC aide Gary Sick has described, "[i]n the next four years after the Nixon-Kissinger visit, the shah ordered more than $9 billion worth of the most sophisticated weaponry in the U.S. inventory, and the arms sale program quickly became a scandal."[55]

The public furor over these and later weapons sales to Saudi Arabia and Kuwait stimulated congressional concerns that secret arms sales to Third World nations would escalate unavoidably into more unwanted overseas commitments, such as in Vietnam. Those concerns encouraged passage in 1974 of new arms export control legislation, which required the president to give Congress advance notice of any offer to sell to foreign countries defense articles and services valued at $25 million or more; it further authorized Congress to veto all such sales within twenty calendar days by a concurrent resolution (which is not subject to presidential veto).[56] Congress later incorporated this two-house legislative veto provision, along with numerous reporting and certification requirements designed to reach commercial sales and third-country transfers of U.S. arms, into the comprehensive International Security Assistance and Arms Export Control Act of 1976. That scheme subjected certain presidentially initiated arms sales to congressional disapproval, but only if a sale both exceeded certain dollar amounts and could not muster majority support in either legislative house.[57]

Although Congress never exercised its legislative veto in the arms export laws, executive-branch officials conceded that the veto imposed "important discipline on all who administer the system—the State and Defense Departments, the White House and National Security Council staffs, Ambassadors in the field, and the manufacturers of defense equipment, as well as foreign military leaders."[58] But the Supreme Court's watershed 1983 decision in *INS v. Chadha* swept away not only the legislative veto in IEEPA, but this congressional veto as well.[59] Several years after *Chadha,* Congress amended the arms statute with a so-called report-and-wait provision. That amendment imposed upon the president a much looser obligation—to report to Congress about planned arms sales and to wait to see whether Congress would nullify the sale by passing a joint resolution of disapproval (a resolution subject to presidential veto).[60] Yet this option—of barring a presidential action essentially by passing a new law that the president could veto—had always been available to Congress. Moreover, executive-branch lawyers successfully embedded into the successor legislation numerous provisions giving the president greater freedom of action in case he found certain proposed transfers to be "in the national security interests of the United States." The revised legislation also left ambiguous whether the executive branch could transfer weapons abroad secretly, if the transfer occurred as part of an intelligence operation conducted under other laws.[61]

The result was that even a joint resolution of disapproval did not bar the president from openly selling arms abroad as long as he could veto that resolution and defeat an override by securing more than one-third of the votes in either chamber of Congress. Nor was the president clearly barred from selling arms abroad covertly as long as he could claim to be acting pursuant to intelligence laws rather than to arms control laws. This precise scenario materialized in 1985 and 1986 when the Reagan administration covertly sold some $30 million in missiles to Iran. At virtually the same time, the executive branch overtly sold nearly nine times that dollar volume in advanced missiles to Saudi Arabia over the objection of large majorities in both houses. A joint resolution disapproving the Saudi deal had passed the House by a vote of nearly six-to-one and the Senate by a vote of more than three-to-one. But after vetoing the resolution, President Reagan persuaded twelve additional senators to support his position, averting a veto override by a single vote.[62] Similarly, two years later, President Reagan successfully concluded a sale of nearly $2 billion in arms to Kuwait over the initial opposition of a Senate majority.[63]

Although members of Congress proposed an amendment to the arms export control laws "designed to restore a balance between the executive and legislative branches on foreign arms transfers," the bill died with the 100th Congress and has yet to be reintroduced.[64] Nor, despite the Iran-contra furor, have any of the laws governing covert arms sales been significantly strengthened. Less than two weeks after taking office, the Bush administration proposed new large-scale arms sales to Bahrain, Egypt, Israel, Kuwait, Morocco, Saudi Arabia, and the United Arab Emirates.[65] Thus, fifteen years after controversial Middle Eastern arms sales had first spurred Congress to enact restrictive arms export legislation, the president retained largely unaltered discretion to conclude controversial arms sales over substantial congressional objection.

Funding Secret Wars

The Boland amendments, which were attached to successive appropriations bills between 1982 and 1986, barred any "agency or entity of the United States involved in intelligence activities" from spending funds available to it "to support military or paramilitary operations in Nicaragua."[66] Yet those amendments did not mark the first time that Congress had invoked its appropriations power to harness executive funding of secret war making. Once again, the prototype for such legislation had been aimed not at Central America, but at Southeast Asia. The unmasking of the Nixon administration's secret Cambodian incursions in 1970 revealed that the president had used his special funds and transfer authorities to allot millions of dollars in secret military aid to Cambodia without prior congressional approval. At one point, the Nixon administration sent Cambodia $7.9 million in military aid and justified it after the fact, making a "retroactive presidential finding" that closely resembled one later made by the general counsel of the Central Intelligence Agency (CIA) during the Iran-contra affair.[67]

In 1971, Congress debated the famous Cooper-Church amendment to the Foreign Military Sales Act, which would have cut off funds for U.S. ground troops, advisers, and air support in and over Cambodia. A similar provision, the Hatfield-McGovern Bill, introduced at roughly the same time, would have terminated the use after December 1970 of any appropriated funds in Vietnam for purposes of military conflict. Although Professor Bickel, for one, expressed no "doubt under the sun . . . on the constitutional foundation for either the Cooper-Church or the McGovern-Hatfield amendment," neither became law.[68] As opposition to the Indochina war grew, in 1973 and 1974, Congress finally enacted seven separate provisions denying the use of funds authorized or appropriated pursuant to various laws to support United States military or paramilitary forces in Vietnam, Cambodia, or Laos.[69] Moreover, as CIA involvement in the Cambodian operations became public, Congress enacted the Hughes-Ryan amendment of 1974, which imposed reporting requirements on the CIA as a prerequisite to its expenditure of appropriated funds.[70]

Yet even these Vietnam-era statutory funding limitations did not totally curtail the executive's foreign military and paramilitary campaigns. Notwithstanding express statutory funding prohibitions barring the use of United States forces to carry out military operations in, over, or off the shores of Cambodia or South Vietnam, within a year President Ford had sent U.S. armed forces to rescue the *Mayaguez* and to evacuate personnel from Vietnam and Cambodia.[71] Even after the Hughes-Ryan amendment became law, secret United States paramilitary aid to Angola persisted. Already "[t]raumatized by Watergate and Vietnam," Congress finally passed the Boland amendments' direct ancestor, the Clark amendment to the Arms Export Control Act of 1976.[72] Until its repeal in July 1985, the Clark amendment did exactly what the Boland amendments later sought to do; it barred aid to private groups that would have the purpose or effect of aiding military or paramilitary operations in Angola.[73] Yet even after the Clark amendment became law, then–Director of Central Intelligence George Bush refused to concede that all U.S. aid to Angola had stopped.[74] Thus, during the Iran-contra hearings, allegations persisted that Oliver North had not only supported the Nicaraguan rebels while the Boland amendments were in force, but had also supported the Angolan rebels while the Clark amendment was in place.[75]

During his congressional testimony, North criticized the Boland amendments by comparing the inadequate U.S. support given to democratic movements in Vietnam, Angola, and Nicaragua. "[O]nce we made the commitment to support the democratic resistance" in each country, he argued, "we should have made that commitment a consistent one."[76] His interrogators could have responded that Congress and the president share the decision on whether to sustain U.S. "commitments" by appropriating funds, and that during each of the three conflicts, Congress had enacted, and the president had signed, a statute that barred continued U.S. military support for the resistance movement. Had the investigators so responded, debate could have ensued over a broader constitutional question, whether executive officials may unilaterally disregard funding decisions regarding U.S. commitments abroad, which Congress and the president have jointly made. But in their single-minded pursuit of the facts, the members of the committees asserted that point only tangentially and with regard to Nicaragua, again overlooking the broader historical lessons of Vietnam.[77]

The NSC Staff Operationalized

Similarly, the operationalization of NSC staff commenced not with the peregrinations of Oliver North or Robert McFarlane's odyssey to Tehran with Bible and birthday cake, but with

Henry Kissinger's secret trip to mainland China nearly two decades earlier.[78] The National Security Act of 1947, which had established both the NSC and the CIA, did not create the NSC as a decision-making, much less a decision-executing, body. Congress no more designed the NSC to execute national security policy than it designed the Council of Economic Advisers to print the nation's money. Instead, the 1947 act unambiguously provided that the NSC's function "shall be to *advise the President* with respect to the integration of domestic, foreign, and military policies relating to the national security."[79] Accordingly, Congress made the president, the vice-president, and the secretaries of state and defense statutory NSC members, with the director of central intelligence, the chairman of the Joint Chiefs of Staff, and the attorney general attending NSC meetings only by invitation.[80] Until the Korean War began, President Truman employed the NSC and its small staff solely as an information-gathering and policy-coordinating entity.[81]

Similarly, the staff position of assistant to the president for national security affairs was not designed to act as a policy advocate or executor. In 1947, Congress established no position called national security adviser, authorizing only the creation of a small executive secretariat to serve as the NSC's staff.[82] In 1953, President Eisenhower created the national security assistant's position under an obscure statute authorizing the appointment of "employees in the White House Office" to set the council's agenda, to brief the president on national security matters, and to supervise the NSC staff.[83] Throughout the Eisenhower era, the president and not the national security assistant presided over NSC meetings; presidential decisions were transmitted for implementation to a separate operations coordinating board, chaired by the undersecretary of state.[84]

By the same token, in 1947, Congress never envisioned that the CIA would formulate, as opposed to execute, intelligence policy. Instead, Congress authorized the CIA to perform only such "functions and duties related to intelligence affecting the national security as the *National Security Council* may from time to time direct."[85] In the CIA's early years, Congress and the NSC mandated that the agency follow three internal control principles. First, Congress expressly denied the CIA "police, subp[o]ena, law-enforcement powers, or internal-security functions," to ensure that it would act as a national security agency, not as a domestic law enforcement unit.[86] Second, an early NSC directive instructed the CIA to employ covert means only in pursuit of announced

American foreign policy ends. Third, subsequent NSC directives established that the CIA's covert activities should proceed only after full consultation and coordination with other executive branch agencies and Congress.[87]

By the early 1960s, however, both the NSC and the CIA had deviated noticeably from their original organizational mandates. In accordance with his personalized leadership style, President Kennedy deinstitutionalized the NSC and incorporated NSC personnel into his personal staff. Kennedy's national security assistant, McGeorge Bundy, soon emerged as one of the president's principal policy advocates and public spokespersons in foreign affairs. Deinstitutionalization continued under Lyndon Johnson with informal Tuesday lunches gradually supplanting the NSC system as the fora for coordinating and supervising particular national security programs.[88] Within this unrigorous structure, the national security assistant's peculiar political and legal status effectively immunized his activities from congressional examination. The national security assistant maintained the protocol rank of a deputy undersecretary, thereby escaping Senate confirmation by being an "inferior Officer," whose appointment Congress had vested "in the President alone" for purposes of the appointments clause of the Constitution.[89] No statute required the assistant to report to Congress and until the Iran-contra affair, each president refused to allow the national security assistant to testify before Congress, claiming executive privilege.[90]

During his 1968 presidential campaign, Richard Nixon hearkened back to the Eisenhower years, vowing to "restore the National Security Council to its preeminent role in national security planning."[91] In his initial presidential press conference, Nixon for the first time referred to National Security Assistant Henry Kissinger as "my *Adviser* for National Security Affairs."[92] Kissinger organized and chaired an NSC review group that oversaw a succession of top-level interagency committees charged with developing policies for particular geographical regions and subject matters, an arrangement that effectively replicated the State Department's own bureaucratic structure. Before Kissinger became secretary of state in name as well as in fact, the NSC staff had expanded to some 120 members, accumulating extraordinary decision-making, then decision-executing, power at the State Department's expense.[93]

Under Kissinger's leadership, the NSC's policy-formulating functions expanded to include numerous policy-executing activities. Kissinger's own operational activities began with his dramatic secret negotiating missions to Vietnam, China, and Berlin, the details of which he kept even from the secretary of state. Kissinger announced the decision that placed American military forces on worldwide alert during the 1973 Yom Kippur War and opened the back channel to the Soviet leadership that ripened into the policy of detente. During the Indochina conflict, Kissinger and his deputy, Maj. Gen. Alexander Haig, directly supervised the secret bombing of Cambodia over the defense secretary's initial objections.[94]

Yet even while the NSC was assuming these operational duties, the CIA had started to assume a greater role in policy formulation. Active CIA intervention in Iran began in the early 1950s with the reinstallation of the Shah as national leader. Even before the Bay of Pigs, the agency had begun executing and formulating policy in Guatemala and Cuba that governed not just intelligence gathering, but covert operations and covert war.[95] The 1964 Gulf of Tonkin incident itself, by most accounts, resulted from overaggressive espionage by a navy destroyer working for a U.S. electronic surveillance unit.[96]

By 1974, the CIA had violated each of the three internal control principles that had guided its creation. During the Vietnam War, the agency conducted secret illegal domestic break-ins, mail intercepts, wiretaps, and domestic surveillance. Congressional investigations uncovered CIA death plots against foreign leaders in Cuba and the Congo and secret CIA military and paramilitary activities in Chile. All of these activities the CIA conducted not only contrary to stated U.S. foreign policy objectives, but also without accountability to either Congress or to the rest of the executive branch.[97] By the early 1970s, it was an open secret that the CIA was running secret wars in Vietnam, Laos, and Cambodia.[98] Indeed, Watergate itself ultimately grew out of our Southeast Asian foreign policy. The now-infamous office break-in was executed by the "plumbers," a White House unit funded with private campaign contributions that was partly staffed by former CIA agents, supported by the CIA, and formed for the purpose of "plugging leaks" by government officials suspected of having exposed the secret bombing of Cambodia.[99]

In short, by 1974, the NSC had taken on significant operational responsibilities and the CIA was firmly entrenched as an important national security policy player. Although both trends abated during the Ford and Carter years, the Reagan administration reinvigorated them. In a foreign policy reorganization announced shortly after he took office, President

Reagan installed William Casey as CIA director, and gave him a status equal to the secretaries of state and defense. William Clark, President Reagan's second national security assistant, abandoned neutral brokering of interagency differences in favor of an active role in developing Middle East, Latin American, and international economic policy. Clark's interventions helped force Alexander Haig's 1982 resignation as secretary of state, which created a vacuum that propelled Director Casey into a primary role in directing Central American covert operations policy.[100] As Robert McFarlane, then John Poindexter, became national security assistant, the NSC maintained dominance over covert operations and crisis management (particularly with regard to counterterrorism), the two warmaking areas that Congress had left unregulated by the War Powers Resolution.[101] As a carryover from the Carter years, the NSC's crisis management-counterterrorism portfolio afforded it principal custody of government policy regarding Iran, effectively depriving top-level decision makers of the State Department's sources of Iranian expertise.[102] Meanwhile, the NSC's covert operations duties gave it increasing line responsibility for managing the secret war in Nicaragua. What the Iran-contra affair revealed was that the NSC and CIA had finally swapped institutional roles. The NSC staff had linked its operational relations with both Iran and the contras by conducting a covert policy that the director of central intelligence had helped to formulate. But by trading places, the two agencies had only brought full circle an inversion of institutional responsibility that first began during the Vietnam era.

Covert Operations

Once the executive's Vietnam-era abuses came to light, Congress sought to prevent future executive adventurism by amending existing intelligence legislation to reach covert activities. Yet even a brief review of this revisionary movement unveils a recurring historical pattern. In late 1974, as revelations of executive misconduct multiplied, the president declared that he would not tolerate illegal activities by intelligence agencies and formed a presidential commission to investigate hidden abuses.[103] Congress enacted a law, the Hughes-Ryan amendment to the Foreign Assistance Act of 1974, which sought to ensure future accountability for covert operations through stiffer certification and reporting requirements.[104] The president then replaced the director of central intelligence and Congress established select, and later permanent, House and Senate committees to study governmental intelligence operations.[105]

Based on those investigations, oversight advocates offered a comprehensive 263-page charter for the intelligence community. But following extensive debate, opponents trimmed it down into the two-page Intelligence Oversight Act of 1980, which made only two significant changes in the law.[106] The Hughes-Ryan amendment had already abandoned the pre-Vietnam practice of denial of presidential responsibility, instead requiring the president to make an explicit statutory "finding" that each covert operation is "important to the national security of the United States." The 1980 law stiffened that reporting requirement by mandating that the executive provide the intelligence committees with prior notice of any "significant anticipated intelligence activity" (including covert operations).[107] In exchange, Congress reduced from eight to two the number of congressional committees to which the president was required to report. In "extraordinary circumstances affecting vital interests of the United States," Congress reduced the members to be notified of pending covert actions to a "Gang of Eight" congressional leaders and allowed the president to act without prior notice as long as he reported "in a timely fashion."[108]

By requiring only that Congress be informed of intelligence activities, the 1980 act "hardly satisfied those who preferred a major statutory charter; it carried a certain ambiguity permitting the president to skirt prior notification; it placed no time limit on covert actions and did not provide for a congressional veto."[109] As finally enacted, the 1980 oversight act did little more than codify the executive practice followed by the Carter administration over the previous four years. The act included almost verbatim the provisions for intelligence oversight contained in President Carter's 1978 executive order restricting intelligence activities.[110] Even so, the Carter administration opposed legislative enactment of those provisions "because the President did not want to give those restraints the force of law."[111] The act's effectiveness therefore hinged upon informal congressional-executive accords and the president's willingness to issue and enforce the executive orders and national security decision directives necessary to discharge his statutory responsibilities.

In the Reagan years, this choice for informality proved costly. The fall of the Shah of Iran and the Soviet invasion of Afghanistan, both viewed as intelligence failures, helped dampen public concern over CIA misconduct.[112] As memories dimmed, the administration began to protest the stringency of existing statutory reporting and consultation requirements. In addition, the new president began unilaterally to modify his predecessor's intelligence directives. For example, President Carter's executive order governing intelligence had required consistency between covert and overt policies by defining "special [that is, covert] activities" as secret "activities conducted in support of national foreign policy objectives abroad *which are designed to further official United States programs and policies abroad.*" In 1981, President Reagan's succeeding executive order quietly amended that order, dropping that important limiting language.[113] Although the new administration issued a National Security Decision Directive requiring that the president approve covert actions by means of written findings, the Justice Department later opined that such executive directives were merely procedures instituted for the "internal use" of the president and his intelligence advisers and could not legally bind him.[114]

Similarly, the committee oversight mandated by the 1980 act softened as the intelligence committees gained familiarity with the agencies they were regulating. Like government agencies "captured" by the private industries they regulate, all "federal agencies exist in a symbiotic relationship with the congressional committees and subcommittees to which they report. . . . [An agency] purchases freedom . . . by playing ball in the areas that are of concern."[115] The comparative laxity of the reporting requirements in the 1980 act forced the House and Senate intelligence committees, like other congressional oversight committees, to pay for CIA information by affording the agency greater discretion. Before long, the Senate intelligence committee's vice-chair was charging that that body, "[l]ike other legislative committees, [had come] to be an advocate for the agency it was overseeing."[116]

By 1984, revelations of covert CIA activities in Central America were quickly multiplying. Nicaragua brought suit against the United States at the International Court of Justice, charging the Reagan administration with actively supporting military and paramilitary activities against it in violation of international law.[117] Intelligence committee hostility toward Director Casey peaked with the April 1984 revelation that the CIA had secretly mined Nicaraguan harbors without giving the committees the statutorily required notice.[118] In response, the Senate initially passed a nonbinding resolution proclaiming that no money could be spent for such purposes. But rather than embody that resolution in binding legislation, the Senate compromised and settled for the so-called Casey accords, which required the director to give the committees notice of new covert actions as soon as practicable. Within days after accepting those "voluntary" reporting requirements, the Reagan administration began planning its secret arms sale to Iran.[119]

As the Iran-contra committees' report revealed, President Reagan authorized the initial arms sales to Iran and ordered his subordinates to keep the contras together "body and soul." Casey directed North to coordinate both sets of activities and endorsed the diversion of the proceeds from the sales into the Enterprise, an "off-the-shelf, self-sustaining, stand-alone" covert organization staffed by private citizens and run with private monies. The president authorized the first shipments of arms to Iran in August and September of 1985 (which took place through Israeli intermediaries) by "oral" findings that were nowhere authorized by the intelligence statutes. The second shipment in November 1985, which was executed in part by the CIA, was subsequently deemed to be authorized by a novel "retroactive" finding generated by the CIA's general counsel (which Vice Admiral Poindexter later admitted destroying). The third finding of 6 January 1986 and its amended version of 17 January 1986 President Reagan admittedly signed, but later claimed he never actually read. Contrary to the internal agency control principles described above, all of the NSC's actions during the Iran-contra affair ran counter to announced U.S. foreign policy objectives and all were conducted without the knowledge of either Congress or virtually all of the executive branch.[120]

In the wake of these disturbing revelations, one might have expected Congress to have learned the lesson of the last war. But in covert operations, as in other fields, the post-Vietnam era largely repeated itself. The president declared that he would not tolerate illegal activities by his national security agencies and formed the Tower commission to investigate the abuses. Congress established select House and Senate committees to study the events. To forestall future Iran-contra affairs, both houses considered amendments to the Intelligence Oversight Act that would have required the president to inform Congress in writing about all new covert operations within forty-eight hours after they began.[121]

Congress's action prompted a predictable executive reaction. To quell public outcry, the president appointed a new CIA director pledged to internal procedural reforms, but opposed to any legislative reform of the agency.[122] The president's lawyers hinted that he would veto the new reporting measure as an unconstitutional limit upon his prerogative to initiate, direct, and control sensitive national security activities.[123] Nor did they foreclose the possibility that if the legislation passed over his veto, the president might direct his director of central intelligence not to implement the law, citing the statute's alleged constitutional infirmities.[124] Needing to secure a two-thirds majority in each house to enact the proposed amendments, the congressional leadership settled for yet another interim informal accord with the president to achieve the same result. Although the president promised that his administration would abide by that accord, he did not purport to bind his successor with it, reiterating his belief "that the current statutory framework is adequate."[125] After the new CIA director had disciplined the officers responsible for the Iran-contra affair, public interest in restrictive intelligence oversight legislation began to subside.[126]

Until the fall of 1988, enactment of the proposed covert action bill remained possible, as the measure passed the Senate by a wide margin and the House bill was reported out of two committees.[127] But less than a week before the House bill was to reach the floor, then–Speaker of the House Wright announced that Congress had "received clear testimony from C.I.A. people that they have deliberately done things to provoke an overreaction on the part of the Government of Nicaragua."[128] The administration did not deny the accuracy of the remark, which the Speaker later claimed derived not from classified congressional briefings but from a former CIA official's public testimony before the International Court of Justice. Nevertheless, administration officials charged that the Speaker had violated House rules governing disclosure of classified information. Meanwhile House Republicans requested an ethics inquiry and sought to amend the pending bill to impose criminal penalties upon any person, including a member of Congress, who leaks classified intelligence information. In response, the House Democratic leadership deferred floor consideration of the covert action bill to avoid providing another forum for the discussion of the Speaker's alleged indiscretion.[129]

As the Bush presidency began, the new Senate majority leader reiterated his desire to enact the covert action bill. But in the first days of the new Congress, with his actions still under review by the House Ethics

Committee, Speaker Wright voluntarily shelved the legislation as "an opening gesture of good faith on our part" toward the new president. In return, President Bush agreed to abide by the spirit and letter of the legislative proposal, but did not commit himself to accept the terms of President Reagan's informal covert action deal. Following Speaker Wright's departure, the intelligence committees and the new president finally concluded yet another set of informal accords.[130]

In sum, the history of the covert action field from Vietnam to Contragate repeats the pattern found in other foreign policy arenas. Scandals regarding executive misconduct have proceeded from revelation to public outrage to blue-ribbon investigations. Those investigations have inspired restrictive legislative proposals whose enactment the president has opposed, offering instead temporary informal accommodations and pledges to replace the responsible officials. As the scandal has faded from public consciousness, legislative solutions have grown increasingly difficult to secure. Congress has found itself left without adequate statutory remedies to prevent or redress the inevitable recurrence of the so-called aberrational event.

THE PATTERN OF HISTORY

If the Iran-contra committees had looked past Watergate to the Vietnam era, they would have seen that the Iran-contra affair was only the tip of a much larger iceberg that crystallized during the Vietnam War. All of the congressional-executive struggles that surrounded the affair merely replicated battles that transpired during that earlier period. That history should have repeated itself across so many spheres of foreign affairs, even after Congress had passed so many statutes to avoid repetition of the Vietnam-era evasions, suggests that the Iran-contra affair exposed systemic, rather than localized, problems in the American foreign-policy process.

Had the Iran-contra investigators asked why we have been forced to relive this history, they would have recognized a pattern familiar to any student of regulation. It was Vietnam that originally spurred Congress to pass the War Powers Resolution in an attempt to regulate overt executive war making. Yet far from eliminating such war making, the War Powers Resolution only drove it underground. The resolution stimulated the executive to substitute emergency economic sanctions for military warfare, to replace overt with covert operations, and to transfer the control of covert operations from the military establishment to the less heavily regulated intelligence agencies.

Abuses by those intelligence agencies then increased congressional regulation of the CIA through special oversight committees, which led to both the partial capture of those committees by that agency and a shifting of its activities during the Iran-contra affair toward an unregulated alternative, the NSC staff. When the NSC staff found its own resources inadequate to execute covert operations, it subcontracted its duties to private agents and financed the payments with contributions from private parties and foreign governments.[131] Statutes requiring the disclosure of public international agreements caused government-to-government deals to be struck privately.[132] Existing laws that limit overt arms sales inspired NSC officials and their delegates to sell arms covertly. After the Boland amendments restricted any official U.S. funding to the contras, military aid was privatized. In short, Congress's postwar efforts to enact legislation that would stop the last war simply channeled executive action into new, unregulated forms of warfare. In a familiar regulatory pattern, each succeeding congressional effort to catch up with executive evasion of its legislative controls served only to shift executive activity into a new pattern of evasion.

If the Iran-contra investigators had recognized this broader historical pattern, they would have seen that new patchwork legislation would not prevent but only alter the form of future Iran-contra affairs. Yet as chapter 1 revealed, the affair's principal investigators disputed the need for even patchwork legislation. The Tower commission simply rejected legislative reform. One of its few structural recommendations—that Congress should combine existing intelligence committees into a smaller joint committee—would only have rendered those committees more vulnerable to CIA capture.[133]

The congressional committees at least offered a collection of legislative proposals, thereby acknowledging the possibility of some structural reform of the foreign policy process. But their decision to lay blame, rather than legislative groundwork, allowed them to avoid specifying a *normative vision* of what the foreign policy process should look like. Indeed, the fact-intensive, personality-oriented nature of the hearings left unclear to many viewers which foreign policy processes were normal and which were aberrational. For example, one might have expected the

committees to begin by hearing testimony from the secretaries of state
and defense to determine how the foreign policy process should operate
ideally. Only then would one have expected them to call North and
Poindexter to demonstrate how thoroughly the players in the Iran-contra
affair had misunderstood and subverted that process. Yet by the account
of two prominent congressional participants, the committees rejected the
option of calling so-called wise men as first witnesses for the remarkable
reason that "they would be too dull."[134] Instead, the committees let the
hearings climax with North and Poindexter's melodramatic testimony,
leaving many observers with the impression that the conduct of those
witnesses had been normal and necessary.[135]

Had the committees viewed the affair against the historical background
outlined above, they would have recognized that they were not dealing
with a collection of unconnected statutory violations. What faced them
instead was a more fundamental assault on the constitutional assumptions
underlying our postwar national security system. Taken together, these
assumptions form a distinct constitutional vision of how governmental
decisions regarding national security issues should be made—what I call
our National Security Constitution. Viewed in light of this normative
vision, the Iran-contra affair represented nothing less than a covert attempt to rewrite the National Security Constitution that we have inherited. Before we return to the Iran-contra affair in chapter 4, we must
examine this National Security Constitution. Where did it come from and
what are its premises?

PART TWO
THE PROBLEM

3 The National Security Constitution We Inherited: From the Founding to the National Security Act

THE NATIONAL SECURITY CONSTITUTION

One cannot read the Constitution without being struck by its astonishing brevity regarding the allocation of foreign affairs authority among the branches. Nowhere does the Constitution use the words "foreign affairs" or "national security." Instead, it creates a Congress, president, and federal judiciary and vests in them powers, some of which principally affect foreign affairs. Only occasionally does it explicitly condition one branch's exercise of a foreign affairs power upon another's, as in its grants to the president of the powers, with the Senate's advice and consent, to make treaties and to appoint ambassadors.[1] More frequently, the document grants clearly related powers to separate institutions, without ever specifying the relationship between those powers, as for example, with Congress's power to declare war and the president's power as commander-in-chief.[2] Most often, the text simply says nothing about who controls certain domains as, for example, the exercise of international emergency powers or the conduct of covert action.

In the few cases where a constitutional phrase clearly designates who shall exercise a particular authority—the president's power to "receive Ambassadors," for example—the textually granted power often appears far more limited than the one we know to have been exercised historically.[3] Perhaps most striking, the relative balance struck in the Constitution's text between the president's few and Congress's many enumerated foreign affairs powers hardly matches our present-day sense of their relative preeminence.[4]

These incongruities suggest that we should look beyond the Constitution's cryptic text to discover the broader constitutional principles that govern how Congress, the courts, and the executive should interact in the foreign policy process. In this chapter, I argue that there lurks within our constitutional system an identifiable National Security Constitution, a normative vision of the foreign-policy-making process that emerges only partially from the text of the Constitution itself. Like America's fiscal constitution and administrative constitution, which other scholars have described, the National Security Constitution comprises that subset of our public law that governs America's national security decision making.[5] The National Security Constitution creates the basic governmental institutions to deal with national security matters, defines the fundamental power relationships between those institutions, and places limitations upon the powers of each branch.

What sources of law make up this National Security Constitution? These sources can be found at three hierarchical levels. First and most obvious, the *text* of the Constitution provides a skeleton for the National Security Constitution by creating the three branches of the federal government and by assigning certain foreign affairs powers to them. But as Charles Black has recognized, a constitution "constitutes" not by merely enumerating individual rights and institutional powers, but more broadly by declaring how an entire government is to be structured. Thus, ultimate judgments regarding how the Constitution allocates particular powers in foreign affairs cannot be reached solely by looking at constitutional text, for the problem is not simply one "of correctly discerning or stating the legitimate bounds of the presidential and the congressional powers respectively." Rather, allocations of authority must be identified by "reasoning from the *total structure* which the text has created."[6] Accordingly, at this first level, the core principles of the National Security Constitution must be ascertained not only through textual exegesis of particular constitutional clauses, but also through inferences drawn from the broader structure and relationships created by the Constitution. Authoritative declarations of these core principles can also be found in those relatively few *judicial decisions* that have construed the basic constitutional structure and text with regard to foreign-affairs matters over the past two centuries.

The historical examination of constitutional structure and relationship that follows suggests that our National Security Constitution rests upon a simple notion: that generally speaking, the foreign affairs power of the United States is a *power shared* among the three branches of the national government. It is axiomatic that the Constitution as a whole rests upon a system of institutional checks and balances. The National Security Constitution grows out of the corollary principle that the system of checks and balances is not suspended simply because foreign affairs are at issue. In foreign as well as domestic affairs, the Constitution requires that we be governed by separated institutions *sharing* foreign policy powers.[7] Under this constitutional power-sharing scheme, the president, Congress, and the courts all play integral roles in both making and validating foreign-policy decisions. As it has evolved, the National Security Constitution assigns to the president the predominant role in that process, but affords him only a limited realm of exclusive powers, with regard to diplomatic relations and negotiations and to the recognition of nations and governments.[8] Outside of that realm, governmental decisions regarding foreign affairs must transpire within a sphere of concurrent authority, under presidential management, but bounded by the checks provided by congressional consultation and judicial review. In short, the structural principle that animates our National Security Constitution is *balanced institutional participation.*

At a second, subordinate hierarchical level, more specific rules governing the legal rights and duties of the three branches in national security decision making can be found in *"framework statutes"*: laws that Congress enacts and the president signs within their zone of concurrent authority, not simply to "formulate policies and procedures for the resolution of specific problems, but rather . . . to implement constitutional policies."[9] Statutes such as the Judiciary Act of 1789, the National Security Act of 1947, the War Powers Resolution of 1973, the Congressional Budget and Impoundment Control Act of 1974, the National Emergencies Act of 1976, and the International Emergency Economic Powers Act of 1977 all "attempt to support the organizational skeleton of the Constitution by developing a more detailed framework for governmental decisionmaking" in foreign affairs.[10] Such legislation therefore reinforces and elaborates the constitutional foundation of power sharing by constructing a statutory superstructure that declares in greater detail how power should be distributed among institutions in specific areas of foreign policy. These statutes specify legal authorities and constraints for particular institutional acts; they provide procedures to evaluate and control particular exercises of delegated powers; and they foster institutional expectations as to how those powers will be exercised in the future. By enacting such framework statutes, the president and Congress jointly generate a body of "subconstitutional" law in foreign affairs, working together both to construe particular constitutional provisions and to effectuate the underlying constitutional principle of balanced institutional participation. Within his limited zone of exclusive constitutional authority, the president can also unilaterally "legislate" by issuing similar *framework executive orders*. [11] But because these framework statutes and orders purport only to declare or reinforce the Constitution and are not themselves constitutional amendments, the courts may hold them unconstitutional in cases where they erect a subconstitutional framework that conflicts with the text or structure of the Constitution itself.

At the third and lowest level in this legal hierarchy stands a body of historical precedent that may be thought of as *quasi-constitutional custom*. This term embraces a set of institutional norms generated by the historical interaction of two or more federal branches with one another: executive practice of which Congress has approved or in which it has acquiesced, formal and informal congressional actions with which the president has consistently complied, and certain vacated judicial opinions that have acted as influential advisory opinions to the other two branches. Each of these historical sources has contributed to the creation of a customary constitutional law in the realm of foreign affairs, not dissimilar to rules of customary law observed by nations in the international arena. [12]

These customary rules represent informal accommodations between two or more branches on the question of who decides with regard to particular foreign policy matters. For that reason, they carry greater normative weight than self-serving justifications that one branch may offer, without another branch's endorsement, to defend its own actions as constitutional. At the same time, however, both the informal process that governs the creation of these customary norms and the difficulties inherent in establishing their existence suggest that they should have only persuasive, not conclusive, force as to what the constitutional allocation of authority in foreign affairs should be. Thus, Justice Frankfurter, concurring in *Youngstown Sheet and Tube Co. v. Sawyer* (the *Steel Seizure* case), declared that "a systematic, unbroken, executive practice, long pursued to the knowledge of the Congress and never before questioned . . . making as it were such exercise of power part of the structure of our government, may be treated as a gloss on 'executive Power' vested in the President by § 1 of Art. II."[13] Congress and its committees have sought to place similar glosses on other constitutional clauses by declaring norms of constitutional conduct through means other than legislation, as they did, for example, in the Iran-contra report's declarations reinforcing the general constitutional principle of power sharing.[14] The lower federal courts have sometimes rendered important opinions affirming on the merits one branch's claim of foreign-affairs authority, opinions that the Supreme Court has subsequently vacated for procedural reasons. Although strictly speaking these vacated opinions carry no precedential weight, the president and Congress frequently cite them against one another as predictions of how a court would rule were a particular constitutional claim ever to arise again in the future.[15]

Although this large body of quasi-constitutional custom fills in the interstices of the textual and statutory skeleton of the National Security Constitution, it is perennially subject to revision. In the same way as nations may modify customary rules of international law by establishing more formal rules in a particular area by treaty, so too can Congress and the president override quasi-constitutional custom by enacting a framework statute or issuing a framework executive order, which can in turn be invalidated or modified by a formal constitutional amendment or judicial decision construing the Constitution. By enacting the Judiciary Act of 1789, for example, Congress and the president "executed" Article III of the Constitution by creating an organic, formal structure of decision making for the federal judiciary; in *Marbury v. Madison,* the Supreme Court later invalidated section 13 of that act as inconsistent with the underlying constitutional provision.[16] Similarly, the Constitution's text gives little guidance as to which branch of government should exercise international emergency economic powers in wartime or nonwartime situations, leaving that question to be resolved by institutional practice (quasi-constitutional custom). As demonstrated in chapter 2, Congress and the president finally addressed that question in the twentieth century by enacting three framework statutes—the Trading with the Enemy Act (TWEA) of 1917, the National Emergencies Act of 1976, and the International Emergency Economic Powers Act (IEEPA) of 1977—a statutory structure which the Supreme Court has generally upheld against constitutional challenge, even while invalidating its provision for a legislative veto.[17]

In sum, the Constitution's structure and text, as construed by judicial decisions, legislative enactments, executive orders, and subsequent historical practice, describe a National Security Constitution whose animating principle is balanced institutional participation. That legal structure both facilitates and constrains the operation of the national security policy process.

This structural vision of a foreign-affairs power shared through balanced institutional participation has inspired the National Security Constitution since the beginning of the Republic, receiving its most cogent expression in Justice Robert Jackson's famous 1952 concurring opinion in *Youngstown.*[18] Yet throughout our constitutional history, what I call the *Youngstown* vision has done battle with a radically different constitutional paradigm. This counterimage of *unchecked executive discretion* has claimed virtually the entire field of foreign affairs as falling under the president's inherent authority. Although this image has surfaced from time to time since the early Republic, it did not fully and officially crystallize until Justice George Sutherland's controversial, oft-cited 1936 opinion for the Court in *United States v. Curtiss-Wright Export Corp.*[19] As construed by proponents of executive power, the *Curtiss-Wright* vision rejects two of *Youngstown*'s central tenets, that the National Security Constitution requires congressional concurrence in most decisions on foreign affairs and that the courts must play an important role in examining and constraining executive branch judgments in foreign affairs. By denying that the other two branches have a legitimate role in foreign affairs, the *Curtiss-Wright* vision rejects the principles of balanced institutional participation and power sharing that lie at the heart of the National Security Constitution.

INTERNATIONAL REGIMES AND CONSTITUTIONAL REGIMES

Because most constitutional law casebooks begin their discussion of foreign affairs power with either *Curtiss-Wright* or *Youngstown,* a newcomer to the field might conclude that the struggle between the paradigms they represent did not commence until 1936.[20] In fact, one can trace four discrete historical eras in the evolution of the National

VERNON REGIONAL
JUNIOR COLLEGE LIBRARY

Security Constitution that date back to the beginning of the Republic: a pre–Civil War period of infancy when America operated on the world's periphery; an adolescence that ended with the turn of the twentieth century during which the United States rose to the status of a dominant regional power; a heady adulthood stretching until World War II, which witnessed America's emergence as a global power; and a period of mature dominance in which America enjoyed the singular status of hegemonic power. Through each of these four eras, *Youngstown's* norm of balanced institutional participation remained the dominant constitutional vision. Proponents of executive discretion periodically launched challenges to it, however, culminating in the period of executive dominance that bred the Vietnam War.

As the previous chapter has shown, Vietnam triggered a congressional reaction against the imperial presidency that led to the enactment of framework statutes in virtually every field of foreign affairs. Yet even this extensive post-Vietnam legislative activity failed to reimprint the *Youngstown* vision firmly upon the National Security Constitution, thus allowing *Curtiss-Wright* to resurface yet again during the Iran-contra affair. But as we have seen, the Iran-contra investigators did not view the affair as indicating the need for a new round of framework legislation. Instead, the investigators largely ignored the struggle between the competing visions of our National Security Constitution, allowing the battle to revive once more between the independent counsel and the Justice Department during the trial of Oliver North. In chapters 7 and 8, I argue that Congress and the president should now correct this oversight by enacting a new framework statute that would effectively redraft the National Security Constitution for a post-Iran-contra age. But to grasp why such redrafting is necessary, we must first gain a deeper understanding of how the National Security Constitution has evolved to this date.

By sketching in broad strokes the life cycle of the National Security Constitution, this chapter does not aim to redescribe comprehensively the history of American foreign policy, a path that has been exhaustively traveled by political scientists and historians alike.[21] Instead, my goal is to examine how the structure of domestic constitutional law has interacted over time with the structure of international politics. More precisely, my inquiry focuses upon how successive regimes of American constitutional decision making in foreign affairs have both influenced and been influenced by evolving international political regimes. A broad examination of that question demonstrates that in each succeeding historical era, judicial decisions, framework statutes, executive orders, and institutional practice have all amended our National Security Constitution to respond to evolving national perceptions of America's changing position in the international arena. Although each successive era has embroidered the basic constitutional tapestry, in each era the core constitutional principle of balanced institutional participation has been preserved.

HOW THE NATIONAL SECURITY CONSTITUTION EVOLVED

Precarious Infancy: America on the Periphery

From the very beginning, our Constitution has been obsessed with the idea of national security: "the government's capacity to defend itself from violent overthrow by domestic subversion or external aggression [and its] . . . ability . . . to function effectively so as to serve our interests at home and abroad."[22] The term "national security" was not officially coined until the cold war.[23] Nevertheless, no fewer than twenty-five of the first thirty-six Federalist Papers concerned national *in*security, with most linking the young republic's international weakness to the incapacity of the national government.[24] Under the Articles of Confederation, the United States suffered a string of failures in foreign policy attributable in good measure to the national government's impotence. In their zeal to avoid creating an American king, the authors of the Articles had unwisely vested executive as well as legislative powers in Congress. Congress was authorized to appoint and supervise ambassadors as well as to approve treaties and to exercise "the sole and exclusive right and power of determining on peace and war."[25] Although Article VI purported to give "the united states in congress" control over the new nation's foreign affairs, the Continental Congress lacked a supremacy power that empowered it to enforce treaty commitments upon the states.[26] Consequently, individual states regularly violated the 1783 Treaty of Paris, which had secured America's independence from Britain. Not only did this noncompliance raise the spectre of renewed British intervention, it jeopardized America's hopes of developing stronger treaty relations with Spain, France, and Holland.[27]

To remedy the Articles' defects, the Founding Fathers framed the constitutional provisions on foreign affairs with two goals in mind—to fashion a stronger national government while holding each branch of that government accountable to the others through a strong system of checks and balances.[28] The two goals were closely related. On the one hand, the Framers overwhelmingly agreed upon the need for increased national power in four areas: taxation, military establishment, regulation of foreign commerce, and treaty enforcement.[29] As Madison put it, "[t]he powers delegated by the proposed Constitution to the federal government are few and defined. . . . [They] will be exercised principally on *external objects,* as war, peace, negotiation, and foreign commerce."[30] At the same time, however, the Framers rejected the option of centralizing the national government's foreign affairs powers in the president alone. Nor did they intend the operation of the system of checks and balances to stop at the water's edge. To the contrary, the Framers fully intended them to apply to both foreign and domestic affairs. In Professor Henkin's words, "the Framers were hardly ready to replace the representative inefficiency of many with an efficient monarch, and unhappy memories of royal prerogative, fear of tyranny, and distrust of any one man, kept the Framers from giving the new President too much head. . . . Every grant to the President . . . relating to foreign affairs, was in effect a derogation from Congressional power, eked out slowly, reluctantly, and not without limitations and safeguards."[31]

Thus, the first three articles of the Constitution expressly divided foreign affairs powers among the three branches of government, with *Congress,* not the president, being granted the dominant role. Article I bestowed upon Congress legislative powers to "lay and collect Taxes, Duties, Imposts and Excises . . . and provide for the common Defence"; to "regulate Commerce with foreign Nations . . . and with the Indian Tribes; [t]o establish an uniform Rule of Naturalization"; to "define and punish Piracies and Felonies committed on the high Seas, and Offences against the Law of Nations; [t]o declare War, grant Letters of Marque and Reprisal, and make Rules concerning Captures on Land and Water"; plus all manner of powers regarding raising, supporting, maintaining, and regulating the army, navy, and militia, which could be exercised both domestically and abroad. The Framers embellished these congressional powers not only with other constitutional grants, but also with Article I's sweeping authorization to Congress of power "[t]o make all Laws which shall be necessary and proper for carrying into Execution the foregoing Powers, and all other Powers vested by this Constitution *in the Government of the United States, or in any Department or Officer thereof.*"[32]

In Article II, the Framers granted the president the commander-in-chief power, the power to receive ambassadors, and the power to appoint ambassadors and make treaties with the advice and consent of the Senate. They pointedly denied him other grants, however, most prominently, the power to declare war, thereby rejecting the English model of a king who possessed both the power to declare war and the authority to command troops.[33] Similarly, the Federalist Papers made clear that the Framers considered it "imprudent to confide in [the president] solely so important a trust" as the treaty-making power.[34] Although the Framers also vested the "executive power" in the president, they expressly incorporated within that nebulous grant neither an exclusive power in foreign affairs nor a general war-making power. Nor, despite expansive claims later asserted by more recent advocates of presidential power, did the Framers intend apparently by that grant to bestow upon the president an unenu-merated inherent authority to take external actions.[35] Article II addi-tionally declared that the president "shall take Care that the Laws be faithfully executed," but by its own terms that phrase more clearly im-posed upon the president a duty rather than a license.[36]

Finally, in Article III, the Framers created a federal judiciary and extended the judicial power of the United States to cases and controver-sies arising under treaties, affecting ambassadors and consuls, and in-volving foreign states, citizens, and subjects. As implemented by the first Congress in one of its first framework statutes, the Judiciary Act of 1789, these authorizations gave the Supreme Court (and such lower courts as Congress might create) an important checking function against the politi-cal branches with regard to a range of foreign matters.[37] Thus, the linchpin of the entire constitutional scheme remained the notion that powers in foreign affairs should be *distributed* among the branches and exercised through balanced institutional participation. As Professor Arthur Bestor notes, "the documents of this formative period of Ameri-can constitutionalism consistently treated the conduct of foreign relations as a *shared responsibility.*"[38]

Even though the Framers carefully refrained from giving the president elastic unenumerated constitutional powers, they fully recognized that "[e]nergy in the executive is a leading character in the definition of good government."[39] The Framers thus anticipated creation of a cabinet gov-ernment. Early drafts of the Constitution actually referred to the Depart-ment of Foreign Affairs and the Department of War by name. In yet another early framework statute, Congress created those two cabinet departments pursuant to the Constitution's explicit reference to "executive Departments."[40] Equally central was the decision of the Framers to establish civilian supremacy over the military. Enumerating the "history of repeated injuries and usurpations" visited upon the colonies by the king of Great Britain, the Declaration of Independence had prominently mentioned the king's efforts "to render the Military independent of and superior to the Civil Power."[41] The Framers therefore named the president, a political and not a military leader, as commander-in-chief. As Justice Jackson would later note in *Youngstown*, "[t]he [Framers'] purpose of lodging dual titles in one man was to insure that the civilian would control the military, not to enable the military to subordinate the presidential office."[42] For similar reasons, the Framers endowed another civilian entity, Congress, with the power to declare war and to make rules for governing the armed forces.[43]

The birth of the National Security Constitution did not occur within a geopolitical vacuum. America's geographical separation from the rest of the world, which played a crucial role in fostering its liberal political tradition, figured equally prominently in the development of America's constitutional traditions.[44] In giving Congress a dominant role in the making of foreign policy, the Framers were aware that "[t]he distance of the United States from the powerful nations of the world gives them . . . happy security."[45] The United States constituted its national government during a global era of nascent British hegemony, which did not fully ripen until 1815. Before 1815, the new country's survival was far from assured. The young republic's physical separation from the Old World and the power struggles that raged in Europe thus permitted it to pursue a largely isolationist foreign policy, one "made possible by the fact of isolation . . . made necessary by the weakness, disunity, and vulnerability that rendered the fledgling state utterly unfit for the strenuous game of power politics [and] made desirable for Americans by their sense of differentiation and moral separation from the European world, their conviction that they had created a fresh and innocent society that could only be sullied by close involvement in European politics."[46]

When, in the early years of the republic, foreign sovereigns inevitably began to breach the cordon sanitaire that the British Royal Navy had imposed between the Old and New Worlds, it quickly became apparent that the Congress was poorly structured to respond. The varied tasks of nation building—recognition of and by foreign states, establishment of diplomatic relations, and conclusion of treaties—all demanded a branch of government that could react quickly and coherently to foreign initiatives. Not only was the office of the president ideally structured for such responsive action, it was filled during those early years by founding presidents of unusual personal force.[47] For that reason, the president's constitutional authorities grew rapidly during this first era, but the growth was confined principally to expansion of his textually enumerated powers in the area of recognition, treaty making, and appointment and reception of ambassadors. Significantly, little claim was heard in those years that the president operated in foreign affairs by dint of an *inherent* unenumerated constitutional authority. The era was marked by sporadic, not steady, aggrandizement of presidential powers in foreign affairs vis-à-vis the Congress, with the presidencies of Washington, Jefferson, Jackson, and Polk marking high points amid identifiable valleys of presidential power.[48]

An examination of executive practice during these early years reveals that most unilateral exercises of presidential authority were driven not by presidential ambition, but by external events—particularly the president's desire to preserve his young nation's neutrality from foreign struggles. President Washington consciously avoided substantive tests of presidential power.[49] Still, he took several notable actions in foreign affairs that appeared to challenge the Federalist vision of power sharing: rejecting Citizen Genet as a foreign emissary; employing special agents to conduct diplomacy; negotiating treaties without prior consultation; withholding documents regarding the Jay Treaty from the House; and issuing the Neutrality Proclamation of 1793 without consulting Congress. Yet virtually all of these decisions were driven by his primary foreign policy priority, "that we avoid errors in our system of policy respecting Great Britain."[50] Moreover, on examination, nearly all of these acts stemmed from Washington's determination to assert sole constitutional responsibility for *communicating* with foreign nations. For example, he based his decision to withhold information about the Jay Treaty from the House not on unanchored principles of executive privilege, but on the House's constitutional exclusion from the treaty process.[51] He took military action only once without express congressional authorization, and even then, Congress arguably endorsed his decision by subsequent acts.[52]

Washington's most controversial foreign policy decision was the Neutrality Proclamation of 1793. Yet that proclamation, a response to Citizen Genet's efforts to draw the United States into France's war with Great

Britain, received overwhelming congressional support.[53] Equally important in gauging the incident's precedential weight as quasi-constitutional custom was the fact that Washington expressly conceded that Congress had the power to change neutrality policy by legislation.[54] By so saying, he prompted Congress in the following year to pass another framework statute, the Neutrality Act, which remains on the books today. In that law, Congress by statute went beyond what the president had sought to do by proclamation. It imposed criminal penalties, enforceable by the courts, upon persons within the United States who begin, or provide the means for, a military expedition against any country with which the U.S. is at peace.[55] The purpose of that law was to prevent individuals from taking actions to disrupt an official foreign policy set by the president and Congress. Thus, "this policy was not a presidential monopoly; it was shared with Congress."[56]

In short, the framework statutes and customary norms established during the Washington presidency worked a substantial de facto amendment of the National Security Constitution. Although the Constitution's drafters had assigned Congress the dominant role in foreign affairs, the president's functional superiority in responding to external events enabled him to seize the preeminent role in the foreign policy process, while Congress accepted a reactive, consultative role. In practical terms, this switch in roles placed the president in a position to propose, leaving the Senate and Congress to dispose. But although the president, and not Congress, now took the lead, the dominant constitutional notion remained one of separated institutions sharing foreign policy powers. The framework statutes passed during this period firmly entrenched Congress, the courts, and the cabinet departments in the foreign-policy-making process. Institutional practice further reveals that though Congress acquiesced in the president's initiating role, the president took equal pains to keep Congress informed and to secure its approval for his actions in foreign affairs.[57]

Yet even as the events of this period reaffirmed the notion of balanced institutional participation, a counter-principle of unchecked executive discretion began to surface. When Washington issued the 1793 Neutrality Proclamation, his act provoked a heated exchange of letters between Hamilton (using the pen name "Pacificus") and Madison (writing under the name "Helvidius"). Foreshadowing *Curtiss-Wright,* Hamilton recited for the first time a broad argument that the president's "executive power" and duty to "take Care that the Laws be faithfully executed" in Article II of the Constitution carried within them the power unilaterally to proclaim neutrality and to prosecute private citizens who violate that proclamation. But once declared, Hamilton's vision was immediately challenged and not embodied into customary law. Defending the Framers' original power-sharing principle, Madison characterized Hamilton's claim as "no less vicious in theory than it would be dangerous in practice" and nowhere "countenanced . . . by any general arrangements . . . to be found in the constitution."[58]

Moreover, the ensuing presidencies of Adams, Jefferson, Madison, and Monroe did not fundamentally alter the basic pattern laid down in the Washington years. Admittedly, those presidents took numerous external measures that Congress had not previously authorized. Adams led the country into its first undeclared war with France; Jefferson effected the Louisiana Purchase and authorized the navy to retaliate against the Barbary Pirates; and Madison and Monroe worked aggressively to seize West Florida. But as the definitive study of the period by Judge Sofaer (later the legal adviser of the Reagan and Bush State Departments) established, "[t]he full picture contains very substantial evidence of [presidential] concern for both the legislative and the popular will." None of these presidents ever claimed that he possessed inherent constitutional powers as chief executive or commander-in-chief that lay beyond legislative control. Nor did any renounce the principle of shared power by claiming that he "may use whatever raw power he has—monetary, diplomatic and military—in the national interest."[59]

Congressional action during this period largely reinforced the president's caution. As the nineteenth century began, Congress maintained strict control of the president's power to raise military forces. For example, in contrast to twentieth-century statutes, such as the International Emergency Economic Powers Act (IEEPA), which delegated sweeping tools of economic warfare to the president based upon his declaration of an emergency, a 1799 statute imposed strict ceilings on the size of cavalry and infantry regiments "unless war shall break out between the United States and some European prince, potentate, or state, in which case it shall be lawful for the President of the United States, at his discretion, to cause the said regiments . . . to be severally completed to their full establishment."[60] However, in other areas—particularly recognition, the use of special envoys, and other matters related to the conduct of diplomatic relations—Congress almost entirely acquiesced in executive prerogatives established during Washington's presidency. Thus, when Congressman (later Chief Justice) John Marshall rose on the floor of the House in 1800 to call the president "the sole organ of the nation in its external relations," his remarks were uncontroversial, not because Congress had accepted a broad presidential monopoly over all foreign relations, but because it had largely acquiesced in the president's narrower dominance over diplomatic communications.[61]

Nor did the constitutional requirement of balanced participation interfere with the president's freedom to declare guiding principles of foreign policy, as President Monroe did in 1823 when he announced to the world the doctrine which bears his name. Although Congress neither authorized nor ratified that unilateral declaration, Monroe never asserted that the doctrine carried with it a unilateral presidential right to commit military forces to protect the hemisphere. Indeed, only one year later, John Quincy Adams rejected Colombia's attempt to invoke the Monroe Doctrine to obtain U.S. joinder in a defensive alliance, stating that "by the Constitution of the United States, the ultimate decision of this question belongs to the Legislative Department of the Government."[62]

The activist presidency of Andrew Jackson did not alter this balance of constitutional authority. For although Jackson's populist presidency remarkably expanded the president's domestic authorities in foreign affairs, Jackson institutionalized a practice of information sharing with Congress and frequently requested legislative authorization of his particular acts.[63] Even in domestic affairs, Jackson was "an exception to the general rule of weak presidents in the nineteenth century. He asserted strong claims, only to see them denied to his successors."[64]

Looking back upon this first era of constitutional history, perhaps its most striking feature is the extent to which the courts actively participated in the delineation and delimitation of the executive's authority in foreign affairs. In 1800, the Supreme Court unanimously upheld John Adams's undeclared war with France in a series of opinions resting not on findings of plenary presidential power, but rather on declarations that Congress had intended to authorize limited hostilities by means other than formally declared war.[65] In *Talbot v. Seeman,* decided the following year, a unanimous Court headed by the newly appointed Chief Justice Marshall found that Congress had authorized an American commander's capture of a neutral ship, reasoning that "[t]he whole powers of war being, by the constitution of the United States, vested in congress, the *acts of that body can alone* be resorted to as our guides in this inquiry."[66] Three years later, in *Little v. Barreme,* Marshall reiterated the point, this time holding that a navy officer who had executed a presidential order during President Adams's undeclared war with France was nevertheless liable to those he had injured in violation of a duly enacted statute. Because "the legislature seem[s] to have prescribed . . . the manner in which this law shall be carried into execution," he concluded, the contrary presidential order could not legalize the officer's act.[67] In yet a third Marshall opinion, *Brown v. United States,* the Court invalidated an executive seizure of British property shortly before Congress declared the War of 1812.[68] As in the three earlier cases, the Court had no trouble finding the case justiciable. On the merits, it ruled that the executive was powerless to confiscate enemy property without legislative authorization. In none of these cases did the Court ever suggest that a legislative effort to regulate the issue in question would unconstitutionally intrude upon an exclusive or inherent presidential prerogative.

Perhaps the most dramatic illustration of the judicial role in foreign affairs during this era was *United States v. Smith,* an 1806 New York federal court case whose facts bear an uncanny resemblance to the Iran-contra affair.[69] Like Oliver North, the defendant Smith was an American colonel charged with aiding a Central American rebel to plan an attack and an indigenous revolt against the rulers of Spanish America (now Venezuela). Smith and the rebel later alleged that President Jefferson and Secretary of State Madison had promised covert, but not overt, assistance for their expedition. Based upon these alleged promises, Smith recruited troops for the rebel enterprise and persuaded private sympathizers to contribute funding and transportation. When the rebel expedition failed, Smith was prosecuted in a New York federal court for violating the Neutrality Act of 1794. Smith defended himself by claiming that the president and cabinet had authorized his acts, and he subpoenaed four cabinet secretaries to prove it.

The case was tried by Supreme Court Justice William Paterson sitting on circuit, along with a district judge. Like Judge Gerhard Gesell in the *North* case, Justice Paterson neither quashed the subpoenas against the cabinet members nor dismissed the case before trial, either as a nonjusticiable political question or for fear that state secrets might be revealed. To the claim that the witnesses' "peculiar privilege of office" immunized them from being called to testify, the justice responded, "You may save yourself the trouble of arguing that point; the witnesses may undoubtedly be compelled to appear." Nor did the justice find Smith immune from prosecution because he had followed superior orders, or dismiss the case on the ground that the Neutrality Act had unconstitutionally invaded the president's prerogatives as chief executive or commander-in-chief. When Smith asserted that the president had authorized him to violate the statute, Paterson ruled (as *Little v. Barreme* had earlier ruled and as Judge Gesell would charge the jury in the *North* case years later) that "[t]he president of the United States cannot control the statute, nor dispense with its execution, and still less can he authorize a person to do what the law forbids." Of Smith's claim that the president could exempt him from the statute under his constitutional powers, the court asked, "Does he possess the power of making war? That power is exclusively vested in congress."[70] Like the Boland amendments, the Neutrality Act had been passed by Congress and the president to avoid enmeshing the United States in foreign conflict. Given that decision, the court concluded, "Whoever violates the law becomes liable to its penalties."[71]

We need not decide whether many, or even any, of the rulings in *Smith* would be decided the same way by a federal court today.[72] For present purposes, the crucial point is that even during America's infancy, the time of its greatest national insecurity, foreign affairs were not treated as exempt from the ordinary constitutional system of checks and balances. To the contrary, the Framers designed the checks and balances scheme to apply *principally* in the realm of foreign affairs. The three branches agreed that even governmental decisions regarding covert actions should be conducted through the scheme of balanced institutional participation mandated by the National Security Constitution—under presidential management, but subject to the checks provided by congressional legislation and judicial review. Congress could and did legislate in ways that imposed meaningful constraints upon executive authority in foreign affairs. Courts reviewed executive conduct on the merits—undeterred by alleged barriers of executive privilege, nonjusticiability, superior orders, or inherent presidential power—to determine its consistency with duly enacted legislation and the overriding constitutional plan.

By the close of the first era, the new nation had moved beyond the task of protecting itself from the outside world toward the affirmative goal of "consolidating the continent."[73] After the annexation of Florida had been effected under Madison and Monroe, Presidents Tyler and Polk authored an almost frantic period of territorial conquest. Polk alone expanded the national territory by nearly 50 percent during his presidency. President Polk dispatched troops to Mexico in 1845 and misrepresented evidence to Congress in order to provoke a declaration of war the following year. By midcentury, the executive branch was increasingly provoking external conflict, claiming an independent war-making capacity and restricting the supply of information flowing to Congress.[74] As Professor Henry Cox notes, rather than protesting, "Congress assented retroactively to unilateral executive actions undertaken without its knowledge or consent, so long as the activities themselves were successful and did not involve fundamental abrogation of constitutional principle."[75] Similarly, the courts made fewer forays into the area and their rulings grew increasingly deferential to executive prerogative. In *Durand v. Hollins,* for example, an American naval commander bombarded a Nicaraguan town to retaliate against an attack by local citizens on an American consul. When an injured American citizen sued the commander, Supreme Court Justice Nelson stated that the question whether the president had a duty to protect American citizens in Nicaragua "belonged to the executive to determine; and his decision is final and conclusive"; neither the president nor his authorized agent were therefore civilly responsible for the consequences.[76] By 1861, the implications were clear. One era of American expansion had concluded, another would soon begin and with it, new and powerful pressures to amend the National Security Constitution.

Uneasy Adolescence: America's Rise to Dominant Regional Power

Even before the outbreak of the Civil War, the United States had become an economic giant, but with relatively underdeveloped military resources. In the 1850s, the country was preoccupied with its domestic problems and its foreign-policy agenda was largely consumed by relations with its neighbors in Cuba and Central America.[77] Abraham Lincoln assumed the presidency as a critic of executive adventurism in foreign affairs, having opined in 1848 that Polk's military actions toward Mexico rivaled "the most oppressive of all Kingly oppressions" that the Framers had sought to suppress.[78] Nevertheless, Lincoln's own presidency was marked by well-chronicled usurpations of constitutional authority: suspension of the writ of habeas corpus; refusal to convene Congress; enlargement of the armed forces beyond congressionally authorized limits; large expenditures without congressional appropriation or authorization; and the blockading of southern ports without a congressional declaration of war.[79] Lincoln invoked both the power of the commander-in-chief and his duty to "take Care that the Laws be faithfully Executed" to deal with the ongoing domestic rebellion. In *The Prize Cases,* the Supreme Court narrowly sustained Lincoln's southern blockade. Although the cases were decided by a five-to-four vote, the Court's opinion evinced a growing judicial receptivity toward expansive claims of executive power. As noteworthy as the Court's holdings on the merits—that President Lincoln had inherent authority to suppress armed insurrection and that Congress had ratified his blockade by subsequent acts—was the Court's hint that the president's decisions could be considered political questions that it ought not review.[80]

As activist as Lincoln's wartime presidency was, it did not amend the National Security Constitution. For Lincoln had not exercised his power in foreign affairs against the insurrectionist southern states; instead, he had expansively employed his domestic statutory and constitutional powers. Congress had passed statutes in both 1795 and 1807 authorizing the president to call out the militia and to use national military and naval forces to suppress internal insurrection against the government of the United States. Furthermore, Article II granted Lincoln the constitutional authority to take care that such legislation be faithfully executed.[81] Although successive presidents liberally employed their powers as commanders-in-chief against rebels, native Americans, pirates, brigands, and slave traders, they did not generally invoke those powers to initiate war making against sovereign states without congressional approval and over congressional objection.[82] Moreover, Lincoln's weak successors, Andrew Johnson and Ulysses Grant, were too beset by impeachment and incompetence, respectively, to continue exercising expanded presidential powers. Congress reacted against Lincoln's activism by reasserting itself against the relatively passive presidents who followed him into office for the balance of the century.[83]

Much of this congressional reaction came on the domestic front as the Reconstruction Congress battled with post–Civil War presidents over issues of removal, nominations, use of appropriations riders, and the president's use of the veto. Invariably, some of those domestic battles spilled over into the realm of foreign affairs. Yet once again, this era did not generate new customary norms that fundamentally altered the National Security Constitution, but now because the *president* refused to acquiesce in congressional assertiveness. In 1867, Congress passed two framework statutes, the Command of the Army Act and the Tenure of Office Act, which were designed to protect military and civilian officials from presidential removal without Senate approval. The impeachment indictment of President Johnson later charged that he had removed his secretary of war in defiance of the latter act. Yet despite this threat, Johnson continued to assert his exclusive constitutional prerogative to remove subordinates, an intransigence that led to a weakening of the Tenure of Office Act by amendment in 1869 and its ultimate repeal eighteen years later.[84] Similarly, in 1867, congressional hostility toward Secretary of State Seward's acquisition of Alaska triggered a House resolution opposing future purchases of territory, placing a damper on expansionist presidential plans. But although subsequent presidents annexed no further contiguous lands for more than a generation, notwithstanding the resolution, they continued to make efforts to obtain land and bases in the Pacific, the Caribbean, Central America, and Greenland.[85] In 1869, the Senate rebuffed President Grant by refusing to advise and consent to his treaty permitting de facto annexation of Santo Domingo. But even then, Grant refused to withdraw the naval force he had previously ordered to implement the "inchoate treaty" and Senate resolutions condemning Grant's military actions failed.[86]

Thereafter, interbranch struggle shifted from the area of war making to treaty making, as the Senate refused to ratify any important treaty outside of the immigration context for nearly thirty years.[87] Writing in 1885, Woodrow Wilson attacked this trend as illustrating the "treaty-*marring* power of the Senate." Wilson's famous book, *Congressional Government,* went on to decry the pattern of the preceding two decades, describing in Walter Lippmann's words, "what happens when the President is weak and helpless . . . [and] how power and responsibility disintegrate when the members of Congress . . . are predominant."[88]

By the end of the nineteenth century, the effective institutional balance of power in foreign affairs had shifted far in Congress's favor. But international pressures were already forcing a transformation of American foreign relations and in the process, spurring the pendulum's return swing.

Although the Civil War had temporarily transformed the United States into a military nation, extensive demobilization occurred after the war. Low-wage immigrant labor, the creation of an intercontinental rail system, and new inflows of foreign capital all enabled America to utilize its vast natural resources for soaring economic growth. Yet as American economic production grew, domestic markets became glutted, leading to new American economic interest in burgeoning markets in East Asia, Latin America, and Africa.[89] As American industrial power grew and extended to markets outside the Western Hemisphere, naval officers and shipbuilders formed a lobby to demand modern naval power to protect global trading routes. Domestic interest groups began urging the president to pursue a more activist diplomacy; public concern developed that congressional intransigence would interfere with the swift conclusion of desired alliances.[90] Driven in part by this private desire for markets, executive officials in the 1890s adopted interventionist measures in Brazil and Chile and clashed with Great Britain over Venezuela's boundaries, actions that aroused little or no congressional protest. By 1896, the United States had undeniably established itself as the dominant hemispheric power. Simultaneously, between 1870 and 1890, the United States fought a string of internal wars against native Americans, "the last step needed to unify and consolidate the United States before Americans could go abroad to become the superpower of the twentieth century."[91]

Because the president was functionally better suited than Congress to respond to the twin trends of outward expansion and internal consolidation, these events served over time to replenish his store of power vis-à-vis Congress. Thus, Professor Cox, summarizing the era, concludes that claims of presidential impotence during this period have been overstated: "Each branch found the necessary tools to strike a healthy balance of legislative and executive powers. . . . [E]ach branch increasingly recognized that actions critical to national security and well-being should not be taken by either without at least a well informed reaction from the other."[92] In the era's closing years, however, administration supporters in Congress began to reassert Hamilton's vision of unchecked executive discretion as a means of reviving what they viewed as diminished presidential power. To defeat statutory attempts to limit presidential executive authority over the armed forces, they contended that the president's constitutional duty to execute the laws carried with it an inherent authority to use physical power to protect the "peace of the United States."[93]

In 1890, the Supreme Court threw some support to this view with expansively worded dicta. *In re Neagle* addressed the virtually fact-specific question whether the president had inherent constitutional power to protect federal judges.[94] Neagle, a United States marshal, had shot and killed the assailant of Supreme Court Justice Stephen Field while acting as Field's bodyguard. Predictably ordering Neagle's relief from state custody, the Court held that the president had inherent constitutional power to authorize the protection of federal judges, thereby validating Neagle's acts and allowing him to invoke the protection of the federal habeas corpus statute. In sweeping language, however, Justice Miller declared that the president's inherent constitutional authority to execute the laws encompassed not only the enforcement of acts of Congress or of treaties of the United States according to their express terms, but also "rights, duties and obligations growing out of the Constitution itself, *our international relations,* and all the protection implied by the nature of the government under the Constitution."[95] Within five years, the Supreme Court had upheld President Cleveland's use of this inherent power rationale to enjoin the Pullman strike for the public good, even without congressional authorization.[96] By 1980, less than a century later, President Carter would be citing *Neagle,* along with *Durand v. Hollins,* as "clearly establish[ing]" the president's "inherent" and "constitutional power to use armed forces to rescue Americans illegally detained abroad" without consulting with Congress.[97]

Heady Adulthood: America as World Power

With the dawn of the twentieth century, a new generation of strong leaders triggered both a resurgence of presidential power and America's increased participation in the world balance of power. The revival began in 1898 with the Spanish-American War and accelerated through Theodore Roosevelt's administration to Woodrow Wilson and World War I. In the Spanish-American War, "Americans first committed themselves to a major role in the international politics of the Far East, first found themselves policing the affairs of the Caribbean, and first fought men of a different color in an Asian guerilla war."[98] With the quick victory of the United States came control over Cuba and the acquisitions of Puerto Rico and the Philippines, which elevated the United States to the status of an imperial power. Blocked by the Senate in his effort to annex Hawaii by treaty, President McKinley accomplished it by joint resolution. Without consulting Congress, McKinley also implemented Secretary of State John Hay's open-door policy and dispatched troops to China as part of a "police action" to help put down the Boxer Rebellion. Although Congress encouraged the Spanish hostilities, the president largely excluded the legislature from the Philippine and China initiatives.[99]

Theodore Roosevelt, America's youngest and most aggressive president, sought to insert the United States into the balance of power in European affairs among Britain, France, and Germany. As he later acknowledged, Roosevelt denied "that what was imperatively necessary for the Nation could not be done by the President unless he could find some specific authorization to do it." Instead, he claimed "that the executive power was limited only by specific restrictions and prohibitions appearing in the Constitution or imposed by the Congress under its Constitutional powers. My view was that every executive officer . . . was a steward of the people."[100]

Roosevelt's stewardship theory, evocative of Hamilton's views in the Pacificus letters and the Court's decision in *Neagle,* left open the question of what "specific restrictions" imposed by the Constitution or Congress might be placed upon a president's powers in foreign affairs. But during his presidency, a compliant Congress and Court did little to test the limits of Roosevelt's theory.[101] Roosevelt intervened in Cuba and Santo Domingo, built the Panama Canal (in the process terminating a treaty with Great Britain), and sent America's fleet around the world despite Congress's express threat to withhold funds. Roosevelt cast himself in the role of international peacemaker, winning a Nobel Prize for his mediation of the Russo-Japanese War and chairing the 1906 Algeciras conference in Morocco, neither of which bore any direct relation to American interests.[102] Finally, Roosevelt put the executive agreement to unprecedented new uses. In addition to a 1904 accord with Santo Domingo asserting U.S. control over its customhouses, he concluded three deals with Japan: the secret Taft-Katsura Agreement of 1905, which approved Japan's military protectorate of Korea; the 1907 Gentlemen's Agreement limiting Japanese immigration to the U.S.; and the 1908 Root-Takahira Accord, which entrenched the status quo in East Asia. Of these, only the Gentlemen's Agreement was concluded with prior congressional authorization and Roosevelt effected the Santo Domingo accord only after the Senate had declined ratification of a similar treaty.[103]

For all of Roosevelt's efforts, in 1909 the United States still stood on the edges of the "great power" system.[104] Roosevelt's successor, William Howard Taft, took a far narrower view of the presidential office. In words reminiscent of Madison's in the Pacificus-Helvidius debate, Taft called Roosevelt's willingness to "ascrib[e] an undefined residuum of power to the President . . . an unsafe doctrine [which] . . . might lead under emergencies to results of an arbitrary character, doing irremediable injustice to private right." Taft, a future law professor and Supreme Court justice, went on to declare that the

> true view of the Executive functions is . . . that the President can exercise no power which cannot be fairly and reasonably traced to some specific grant of power or justly implied and included within such express grant as proper and necessary to its exercise. Such specific grant must be either in the Federal Constitution or in an act of Congress passed in pursuance thereof. *There is no undefined residuum of power which he can exercise because it seems to him to be in the public interest.*[105]

Consistent with this view, Taft substantially contracted unilateral foreign policy initiatives, largely confining his "dollar diplomacy" to modest moves toward China and Latin America.[106]

Long before becoming president, Woodrow Wilson had espoused a different view: "When foreign affairs play a prominent part in the politics and policy of a nation, its Executive must of necessity be its guide: must utter every initial judgment, take every first step of action, supply the information upon which it is to act, suggest and in large measure control its conduct."[107] Inspired by his desire to "make the world safe for democracy," Wilson "became the greatest military interventionist in U.S. history . . . order[ing] troops into Russia and half a dozen Latin American upheavals," including Mexico, Haiti, Santo Domingo, and Cuba.[108] Because Wilson conceived of the presidency as a form of prime ministership, he generally sought congressional approval for his acts. But he did not hesitate to commit troops first and obtain approval later, as he did in 1914 during the Vera Cruz affair. After Congress declared war against Germany in 1917, Wilson announced his Fourteen Points to Congress and dispatched an expedition to Siberia under his commander-in-chief power, virtually without consulting Congress.[109]

Predictably, World War I proved to be another powerful engine for the growth of presidential power. But once again, the president's activism failed to imprint principles of presidential dominance permanently upon the National Security Constitution. As the war ended, a period of forceful congressional reaction set in, culminating in Wilson's repeated failure to win two-thirds Senate approval for the Treaty of Versailles, which established the League of Nations. Unlike McKinley, who named three senators as members of the peace commission that negotiated the end of the Spanish-American War, Wilson took no senators with him to the Paris Peace Conference that negotiated the Versailles Treaty, thereby impairing his subsequent efforts to rally sufficient congressional support to implement his plan. Moreover, Senate procedures not only allowed the Senate Foreign Relations Committee to adopt crippling reservations to the treaty by majority votes, but they also gave its chairman, Henry Cabot Lodge, unusual power to undercut the treaty, thereby keeping the United States in a legal state of war until 1921.[110] Much the same fate befell the executive's attempt to win advice and consent to ratification of the charter of the Permanent Court of International Justice.[111] During the interwar years, which straddled the Great Depression and the presidencies of Harding, Coolidge, and Hoover, congressional government strongly reasserted itself. Wary of reliving Wilson's fate, the new Republican presidents accentuated an international economic diplomacy that focused less on negotiating treaties that would be subject to Senate approval than upon securing arrangements with private banks that would rebuild a war-torn Europe. Congress took the lead in freeing the Philippines, passing one bill to do so over Hoover's veto, and began to reexpress strong isolationist sentiments, leading to a series of neutrality statutes in the mid-to-late thirties.[112]

As in the post–Civil War years, the first decades of the twentieth century thus marked a modulation, but not a fundamental transformation, of the basic premises of the National Security Constitution. By executive practice, the president increasingly dominated foreign affairs decision making, but Congress's acquiescence in that trend was neither unequivocal nor permanent. Although Presidents Theodore Roosevelt and Wilson offered expansive views of their foreign-affairs authority, their successors did not accept those views uncritically as either constitutional orthodoxy or as guides to action. Congress and the courts continued to defer to presidential judgments, particularly when the president deemed swift military action necessary. But as Professor Ely has observed, such decisions were

> subject always to the core command underlying the constitutional accommodation . . . that he come to Congress for approval as soon as possible and terminate military action in the event such approval is not forthcoming. . . .

[T]his constitutional understanding was quite consistently honored from the framing until 1950. And when certain Presidents did play fast and loose with congressional prerogatives . . . they obscured or covered up the actual facts, pleading public fealty to the constitutional need for congressional authorization of military action. *It is therefore difficult to cite the occasional nonconforming presidential actions of this period in support of some adverse possession-type theory that they had gradually altered the constitutional plan.*[113]

Although Congress generally supported presidential activism during the early part of this period, it did not blindly acquiesce in those initiatives. Toward the end of the era it fully exercised its power-sharing role, particularly in the realm of treaty ratification. Although the president resorted with increasing frequency to executive agreements over treaties, the vast majority were agreements that Congress approved by legislation or treaty, not agreements concluded upon the president's sole constitutional authority.[114] Admittedly, judges occasionally flirted with notions that certain executive acts were nonjusticiable, or could be sustained under inherent, unenumerated presidential power, in what lawyers call *obiter dicta* (general statements unnecessary to the decision of particular cases). But the Supreme Court neither declared a broad political question doctrine in foreign affairs nor recognized a pervasive, inherent "executive power" in the key holding of any case. Indeed, although the Supreme Court had previously deferred when the president and Congress had acted together in wartime—treating domestic wartime legislation that permitted Prohibition, press censorship, and the suppression of radicals enacted during wartime as largely exempt from judicial review—the Court reversed that trend from 1919 to 1924, reasserting the principle that "the Constitution applies even to action taken in the name of war."[115]

In short, by 1933, neither institutional practice, legislative act, nor judicial decision had fundamentally altered the shape of the National Security Constitution. The constitutional principle of balanced institutional participation had provided the president with considerable flexibility to act as the primary expositor and initiator of foreign policy decisions. The constraining power that principle gave the courts and Congress enabled them to adjudicate and legislate to redress presidential overreaching. Although the other branches had acquiesced sufficiently in presidential initiatives to establish his preeminent role in foreign affairs, none of the three branches had yet made what Charles Black has called "[t]he one fundamental error . . . that of supposing that the modern expansion of presidential power is based on the Constitution by itself, and is hence inaccessible as a matter of law to congressional correction."[116]

Mature Dominance: America as World Hegemon

Bruce Ackerman has spoken of 1937 as an American "constitutional moment," when the New Deal legitimated the activist state and fundamentally altered America's constitutional politics.[117] Yet the same era also redefined the constitutional politics of American foreign affairs. For it was during Franklin Roosevelt's four terms in office that the president became the most prominent leader of the world as well as of America. As much as any other event, *United States v. Curtiss-Wright Export Corp.*, a 1936 Supreme Court decision, helped consolidate Roosevelt's transformation of the president's authority in foreign affairs.[118] In *Curtiss-Wright*, private parties challenged the president's right, pursuant to a joint resolution of Congress, to prohibit arms sales to belligerents in Latin America. Writing for the Court, Justice Sutherland not only upheld the executive act, but also announced a most sweeping theory to support the president's unenumerated constitutional authority to conduct foreign affairs.

Justice Sutherland began with a historical examination of the origins of the foreign affairs powers. Echoing Theodore Roosevelt, Justice Sutherland suggested that the "investment of the federal government with the powers of external sovereignty did not depend upon the affirmative grants of the Constitution. The powers to declare and wage war, to conclude peace, to make treaties, to maintain diplomatic relations with other sovereignties if they had never been mentioned in the Constitution, would have been vested in the federal government as necessary concomitants of nationality."[119] Quoting from John Marshall's 1800 speech to the House of Representatives, he went on to declare that this "extraconstitutional" power was vested entirely in the president.

> Not only, as we have shown, is the federal power over external affairs in origin and essential character different from that over internal affairs, but *participation in the exercise of power is significantly limited*. In this vast external realm with its important, complicated, delicate and manifold problems, *the President alone* has the power to speak or listen as a representative of the nation. . . .
>
> [W]e are here dealing not alone with an authority vested in the President by an exertion of legislative power, but with such an authority plus *the very*

delicate, plenary and exclusive power of the President as "the sole organ of the
federal government in the field of international relations"—a power which
does not require as a basis for its exercise an act of Congress, but which, of
course, like every other governmental power, must be exercised in subordination to the applicable provisions of the Constitution.[120]

In the years following the Court's decision, *Curtiss-Wright* has received withering criticism.[121] As the decision's numerous critics have
recognized, Sutherland's key language was dicta, for Congress had
passed a joint resolution in the case that expressly authorized the president to take the action under challenge.[122] These commentators have
further demolished the historical accuracy of Justice Sutherland's extra-
constitutional theory of paramount unenumerated presidential power in
foreign affairs.[123] Moreover, carefully read, the opinion contains important words of limitation. By saying that "the President alone has the
power to *speak or listen* as a representative of the nation," Justice
Sutherland could be read as recognizing only the well-established exclusive presidential power to negotiate, and not a novel executive power
to conclude agreements, on behalf of the United States. Similarly, his
conclusion that the president's sole organ power "must be exercised in
subordination to the applicable provisions of the Constitution" would
suggest that it does not override congressional powers granted by the
Constitution or individual rights recognized in the Bill of Rights.[124]

Notwithstanding these obvious defects, later presidents have sought to
treat *Curtiss-Wright* as what Ackerman would call an "amendment-ana-
logue"—an effective *judicial* amendment of Article II of the Constitution to add to the powers enumerated there an indeterminate reservoir of
executive authority in foreign affairs.[125] Among government attorneys,
Justice Sutherland's lavish description of the president's powers is so
often quoted that it has come to be known as the " '*Curtiss-Wright,* so I'm
right' cite"—a statement of deference to the president so sweeping as to
be worthy of frequent citation in any government foreign-affairs brief.[126]

I defer until chapter 6 a fuller description of the impact that *Curtiss-*
Wright has had upon the courts in recent foreign-affairs cases. For present
purposes, the significant point is that *Curtiss-Wright* painted a dramatically different vision of the National Security Constitution from that
which has prevailed since the founding of the Republic. As elaborated by
the Framers and construed through the first three eras of American foreign policy, the National Security Constitution envisioned a narrowly

limited realm of exclusive presidential power in foreign affairs. The president's exclusive realm embraced his textually enumerated powers and his "sole organ" power as John Marshall originally meant the term, namely, his mastery of our diplomatic communications with the outside world. Outside that realm of exclusive presidential authority, most decisions in foreign affairs would occur in a sphere of concurrent authority, under presidential management, but subject to congressional consultation and oversight and judicial review. Within that sphere of concurrent authority, the courts would closely examine congressional enactments to determine whether they permitted the president to undertake particular actions.

Curtiss-Wright, by contrast, viewed the entire field of foreign affairs as falling under the president's inherent authority. While accepting the notion that the president should manage foreign policy—a tradition that had begun with Washington—the *Curtiss-Wright* opinion rejected the attendant condition of congressional consultation and participation. As one critic put it, Justice Sutherland's theory that the president "possesses a secret reservoir of unaccountable power" that flows from external sovereignty and not the Constitution represented "the furthest departure from the theory that [the] United States is a constitutionally limited democracy."[127] If the president actually possessed such extensive extra-constitutional powers, it is unclear why his actions in foreign affairs should ever be subjected to the consent of the governed.

Significantly, nothing in *Curtiss-Wright* itself suggested that executive actions in foreign affairs should be immune from judicial review. To the contrary, in *Curtiss-Wright,* Justice Sutherland reviewed the president's action and upheld it on the merits. Yet, as elaborated in chapter 6, over time the *Curtiss-Wright* vision would mysteriously come to embrace another notion previously suggested, but never broadly adopted, by the Supreme Court—that once courts have determined that foreign affairs are at stake, they should dismiss challenges to executive acts as political, not legal, questions.[128]

Curtiss-Wright was not the Court's only foray into foreign affairs during these years. The following term, in *United States v. Belmont,* Justice Sutherland upheld the constitutional validity of the Litvinov Assignment, an executive agreement made by President Roosevelt in 1933, as part of a single transaction that had resulted in the recognition of the Soviet Union.[129] Five years later, in *United States v. Pink,* the Court confirmed that holding, declaring that "[p]ower to remove such obstacles to full recognition . . . certainly is a modest implied power of the President who is the 'sole organ of the federal government in the field of international relations.' "[130]

When *Curtiss-Wright* and *Belmont* were decided, the president's power vis-à-vis Congress remained at a relatively low ebb. Yet combined with executive practice during the years leading to World War II, the decisions provided the constitutional rationale for a truly dramatic expansion of presidential power. Three years after *Belmont,* President Roosevelt concluded the notorious destroyers-for-bases deal with Great Britain, relying on his commander-in-chief power, his *Curtiss-Wright* authority, and two statutes of dubious relevance.[131] In early 1941, Roosevelt employed executive agreements to send American troops to Greenland and Iceland, declared a state of unlimited national emergency, and ordered the navy to convoy American ships and to shoot Nazi U-boats on sight, all without express congressional consent.[132] After Pearl Harbor, Congress's declaration of war authorized FDR to lead the nation into an all-out war. That conflict did not conclude until after President Truman had twice dropped the atomic bomb, seeking no congressional consultation and relying on his commander-in-chief power.

Looking back, it seems clear that Roosevelt's activist presidency triggered an extrovert phase in American foreign policy, which was marked by wars, military spending, treaty making, and international summitry.[133] During this era, which began before Pearl Harbor and ended with Vietnam, the United States assumed unchallenged status as the world's "hegemon," its great power. During these years, the president emerged as America's leader and America emerged as the world's leader. When World War II ended, America acted through its president to erect the entire postwar multilateral political and economic order. The era was marked by the creation of international institutions governed by written constitutions. On the political side, the United Nations and its regional and functional agencies were created. On the economic side, the United States helped establish the so-called Bretton Woods System, which provided the World Bank to stimulate international development and reconstruction; the International Monetary Fund to monitor the balance of payments; and the General Agreement on Tariffs and Trade (GATT) to manage international trade.[134] The president spurred an optimistic vision of world public order with an orgy of treaty making, which secured our participation in international organizations and led us into the brave new world of multilateralism.

Even as the United States was seeking to transform the world, Franklin Roosevelt was transforming the domestic structure of the presidency. Although, as we have seen, presidential power had sporadically expanded since the beginning of the Republic, Roosevelt's presidency marked a change not simply of degree, but of kind. Roosevelt became our first "plebiscitary president," a term Professor Theodore Lowi has coined to describe a presidency in which "[t]he lines of responsibility run direct to the White House, where the president is personally responsible and accountable for the performance of government."[135] Roosevelt personalized his role in world leadership through summitry and personalized his role as America's leader through frequent press conferences and fireside chats.[136]

Equally important, Roosevelt did not simply centralize national power unto himself, he institutionalized it into a bureaucracy that would wield executive power. When Roosevelt took office, his personal staff consisted of only a press secretary and a few special assistants. But following the recommendations of the President's Committee on Administrative Management, Roosevelt created an Executive Office of the President that would eventually embrace the Council of Economic Advisers in 1946; the National Security Council in 1947; the Special Trade Representative in 1963 (now the U.S. Trade Representative); the Council of Environmental Quality in 1970; the Office of Management and Budget (previously the Bureau of the Budget) in 1970; and the White House Office of Science and Technology Policy in 1976.[137] During Theodore Roosevelt's administration, the White House staff consisted of only thirty-five people; by the time Ronald Reagan left office, the White House staff had swelled to 3,366.[138]

In short, growing American hegemony and growing presidential power fed upon one another. Together, they created strong pressures for the transformation of the National Security Constitution along the lines suggested in *Curtiss-Wright*. As America emerged from World War II, the question became how the courts and Congress would respond to the president's broad assertions of authority in foreign affairs. The first sound from the courts was one of deference. In *Chicago & S. Air Lines, Inc. v. Waterman Steamship Co.*, the Court refused to examine the basis for presidential orders under the Civil Aeronautics Act granting or denying licenses for foreign air routes. In so holding, the Court announced broad dicta declaring that "the very nature of executive decisions as to foreign policy is *political, not judicial.* . . . They are decisions of a kind for which the Judiciary has neither aptitude, facilities nor responsibility and which ha[ve] long been held to belong in the domain of political power *not subject to judicial intrusion or inquiry.*"[139] But ruling against presidential prerogative in the *Steel Seizure* case only four years later, Justice Jackson, *Waterman*'s author, acknowledged that *Waterman* did not validate a presidential exercise of inherent constitutional powers, only a "wide definition of presidential powers under *statutory authorization.*"[140] Nevertheless, like *Curtiss-Wright*, *Waterman*'s sweeping language has fostered a judicial deference argument that has been urged upon courts up to and including the one that tried Oliver North.[141]

Congress's reaction to the newly powerful presidency proved more complex than the Court's. In the initial postwar years, it appeared that Congress might recreate the Treaty of Versailles experience and reject multilateralism, recreating the isolationist role that it had played during the interwar years. At first, the Senate followed that pattern by refusing to ratify the Charter of the International Trade Organization (ITO), the Genocide Convention, or other conventions on human rights. In 1946, the Senate also imposed the notorious Connally Reservation on the U.S. acceptance of the compulsory jurisdiction of the International Court of Justice.[142] Despite initial protests, the president ultimately abided by all of these congressional actions. But in other foreign policy areas, Congress soon demonstrated that it could work together with the president to promote multilateral cooperation. Between 1947 and 1950, for example, while Arthur Vandenberg chaired the Senate Foreign Relations Committee, the Senate gave its advice and consent to the Charter of the United Nations, the Marshall Plan, the NATO Treaty, and to U.S. entry into a host of other international organizations and security arrangements.[143]

Perhaps the archetype of executive-legislative cooperation during this period was the body of framework statutes enacted to govern U.S. participation in the international trading system.[144] This domestic legal regime revealed that executive practice and judicial decisions were not the only means available to amend the National Security Constitution. *Framework legislation* offered an alternative way to maintain executive flexibility in foreign affairs, while reducing congressional-executive conflict by promoting interbranch dialogue through enforced statutory consultation. Before 1930, Congress had largely refused to delegate responsibility for international trade to the president, instead insisting upon setting every tariff level itself. Because congressional logrolling and horse trading had contributed to every individual duty rate, the infamous Smoot-Hawley Tariff Act of 1930 had set the most protectionist tariff levels in United States history, triggering a series of retaliatory measures by United States trading partners that fueled the worldwide depression.[145] To avoid similar fiascoes, Congress enacted the Reciprocal Trade Agreements Act of 1934, which delegated broad advance authority to the president to negotiate and conclude reciprocal tariff-cutting agreements with foreign nations without further congressional reference. To preserve its check on presidential initiative, however, Congress legislated a "sunset" provision that terminated the president's negotiating authority after three years.[146]

The regime of the Reciprocal Trade Agreements Act proved successful both as a domestic political compromise and as a way to promote U.S. adherence to evolving norms and structures of international trade law. Successive Congresses extended the president's authority under the act nine times between 1937 and 1958, each time extracting a variety of concessions from the president as the price of renewed negotiating authority. Meanwhile, the broad advance delegation permitted the president to negotiate and accept thirty-two bilateral agreements between 1935 and 1945 and to consummate the postwar entry of the United States into multilateral trade management through the acceptance of GATT.[147] Thus, America's experience with framework statutes in the trade field demonstrated that a domestic structure of balanced institutional participation could coexist with an international regime of multilateralism, even if both are dominated by the American president.

By 1947, the primary focus of American foreign policy was not on international trade, but on the perception of rising Soviet expansionism. In July of that year, under the nom de plume "X," George Kennan published a famous article in *Foreign Affairs,* contending that the only way to check Soviet expansion was by "containing" it through "the adroit and vigilant application of counter-force at a series of constantly shifting geographical and political points." Although later questioned by some, including Kennan himself, the policy of containment "quickly became the quasi-official statement of American foreign policy."[148]

The question then arose whether the existing structure of foreign-policy decision making was adequate to implement such a policy. After substantial deliberations, the legislative and executive branches produced a new framework statute designed to reshape the national security decision-making structure for the postwar years. Because that law was designed to unify the president's capacity to make and coordinate national security decisions, it was known informally as the "Unification Act."[149] Its formal name was the National Security Act of 1947. Together with Justice Jackson's 1952 concurring opinion in *Youngstown,* that framework statute would help to shape the National Security Constitution into its current form.

4 The Iran-Contra Affair as an Assault on the Postwar National Security Constitution

To grasp the full constitutional import of the Iran-contra affair, we must first understand the assumptions underlying our postwar national security system. Undergirding that system are complementary visions of how governmental decisions regarding national security issues should be made: a policy vision embodied in the National Security Act of 1947 and the statutes that have built upon it, and a constitutional vision guided by those statutes and Justice Jackson's 1952 concurring opinion in *Youngstown Sheet & Tube Co. v. Sawyer* (the *Steel Seizure* case).[1]

THE NATIONAL SECURITY SYSTEM: THE POLICY VISION

In 1947, America emerged from World War II only to find itself enmeshed in a cold war, the ideological and historical dimensions of which have been thoroughly examined.[2] The Truman Doctrine, the Marshall Plan, military alliances such as NATO, SEATO, Cento, and ANZUS, the Inter-American Defense System, and the Mutual Defense Assistance Program all formed interrelated substantive planks of Truman's foreign-policy response. At the same time, however, World War II had revealed the need for greater centralized management of both military and intelligence services.[3]

The central innovation of the 1947 National Security Act was its recognition that the management of this complex structure of agencies and alliances required a unified national security system, centered in the executive branch. The act therefore sought to place American governmental decisions regarding war making, intelligence, covert operations, military sales, and military aid under the executive's unified and coordinated control.[4] As originally structured by the act, the national security system had two key features. First, the system was designed to be personally managed by a strong plebiscitary president with the support of a bureaucratic institutional presidency. Second, the system was intended to operate not just in times of declared war, but also during a "false peace." Thus, the system was meant to be flexible enough not only to meet the pressing demands of the cold war, but to cope with new and unknown challenges that were yet to come: for example, overt undeclared wars, such as the Korean conflict, and overt creeping wars, such as the Vietnam War, that start and build before anyone is fully aware.

In much the same way as the Administrative Procedure Act of 1946 imposed the concept of due process of administration upon the domestic actions of executive officials, the National Security Act of 1947 formalized the principle of accountable, centralized presidential *management* of the external acts of those officials.[5] The system envisioned that overt wars would be managed by military officials subject to civilians under the control of the president and that covert intelligence gathering would be carried out by agencies directed by the president with the advice of the National Security Council (NSC).

The statutory requirement that overt wars be conducted by military officials under civilian control simply reaffirmed one of the charter principles of the National Security Constitution. The National Security Act converted the Department of War into a Department of Defense, comprising all three military departments, and integrated all military services under the command of a Joint Chiefs of Staff. Congress then subjected the Joint Chiefs to "unified direction under civilian control of the Secretary of Defense," who was in turn answerable to the civilian president.[6] In subsequent statutes, Congress forcefully reiterated the principle of civilian control in prophylactic statutory requirements that the secretary of defense and his deputies be individuals "appointed from civilian life" who had not served as active military officers for at least ten years.[7]

Similarly, the statute effected a long-awaited institutionalization and consolidation of the intelligence-gathering function in a Central Intelligence Agency directed by the president and advised by the NSC. Government spying had gone on sporadically since at least the days of Nathan Hale; by the 1880s the armed services had established permanent intelligence units. Shortly before Pearl Harbor, President Roosevelt established the first central office to coordinate government intelligence, which he later named the Office of Strategic Services (OSS). But when World War II ended, the OSS was disbanded, only to be revived by executive order less than a year later.[8] By formally creating the Central Intelligence Agency (CIA) in the 1947 act, Congress finally gave its imprimatur to executive intelligence gathering, which already had been proceeding systematically for some sixty years. At the same time, however, Congress sought to preserve a crucial distance between the CIA and the military by mandating that the director and deputy director could not both simultaneously be military officers and that those officials could not, during their CIA service, operate within the military chain of command.[9]

What remains unclear, however, is whether in 1947 Congress intended to authorize either the CIA or the president to exercise a covert *war making* function as opposed to an intelligence-gathering function. In 1947 Congress charged the CIA principally with collecting, evaluating, disseminating, and advising on intelligence, but also gave it the ambiguous authority "to perform *such other functions and duties related to intelligence affecting the national security* as the National Security Council may from time to time direct."[10] A drafter of the 1947 act recently testified that, by this language, Congress intended the CIA to perform covert operations, but expected them "to be restricted in scope and purpose."[11] Yet Congress never formally acknowledged that the CIA engaged in activities other than intelligence gathering until a generation later when it enacted the Hughes-Ryan amendment of 1974.[12] Shortly thereafter, the Church committee concluded that in 1947, Congress had never expressly intended to authorize covert action at all.[13] Some executive branch attorneys have responded by claiming that express congressional authorization of covert actions is superfluous, because such activities fall within the scope of the president's exclusive constitutional authority and can be taken pursuant to his independent directive.[14] But that claim misunderstands that intelligence gathering and covert activities are not constitutionally identical. The president may have exclusive constitutional powers to gather intelligence through the diplomatic process, but many covert activities also fall within Congress's constitutional power over foreign commerce. To the extent that covert action takes military or paramilitary forms, it constitutes war making and would thus appear to fall at least within the realm of shared powers of the two branches.[15] Thus, assuming that the 1947 act permitted the CIA to conduct covert operations at all, there seems little doubt that Congress expected such operations to be tightly controlled by the president and the NSC, subject to the three internal control principles that have been described in chapter 2.

The 1947 act's most glaring omission was its failure to mention the role of either Congress or the courts in foreign policy decision making. Congress had partially addressed the issue the previous year by passing the Legislative Reorganization Act of 1946. That law had restructured and reduced the number of standing congressional committees, directed them to exercise "continuous watchfulness" over executive agencies, and authorized committees to seek expert advice from appointed, professional committee staff and the Congressional Research Service. Thus, in James Sundquist's words, "[t]he picture was clear: the president would prepare the unified and coordinated [national security] policy; if legislation or appropriations were required, the Congress would review and respond."[16]

In the years after Vietnam, Congress enacted a wave of foreign affairs framework statutes, which dramatically reasserted its right to participate in nearly all arenas of foreign policy decision making.[17] As recounted in chapter 2, those framework statutes expressly allocated policy-making responsibility not just vertically within the executive branch, but also horizontally between the president and Congress. By imposing on the president a range of notification, reporting, and certification requirements, those statutes sought to ensure that the president and Congress would jointly agree upon broad foreign policy objectives. Furthermore, they envisioned that the president, with the aid of the NSC, would coordinate a full internal debate within the executive branch and secure a consensus among the major foreign policy bureaucracies (particularly the Departments of State and Defense). Thereafter, he would propose particular policy initiatives to Congress to carry out those objectives. Experts outside the executive branch—particularly the congressional committees and their staffs—would then consider and test the wisdom of those initiatives. With committee approval, the relevant executive agencies would carry out those initiatives. The various finding requirements in the intelligence laws, the consultation provisions in the statutes on war making, emergency economic powers, arms sales, and military aid, and the omnipresent legislative-veto provisions were all designed to ensure that policy execution would be subject to congressional consultation, oversight, and a meaningful opportunity for objection. While a particular policy initiative was being executed, the president was expected to seek political support for it from both Congress and the public, giving each access to all the information necessary to evaluate the wisdom and legality of the action.

THE NATIONAL SECURITY SYSTEM: THE CONSTITUTIONAL VISION

Justice Jackson's famous concurrence in the *Steel Seizure* case, issued five years after the passage of the National Security Act, complemented this policy vision of the national security system by articulating a constitutional vision of how Congress, the courts, and the executive should interact in the foreign policy process. In subsequent decisions, the full Court has now embraced Jackson's concurring opinion as the lodestar of its separation-of-powers jurisprudence.[18] Nevertheless, the opinion's enduring value derives less from its precedential weight than from the unusual clarity with which it articulates the concept of balanced institutional participation that underlies the National Security Constitution.

By the time *Youngstown* reached the Court, the cold war had markedly intensified, with both the national and the international mood reflecting the change. President Truman had actively implemented the containment policy in Greece and Turkey and after the fall of Czechoslovakia in 1948, had authorized the CIA to conduct covert operations in Italy.[19] The national mood had become one of perpetual crisis.[20] In that atmosphere, it grew increasingly difficult for the president to reconcile basic constitutional principles with George Kennan's recommendation favoring "adroit and vigilant application of counter-force" wherever communism should rear its head. Walter Lippman wondered, in his biting response to Kennan's "X" article, "is [the president] going to ask Congress for a blank check on the Treasury and for a blank authorization to use the armed forces? Not if the American constitutional system is to be maintained."[21] In an influential book entitled *Constitutional Dictatorship,* written in 1948, Clinton Rossiter insisted that the cold war had made constitutional revision necessary: "[I]n time of crisis, a democratic, constitutional government must be temporarily altered to whatever degree is necessary to overcome the peril. . . . [The government] is going to be powerful or we are going to be obliterated."[22]

By the time North Korea had invaded South Korea in June 1950, world politics had become firmly bipolarized. Almost by definition, any world event that engaged the national interest of either the Soviet Union or the United States automatically engaged the interest of the other.[23] Thus, although Secretary of State Dean Acheson had pointedly excluded Korea from America's "line of defense" in the Pacific only five months earlier, President Truman responded to the Korean invasion by committing American troops to combat without consulting Congress, relying not on a declaration of war, but on his constitutional powers as president and commander-in-chief. Senator Robert Taft declared that Truman "had no authority whatever to commit troops to Korea without consulting Congress" and one member of Congress introduced a Boland amendment-type funding restriction to terminate the conflict. But Congress could generate no binding resolution to challenge the president's act.[24]

By April 1952, tens of thousands of U.S. troops had already been killed in Korea, General Douglas MacArthur had been fired, and no end to the Korean "police action" was in sight. Fearing that a nationwide steel strike would stop the flow of war matériel to Korea, President Truman ordered his commerce secretary to seize the steel mills, citing his inherent powers as president and commander-in-chief. When the challenge of the steel companies to that action arrived at the Supreme Court, the president was strongly favored to win. As one contemporaneous commentator suggested, the president could cite in his favor language from federal-court decisions ranging from *The Prize Cases* to *Curtiss-Wright,* which suggested that he possessed inherent constitutional authority to protect the "peace of the United States" from external threat.[25] Furthermore, as Justice Jackson's then–law clerk, William Rehnquist, recalled, all nine of the sitting justices had been appointed by either Roosevelt or Truman and "had swept aside past decisions that had limited the power of government, whether federal or state, to regulate economic and social affairs."[26] Indeed, the most likely candidate to support the president's decision appeared to be Justice Jackson himself. Only four years earlier, Jackson had authored the pro-executive *Waterman* decision. As Franklin Roosevelt's attorney general, he had written numerous opinions upholding presidential actions, including the 1940 opinion that supported the destroyers-for-bases deal with Great Britain.[27]

Despite the president's advantages, the *Youngstown* Court rejected his constitutional claims by a resounding six-to-three vote, invalidating the seizure as an unconstitutional usurpation of legislative authority. After the fact, some have sought to minimize *Youngstown*'s relevance for foreign affairs by seeking to characterize it as a domestic labor dispute.[28] Yet even assuming that foreign and domestic affairs could ever be so neatly compartmentalized, each of the participating justices plainly recognized the external implications of the decision. After a lengthy catalogue of "our responsibilities in the world community" and past exercises of presidential authority, Chief Justice Fred Vinson's dissent recalled Theodore Roosevelt's stewardship theory of presidential power. He concluded that a "practical construction of the 'Take Care' clause . . . [as] adopted by this Court in *In Re Neagle, In Re Debs* and other cases" should therefore authorize Truman's acts.[29] Justice Hugo Black's opinion for the Court squarely rejected that view, declining to embed into holding the "inherent power" dicta of the cases relied upon by both the dissent and the president. Nor did the Court choose to sustain the president's actions under Article II's grant of "executive power" or his commander-in-chief power, or any other constitutional claim of exclusive executive authority.[30] Instead, in a strangely formalistic opinion, Black held that Congress had the exclusive constitutional prerogative to engage in lawmaking and that the president's acts—which were not authorized by any congressional statute—transgressed that prerogative.[31]

Each of the separate concurrences in the case took a more flexible view of separation of powers, thereby reaffirming the basic understandings underlying the National Security Constitution. Justice William O. Douglas, in particular, denied that either the press of international events or the president's institutional superiority to respond could justify his deviation from the constitutional principle of shared power. "All executive power has the outward appearance of efficiency," Douglas acknowledged, "[b]ut . . . '[t]he doctrine of separation of powers was adopted . . . not to promote efficiency but to preclude the exercise of arbitrary power.' " Similarly, Justice Felix Frankfurter read the Constitution's structural principle of separation of powers as a limit upon the breadth of the president's unenumerated powers. After examining past instances of similar executive practice, he found that they did "not add up, either in number, scope, duration or contemporaneous legal justification . . . [n]or do they come to us sanctioned by long-continued acquiescence of Congress" sufficient to accord them "decisive weight" as quasi-constitutional custom.[32]

It was Justice Jackson's now-classic concurring opinion, however, that most cogently expressed the core notion of the National Security Constitution—a flexible theory of decision making premised upon separated institutions sharing powers: "Presidential powers are not fixed but fluctuate, depending upon their disjunction or conjunction with those of Congress." Using congressional action as a guide, he went on to establish the three-tiered hierarchy of presidential actions that is now so familiar to first-year law students:

1. When the President acts pursuant to an express or implied authorization of Congress, his authority is at its maximum, for it includes all that he possesses in his own right plus all that Congress can delegate. . . .

2. When the President acts in absence of either a congressional grant or denial of authority, he can only rely upon his own independent powers, but there is a zone of twilight in which he and Congress may have concurrent authority, or in which its distribution is uncertain. . . .

3. When the President takes measures incompatible with the express or implied will of Congress, his power is at its lowest ebb, for then he can rely only upon his own constitutional powers minus any constitutional powers of Congress over the matter.[33]

Read against the constitutional history and practice described in chapter 3, Jackson's *Youngstown* concurrence squarely rejected the *Curtiss-Wright* vision and powerfully reaffirmed the National Security Constitution as it had evolved. Read together with the Constitution's text and subsequent framework statutes, Jackson's opinion specifies enduring principles regarding, first, Congress's role in the foreign policy decision-making process; second, the role of the courts; and third, normative principles to guide foreign policy decision making within the executive branch.

Justice Jackson's opinion first defined Congress's role in national security decision making, in part by specifying what powers it does not have. In essence, Jackson's three-part schema recognized that the Constitution grants the president "conclusive and preclusive" power in certain limited areas. Although Jackson did not attempt to define the scope of the president's sole constitutional authorities precisely, he included within them the president's textually enumerated powers, as construed with "the scope and elasticity afforded by what seem to be reasonable, practical implications instead of the rigidity dictated by a doctrinaire textualism."[34] Outside of these narrow pockets of exclusive presidential authority, he suggested, Congress must have an opportunity to participate in the setting of broad foreign policy objectives or those objectives cannot truly be called policies of the *United States*. Indeed, Jackson's tripartite categorization—which turns crucially on the degree of congressional endorsement of executive acts—would become meaningless if the president could constitutionally deny Congress the opportunity to approve or disapprove actions in foreign affairs that he takes within the scope of concurrent congressional-executive authority.

When the president and Congress jointly agree upon broad foreign-policy objectives in a particular area and Congress has by statute expressly authorized the president to proceed, presidential initiatives taken to implement those broader objectives fall within Jackson's category one, that is, they are "supported by the strongest of presumptions and the widest latitude of judicial interpretation, and the burden of persuasion would rest heavily upon any who might attack it." But when Congress has not specifically authorized a particular initiative, the case drops down to Jackson's category two, where the dispositive questions become whether the initiative has occurred within a constitutional zone of concurrent congressional-executive authority and, if so, whether Congress and the president have in fact agreed about the broad policy objectives that initiative was designed to serve. Here, Jackson suggested, both constitutional text and congressional and executive practice are relevant. For in cases where the president and Congress share "concurrent authority, or in which its distribution is uncertain . . . congressional inertia, indifference or quiescence may sometimes, at least as a practical matter, enable, if not invite, measures on independent presidential responsibility."[35]

Jackson turned finally to the case in which Congress has expressly or impliedly objected to the president's actions. In most cases of this type, Jackson's category three would require the president to abstain from acting (as the Court ordered in *Youngstown*) and either to modify his policy initiative or to seek additional congressional support for his original proposal. The exception would be the rare case in which the president has exclusive constitutional power to execute a foreign-policy initiative without congressional approval, as, for example, in unilaterally choosing to recognize a foreign government. In such a case, Justice Jackson suggested, a court could "sustain exclusive presidential control . . . [but] only by disabling the Congress from acting upon the subject."[36]

Second, having defined Congress's role in the national security process, Jackson's opinion defined a pivotal role for the courts as arbiters within the process. When others challenge the president's sweeping claims of exclusive control over matters of foreign affairs, Jackson suggested, the courts should not abstain, but "must . . . scrutiniz[e those claims] with caution, for what is at stake is the *equilibrium* established by our constitutional system." Furthermore, he intimated, courts should not invoke constitutional bases to uphold presidential actions when express statutory authorization is present. Thus, Jackson read *Curtiss-Wright* not as a constitutional decision, raising the broad "question of the President's power to act without congressional authorization," but rather, as a case raising the narrower "question of his right to act under and in accord with an Act of Congress." Finally, even while recognizing the dramatic accretion of presidential power in the postwar era and the peculiar need for flexibility, secrecy, and dispatch in foreign affairs, Justice Jackson rejected the president's "[l]oose and irresponsible use of adjectives" such as "'[i]nherent' powers, 'implied' powers, 'incidental' powers, 'plenary' powers, 'war' powers and 'emergency' powers."[37] Nor did he find foreign-policy matters so different from domestic affairs that the courts must necessarily defer whenever the president invokes his commander-in-chief power, his general executive power, or his inherent emergency powers in foreign affairs.[38] Thus, far from excluding the judiciary from the national security process, as the *Curtiss-Wright* vision would have done, Justice Jackson reaffirmed the vital role of the federal courts in maintaining institutional balance within the national security system.[39]

Read together with the 1947 National Security Act, a third noteworthy feature of Jackson's *Youngstown* concurrence is its suggestion of quasi-constitutional principles regarding lines of authority and internal accountability *within* the executive branch. These principles may be thought to describe a "due process of foreign policy administration" parallel to those found in the Administrative Procedure Act, namely, rules to constrain the discretion of executive foreign-policy-making officials. In 1947, Congress designed the National Security Act to consolidate the president's control over the national security apparatus by establishing "a clear and direct line of command."[40] By always speaking in terms of "the president," Jackson's tripartite analysis implicitly assumed that the executive acts being challenged were either the president's own or were those carried out in his name and with his clear approval. Under this assumption, an act of an executive official cannot carry the weight of presidential authority unless the president either directly controls or approves that act through a clear line of authority. Thus, individuals on the NSC staff could not lawfully invoke the president's constitutional authority to justify their own covert actions unless they could also demonstrate that they were acting under direct presidential order or under a line of executive supervision that led directly to the president. Nor could the executive branch defend as "presidential" decisions that were in fact reached by an unsupervised entity within the government rather than through a genuine process of intraexecutive branch debate.[41]

In 1947 Congress directed the president not only to coordinate through the NSC the development and implementation of national security policy, but also to keep his subordinate foreign-policy bureaucracies carefully separate. Coupled with the president's constitutional responsibility to "take Care that the Laws be faithfully executed," that legislative directive imposes upon the president a solemn duty to maintain civilian control of the military and to establish intrabranch procedures that will enable him to supervise the foreign affairs bureaucracies.[42] In addition, subsequent developments in administrative law may be read to bar executive branch agencies created by Congress from subdelegating to inappropriate entities their governmental responsibilities for foreign policy making or execution. Under this reasoning, both the NSC and the CIA act unlawfully when they deviate from those foreign policy tasks which Congress expressly created them to perform. Similarly, the president and his subordinates act unlawfully when they delegate their national security functions to private citizens or governmental entities that were created to operate outside the existing national security apparatus.[43]

Jackson concluded his opinion by adding to these principles of internal accountability a rule of public accountability. When the president acts in accordance with authority delegated by Congress, "[t]he public may know the extent and limitations of the powers that can be asserted, and persons affected may be informed from the statute of their rights and duties." This language suggests an obligation of the president to preserve the accountability of his bureaucracies to Congress and to provide the people and their representatives with at least as much information as is necessary to evaluate the wisdom and legality of his actions.[44] Far from being onerous, this requirement is critical to sound foreign policy making. Eugene Rostow, a strong advocate of executive power, rebutted George Kennan's claim that Congress's constitutional role "makes it impossible for the United States to function effectively as a great power" by saying: "Our constitutional system for developing and carrying out our foreign policy rightly requires the cooperation of the President and of Congress, *and the full understanding of the people*. . . . [N]o nation, and surely no democratic nation, can carry out a sustained policy of any importance, especially one that may involve the catastrophe of war, unless public opinion understands and accepts it."[45]

Simply put, Justice Jackson's *Youngstown* opinion reaffirmed the centrality of "the *equilibrium* established by our constitutional system."[46] By so saying, he firmly rejected *Curtiss-Wright* and embraced the principle of balanced institutional participation in foreign affairs that has guided the National Security Constitution since its founding. In the years since *Youngstown* was decided, congressional framework statutes have confirmed Congress's constitutional right both to participate in the setting of foreign policy objectives and to receive the information and consultation necessary to make its participation meaningful. The proliferation of post-Vietnam era statutes mandating some form of reporting and consultation and the high degree of executive compliance with those mandates buttress the claim that reporting and consultation requirements have now attained quasi-constitutional status. For example, even when President Nixon vetoed the War Powers Resolution in 1973, he expressly approved the act's consultation requirements as "consistent with the desire of this Administration for regularized consultations with the Congress," not only with regard to troop commitments, but "in an even wider range of circumstances." Although subsequent presidents have not treated these reporting requirements as legally binding, as a matter of institutional practice, they have almost invariably complied with them.[47] Similarly, Congress has required the president not just to report but also to consult, by embedding in the post-Vietnam intelligence and arms export control statutes "presidential finding" requirements, which eliminate the possibility of presidential deniability.[48] By ignoring those reporting and finding requirements during the Iran-contra affair, the executive branch violated framework legislation designed to promote institutional practice establishing a "customary constitutional norm" of reporting and consultation in foreign affairs.

In sum, although the cold war, the 1947 Act, and *Youngstown* all embroidered the National Security Constitution, its core principles remained intact to protect and facilitate the constitutional functioning of the new national security system. Justice Jackson's *Youngstown* opinion rejected the *Curtiss-Wright* vision of unrestrained executive discretion in favor of a normative vision of the policy-making process in which the three branches of government all play integral roles. In zones of concurrent constitutional authority, the president and Congress must share information about and jointly agree upon the broad foreign policy objectives of the United States. The president must then coordinate full internal debate among the decision-formulating entities of the executive branch in order to propose particular policy initiatives to Congress to fulfill those broad objectives. When Congress has endorsed particular initiatives, the appropriate decision-executing agencies must execute them in accordance with law, under direct presidential supervision, and subject to the watchful eyes of Congress, the public, and the courts.

POLICY INVERSION: WHAT REALLY WENT WRONG DURING THE IRAN-CONTRA AFFAIR

If this is how American foreign policy should be made, then during the Iran-contra affair, the Reagan administration apparently conducted a major foreign policy initiative in precisely the opposite manner. The Iran-contra affair occurred in two constitutional areas of shared congressional-executive authority—military aid and covert operations.[49] Before the affair began, the president made two deals with Congress in each of these areas that set the nation's broad foreign policy objectives. Acting together, the president and Congress reached substantive policy agreements not to negotiate with terrorists over hostages and, through congressional passage and presidential signature of the Boland amendments, not to fund military activities by the contras. Furthermore, by congressional enactment and presidential signature of the arms export control and covert operations statutes, the branches reached a related procedural accord: that the president would personally participate in decisions authorizing covert operations and arms sales and that he would always keep Congress informed of those decisions. Yet during the Iran-contra affair, the president secretly breached both the substantive and the procedural accords. Without consulting with Congress, the president unilaterally endorsed two opposite policy objectives—release of the hostages in Lebanon by virtually any means and private support for the contras. By so doing, he denied Congress its constitutional entitlement to participate in the setting of broad foreign policy objectives as well as its attendant rights to information and consultation.

If the Tower commission and the Iran-contra committees are to be believed, the president authorized the initial phases of the initiative, then disengaged from the process of decision making. Acting without the knowledge of the major foreign affairs bureaucracies and allegedly without the awareness of the president or the vice-president, the CIA (a decision-executing entity) then helped to formulate the details of a policy initiative to meet those objectives.[50] The national security assistant and his staff (an advisory entity that included active military officers) then executed that initiative with the aid of private parties and third countries, without meaningful internal debate within the executive branch and in violation of internal agency control principles. All of these actions were taken without the legally required congressional notification, knowledge, or oversight. The executive branch then concealed the existence of the entire affair from both Congress and the public, manipulating information to dampen public debate.

The Iran-contra affair thus ran afoul of both the constitutional and policy visions of the national security process described above. The affair proves remarkable not simply because the president failed to take care that individual laws were faithfully executed, but because he condoned a near-total subversion of the U.S. foreign policy process. By the president's own account, the only constitutionally authorized players in that process—the president, the vice-president, and Congress—as well as the only other statutory NSC members, the secretaries of state and defense, were almost entirely excluded from decision making. Both secretaries later testified that two nonstatutory NSC members, the director of the Central Intelligence Agency and the national security assistant, had supported their exclusion from deliberations regarding an operation that was central to the mission of both of their cabinet departments.[51]

Moreover, within the executive branch, the decision-making and implementing process was turned upside down, as the CIA formulated and the NSC executed policy without presidential supervision. The two central actors in the affair, North and Poindexter, were both active military officers; two others—the former national security adviser Robert McFarlane and Richard Secord—were recently retired military officers, as were numerous other functionaries in the Iran-contra Enterprise. Thus, the affair violated each of the legal principles that make up the due process of foreign policy administration described above. Executive officials claimed presidential authority for actions that the president had not directly approved; foreign policy making and execution were delegated to private entities and foreign governments; military personnel ran foreign policy; and the president failed either to supervise his own foreign-affairs apparatus or to preserve that apparatus's accountability to Congress and the people.

Had the Iran-contra committees stated their analysis in these terms, they would have encountered far less difficulty in demonstrating the correctness of their two central conclusions—that individual laws were broken and that "[t]he Administration's departure from democratic processes created the conditions for policy failure."[52] Once the constitutionally prescribed foreign policy process became inverted, it was only a matter of time before the spirit, if not the letter, of particular laws that were meant to constrain that process were also violated. Nor can it be a surprise that the outcome of such an inverted process was a fundamentally unsound foreign policy initiative. As the chairman of the House select committee pointed out at the close of the congressional hearings, the arms-for-hostages "policy achieved none of the goals it sought. The Ayatollah got his arms, more Americans [were] held hostage . . . than when [the] policy began, [and the] subversion of U.S. interests throughout the region by Iran continues."[53]

All of this assumes, of course, that the factual picture drawn by the Tower commission and the Iran-contra committees was basically accurate. Yet information newly disclosed during the trial of Oliver North suggested that both Presidents Reagan and Bush were, in fact, far less disengaged from the events surrounding the affair than the executive and congressional investigators had previously concluded. Under this revisionist view, the president and vice-president did not passively condone, but rather, actively authorized the evasion of the Boland amendments by their subordinates, by offering third countries aid as a quid pro quo for the support of those countries for the contras.[54] Only time will tell whether additional facts will emerge to establish or discredit this alternative hypothesis. But the search for more facts should not obscure a basic reality—that as a constitutional matter, the smoking gun has already been found. Even under the Tower commission and the Iran-contra committees' factual presentations, the Iran-contra affair represented a frontal executive branch assault upon the principle of power sharing that underlies the National Security Constitution. Conclusive proof that the president or vice-president or both had personally led or directed that covert assault would make the assertion of unchecked executive discretion more ominous and extreme. Such documentation might alleviate concerns about the president and vice-president's control of the executive branch, but would do so only by substantiating their intent to deceive and exclude the other governmental branches from national security decision making. Additional evidence of presidential involvement in schemes to circumvent the Boland amendments might exculpate individual subordinates, but in the process would confirm the president's deliberate evasion of the constitutional principle of balanced institutional participation.

Whether or not the president authorized the executive acts taken during the Iran-contra affair, the broader lesson should be clear: Congress's ambitious attempts during the post-Vietnam era to reassert its constitutional role in foreign policy making have met with limited success. In statute after statute enacted during that period, Congress sought to impose upon the president restrictions whose fundamental premises he apparently did not accept. Although the president signed nearly all of those statutes, executive officials later jumped through real or perceived loopholes in the statutes or simply defied them. The president's growing willingness to break his deals with Congress has undercut Congress's post-Vietnam attempts to increase its participation in foreign policy making, thereby disrupting the institutional equilibrium envisioned by the National Security Constitution.

Why have our national institutions failed in recent years to preserve voluntarily the balanced institutional participation envisioned by the National Security Constitution? Why has Congress not been able to force the president to keep his bargains in foreign affairs? Why have these painstakingly negotiated statutes proved to be porous? Whenever Congress and the president differ over foreign policy, why does the president almost always seem to win? In the end, these structural inquiries, not questions of individual responsibility, remain the real unanswered questions of the Iran-contra affair. Unless we consider and answer these questions, we can have no guarantee that the Iran-contra affair will not happen again.

5 Why the President Almost Always Wins in Foreign Affairs: Executive Initiative and Congressional Acquiescence

Why does the president almost always seem to win in foreign affairs? The reasons may be grouped under three headings, which not coincidentally mirror general institutional characteristics of the executive, legislative, and judicial branches. First, and most obviously, the president has won because the executive branch has taken the initiative in foreign affairs and has often done so by construing laws designed to constrain his actions as authorizations. Second, the president has won because, for all of its institutional activity, Congress has usually complied with or acquiesced in what the president has done, through legislative myopia, inadequate drafting, ineffective legislative tools, or sheer lack of political will. Third, the president has won because the federal courts have usually tolerated his acts, either by refusing to hear challenges to those acts or by hearing the challenges and then affirming presidential authority on the merits.

This simple, three-part combination of executive initiative, congressional acquiescence, and judicial tolerance explains why the president almost invariably wins in foreign affairs. Indeed, this three-part reasoning enters directly into the calculus of an executive branch lawyer asked to draft a legal opinion justifying a proposed foreign affairs initiative. If asked, for example, whether the president can impose economic sanctions on Libya or can bomb Colonel Qaddafi's headquarters, the president's lawyer must answer three questions: (1) Do we have the legal authority to act? (2) Can Congress stop us? and (3) Can anyone challenge our action in court? Or, to use the framework outlined above: (1) Do the Constitution and laws of the United States authorize the president to take this executive *initiative?* (2) If the executive branch takes the initiative, will Congress *acquiesce?* and (3) If Congress does not acquiesce and challenges the president's action (or if a private citizen sues), will the courts nevertheless tolerate the act, either by refusing to hear the challenge or by hearing it and ruling in the president's favor? In this chapter, I consider the first two questions; in chapter 6, I take up the third.

EXECUTIVE INITIATIVE

What drives the executive branch to take the initiative in foreign affairs? Most critics of the Iran-contra affair have offered no explanation, simply assuming that the president's men were overzealous, foolish, misguided, or evil. However true these explanations might be, two institutional explanations—based on domestic constitutional structure and international regime change—plausibly supplement them.

The simple yet sensible domestic explanation, offered by Charles Black, attributes executive seizure of the initiative in foreign affairs to the structure of the Constitution. Although, as we have seen, Article I gives Congress almost all of the enumerated powers over foreign affairs and Article II gives the president almost none of them, Congress is poorly structured for initiative and leadership, because of "its dispersed territoriality of power-bases and . . . its bicamerality." The presidency, in contrast, is ideally structured for the receipt and exercise of power: "[W]hat very naturally has happened is simply that power textually assigned to and at any time resumable by the body structurally unsuited to its exercise, has flowed, through the inactions, acquiescences, and delegations of that body, toward an office ideally structured for the exercise of initiative and for vigor in administration. . . . The result has been a flow of power from Congress to the presidency."[1]

The notion that the presidency is institutionally best suited to initiate government action is hardly new. To the contrary, the notion dates back to Hamilton's statement that "[e]nergy in the executive is a leading character in the definition of good government."[2] Nor, in theory, is there anything wrong with the president initiating international action. As in the domestic context, a plebiscitary president is uniquely visible, and hence accountable, to the electorate. He is the only individual capable of centralizing and coordinating the foreign policy decision-making process. He can energize and direct policy in ways that could not be done by either Congress or his own bureaucracy.[3] His decision-making processes can take on degrees of speed, secrecy, flexibility, and efficiency that no other governmental institution can match. As Justice Sutherland declared in *Curtiss-Wright* (quoting from a Senate Report): "The President . . . manages our concerns with foreign nations and must necessarily be most competent to determine when, how, and upon what subjects negotiation may be urged with the greatest prospect of success. . . . The nature of transactions with foreign nations, moreover, requires caution and unity of design, and their success frequently depends on secrecy and dispatch."[4] Over time, these structural considerations have largely explained why the president has assumed the preeminent role in foreign affairs, despite the clear textual preference of the Framers for Congress.

But the structural fact that the president may more easily exercise foreign affairs power than Congress does not explain why he *chooses* to wield it. As suggested in chapter 3, the explanation may lie not simply in constitutional structure, but rather in the complex relationship between domestic constitutional regimes and international regimes.[5] Theorists of international relations might explain the president's activist choices in terms of the rise and fall of American hegemony during the postwar era. As the discussion in chapter 3 demonstrated, Franklin Roosevelt's personalization and institutionalization of the presidency initiated an extrovert phase in American foreign policy, which marked America's emergence as the world's hegemonic power. During those years, which began before Pearl Harbor and ended with Vietnam, the president led America to erect the entire postwar multilateral political and economic order. An entire generation of Americans grew up and came to power believing in the wisdom of the muscular presidential leadership of foreign policy.[6]

The activist logic of this extrovert era made presidential initiatives virtually inevitable. Yet Vietnam caused an entire generation to rethink its attitude toward foreign policy. National elites became less willing to intervene to defend other nations and to bear the costs of world leadership.[7] Why, then, have presidential initiatives not only continued, but appeared to accelerate, during the post-Vietnam era?

In recent years, many distinguished scholars have made the claim that

America is losing its hegemonic grip upon the world. Political economists David Calleo, Robert Gilpin, Robert Keohane, and Stephen Krasner, the historian Paul Kennedy, and economists Charles Kindleberger and Mancur Olson have all recently examined the implications for world order of declining American hegemony. Although other distinguished scholars, including Samuel Huntington, Joseph Nye, Bruce Russett, and Susan Strange, have questioned the empirical basis underlying these claims of lost American hegemony, several policy analysts have steadfastly asserted the same claim.[8]

The common strand that runs through this burgeoning literature is the suggestion that America is moving into a fifth historical era in its relationship with the rest of the world. This new phase moves beyond the four eras identified in chapter 3 into a posthegemonic era in which the United States will act as an engaged global participant but will lack its former power to dominate singlehandedly the flow of international events.

Put simply, America's declining role as world hegemon has forced changes in the postwar structure of international institutions, which have in turn stimulated further presidential initiatives. In the place of formal multilateral political and economic institutions, which enact bodies of positive international law through treaties, have arisen new, informal regional and functional regimes. Those regimes, which the United States may not dominate but in which it must participate, now manage global economic and political events through bargaining and "soft," quasi-legal pronouncements. Examples on the political side include the international human-rights regime, the international peacekeeping and nuclear nonproliferation regimes, and an evolving international dispute-resolution regime. On the economic side, the United States participates in the Group of Seven nations to manage exchange rates; in the Coordinating Committee on Multilateral Export Controls (CoCom) to manage strategic export trade; and in a debt regime that includes private bankers, multilateral organizations, and the informal Paris and London clubs for debt rescheduling, to give just a few examples.[9] Within these regimes, the United States can no longer simply suppress conflicts of national interest; it must constantly manage relations even with close historic allies through repeated applications of economic carrots and political sticks. For example, recent developments in the world trading system have stimulated the United States to turn to an array of unilateral economic sanctions, bilateral free trade agreements and investment programs, and plurilateral monetary bargaining within the Group of Seven, in addition to (and often in lieu of) its traditional multilateral bargaining within the framework of the General Agreement on Tariffs and Trade (GATT). The rise of new and unanticipated problems not subject to the control of any nation-state, such as global terrorism and the debt crisis, have increasingly forced the United States into a reactive international posture.[10]

Given the president's superior institutional capacity to initiate governmental action, the burden of generating reactive responses to external challenges has almost invariably fallen on him. It is of course true, as suggested in chapter 2, that post-Vietnam congressional reforms also stimulated a resurgence of congressional interest and activism in foreign policy. Key foreign affairs committees have recently gained dramatically in both expertise and influence and the number of informal congressional foreign-policy caucuses has risen dramatically. Yet, ironically, those same reforms have left Congress too decentralized and democratized to generate its own coherent program of foreign policy initiatives.[11] Increasingly, Congress has exhibited its interest and activism in foreign affairs by exerting pressure on the president through means short of legislation. Particularly in fields such as international trade, which directly affect congressional constituencies, Congress has forced the president into a range of preemptive strikes to respond to or forestall even more drastic congressional activity. Recent well-publicized examples include the executive order imposing sanctions upon South Africa in order to preempt congressional enactment of comprehensive antiapartheid legislation; executive decisions in response to congressional pressures to close Palestinian Liberation Organization (PLO) offices in the United States and to deny PLO leader Yasir Arafat a visa; the expanded use of section 301 of the Trade Act of 1974 and so-called Super 301 of the 1988 Omnibus Trade and Competitiveness Act to open foreign markets; and the reluctance to fund the United Nations, a reflection in part of pressure imposed by Congress's enactment of the Kassebaum amendment.[12]

The same public opinion that has empowered the plebiscitary president has simultaneously subjected him to almost irresistible pressures to act quickly in times of real or imagined crisis. "Mass pressure on plebiscitary presidents requires results, or the appearance of results, regardless of the danger."[13] In many ways, the recent wave of treaty breaking and bending chronicled in chapter 2 reflects a reactive presidential role in leading both America's flight from international organizations and its movement toward alternative mechanisms of multilateral cooperation.

Similarly, President Reagan's use of short-term military strikes and emergency economic powers (to respond to terrorism); longer-term military commitments in Lebanon and the Persian Gulf (to respond to requests for peacekeeping); arms sales (to respond to military tensions in the Middle East); and covert actions (to effectuate neocontainment policies in Central America and Angola) reflect the modern American perception that crisis situations uniquely demand a presidential response.

Thus, the relative weakening of America in the world arena appears unexpectedly to have promoted an increase, rather than a decrease, in executive initiatives. In so suggesting, I do not deny the political scientists' insight that once such a crisis has been presented to the president, powerful domestic factors such as ideology, political philosophy, "groupthink," or bureaucratic politics will combine to help drive his response.[14] My overriding claim, however, is that a pervasive national perception that the presidency must act swiftly and secretly to respond to fast-moving international events has almost inevitably forced the executive branch into a continuing pattern of evasion of congressional restraint.

This pattern has afflicted presidents of both political parties, without regard to whether they have generally been viewed as weak or strong, reckless or law-abiding. During the Iranian hostage crisis of 1979–81, for example, President Carter reacted to both international and domestic pressures by conducting one of the most dramatic exercises of presidential power in foreign affairs in peacetime in United States history. During the 444 days that the U.S. hostages were held captive, he declared a national emergency under the International Emergency Economic Powers Act (IEEPA); imposed a trade embargo and an extraterritorial-assets freeze; cut off lines of communication and embargoed travel to Iran; sued Iran in the International Court of Justice; expelled Iranian diplomats; forced Iranian students to report to local immigration offices for visa checks; made a disastrous attempt to rescue the hostages by force; and concluded a wide-ranging executive agreement that suspended all private property claims against Iran, while consigning American commercial claimants to arbitration before a newly established international tribunal. But when Carter left office, he was widely viewed not as an imperial president, but as the weakest, most reactive president in recent memory. As one commentator observed, describing Carter's disastrous military attempt to rescue the hostages, "[p]ublic opinion had forced upon the president an act of the sheerest adventurism."[15]

In the end, an unholy synergy between the executive branch's ideological imperatives, international incentives, and domestic latitude to act drove it toward the Iran-contra affair. A president dependent upon public opinion and sensitive to congressional pressure sought to respond to two perceived external threats—the taking of American hostages in Lebanon and the rise of a communist regime in Nicaragua. In the same way as Oliver North saw the choice as one between "lies and lives," President Reagan saw the choice as between lives and law. As he reportedly told his secretary of state, "the American people will never forgive me if I fail to get these hostages out over this legal question."[16] As with earlier presidents, Reagan's commitment to action led him to condone an errant flow of decision-making power, not just from Congress to the executive branch but *within* the executive.[17] In his administration, power flowed away from the larger, more accountable but more cumbersome foreign-affairs bureaucracies, such as the State and Defense departments, toward institutions such as the Central Intelligence Agency (CIA) and the National Security Council (NSC), which are closer to the Oval Office and more capable of swift, secret, and flexible action. To be sure, the resulting covert transfer of power to subexecutive entities facilitated swift and secret action. But at the same time, it inevitably sacrificed the technical expertise, institutional judgment, bureaucratic support, and bipartisan political approval that comes from consultative inter- and intrabranch decision making in accordance with the National Security Constitution.

CONGRESSIONAL ACQUIESCENCE

In light of the president's strong institutional incentives to take initiatives, why in recent years has Congress so consistently failed to check or restrain him? The short answer is that, despite the initial flurry of post-Vietnam legislation, Congress has persistently acquiesced in executive efforts to evade that legislation's strictures. That acquiescence has institutional roots in legislative myopia, inadequate drafting, ineffective legislative tools, and an institutional lack of political will. The case in point is the War Powers Resolution of 1973, which has failed in its intended purpose for each of these four reasons.

Legislative Myopia

The first reason, already illustrated, is that Congress legislates to stop the last war. As explained in chapter 2, the War Powers Resolution was drafted principally to halt creeping wars like Vietnam, not short-term military strikes or covert wars of the kind that dominate modern warfare. Similarly, the covert action reform legislation that recently died in Congress would not have truly reformed the intelligence apparatus; it would have only finely tuned existing statutes to prevent the president from indefinitely delaying reports to Congress, which any future president mindful of the Iran-contra affair would take care to avoid even without legislation.

Why does Congress legislate this way? All explanations of congressional behavior, of course, must begin and end with politics. The institutional roots of congressional myopia lie in each phase of the legislative process.[18] As Professor Fiorina has observed, Congress legislates retrospectively in large part because voters vote that way.[19] Like other legislation that attempts to be public regarding, proposed foreign affairs legislation is fully subject to undue influence or political veto by special-interest groups. The trade field, of course, is the most extensively studied arena of private-interest-group influence upon Congress in foreign affairs. But in other areas, the defense and foreign-aid lobbies have proved to be highly successful in promoting the maintenance of military spending and military aid. The Israel lobby has exercised well-publicized influence over Middle East, Arab boycott, and arms sale policy. Even the intelligence committees are subject to lobbying by interest groups such as the Center for National Security Studies and the Association of Retired Intelligence Officers.[20]

Occasionally, these interest groups will press for, rather than against, legislative action. The international human-rights lobbies, for example, successfully pressed for legislative action in obtaining the ratification of the Genocide Convention and the enactment of the South African sanctions bill. An influential ad hoc national interest group composed of students, parents of potential draftees, and alumni of the 1960s civil-rights movement rose up to demand legislation to end the Vietnam War.[21] But more frequently, powerful interest groups will press to defeat or narrow pending legislation, thereby burying broader public-policy reform objectives amid a welter of provincial or ethnic-group concerns.

Even when interest groups successfully press individual members of Congress to act, rather than simply to refrain from action, there is no assurance that those members will take the broad view. The need of members to be seen as addressing this year's problem encourages them to address last year's problems by tinkering with existing statutes rather than by investing energy in introducing and passing large-scale reform programs. In 1973, for example, Senator Eagleton attempted to expand the War Powers Resolution to reach paramilitary forces under civilian command, but his efforts failed because his colleagues did not wish to legislate against speculative problems. As Professor Mayhew has noted, the desire of congressional members to choose legislative devices that can be easily explained to constituents leads to a "congressional penchant for the blunt, simple action," which may be insufficiently sensitive to the complexities of the underlying problem.[22] Congress's taste for the symbolic, easily comprehended legislative fix explains its decisions to enact a War Powers Resolution with an automatic sixty-day withdrawal provision; to consider carefully the Gephardt amendment to the 1988 trade bill (which, like the Gramm-Rudman-Hollings budget-balancing act, took an automatic phased numerical approach to reduction of the trade deficit); and to propose intelligence reform legislation after the Iran-contra affair that declared a simple, mandatory forty-eight-hour notice rule for all covert operations. The result of these institutional influences is that Congress lags behind public opinion in enacting major legislation and tends to wrap its policies in packages with largely symbolic value that offer particularized benefits to organized interest groups.[23]

Even when courageous congressional members overcome this institutional particularity and introduce sweeping legislative reforms, they must deal with committees. The competing objectives of the committees sharing jurisdiction over any omnibus bill or of members within particular committees may impede the coalition formation necessary to bring that bill to the floor. Committee chairs, who are still generally chosen based on seniority, may be less ready to challenge the president than more junior members, who may be subcommittee chairs at best. Thus, as in the case of the Boland amendments, several years of internal committee battles may ensue before the committee chair is willing to support, much less lend his or her name to, legislation that restricts presidential prerogative.[24]

The fate of the 1988 intelligence oversight reform legislation, the only Iran-contra legislation to progress during the last Congress, provides a good illustration of these legislative problems. As recounted in chapter 2, that bill was long delayed in coming to the floor, in part because it was referred for markup to both the House Intelligence and the House Foreign Affairs committees. Yet even after the committees finally reported the bill out late in the session, it was not brought to a floor vote; when it was reintroduced early in 1989, the leadership shelved it for extraneous political reasons. Even in the rare case where a floor vote occurs and floor majorities can be mustered in a bill's support, the Senate's rules require only forty-one votes to sustain a filibuster and defeat legislation.[25] Should the president veto the bill, as he threatens to do with most proposed legislation that would limit his freedom in matters of foreign affairs, the number of senators required to sustain the veto drops even further to thirty-four. For that reason, the supermajorities needed to overcome filibusters and vetoes usually coalesce around only those specific incremental changes that would correct known policy defects.

Bad Drafting

Even when enacted, legislation expressly designed to check executive adventurism has often failed because of faulty draftsmanship. The War Powers Resolution, the most ambitious piece of foreign-affairs framework legislation enacted in the post-Vietnam era, offers three particularly glaring examples. First, the resolution's consultation requirements oblige the president to consult "in every possible instance," but then allow the president to decide what that term should mean. Thus, although prior consultation was clearly "possible," neither President Carter nor President Reagan consulted with Congress before sending troops to Iran and Grenada.[26] Second, the resolution requires the president to consult with "Congress" before he sends troops abroad, but nowhere specifies how many members must be consulted or how far in advance. When President Reagan sent warplanes to bomb Libya in April 1986, for example, he consulted with only fifteen congressional leaders and even then only after the planes were already in the air.[27] Third and most curious, depending upon the situation the resolution permits the president to file three different types of reports to Congress upon committing armed forces abroad—whenever U.S. armed forces are introduced "into hostilities" or imminent hostilities; into foreign territory, airspace, or waters equipped for combat; or in numbers that substantially enlarge a preexisting combat unit. Yet the law's sixty-day clock for removing those troops runs automatically only from the date when a so-called hostilities report is submitted or "required to be submitted" and not when one of the other two types of report has been filed.[28] Simply by his choice of report, the president can thus satisfy the resolution's procedural reporting obligation, while evading the resolution's substantive obligation to remove those troops within sixty days.

Some of these drafting errors were simply inadvertent. The legal counsel to the Senate Foreign Relations Committee during consideration of the War Powers Resolution recalls that the third drafting error described above was simply "unnoticed at the time the resolution was enacted."[29] Such inadvertence may also have institutional roots, however. Professor Mayhew has observed that once members decide to vote for a bill and exhaust its "credit-claiming" possibilities, they often "display only a modest interest in what goes into bills or what their passage accomplishes."[30] Other drafting errors—the perpetuation of the in-every-possible-instance language, for example—have resulted from the legislative tendency to draft new laws simply by transplanting boilerplate language from other post-Vietnam era statutes.[31]

Perhaps what appears most frequently to outsiders to be poor drafting stems, in fact, from political deals or compromises struck among members of Congress; among staffers; members and staffers; congressional and executive staffers; members and executive officials; or among the drafting entities within the executive branch itself. Particularly when the president threatens a veto, a peculiar Capitol Hill ritual known as "being pecked to death by ducks" transpires, whereby more stringent procedural provisions are substantially watered down in conference in an often futile effort to avert the president's veto. This phenomenon accounts, for example, for the numerous loopholes in the 1986 South Africa sanctions bill, which passed into law over a presidential veto.[32] In much the same way, the 1980 Intelligence Oversight Act described in chapter 2, which was originally drafted to require prior notice in all cases, was watered down to require only "timely" notice, language which lent itself to easy twisting during the Iran-contra affair.

Whatever the cause, the cumulative effect of these drafting failures has been to prevent the War Powers Resolution from being self-executing. Rather than put the pressure where it should be—on the president to start thinking about removing armed forces sixty days after he has committed them to a hostile situation—the War Powers Resolution now puts pressure on Congress to declare that United States forces are "in hostilities" in order to trigger the sixty-day clock for troop removal. If Congress as a whole is unwilling to make that declaration, aggrieved members must file suit in federal court seeking a judicial declaration that the resolution has been triggered, an option which thus far has yielded them no relief.[33] In chapter 2 the ironic result was revealed. Even though Congress designed the War Powers Resolution to stop the last war—subtly escalating conflicts like Vietnam—in recent years, the resolution's drafting flaws have undercut its effectiveness in restraining just such creeping escalation in Lebanon, Central America, and the Persian Gulf.

Ineffective Tools

Why have Congress's legislative solutions not worked even when Congress has both foreseen a problem and properly drafted provisions to address it? As chronicled in chapter 2, post-Vietnam era statutes applied an array of innovative procedural devices to bring executive action under control, including statutory sunset provisions, reporting and consultation requirements, committee oversight procedures, legislative vetoes, and appropriations limitations. Each of the statutes whose enactment has been described—the War Powers Resolution, the Case-Zablocki Act, IEEPA, the Arms Export Control Act, the Hughes-Ryan amendment, and the Intelligence Oversight Act—was designed not only to restrain executive discretion, but also to increase congressional input into key foreign-policy decisions. But if the Iran-contra affair teaches anything, it is that most of these procedural devices simply have not worked, particularly when executive officials are intent upon evading them and courts are unwilling to enforce them.

Each of these devices has its defects. As Dean Guido Calabresi has recognized, mechanical sunset laws force Congress to redo its work every few years and "gives a tremendous weapon to those who oppose regulation itself; the force of inertia shifts to their side." Not only does time not serve as an adequate measure of how obsolescent a statute may be, complex legislative compromises will inevitably be difficult to replicate when a statute is sunsetted.[34] The War Powers Resolution experience shows that reporting and consultation requirements lack teeth and are all too easily evaded. Committee oversight invites committee capture and can usually be conducted only after the executive action has been completed.[35] The only supervisory methods that have proved their bite in foreign affairs—particularly in the areas of arms sales, transfer of nuclear materials, and covert action—have been the legislative veto and the appropriations cutoff.[36]

Legislative vetoes are simple or concurrent resolutions that have been approved by a majority of one or two houses, respectively, but that have not been presented to the president for signature or veto.[37] As we saw in chapter 2, these provisions were the linchpins of the post-Vietnam era framework legislation. Yet in 1983, the Supreme Court issued a sweeping decision, *INS v. Chadha,* which denied such vetoes legal effect.[38] Moreover, in the first years after *Chadha,* the Court embroidered it with a series of formalistic rulings whose broad language, read literally, would limit any congressional attempt to regulate executive exercises of delegated power by means other than legislation.[39] A fuller account of *Chadha* and its progeny will be taken up in chapter 6. For present purposes, the key point is that *Chadha* announced wide-ranging separation-of-powers language, which could be read to restrict Congress's future authority to check presidential discretion in foreign affairs by using methods functionally similar to the legislative veto.

Moreover, as the saga of the Boland amendments has revealed, the alternative technique of appropriations cutoff does not necessarily ensure good executive behavior. When tacked to massive continuing appropriations measures, such limitations carry the political advantage of being nearly veto-proof.[40] At the same time, however, they possess the disadvantage of being subject to yearly reconsideration and modification. When, as in the case of the Boland amendments, the language of the restriction becomes more and less inclusive over time, executive officials can claim that the provision's vagueness impairs their ability to determine whether particular activities are proscribed.[41]

More explicitly drafted appropriations limits might not, however, have more teeth. Two recent inconclusive Supreme Court rulings have left unclear how far Congress may go in exercising or enforcing its appropriations power to constrain the president's authorities in foreign affairs. More than forty years ago, in *United States v. Lovett,* the Court held that Congress could not use its appropriations power to effect a bill of attainder under Article I, § 9, clause 3 of the Constitution.[42] Although the Court has never extended *Lovett* beyond the bill of attainder context, presidential supporters have argued by analogy that the Boland amendments placed overly strict conditions upon presidential expenditure of authorized funds and thereby encroached unconstitutionally upon the executive's inherent authority to conduct foreign affairs.[43] Some commentators have argued that Congress may not constitutionally refuse to appropriate funds for the president to execute his exclusive, enumerated authorities in foreign affairs.[44] Until very recently, however, no federal court had ever invalidated an appropriations statute on the ground that it unconstitutionally impinged upon the president's ill-defined *unenumerated* foreign affairs authority, as described in *Curtiss-Wright*. In *Federal Employees v. United States,* however, a district court invoked the amorphous "role of the Executive in foreign relations" to invalidate a statute precluding the use of appropriated funds to implement or enforce government nondisclosure agreements. On appeal, the Supreme Court vacated and remanded that judgment for procedural reasons. While the ruling removed district court precedent from the books, it also left both the underlying issue unresolved and the president free to challenge future appropriations limitations on executive branch actions as unconstitutional exercises of Congress's power of the purse.[45]

Indefinite judicial resolution has kept suspended constitutional objections not just to congressional creation of appropriations limits, but also to the enforcement of such limits on the executive by the comptroller general. It appeared that the Supreme Court would clarify the constitutionally permissible scope of the comptroller general's authority when it recently consented to hear a case raising a constitutional challenge to his statutory authorities under the Competition in Contracting Act. Subsequently, however, the litigants agreed voluntarily to dismiss the case, leaving unresolved whether Congress may constitutionally direct the comptroller general to enforce executive compliance with spending limitations in foreign affairs.[46]

As the Iran-contra affair revealed, the executive branch may also seek to escape Congress's power of the purse altogether by soliciting private entities to support U.S. foreign policy initiatives with wholly private monies. Although the Iran-contra committees concluded that the Constitution prohibits such private solicitations *"where the United States exercises control over the receipt and expenditure of the solicited funds,"* executive officials could foreseeably circumvent that conclusion by soliciting third parties directly to support foreign initiatives and by arguing that the solicited private monies never became part of the "public fisc" that is subject to Congress's appropriations power.[47] Oliver North made such a claim during the congressional Iran-contra hearings when he acknowledged urging private citizens to support the contras, while maintaining that "[w]e lived within the constraints of Boland, which limited the use of *appropriated* funds."[48]

Even when undeniably managing government monies, the president has developed over time a whole range of devices to exploit spending loopholes in the appropriations process. When Congress grants the president statutory "drawdown" authority, he may withdraw certain funds simply by determining that such withdrawals are vital to the security of the United States. Similar statutory provisions allow the president access to special or contingency funds based upon nebulous findings that the use of those funds is "important to the security of the United States" or "to the national interest." When given statutory "transfer" and "reprogramming" authority, the president may transfer to one appropriations account funds initially appropriated for another or may reprogram appropriated funds *within* a single appropriation account, often without specific statutory authority.[49] Even before the Iran-contra affair broke, the Reagan administration had shown that these authorities could be used in combination to sustain the Central American conflict without seeking new appropriations. In the early 1980s, the Reagan administration used drawdown authority over special funds to increase military aid to El Salvador by nearly five times the amount actually appropriated in a given year and routinely used the reprogramming authority to fund Central American projects that Congress had not approved.[50]

For all of these defects, the appropriations limitation remains one of Congress's few effective legal tools to regulate presidential initiatives in foreign affairs. Even the most creative president cannot exploit spending loopholes indefinitely. Moreover, each of the open legal questions described above should, in my judgment, be resolved in favor of Congress's appropriations power if Congress's exclusive power over the purse is to have continuing meaning in the context of foreign affairs. But even if the courts rule for Congress on these matters, for purposes of Justice Jackson's category three, Congress will retain only two meaningful ways to oppose a presidential initiative—by disapproving the president's action by joint resolution or by voting an unambiguous and complete denial of appropriated funds for the disfavored program.[51] But in either case Congress would then need to override the president's inevitable veto by a two-thirds vote in each house. In the end, both solutions only trade one problem for another, for each requires Congress to exercise a measure of political will that it has rarely been able to muster.

Political Will

Congress could regularly block executive decisions by joint resolution or appropriations cutoff, so long as it could override a presidential veto by a two-thirds vote. Yet over the years, Congress has overridden only 7 percent of the presidential vetoes (excluding pocket vetoes) exercised between 1789 and 1989.[52] Why has Congress not overridden vetoes more often? In many cases, a critical mass of congressional members has simply been unwilling to take responsibility for setting foreign policy, preferring to leave the decision—and the blame— with the president. As Senator Fulbright recalled, long before the mid-1970s, "[a] majority [of Congress] may have wished to end the war [in Indochina], but less than a majority of the two Houses were willing to take the responsibility for ending it."[53]

The size of the critical mass necessary to kill legislation varies from bill to bill. In committee, sometimes even a single member can prevent a bill from reaching the floor; in the Senate, forty-one votes (less than a majority) can defeat cloture. Even in those cases in which a majority in both houses is willing to take a stand against the president, Congress often falls victim to simple numbers. For if Congress must muster a two-thirds vote in both houses to override a veto, only thirty-four senators can undercut its efforts. It is a crippled president indeed who cannot muster at least thirty-four votes for something he really wants, especially in foreign affairs. Even in the waning days of his administration, for example, President Reagan secured forty-two votes for the confirmation of Robert Bork as a Supreme Court justice; early in his term, President Bush won forty-seven votes for the ill-fated nomination of John Tower as secretary of defense. President Reagan also succeeded in defeating Congress's effort to override his veto of the 1988 trade reform legislation, essentially by securing the votes of two senators, even though the House had voted overwhelmingly for an override.[54]

Professor Black has calculated that, assuming equal defections across party lines, a House of Representatives would need 308 Democrats and 127 Republicans to be veto-proofed against a Republican president. At this writing, even the large Democratic majority facing President Bush falls more than fifty votes short of this number.[55] In theory, all members would have an incentive to enhance the power of Congress by enforcing an alternative solution—a binding political agreement to override any presidential veto regardless of its substance.[56] Yet even in a repeat-player game, such an accord simply would not hold up, for those members who favored the president's position on any particular bill would always have an incentive to defect and support the president, even if their defection would weaken Congress's long-run strength vis-à-vis the president. For precisely this reason, Congress has been unable to circumvent the Supreme Court's decision in *Chadha* by entering a political compact to reenact all legislative vetoes by joint resolution regardless of their content.[57]

Collective-action problems aside, individual members face voting dilemmas when the president violates congressionally imposed procedural constraints in pursuit of substantive policies that they favor. When the Reagan administration sent troops to Grenada and bombers to Libya without complying with the terms of the War Powers Resolution, for example, advocates of his policy decision remained quiet rather than contest his procedural violation.[58] Similarly, parliamentary manipulation by the president's congressional allies may force objecting legislators into untenable voting postures. In 1987, Senator Lowell Weicker, an opponent of the president's Persian Gulf policy, initially voted against a weak resolution protesting the president's acts on the ground that it implied that the War Powers Resolution was not self-enforcing. He ultimately decided to vote for it, simply to ensure that Congress would register some objection to the president's noncompliance with the War Powers Resolution in the Persian Gulf.[59] Nor is it unprecedented for a member who led a drive to override the president's veto to vote to sustain the veto, simply to preserve his right to call for the bill's reconsideration.[60]

Some legislative restraints are rarely applied simply because they leave members too vulnerable to political criticism. Appropriations cutoffs, for example, expose legislators to charges of having stranded soldiers in the field. Even though Congress had constitutional authority through its power of the purse to terminate United States involvement in Vietnam long before 1973, "a large majority of Congress felt it could not break with the President without jeopardizing the lives of American troops."[61] Even when Congress has successfully forced the president to the bargaining table on a question of foreign affairs, as it did with regard to the 1982 commitment of forces to Lebanon, the president has usually been able to demand concessions or future support in exchange for agreeing to modify his conduct.[62] Thus, once again, the president remains largely free to execute his initiatives without congressional check, except in those rare cases where he is politically weak and where Congress's political will is unusually unified.

6 Why the President Almost Always Wins in Foreign Affairs: The Problem of Judicial Tolerance

Neither the executive's lack of self-restraint nor Congress's failure directly to enforce its will on the president precludes third parties from enforcing that will through the federal courts. But however attractive this strategy may be in theory, it fades in the face of a string of recent executive branch victories before the Supreme Court on questions of foreign affairs. Since Vietnam, the Supreme Court has intervened consistently across the spectrum of United States foreign policy interests to tip the balance of foreign-policy-making power in favor of the president. Whether on the merits or on justiciability grounds, the courts have ruled for the president in these cases with astonishing regularity.

THE MERITS

Given the outcome in *Youngstown,* one might have expected subsequent presidents to have encountered less universal success in the courts. But an examination of the president's judicial victories since Vietnam reveals that he owes much of his success to a subtle judicial revival of the *Curtiss-Wright* theory of the National Security Constitution. That *Curtiss-Wright* has not only survived *Youngstown,* but now challenges it once again, reminds us that the history of the National Security Constitution has been a tale of three branches, not two. The player whose role in this foreign-policy drama has most frequently been overlooked has not been Congress or the president, but the federal judiciary.

As shown in chapter 3, in the first era of our constitutional history, the courts played an important and active role in preserving the constitutional principle of balanced institutional participation. Through the next two eras, the courts grew increasingly deferential toward presidential power, at times issuing expansive dicta in support of inherent executive discretion. That trend culminated with the Court's recognition of the president's unenumerated sole-organ power in *Curtiss-Wright* in 1936 and its validation of his exclusive recognition powers in *Belmont* in 1937 and *United States v. Pink* in 1942. Yet even through these years of deference, the Court remained willing to review the president's conduct on the merits, despite occasional hints that political decisions should not be subject to judicial review. One year after the founding of the national security system in 1947, dicta in *Chicago & S. Air Lines, Inc. v. Waterman Steamship Co.* strongly asserted the nonreviewability principle, but in *Youngstown* both the Court and Justice Jackson's concurrence announced renewed commitment to the principle of balanced institutional participation.

In the decades since then, however, the pendulum has swung back in the opposite direction. Particularly since the Vietnam War, the federal courts, through both action and inaction, have adopted an increasingly deferential attitude toward presidential conduct in foreign affairs. By resurrecting *Curtiss-Wright* after Vietnam, the courts have repeatedly upheld the president's authority to dominate foreign affairs. By applying a *Curtiss-Wright* orientation to tip particular decisions in favor of executive power, their actions have posed a potent, growing threat to *Youngstown*'s vision of the National Security Constitution.

Curtiss-Wright and *Youngstown* sketched dramatically different visions of the National Security Constitution. *Curtiss-Wright* was decided during the rise of the imperial presidency and the American empire. By giving constitutional legitimacy to the concept of presidential dominance in foreign affairs, it contributed forcefully to the model of activist presidency fostered by Franklin Roosevelt. The vision of *Curtiss-Wright* carried the nation through World War II, a time when the nation drew together of necessity and Congress and the president shared a consensus about national ends. The president and Congress then designed the national security system in 1947 to sustain that national consensus in the cold war years through a model of management by an institutional and plebiscitary presidency. But when President Truman used that system to extend the national security state and to lead the nation into the unpopular, undeclared Korean war, the *Youngstown* Court reaffirmed the limits that the National Security Constitution placed upon his authority.

Youngstown both reiterated limits upon exclusive presidential powers in foreign affairs and specified roles for congressional consultation and judicial review in distributing concurrent constitutional authority. It imposed a constitutional vision that fostered both dialogue and consensus between Congress and the president about substantive foreign-policy ends. In *Youngstown* itself, both Justice Black's opinion for the Court and Justice Jackson's concurrence read *Curtiss-Wright* as resting not on inherent presidential power, but on whether Congress had authorized the executive action under challenge.[1] By so saying, both opinions suggested that, even in foreign affairs, executive decisions based on legislative consent will more likely express the consent of the governed than those generated by the executive bureaucracy alone.

During the Warren Court years, the *Youngstown* theory took hold powerfully. The Eisenhower and Kennedy administrations provoked relatively few conflicts with Congress in foreign affairs. Most of the disputes in foreign affairs that came before the Court during this era involved not interbranch conflicts, but allegations that government conduct had infringed upon individual rights. In such cases, the Warren Court carefully scrutinized statutes cited by the executive for signs not only of legislative consent to the president's actions, but also to determine whether Congress and the president acting together had entrenched upon protected constitutional rights.[2] Justice Douglas most clearly articulated this judicial method in *Kent v. Dulles,* where the Warren Court declared that judges must find a clear statutory statement that Congress has authorized the executive act in question before deciding whether to condone an executive infringement upon an individual's constitutional right to travel.[3] This "clear statement" principle underscores the importance of legislative consent to executive acts in foreign affairs, particularly when individual rights are at stake. For as Professors Harold Edgar and Benno Schmidt recognized, the clear statement principle demands that rules regulating individual rights "reflect the political consent and public participation embodied in legislation, rather than the self-interested bureaucratic discretion that is likely to be the character of executive action."[4]

The Vietnam War disrupted both the dialogue and the foreign-policy consensus between Congress and the president that *Youngstown* had sought to foster. When Congress responded to the president's Vietnam-era abuses by embedding the *Youngstown* vision in a series of framework statutes, the Burger Court threw its weight toward *Curtiss-Wright,* which reemerged as the touchstone of the Court's foreign affairs jurisprudence. Rather than play a sensitive balancing role between the two political branches, the Court responded to Congress's post-Vietnam questioning of presidential power by muffling debate and uncritically supporting the executive.

The first traces of this pattern appeared in 1971 when the Court rejected the efforts of the Nixon administration to enjoin publication of the Pentagon papers without statutory authorization.[5] Although the votes of the First Amendment absolutists then sitting on the Court sealed the president's defeat in the *Pentagon Papers* case, the separate opinions unveiled a strong undercurrent favoring the *Curtiss-Wright* vision of executive supremacy in foreign affairs.

Three justices rejected the president's claims on First Amendment grounds and a fourth did so primarily because congressional authorization was absent. But the three dissenters would have upheld the president's power, resting on *Curtiss-Wright.*[6] Moreover, the two swing justices, Stewart and White, not only acknowledged the need for executive supremacy in foreign affairs, but openly contemplated other situations in which they might be willing to approve a prior restraint against publication based on national security claims. Justice Stewart declared that "[i]f the Constitution gives the Executive a large degree of unshared power in the conduct of foreign affairs and the maintenance of our national defense, then under the Constitution the Executive must have the largely unshared duty to determine and preserve the degree of internal security necessary to exercise that power successfully."[7] Less than a decade later, in a suit the government later dropped, a lower federal court relied on Justice Stewart's opinion to enjoin publication of a magazine article whose subject matter later appeared elsewhere.[8]

Since the *Pentagon Papers* case, the executive supremacy undercurrent has resurfaced, as the Burger Court has resurrected *Curtiss-Wright,* not so much in constitutional interpretation as in the realm of statutory construction. Against *Youngstown*'s theme of legislative consent, *Curtiss-Wright* counterposed the principle of executive discretion. In that case, Justice Sutherland rejected a claim that the statute under challenge constituted an unlawful delegation of legislative power to the executive, stating: "[I]f, in the maintenance of our international relations, embarrassment . . . is to be avoided . . . congressional legislation which is to be made effective through negotiation and inquiry within the international field must often accord to the President *a degree of discretion and freedom from statutory restriction which would not be admissible were domestic affairs alone involved.*"[9] In the 1970s and 80s, executive branch attorneys urged that language upon courts construing statutes on foreign affairs as a canon of deferential statutory construction. Even when Congress has enacted statutes designed to limit executive power in foreign affairs, executive branch attorneys have liberally construed statutory loopholes—as they did during the Iran-contra affair—to permit or authorize executive initiatives that Congress never anticipated.[10]

The Burger Court had several opportunities to read *Curtiss-Wright* strictly and thereby to rein in this executive practice. On each occasion, however, it ruled in the president's favor, approving rather than rejecting his self-serving construction of the statute in question.[11] Late in the Carter administration, the Supreme Court decided *Snepp v. United States,* in which the Central Intelligence Agency (CIA) sued a former CIA agent for writing a book without the preclearance that was required under the terms of a nondisclosure agreement. Without briefing or oral argument on the question, the Court chose to award the government both a permanent injunction barring Snepp from speaking or writing without preclearance and an unprecedented postpublication constructive trust to recover the profits of the book. Without citing *Youngstown* or asking the *Kent v. Dulles* question—whether Congress had specifically authorized courts to restrain authors' rights by creating either prepublication injunctions or postpublication constructive trusts—the Court dismissed Snepp's First Amendment claims in a footnote and inferred legislative authority for the CIA's acts from general language in the 1947 National Security Act.[12]

In the first foreign-affairs case of the Reagan era, *Dames & Moore v. Regan,* the Supreme Court upheld President Carter's authority to nullify judicial attachments, transfer frozen Iranian assets, and suspend private commercial claims against Iran as part of a sole executive agreement to free the American hostages in Iran. Dames & Moore, a company owed money by Iran, charged that the executive branch had violated its Fifth Amendment rights by taking its claims against Iran and voiding its prejudgment attachments upon Iranian assets without paying just compensation. In an opinion issued barely a month after the complaint was filed, Justice Rehnquist, writing for a nearly unanimous Court, largely rebuffed these claims. The Court held that the International Emergency Economic Powers Act (IEEPA) had authorized the nullification and transfer, but could find no express IEEPA authority for the president's suspension of private claims. Nevertheless, Justice Rehnquist relied on the absence of express congressional disapproval of the president's action, the fact of IEEPA's existence, and a history of unchecked executive practice to conclude that Congress had endorsed the president's initiative, thus bringing the case within Jackson's category one.[13] He further held that the nullification of the attachments did not constitute a taking and that the remaining takings claims were not ripe for judicial review.[14]

Justice Rehnquist's opinion purported "to lay down no general 'guidelines' covering other situations not involved here."[15] Nevertheless, his opinion introduced a disturbing three-part technique of statutory construction, which the Supreme Court has applied to many statutes on foreign affairs that have subsequently come before it. First, notwithstanding *Kent v. Dulles,* Justice Rehnquist did not demand a "clear statement" that Congress had authorized the president to suspend individual claims, despite the undeniable impact of the president's act on individual rights. He thereby permitted executive discretion to override individual rights without a clear expression of legislative consent to do so. Second, he read IEEPA's language as unambiguously authorizing some of the executive acts under challenge, thereby ignoring the legislative history of the statute, which, as explained in chapter 2, clearly evinced the contrary legislative intent to narrow presidential power. Third, rather than construe IEEPA's silence regarding the suspension of claims as preempting the president's claim of inherent power to act, Justice Rehnquist construed a history of unchecked executive practice, the fact of IEEPA's existence, and the absence of express congressional disapproval of the president's action to demonstrate that Congress had *impliedly* authorized the act, thereby elevating the president's power from the twilight zone—Jackson's category two—to its height in Jackson's category one. By so holding, he effectively followed the dissenting view in *Youngstown,* which had converted legislative silence into consent, thereby delegating to the president authority that Congress itself had arguably withheld.[16]

It is hard to fault the result in *Dames & Moore,* given the crisis atmosphere that surrounded its decision and the national mood of support for the hostage accord. Yet given Rehnquist's own past experience with *Youngstown,* where the president had taken similarly drastic action without national support, the Court should have demanded more specific legislative approval for the president's far-reaching measures. [17] The hostages had returned home months earlier and the hostage accord had given the United States government six months before the frozen Iranian assets were to be transferred—plenty of time for the president to ask a supportive Congress for a swift joint resolution of approval. Yet by finding legislative "approval" when Congress had given none, Rehnquist not only inverted the *Steel Seizure* holding—which had construed statutory nonapproval of the president's act to mean legislative disapproval—but also condoned legislative inactivity at a time that demanded interbranch dialogue and bipartisan consensus.

Dames & Moore also sent the *president* the wrong message. In responding to perceived national crises, the Court suggested, the president should act first, then search for preexisting congressional blank checks, rather than seek specific prior or immediate subsequent legislative approval of controversial decisions. [18] Thus, *Dames & Moore* championed unguided executive activism and congressional acquiescence in foreign affairs over the constitutional principle of balanced institutional participation.

Had the Court subsequently given *Dames & Moore* the narrow reading originally intended, its holding could have been limited to its highly unusual facts. But in later years, the Burger Court chose to extend each prong of the dubious method of statutory construction used in *Dames & Moore*. In *Haig v. Agee*, a case decided less than a week before *Dames & Moore*, Chief Justice Burger upheld the secretary of state's revocation of an author's passport based upon a dubious reading of the Passport Act, giving similarly short shrift to the individual rights infringed by the executive action. Citing *Curtiss-Wright*, the Court ignored the principle of balanced institutional participation, suggesting that "in the areas of foreign policy and national security . . . congressional silence is not to be equated with congressional disapproval." [19] Three years later, in *Regan v. Wald*, the Court applied the *Dames & Moore* technique of statutory construction to uphold President Reagan's power to regulate travel to Cuba under IEEPA's grandfather clause, despite unambiguous statutory language and legislative history to the contrary. [20] *Wald* went beyond *Dames & Moore*, insofar as it construed an ambiguous statute to override not simply property rights, but also the right to international travel guaranteed by the due process clause of the Fifth Amendment. Although the Court of Appeals had properly applied *Kent v. Dulles*'s "clear statement" principle and found insufficient evidence of legislative consent, Justice Rehnquist refused to do the same, now citing *Curtiss-Wright* to mandate "traditional deference to executive judgment '[i]n this vast external realm.' "[21]

What made the Court's deference in *Wald* even more remarkable was that the president could have sustained his Cuba travel restrictions without seeking renewed congressional consent simply by declaring a new national emergency under IEEPA (as he did shortly thereafter against Nicaragua, Libya, South Africa, and Panama). Such a declaration would have occasioned national discussion of whether—after more than two decades of emergency controls—our relations with Cuba still constituted a national emergency warranting continued travel restrictions. That question was not merely academic, given that President Carter had licensed travel to Cuba for the five years before 1982 when President Reagan reimposed travel controls.[22] But by "grandfathering" preexisting statutory power, the Court again exalted executive discretion over legislative consent, once again allowing both the president and tionsess to avoid making fresh judgments on that important foreign-policy question.

In 1983, the Court dramatically expanded the third prong of its *Dames & Moore* statutory analysis with its decision invalidating legislative vetoes, *INS v. Chadha*. *Chadha* construed Article I, § 7 of the Constitution to require that any congressional action that is "legislative in purpose and effect"—in the sense that it "alter[s] the legal rights, duties, and relations of persons . . . outside the Legislative Branch"—be both approved by a majority of both houses and presented to the president.[23] Because two-house vetoes (concurrent resolutions) meet only the first requirement and because one-house vetoes (simple resolutions) satisfy neither, the Court's reasoning invalidated both types of legislative vetoes. Although some commentators have suggested that some legislative vetoes survive *Chadha,* the Court's reasoning admits of no exceptions, thereby barring Congress from vetoing any presidential action in foreign affairs of which it may disapprove.[24] In the realm of foreign affairs, *Chadha* struck down the legislative veto provisions in the War Powers Resolution, the Arms Export Control Act, the Nuclear Non-Proliferation Act, the National Emergencies Act, and IEEPA.[25] Thus, Congress may now disapprove an executive act in those areas only by passing a joint resolution in both houses and presenting it to the president, who would of course be entitled to veto it. As demonstrated in chapter 2 in the context of

arms sales, the president may consequently make numerous major foreign-policy decisions under the cloak of congressional approval when in
fact he possesses support from only the thirty-four senators needed to
sustain his veto against an override.

Read together, *Dames & Moore* and *Chadha* dramatically alter the
application of Justice Jackson's tripartite *Youngstown* analysis in cases on
foreign affairs. As we have seen, Justice Rehnquist's *Dames & Moore*
reasoning authorizes judges to construe congressional inaction or legislation in a related area as implicit approval for a challenged executive
action. Yet under *Chadha,* Congress may definitively *disapprove* an
executive act only by passing a joint resolution by a supermajority in both
houses that is sufficient to override a subsequent presidential veto. These
rulings create a one-way "ratchet effect" that effectively redraws the
categories described in Justice Jackson's *Youngstown* concurrence. By
treating ambiguous congressional action as approval for a challenged
presidential act, a court can manipulate almost any act out of the lower
two Jackson categories, where it would be subject to challenge, into
Jackson's category one, where the president's legal authority would be
unassailable. Yet because *Chadha* demands an extraordinary display of
political will to disapprove a presidential act, Congress can only rarely
return those acts to Jackson's category three where a court may declare
them invalid. Thus, these decisions effectively narrow Jackson's category three to those very few cases on foreign affairs in which the president
both lacks exclusive constitutional powers and is foolish enough to act
contrary to congressional intent clearly expressed on the face of a
statute.[26]

Coupled with *Chadha,* Justice Rehnquist's statutory interpretation in
Dames & Moore radically undercuts the *Youngstown* vision of balanced
institutional participation in the national security process. The decisions
enhanced the president's power against Congress by making it easier to
find congressional approval and more difficult for Congress to express its
institutional opposition to particular executive acts. The decisions simultaneously strengthened the president vis-à-vis the courts by effectively
requiring them to apply special deference to executive acts in foreign
affairs, a requirement that Justice Jackson had soundly rejected in
Youngstown itself.

Nor is it clear that the reasoning of *Chadha* and *Dames & Moore* can be
reconciled with one another. In *Dames & Moore,* Justice Rehnquist

derived implied congressional approval for the president's act from two sources—congressional acquiescence in past executive practice and the absence of specific congressional disapproval.[27] Yet *Chadha* declared that any congressional action that alters the "legal rights, duties, and relations of persons" outside the legislative branch must be both approved by a majority of both houses and presented to the president.[28] *Dames & Moore* read legislative silence to enhance the legal rights of the president to diminish the legal rights of other persons outside the legislative branch, all without requiring either of these formalities of legislation.

Chadha's broadest impact in foreign affairs derives not from what it says the president may do, but from what it implies Congress may not do. As construed in light of *Bowsher v. Synar*, decided two terms later, *Chadha* sketched a formalistic theory of separation of powers, which rests on four basic premises: first, that constitutional powers are functionally definable as inherently executive, judicial, or legislative in nature; second, that the Constitution allocates certain powers exclusively to the executive branch, thereby denying them to the other two branches; third, that Congress has limited constitutional discretion to regulate executive action by means other than formal legislation; and fourth, that these separation-of-powers concerns require that specific constitutional provisions—such as the appointments clause or the presentment clauses—be construed to invalidate even those legislative control devices that plainly promote administrative efficiency or political compromise.[29] Should the Court choose to embellish *Chadha*'s theory with a *Curtiss-Wright* gloss—that the power to conduct foreign affairs is an inherently executive one, which Congress and the courts may not exercise or restrain by legislation or judicial decision—then the vision of balanced institutional participation that is central to the National Security Constitution would be destroyed completely.

Fortunately, in two recent cases decided outside the realm of foreign affairs, the Court has exhibited signs of retreating from *Chadha*'s formalism. In *Morrison v. Olson* and *Mistretta v. United States,* the Court declined to extend the formalistic separation-of-powers theory of *Chadha* and *Bowsher* to invalidate new laws—in *Morrison,* the independent counsel provisions of the Ethics in Government Act and in *Mistretta,* the new federal guidelines issued by the U.S. Sentencing Commission. In both cases, the Court's opinion eschewed *Chadha*'s formalistic approach in favor of a more flexible, functional separation-of-powers analysis that would permit a broader interbranch sharing of powers.[30] Thus, in both cases, the Court did not ask the formalistic question, whether the powers being exercised were exclusively executive or legislative, asking instead a functional question, whether the challenged legislation had aggrandized or encroached upon the president's ability to perform duties "central to the functioning of the Executive Branch."[31]

Nor, upon reflection, is it at all clear why *Chadha*'s formalism should invariably redound to the president's benefit. After all, it is the president, not Congress, who more frequently engages in foreign affairs activities that are not authorized by the text of the Constitution.[32] Moreover, the president often promises Congress a measure of control as the price for winning desired statutory authority. By depriving Congress of formal devices such as the legislative veto, which allow it to control delegated authority, *Chadha* may simply encourage Congress to withhold future delegations, to take back statutory foreign affairs powers that it has previously delegated to the president, or to construct informal, non-statutory legislative vetoes of the type to which President Bush consented in his March 1989 "Good Friday accords" with Congress to secure continued contra aid.[33] Finally, as will be suggested in chapter 7, a strict application of *Chadha*'s formalistic reasoning would permit Congress to employ throughout its legislation on foreign affairs congressional control devices that are functionally more intrusive than the legislative veto—for example, a fast-track statutory approval device similar to those found in the international trade statutes—but which do not run afoul of *Chadha*'s literal holding.[34]

Whatever hopeful signs one may glean from the Court's most recent constitutional decisions, there can be little doubt that the Court's recent *Curtiss-Wright* orientation toward statutory construction now challenges the *Youngstown* vision of balanced institutional participation. In *Weinberger v. Catholic Action of Hawaii/Peace Education Project,* decided one term after *Dames & Moore,* the navy refused to confirm or deny that it had stored nuclear weapons at a Hawaiian facility, claiming that that information was classified. Less than a decade earlier, Congress had passed the 1974 Freedom of Information Act amendments, which required the courts to make a de novo determination of whether such a classification was proper. Nevertheless, Justice Rehnquist accepted the government's claim of a national security interest at face value, without conducting such a review or even considering Congress's intent that classification decisions of the executive receive close judicial scrutiny.[35] In *Japan Whaling Association v. American Cetacean Society,* the Court similarly undercut legislation designed to place stringent limits upon executive discretion.[36] Congress had passed two amendments to fisheries statutes, imposing a mandatory duty on the secretary of commerce to certify to the president any fishing operations by foreign nationals that "diminish the effectiveness" of an international fishery conservation program.[37] Although the International Whaling Commission had established a "zero quota" against the taking of whales in accordance with an international treaty, the commerce secretary chose not to certify Japan's whaling activities, based upon an executive agreement whereby the United States permitted Japan to keep whaling at certain harvest levels for a fixed period of years. In a dissent joined even by Justice Rehnquist, Justice Marshall charged that the secretary had "exceeded his own authority," had "substitute[d] . . . his judgment for Congress' on the issue of how best to respond to a foreign nation's intentional past violation of quotas . . . [and] flouted the express will of Congress."[38]

Since *Japan Whaling,* the Rehnquist Court has largely continued to support the expansive executive claims of foreign affairs power. Although the Court recently ruled twice against the executive in cases bearing on foreign affairs, in neither case did it deny the executive's claim of substantive authority.[39] Its most expansive recent declaration of deference to executive discretion came in *Department of Navy v. Egan,* in which the navy discharged an employee after revoking his security clearance without a hearing. As in *Curtiss-Wright* and *Waterman,* the Court's strict holding rested on narrow statutory grounds—that the statute empowering the Merit Systems Protection Board gave the board no authority to review the substance of the underlying security-clearance determination. But in ruling that executive agencies like the navy had inherent discretion to make judgments regarding security clearances, the Court issued broad proexecutive dicta, declaring that the president's "authority to classify and control access to information bearing on national security and to determine whether an individual is sufficiently trustworthy to occupy a position in the Executive Branch . . . flows primarily from . . . [the president's commander-in-chief power] *and exists quite apart from any explicit congressional grant.*"[40] The dissent, by contrast, echoed *Kent v. Dulles,* finding no evidence that Congress or the president had expressly agreed by statute that alleged security risks should be discharged without any sort of hearing. Instead of looking for proof of such balanced participation, the dissent charged, the majority had effectively applied the Court's *Dames & Moore* technique to "assum[e] such a result from congressional 'non-action.' "[41]

Significantly, Congress designed none of these statutes to shift the balance of decision-making power in foreign affairs from Congress toward the president. Several statutes, such as the fisheries amendments and IEEPA, were enacted for precisely the opposite purpose. But the Supreme Court's reading of these statutes has enhanced presidential power by encouraging lawyers throughout the executive branch to construe their agency's authorizing statutes to permit executive initiatives extending far beyond the intended scope of those statutes.

In reaching these decisions, the Burger and Rehnquist Courts have rejected virtually every doctrinal technique offered them to narrow the substantive scope of executive power. When urged to apply the non-delegation doctrine to invalidate a grant of power to the president, the Court has held that that doctrine did not apply equally to foreign affairs.[42] When asked to construe the existence of a statute in the field to preempt a claim of inherent presidential power to make foreign policy, the Court has refused.[43] When asked to read narrowly a statute that impinged on constitutional rights, the Court has refused to apply the "clear statement" rule.[44] When urged to uphold the constitutionality of a congressional control device, the Court has invalidated it.[45]

In short, far from maintaining a rough balance in the congressional-executive tug-of-war, the Court's decisions on the merits of foreign-affairs claims have encouraged a steady flow of policy-making power from Congress to the executive. Through unjustifiably deferential techniques of statutory construction, since Vietnam the courts have read *Curtiss-Wright* and its progeny virtually to supplant the constitutional vision of *Youngstown*. As a result, in the years leading up to the Iran-contra affair, the courts became the president's accomplices in an extraordinary process of statutory inversion. It is hardly surprising, then, that Oliver North should have cited *Curtiss-Wright* to Congress as the legal basis justifying all of his actions during the Iran-contra affair.[46]

JUSTICIABILITY

Perhaps even more important than these rulings on the merits have been the many cases in which the Court has condoned executive initiatives in foreign affairs by refusing to hear challenges to the president's authority. In *Goldwater v. Carter,* the Court dismissed congressional challenges to presidential treaty breaking, with various justices finding the challenges not ripe or presenting nonjusticiable political questions.[47] In *Burke v. Barnes,* the Court dismissed as moot a congressional challenge to President Reagan's pocket veto of a foreign-aid bill that would have required him to certify El Salvador's progress in protecting human rights.[48] These Supreme Court decisions stand atop a much larger collection of lower federal court cases that, over the years, have refused to hear challenges to the legality of the Vietnam War and to various aspects of the Reagan administration's support for the contras.[49]

Even when the courts have not relied on nonjusticiability doctrines tied to the nature, ripeness, or mootness of the question presented, they have invoked the identity of the plaintiff, the defendant, the cause of action, and the requested relief as grounds for dismissing the case. Recent decisions have erected standing bars to suits regarding foreign affairs brought by aliens, citizens, taxpayers, and members of Congress.[50] Courts have held government officials immune from suits by citizens for monetary damages.[51] They have held the United States government and recently, private parties who contract with the government, immune from suits by members of the armed forces for all manner of injuries.[52] They have dismissed state, federal, and international-law claims against federal defendants for want of a cause of action.[53] Even when they have conceded a right, they have denied claims for both monetary and equitable remedy on fuzzy "equitable discretion" grounds.[54] In recent years, lower courts have dismissed so many challenges to executive conduct by so many carefully selected plaintiff groups that their opinions now seem to pick and choose almost randomly from among the available abstention rationales.[55] In contrast, when Congress has raised similar defenses to suits brought by the executive branch, the Court has uniformly rejected them.[56] In recent times the Court has been almost "totally deferential in reviewing challenges to executive conduct, but . . . very willing to declare unconstitutional congressional statutes as violating separation of powers."[57]

In chapter 9, I address and challenge the prudential concerns that have led the courts to defer so broadly to the executive in foreign affairs. For present purposes, it suffices to say that however powerful these rationales may be, they provide no intellectual support for the sweeping statements of judicial abdication that have recently begun to appear in the *Federal Reporters*.[58] Nor do they explain the persistent reluctance of the courts to look behind talismanic executive assertions of national security, military necessity, or the need for judicial deference to the political branches in matters of military discipline and military affairs.[59] Finally, they do not explain the troubling confusion that judges have exhibited in attempting to distinguish cases in which they find the president's conduct unreviewable from those in which they review his conduct and find it authorized.[60]

As chronicled in chapter 3, the trend toward executive insulation from judicial review in foreign affairs is a relatively recent development, which finds little support in our constitutional traditions. Since the founding of the National Security Constitution, the courts have played a pivotal role in maintaining the constitutional equilibrium of the national security system. That role has required judges to police the boundaries of the branches' authority in foreign affairs to maintain the constitutional principle of balanced institutional participation. Particularly when Congress legislates a framework statute governing executive decisions, those decisions should remain fully subject to judicial review.[61] Thus, the recent foreign-affairs cases in which courts have abstained from such review ultimately betray not doctrinal fidelity, but reflexive timidity.

THE ROAD TO THE IRAN-CONTRA AFFAIR

The broader lesson that emerges from this study of executive initiative, congressional acquiescence, and judicial tolerance in the post-Vietnam era is that under virtually every scenario the president wins. If the executive branch possesses statutory or constitutional authority to act and Congress acquiesces, the president wins. If Congress does not acquiesce in the president's act, but lacks the political will either to cut off appropriations or to pass an objecting statute and override a veto, the president again wins. If a member of Congress or a private individual sues to challenge the president's action, the judiciary will likely refuse to hear that challenge on the ground that the plaintiff lacks standing; the defendant is immune; the question is political, not ripe, or moot; or that relief is inappropriate. Even if the plaintiffs somehow surmount each of these obstacles and persuade the courts to hear their challenge on the merits, the courts will usually rule in the president's favor. In sum, whatever the scenario, the bottom line stays the same. The president almost always seems to win in foreign affairs.

One need not be a cynic to recognize that this doctrinal tangle has afforded presidential judgment extraordinary insulation from external scrutiny. Thus, it should not surprise us when an institutional presidency so rarely held accountable for its acts stops trying to keep account. During the Iran-contra affair, several interrogators expressed disbelief that the president's subordinates thought they could get away with what they were doing.[62] But their arrogance was not born of ignorance, but of habit. National Security Council secretary Fawn Hall's suggestion that "sometimes you have to go above the written law" was not a new thought.[63] Ten years earlier, an unchastened Richard Nixon told an interviewer, "When the President does it, that means that it is not illegal."[64]

PART THREE
THE PRESCRIPTION

7 Restoring the National Security Constitution: Some Guiding Principles

If the foregoing chapters have explained why, in recent years, the president almost always wins in foreign affairs, two obvious questions arise. First, why does the president sometimes lose in foreign affairs, as he plainly did during the Iran-contra affair itself? Second, when the president wins, does the country also win?

To both questions, I would argue, the answer is the same. In the long run, winning usually becomes losing. American foreign policy grows out of a long-term political process premised upon notions of balanced institutional participation and power sharing. In the same way as one spouse cannot and should not win in a marriage, one branch of government cannot and should not permanently defeat another in a constitutional system where separated institutions share foreign policy powers. Thus, as revealed in chapter 3, over time too many short-term presidential victories will almost inevitably trigger a reactive era of presidential defeat. As both the Iran-contra affair and Vietnam have further demonstrated, too many presidential victories tend to foster a pattern of secretive, unilateral, executive decision making that eventually leads the country to defeat. A foreign policy system domineered by the executive and beset by chronic conflict among the branches of government ultimately serves the long-term interests of neither the executive branch nor the nation as a whole.

HOW "WINNING" BECOMES LOSING

As we have seen, Congress's post-Vietnam framework statutes have failed to enforce the principle of balanced institutional participation, the core of the National Security Constitution. With the crucial collaboration of the courts, the president appears to have won consistently against Congress during the post-Vietnam era.

Yet on closer inspection, many of the president's recent victories in foreign affairs prove far more illusory than they appear at first glance. In the American foreign-policy process, wins and losses are often incremental, anticipated rather than imposed, and traded in intricate, low-visibility ways. However impressive the president's recent court victories may be, they cumulatively occupy only a small corner of the foreign-policy spectrum. Even when Congress has sustained presidential vetoes, those vetoes have only rarely directed affirmative policies. Take, for example, President Reagan's veto of the 1988 omnibus trade reform bill, based upon his opposition to a provision requiring employers to give their employees sixty days' notice of expected plant closings. Congress narrowly failed to override that veto, but then separately repassed only slightly modified versions of both the omnibus package and the plant-closing bill. Under severe pressure from members of his own party, the president signed the first and allowed the second to become law without signing it, causing his trade representative to concede that the president's initial veto had accomplished virtually nothing.[1]

Nor, as we have seen, do intense periods of presidential activity invariably signal presidential victory. The Reagan administration's closing flurry of counterterrorist acts, antiapartheid sanctions, and retaliatory trade measures were all ostensibly initiated by the president, but were in fact largely driven by congressional pressure or external events. Apparently successful executive end-runs around Congress have often been answered, months or years later, by new congressional restraints. Perhaps the starkest illustration has been the president's decision to adopt unilaterally a broad "reinterpretation" of the 1972 Anti-Ballistic Missile (ABM) Treaty, which was designed to give him greater freedom to develop a Strategic Defense Initiative (SDI) program. Although the president initially declared that his reinterpretation authorized SDI development, outcry over the attempted reinterpretation by both Congress and our allies prompted him to announce that the United States would continue to comply voluntarily with the treaty's preexisting narrow interpretation.[2]

Meanwhile, as elaborated in chapter 2, the controversy yielded many counterproductive effects for the president: the imposition of legislative conditions upon Defense Department appropriations; the Senate's ABM Treaty Interpretation Resolution; the Byrd amendment to the Intermediate Nuclear Forces (INF) Treaty; and the waiver of executive privilege on a wide range of secret negotiating documents.[3]

The administration's recent efforts to expand executive freedom in the treaty process have not only proved counterproductive domestically, they have failed to advance our national positions in the international arena. Because the United States is a party to a network of closely interconnected treaties, unilateral administration decisions to break or bend one treaty have forced it into vicious cycles of treaty violation. For example, in 1984, the administration hastily modified its 1946 declaration accepting the compulsory jurisdiction of the International Court of Justice in an effort to divest the court of jurisdiction over a suit being brought against the United States by Nicaragua. That decision was not only later held to be legally ineffective, but almost certainly weakened the American position that the court lacked jurisdiction without the modification. Once the court rejected the U.S. position at the jurisdictional phase of the suit, the Reagan administration had little choice but to withdraw from the court's compulsory jurisdiction altogether, breaking an acceptance issued nearly four decades earlier. Predictably, that decision was followed by the court's adverse judgment on the merits, which formed the basis for both Nicaragua's new claim that the United States has breached its international obligation to respect World Court judgments and domestic litigation by American citizens living in Nicaragua against United States officials.[4] Unfortunately, this wave upon wave of executive treaty bending fostered an impression of a United States contemptuous of both its treaties and its treaty partners at precisely the time when the administration was seeking to mobilize those partners to address problems it simply could not solve by itself: the Central American peace process, trade imbalances and currency coordination, international terrorism, and Middle East security policy.[5]

All of these outcomes bear witness to the false promise of a foreign policy-making system overly dominated by the executive. As the Iran-contra affair revealed, secretive, unilateral, executive decision making, missing the representative qualities derived from congressional participation and the legal constraints imposed by judicial supervision, guarantees neither wise nor efficient foreign-policy making. History suggests that too many years of foreign policy dominance by any single branch of government will foster reactive interbranch conflict that will ultimately jeopardize the long-term interests of the nation as a whole. As Alton Frye has observed, Professor Corwin's oft-quoted description of the Constitution as an "invitation for Congress and the President to struggle for the privilege of directing American foreign policy" misses the real point that "[t]he objective of the struggle is not control but wise policies acceptable to the American people."[6] Internecine political warfare can only harm the national interest when interbranch disputes determine critical national positions in the international realm. Congressman Lee Hamilton put the point well when he told Oliver North at the close of North's congressional testimony: "You said . . . the Congress would declare itself the winner [in the Iran-contra affair]. . . . but may I suggest . . . [w]e all lost. The interests of the United States have been damaged by what happened."[7]

A NATIONAL SECURITY CHARTER

Since the Founding, our informal National Security Constitution has embodied the constitutional premise of balanced institutional participation. But by working a nearly successful assault upon that constitution, the Iran-contra affair vividly demonstrated that our existing legal structure no longer affords the national security system sufficient protection. No legal structure can endure if it attempts to regulate without accounting for the incentives of the regulated individuals and institutions.[8] Yet, as argued in chapters 5 and 6, the current structure of our national security system gives the executive branch incentives to act; Congress, incentives to acquiesce; and the courts, incentives to refrain from passing judgment on the conduct of the other two branches. The synergy among these institutional incentive structures, not the motives of any single branch, best explains the recurring pattern of executive adventurism and interbranch conflict in our postwar foreign policy.

Although individual presidents certainly bear much of the blame for this vicious cycle, in an important sense, they have equally been victims of it. As earlier chapters outlined, the current foreign-policy decision-making process places too great a burden upon the president and the presidency, while allowing Congress and the courts too easily to avoid constructive participation in important national decisions. Consequently, in the years from Vietnam to the Iran-contra affair, the president regularly broke his bargains with Congress in foreign affairs and neither Congress nor the courts forced him to keep those bargains.

Nor does this problem appear likely to abate, despite post-Iran-contra changes in executive branch personnel and renewed pledges of bipartisanship. As argued in chapter 5, as American hegemony diminishes internationally, the occasions for executive initiative are likely to increase, not decline. The current probability that Congress will acquiesce and that the courts will tolerate such initiatives will impose few costs on any president who stretches legislative bargains in a haste to act.

Those who view the Iran-contra affair as an aberration reject legislative reform on the ground that our national security system is ultimately self-regulating. Those who view the affair as an exercise in congressional folly oppose new laws because they consider that system to be overregulated. But to those who view the Iran-contra affair as evidence of systemic flaws in the national security process, the affair has confirmed that the process is inadequately regulated.

The momentum of the Iran-contra affair, coupled with the Democrats' renewed control of Congress after November 1986, presented Congress with a rare window of opportunity to revamp existing national security regulation and to reinsert itself and the courts in the foreign-policy-making process. In the late 1970s, Congress exploited a similar opportunity by legislating a broader ongoing role for itself across the realms of foreign policy, a role which the executive branch subsequently undercut. The Iran-contra watershed has offered the legislators a similar opening, which Congress has thus far almost entirely squandered.[9] But if the administration and Congress wish to learn the lessons of the last war, they should now consider new omnibus legislation, designed to redefine broadly the roles of Congress, the president, and the courts in national security matters.

What the Iran-contra affair underscores is the need for a new national security charter—an omnibus statutory amendment to the National Security Constitution—in the form of a framework statute designed to regulate and protect many aspects of the foreign-policy-making process.[10] Unlike the current patchwork of laws, executive orders, national security directives, and informal accords that govern covert and overt war making, emergency economic power, foreign intelligence, and arms sales, such a statute would act as a statutory successor to the National Security Act of 1947. An ideal statute would reenact, in five separate titles—the War Powers Resolution, the International Emergency Economic Powers

Act, the arms export control laws, the Intelligence Oversight Act, and the National Security Council (NSC) provisions of the 1947 act.[11] At the same time, the charter would repeal other lingering statutes that have fallen into desuetude. Accompanying procedural titles would address modes of congressional-executive consultation in international agreement making, internal and external agency control procedures, and provisions for judicial review of executive action. Perhaps most important, the legislation would create new congressional structures and effect certain modest, but important, revisions in internal House and Senate rules.

Such a framework statute could and should incorporate many of the legislative proposals contained in the Iran-contra committees' majority report.[12] For as explained in chapter 1, the fault of those proposals lies not in their substance, but in the committees' failure to articulate how the proposals jointly constitute a legislative strategy for attacking the deeper institutional causes of the affair. The recent history recounted in chapter 2 suggests that without such a strategy, interstitial efforts to amend particular foreign-affairs laws will inevitably fail, serving only to push executive conduct toward new statutory lacunae and pockets of unregulated activity.

The remainder of this chapter offers general principles that should animate such a national security charter. In chapter 8 I sketch how those general principles might be applied in specific issue areas. In the ninth and concluding chapter, I anticipate and respond to likely objections to the charter proposal and speculate more broadly about the future of the National Security Constitution.

PRINCIPLES TO GUIDE REFORM

More important than any particular legislative proposal should be a broader national recognition that executive practice has recently gained undue predominance as a source of customary constitutional law in the area of foreign affairs. As described in chapter 3, since the Founding, the provisions of the Constitution regarding foreign affairs have never been subject to formal constitutional amendment. Instead, periodic framework legislation, judicial decisions, and executive practice accepted by the other branches have adapted our National Security Constitution to meet changing times. The framework statutes and customary norms established during the early years of the Republic worked the first de facto amendment of the National Security Constitution, by shifting the president's role in foreign affairs from the secondary one assigned him by the Framers to the dominant role he now plays. During succeeding historical eras, executive practice endorsed by judicial decision and congressional approval consolidated the president's exclusive authority over recognition, diplomatic relations, and negotiations, while approving new constitutional modes of agreement making. But when *Curtiss-Wright's* dicta, coupled with unprecedented presidential activism in the years after World War II, threatened to expand those zones of exclusive presidential discretion even further, new framework legislation—the 1947 National Security Act and the post-Vietnam foreign-affairs statutes—and an authoritative judicial decision—the Court's 1952 ruling in *Youngstown*—reaffirmed the constitutional primacy of balanced institutional participation.

As recounted in chapter 2, however, since Vietnam, the institutional balance has once again shifted decidedly toward executive power. In chapters 5 and 6, I detailed how congressional acquiescence and judicial tolerance in the post-Vietnam era have combined to elevate this pattern of executive dominance to the status of quasi-constitutional custom. The Iran-contra affair graphically illustrated the defective results of this informal method of constitutional amendment. To allow executive practice to remake constitutional law perpetually in this area inevitably permits successive presidents to rewrite the National Security Constitution based upon their shifting views of the exigencies of the external world. More troubling, such a practice allows the president's agents to claim constitutional legitimacy for arbitrary, unsupervised, and even unauthorized exercises of executive discretion.

Nor does it make sense for the National Security Constitution to be updated solely by sporadic judicial review.[13] As Justice Jackson observed, when judges "review and approve [executive action that oversteps the bounds of constitutionality], that passing incident becomes the doctrine of the Constitution. There it has a generative power of its own, and all that it creates will be in its own image."[14] In Corwin's words: "The best escape from presidential autocracy in the age we inhabit is not . . . judicial review, which can supply only a vacuum, but timely legislation."[15]

Consistent with the guiding principle of balanced institutional participation, the process of reconstituting our National Security Constitution over time should thus be confided in no single branch, but in all three branches working together: in a Congress that enacts a framework statute defining institutional responsibilities in foreign affairs; in a president who helps draft and apply the statute; and in courts who construe the charter and draw boundaries between lawful and unlawful conduct. Enactment of national security framework legislation designed to promote occasional judicial decisions would supply two countervailing sources of constitutional law in this area, which would serve as much-needed counterweights to unchallenged executive practice. Even rudimentary legislation in this area would replace the barnacled 1947 National Security Act with a more recent, considered statement—made jointly by Congress and the president and construed by the courts—of how national security policy should be made in the future.

Any charter legislation should aim, primarily, to reaffirm the core constitutional notion of balanced institutional participation, not to encourage congressional micromanagement or improvident judicial activism in foreign-policy matters. Thus, any reform legislation should acknowledge the executive's leading constitutional role in foreign affairs, at the same time as it seeks to reduce the isolation that currently surrounds executive branch activities, to enhance internal executive branch deliberations, and to increase congressional-executive dialogue while foreign-policy objectives are being set and initiatives implemented. The goal of the reform effort should be to assign institutional responsibility by clarifying the legal and constitutional framework within which foreign-policy decisions shall be made.

One final prescriptive implication of my analysis is that no national security reform legislation can redress the problems described above by focusing solely upon organizational problems within the White House. As argued in chapters 5 and 6, the sources of executive adventurism lie not only there, but also in the outside world and in the operation of the two coordinate branches of government. Admittedly, Congress cannot legislate executive self-restraint, legislative will, or judicial courage. But Congress can and should seek to alter recurrent patterns of executive behavior by restructuring the institutional attributes that now create almost irresistible incentives for executive officials to act irresponsibly while imposing few costs on their conduct. Any national security reform bill should therefore target the institutional sources of executive adventurism, congressional acquiescence, and undue judicial tolerance—all of which have contributed to recent executive excesses. The goal of a national security reform bill should be to restructure existing laws not only to restrain executive initiative, but also to revitalize both Congress and the courts as institutional counterweights to the presidency.

Restraining the Executive: Internal and External Accountability

Since 1949, more than a dozen private and public studies have sought to determine how best to organize the foreign policy apparatus of the executive branch.[16] The Iran-contra affair underscores the need to develop more efficient policy-making mechanisms, as well as more effective internal and external checks upon executive adventurism.

Congress's effort to promote executive self-restraint should be guided by the principles of *internal and external accountability.* Wherever possible, the legality of proposed foreign-policy initiatives should be tested by processes of adversarial review both within and without the executive branch. Moreover, Congress should seek to specify the content of the president's responsibility to "take Care that the Laws be faithfully executed" in foreign affairs by making explicit the "due process principles of foreign policy administration" regarding internal executive branch accountability that are currently implicit in our National Security Constitution.[17]

Alexander George has made the case for creating a decision-making system that encourages the clash of the competing foreign-policy views to be presented to the president for final decision. Apparently, the Bush administration has already sought to apply this multiple-advocacy approach with regard to domestic policy decision making.[18] This adversarial approach, extended to test the legality as well as the substance of foreign policy initiatives, would have discouraged the proliferation of secret, unchallenged agency legal opinions that allowed the Iran-contra affair to proceed. Two such legal opinions have received particular public attention—one by the CIA's general counsel permitting the president to make an intelligence finding retroactively and another, cursory opinion by the hapless counsel to the Intelligence Oversight Board, which declared the Boland amendments inapplicable to NSC activities. Apparently, neither of these legal opinions was ever subjected to centralized executive branch review. As President Reagan's White House counsel later recalled, "[o]ne of the real problems with the entire Iran-contra episode was that not only was it not well-lawyered, but it was *not lawyered* in most respects."[19]

To ensure that executive initiatives will not commence based upon a single counsel's questionable reading of his or her agency's organic statute, Congress could act on two fronts. First, it might choose to require an interagency review of legal opinions that authorize covert actions. Such interagency review would mimic the centralized review of agency rulemaking that the Office of Management and Budget has conducted since the Reagan administration. [20] The task of obtaining and coordinating competing legal analyses could be confided in the White House counsel's office or in the newly established office of the legal counsel to the NSC. Alternatively, it could be conducted by particular agency general counsels, such as the State Department Legal Adviser's Office or the General Counsel's Office of the CIA. [21] Ideally, such review would be conducted by the Office of Legal Counsel of the Justice Department, which is not only farther from the president, but should also be less prone to influence by any particular agency's policy mission.

Justice Department review of executive initiatives in foreign affairs would be fully consistent with historical tradition. In the First Judiciary Act of 1789, Congress authorized the attorney general to render opinions on questions of law to the president and the heads of the executive departments, a responsibility which the attorney general has over time delegated to the Office of Legal Counsel. [22] That office, which has been headed by current Supreme Court Justices William Rehnquist and Antonin Scalia, has historically discharged its opinion-giving function with great distinction. [23] But as a former assistant attorney general recently described, even before the Iran-contra affair, the Reagan administration unwisely restricted the attorney general's participation in the approval and review of sensitive foreign policy and intelligence matters: "The cumulative effect of these restrictions was to minimize the ability of the Attorney General to participate in the deliberations or to render meaningful legal advice. He was even asked at times to render off-the-cuff oral advice on complex legal situations. The obvious desire was to be able to claim that the Attorney General had given a legal seal of approval to various proposals without permitting them to undergo real legal scrutiny." [24]

To avoid recurrence of this problem, a new charter could strengthen internal legal accountability by making the attorney general a statutory, rather than simply an invited, member of the NSC. That statutory duty would closely relate to the attorney general's other national security duties, which include supervision of the Federal Bureau of Investigation (FBI) (and all of its foreign counterintelligence operations), as well as authorization of national security wiretaps and other government activities under the Foreign Intelligence Surveillance Act. Following the recommendation of the Iran-contra committees, the White House and intelligence agencies should transmit all proposed intelligence findings to the attorney general for legal review before submitting them to Congress.[25] In addition, Congress could modify the finding requirements in all relevant statutes to require the transmission of such findings to Congress not only with the president's signature, but also with the attorney general's certified approval as to form and legality, a prerequisite that currently attaches to all executive orders.[26]

Congress could enhance external legal accountability by considering a second, more far-reaching possibility—requiring confidential submissions of executive branch legal opinions that justify particularly controversial actions to the intelligence committees so that they may be subjected to external adversarial review by the committee legal staffs. Far from being unprecedented, a version of this process recently transpired with respect to the State Department legal adviser's opinion advocating a broad reinterpretation of the Anti-Ballistic Missile Treaty. For justiciability reasons, that opinion will almost certainly never be tested in a court.[27] Accordingly, the chairman of the Senate Armed Services Committee, Senator Nunn, opted to test the administration's interpretation adversarially through extensive congressional hearings.[28] Similarly, during the Iran-contra hearings, the president authorized the release of numerous executive branch legal opinions to the select committees, whose report went on to challenge or support the legal analysis contained in a number of the opinions.[29]

Obviously, congressional review of agency legal opinions should be the exception, not the rule, particularly when such opinions discuss sensitive classified information. Each house could modify its internal rules to set forth special threshold circumstances under which a committee, house, or both houses could demand an executive branch legal opinion, in the same way as current rules define conditions under which such entities may demand factual information that lies within the control of the executive branch. To protect against inadvertent congressional disclosures, the new law could incorporate provisions from both Senate Standing Rule 36 and the resolution establishing the Senate Iran-contra committee, which order stiff sanctions against congressional members or staffers who inappropriately release confidential information.[30]

Devising more accountable lines of command within the executive branch is a more intractable problem, whose ultimate solution rests more appropriately with the president than with Congress. As demonstrated in chapter 2, struggles between the secretary of state and the national security assistant for foreign-policy prominence have recurred at least since the Nixon administration. Although Henry Kissinger's elevation to secretary of state briefly abated that struggle, two recent secretaries, Cyrus Vance and Alexander Haig, resigned in no small part because of continuing tensions with the national security assistant. Those tensions have been moderated, but hardly eliminated, during the Bush administration.[31] Most presidents and commentators have agreed—correctly, in my view—that the secretary of state should be the president's principal foreign-policy adviser. At the same time, however, they have also recognized the powerful institutional pressures that drive presidents to build the policy-making apparatus around themselves, relying principally upon the NSC.[32] Reform proposals have thus run in two directions. Some commentators have urged debureaucratization of the State Department.[33] Others, including both the Tower commission and the Iran-contra committees, have recommended reformation of the NSC's policy-making role.[34]

As long as the current uneasy division of labor between the NSC and the State Department prevails, Congress should pursue two aims: first, to promote the president's discharge of his constitutional responsibilities to "take Care that the Laws be faithfully executed" by more widely requiring his personal involvement in the most important foreign-policy decisions and second, to enhance both the external and internal accountability of NSC staff. To encourage personal presidential involvement, Congress could extend the presidential findings requirements in the intelligence laws to all forms of covert action, including those that involve arms transfers, emergency economic powers, military aid, or uses of armed force. Similarly, new legislation could modify existing findings requirements in several ways, as suggested by the Iran-contra report—to reach more agencies, to identify all participants in covert actions, to recertify those findings periodically, and most important, to require that all findings be in writing, personally signed by the president, and reported by the president himself (not the agency heads) directly to the intelligence committees.[35]

To reinforce the external accountability of the NSC, Congress should require that the national security assistant be subject to Senate confirmation as well as to regular appearances at oversight hearings. Senate confirmation would require the national security assistant to establish personal contact with, as well as direct accountability to, the relevant congressional committees. Following the recommendation of the Iran-contra committees, the legislation requiring Senate confirmation of the national security assistant should also require the president to make periodic confidential reports to a core consultative group of legislators regarding NSC activities.[36]

To promote internal accountability, Congress should reinforce the constitutional principle of civilian control of the military in the event that the national security assistant should continue to play a major role in the development of defense policy and strategy. The most sensible way would be to impose an express statutory requirement that the national security assistant be a civilian, rather than a military officer. Three of President Reagan's six national security assistants—Col. Robert McFarlane, Vice Adm. John Poindexter, and Lt. Gen. Colin Powell— were active military officers. Active military officers have also held important lower political posts in the NSC, including, most prominently, Major Gen. Alexander Haig (later White House chief of staff) and Lt. Col. Oliver North. In the fall of 1986, the NSC staff included nineteen active-duty officers and numerous retired officers.[37] By most accounts of the Iran-contra affair, North and Poindexter managed elaborate covert transfers of military weapons with little or no supervision by civilians, including the president. As noted in chapter 4, Congress has embodied the constitutional principle of civilian control over the military in prophylactic statutes that separate the CIA directorate from the military and place the military departments under the civilian control of the defense secretary and his deputies, who in turn answer to the civilian control of the president. As long as the CIA continues to engage in covert warmaking operations and the NSC continues to supervise those operations, the same constitutional principle would seem to compel the requirement that the national security assistant also be a civilian. Congress could thus incorporate into the proposed national security charter little-noticed legislation that was introduced in the last Congress and supported in principle by the chairman of the Joint Chiefs of Staff, that would have formally barred active military officers from service as national security assistant.[38] In the same provision, Congress should implement a recommendation of the Iran-contra committees that would place time limits upon how long an active military officer may be assigned to the NSC staff.[39]

Finally, one simple way in which any president could enhance the political accountability of his or her national security assistant—even without congressional action—would be to appoint the vice president to the post. This idea briefly surfaced during the 1988 presidential campaign, when rumors arose that Democratic nominee Michael Dukakis might name Senator Sam Nunn as both his vice-presidential running mate and his national security assistant.[40] While some commentators suggested constitutional obstacles to such a proposal and others questioned the qualifications of particular vice presidents to perform the national security assistant's duties, such a decision would reap several identifiable advantages. Not only would it preserve and clarify the civilian chain of command and integrate the vice president more thoroughly into the administration's work, it would also render the national security assistant directly accountable to both the electorate and to the Senate, over which the vice-president already presides and in whose halls he has an office. The vice president is already a statutory member of the NSC; some presidents, particularly Ford and Carter, have given their vice presidents substantial responsibilities in foreign affairs.[41] Perhaps most important, an appointment as national security adviser would potentially upgrade the vice-presidency by making the office more attractive to politicians of presidential caliber. Service in both positions would more fully prepare the vice-president for possible future presidential service, not a trivial consideration given that more than one-third of our presidents (including our present one) previously held the vice-presidential office.[42]

Revitalizing Congress: Centralized Decision Making, Legal Advice, and Information Sharing

When Congress enacted the National Security Act in 1947, its greatest error was its failure to address its own role in the national security system. Although Congress partly redressed this oversight in the wave of statutes it enacted in the decade after Vietnam, the institutional changes that transformed Congress during those years largely diffused power, transferring substantial power from the congressional leadership to subcommittee chairs and the rank and file. This dispersion of decision-making capacity has doubly undercut Congress's ability to create a centralized delivery system in foreign affairs: first, by hampering Congress's capacity as a whole to confront the president, and second, by rendering Congress less able to withstand interest-group influence.[43] To overcome these institutional deficiencies, Congress should now channel its reform efforts in three directions—toward creating counterarenas of *centralized foreign affairs expertise* within Congress that may act to counter the president; toward building a central repository of *legal advice* within Congress regarding international and foreign-relations law; and toward equalizing *access to sensitive information* that otherwise lies solely within the executive's control.

A Core Consultative Group By first creating a core group of members, with whom the president and his staff could meet regularly and consult on national security matters, Congress could provide the executive with the benefit of its deliberative judgments without demanding unacceptable sacrifices in flexibility, secrecy, or dispatch. A bill to amend the War Powers Resolution, introduced in the Senate during each of the last two sessions of Congress by Senators Byrd, Nunn, Warner, and Mitchell, represents a promising attempt to achieve such centralization.[44] That bill would require the president, before using force, to consult with a "Gang of Six," consisting of the majority and minority leaders of both houses, the Speaker of the House, and the president pro tempore of the Senate. In addition, the bill would oblige the president to maintain continuing consultations with a "permanent consultative group" composed of the Gang of Six, plus the chairs and ranking minority members of the armed services, foreign affairs, and intelligence committees of each house. This latter group would be consulted for the purpose of designing legislative remedies to terminate or approve particular military involvements. The group would have formal authority to invoke the War Powers Resolution even if the president chose not to do so; its legislative proposals would be accorded a special fast-track status in the legislative process.

One serious objection to the Byrd-Nunn-Warner-Mitchell proposal is that it would exclude from the core consultative group the very subcommittee chairs who gained power during the post-Vietnam congressional reforms, that is, younger members who would more likely be expert on particular foreign-policy issues and who would perhaps be more willing than the leadership to challenge the substance of the president's decisions. As we saw in chapter 1, the House leadership's decision to restrict

House Iran-contra committee membership chiefly to powerful committee chairs was one factor impeding its investigation. This problem could be redressed by modifying the Byrd-Nunn-Warner-Mitchell proposal to include within the core consultative group the Gang of Six, but to allow the balance of the membership to revolve annually or biennially among key subcommittee chairs or ranking minority members from each of the participating committees. Indeed, a bipartisan group of senators has recently proposed a similar, informal plan for monthly foreign and national security policy meetings between the president and ten congressional leaders.[45]

With this modification, the core consultative group would spawn numerous advantages. Even if consultation with such a group might marginally delay presidential responses, "[t]here are few crises short of battlefield disasters and the instant calamity of a nuclear strike in which properly briefed members could not play a valuable part."[46] Moreover, unlike a special legislative committee, which would be susceptible to capture by the executive entity or interest group being regulated, this core group would consist of congressional leaders who would be directly accountable to the entire membership and who would thus have the stature to express to the president views unlikely to come from his own subordinates. The fact that the group's members would be designated, not self-selected, would reduce the likelihood that members unusually prone to special-interest-group pressures would predominate. At the same time, because part of the group's membership would rotate, it would always combine activist younger subcommittee chairs with more distinguished, but perhaps more cautious, senior hands.

The creation of such a core consultative group would ultimately serve not only the long-term interest of Congress, but also of the executive. It would eliminate the president's chronic complaint that in emergencies, statutory consultation requirements impose an intolerable burden upon the president to find members with whom to consult.[47] In the most extreme situations, the number of members consulted could even be reduced to a subgroup of the core group, perhaps a group of four that include the ranking minority and majority leaders in each house (or alternatively, the chair and ranking member of the House and Senate intelligence committees, who perhaps have even greater expertise in deciphering cryptic executive notifications). Even in the most urgent situations, however, the group consulted should never fall below this number, on the assumption that any action that could not secure at least their minimal backing should not proceed. If Congress were to mandate regular confidential meetings between its core consultative group and the president or his principal cabinet officers at the start of each new administration, a practice of true consultative decision making between the branches would be far more likely to evolve.[48]

A Congressional Legal Adviser Second, Congress should consider creating an entity, comparable to the comptroller general and his or her staff, to monitor the output of the executive's national security apparatus. A number of years ago, Alton Frye similarly proposed that Congress create an office of the "Foreign Policy Monitor," who would be appointed for an extended term and subject to removal by a majority vote of either house. Such a monitor, in Frye's view, could perform three valuable tasks: "to alert the Majority and Minority Leaders of both houses of impending issues and decisions regarding which they might wish to request full consultation [with the president]; to identify for senior executive officials potential problems on which they might wish to seek legislative counsel; [and] to brief appropriate congressional leaders in advance of major consultations in order to make such exchanges more focused and meaningful."[49]

I would amend Frye's proposal to include a central legal staff within that unit, headed by a congressional legal adviser, to correspond to the legal adviser's office in the State Department or the Office of Legal Counsel in the Justice Department.[50] The congressional legal adviser could be an elected officer of the House, like the clerk or the parliamentarian, or an attorney agreed upon by a consensus decision of both parties, such as the director of the Congressional Budget Office. The legal adviser's task would be to coordinate the work of the various international-affairs committee staff counsels, to act as a liaison between executive legal staffs, and to brief and advise the core consultative group on questions of international and foreign-relations law. Far from being redundant, the congressional legal adviser would fill a role not currently played by any of the legal offices extant within Congress: the counsel to the numerous foreign-policy committees, the Office of Legislative Counsel, the Senate legal counsel and the general counsel to the clerk of the House, the legal and American Government divisions of the Congressional Research Service, or the house parliamentarians. The legal adviser's primary role would not be legislative drafting (the role currently played by the Office of Legislative Counsel); litigation (which is handled by the counsel to the House clerk and the Senate legal counsel); legal research (the Congressional Research Service's task); nor interpretation of internal house rules (the job of the parliamentarians). Instead, the adviser would play a counseling function similar to that currently played by the staff counsels to the foreign affairs or intelligence committees (who need not be lawyers), with one crucial difference—the legal adviser would not be beholden to any particular committee or chair, but would represent Congress as a whole.

The congressional legal adviser would therefore exercise a jurisdiction encompassing all of the issues of constitutional, foreign relations, and international law that are currently scattered across the judiciary, armed services, foreign affairs, intelligence, commerce, and government operations committees. The legal adviser's central task would be to render legal opinions to Congress regarding both presidential and congressional conduct. By internal rule, Congress could both authorize and require the legal adviser (or the staff counsel of the relevant congressional committee) to issue a "counterreport" whenever the executive branch transmits a declaration of national emergency, a war powers report, or an intelligence finding. These counterreports could then be subject to an immediate congressional vote (under the fast-track procedure described in greater detail below), which would establish a contemporaneous written record either accepting or rejecting the president's legal justification, against which any future executive claim of congressional acquiescence could be immediately tested.

Issuance of such counterreports by a quasi-independent congressional entity would not be unprecedented. In effect, these reports would form legal analogues to the independent cost assessments that the Congressional Budget Office currently provides to the foreign-affairs committees regarding the likely cost of proposed administration programs.[51] Similarly, in 1986, Congress created an independent, five-person commission to monitor and report on Central American negotiations and the internal reform efforts of the contras and to submit reports regarding those matters for congressional comparison with similar reports statutorily required of the president.[52] The legal adviser's office that I propose would have a continuing institutional mission to prepare comparable reports that would contain a legal rather than a policy analysis. Nor would this new entity require dramatic institutional changes. To the contrary, the legal adviser's office could be created by merging or affiliating existing congressional legal offices, thereby centralizing and reorganizing much of the legal expertise that already exists within Congress. Like the core consultative group, its long-term goal would be to promote continuing interbranch dialogue by encouraging congressional and executive legal staffs to foster common constitutional understandings regarding issues of foreign affairs that would rarely be resolved in court.

Equalizing Access to Information Third and finally, Congress should seek to enhance its access to both the classified and unclassified information regarding national security matters that the executive currently controls. "The principal inefficiency in our system," Professor Henkin has argued, "is the distorting effect on the congressional function resulting from the President's monopoly of information and communication."[53] Under current law, classification of United States government information rests not with Congress, but with the president. But like other claims of plenary executive authority, presidential claims to exclusive control over national security information are of surprisingly recent vintage.

The earliest framework statutes creating the Departments of State and War contained general provisions regarding the custody of departmental papers, but Congress did not specifically or broadly empower the president to prescribe regulations regarding the communication of information until 1856.[54] Although the Supreme Court suggested in 1988 that the president's "authority to classify and control access to information bearing on national security . . . exists quite apart from any explicit congressional grant," it has not held that this authority rests *exclusively* in the president.[55] To the contrary, in *Nixon v. Administrator of General Services,* the Court recognized Congress's valid role in creating the "abundant statutory precedent for the regulation and mandatory disclosure of documents in the possession of the Executive Branch," which "has never been considered invalid as an invasion of [executive] autonomy."[56] Since 1911, Congress has enacted several statutes to govern the release of classified documents, most prominently, the Espionage Act of 1917, the Atomic Energy Act of 1946, the Internal Security Act of 1950, and the Classified Information Procedures Act of 1980, whose role in Oliver North's trial is described in chapter 1.[57]

It was not until shortly before World War II that the president began to set classification standards for the entire government by executive order.[58] Until 1982, successive executive orders had steadily narrowed the bases for withholding information, but the Reagan administration's classification order "clearly reverse[d] this trend by expanding the categories of classifiable information, mandating that information falling within these categories be classified, making reclassification authority available, admonishing classifiers to err on the side of classification, and eliminating automatic declassification arrangements."[59] Increased congressional exclusion from classified information has both buttressed executive claims to superior knowledge in foreign affairs and fostered uninformed legislative judgment in those decisions in which Congress does participate.[60]

To overcome this information gap, Congress should act to ensure its core consultative group access to various forms of national security information that would otherwise remain solely in the executive's hands. The Espionage Act, for example, criminalizes the unauthorized communication of certain classified information, but specifies that "[n]othing in this section shall prohibit the furnishing, upon lawful demand, of information to any regularly constituted committee of the Senate or House . . . or joint committee thereof."[61] Congress could incorporate a broader version of this provision into its framework statute, if necessary restricting congressional access, as it has done in other statutes, to identified committees or to its core consultative group.[62]

Such a statute would not work undue violence upon the doctrine of executive privilege. For although the Supreme Court declared in *United States v. Nixon* that utmost judicial deference must be paid to a claim of privilege based on a need to protect military, diplomatic, or sensitive national security secrets, Professor Henkin has properly observed that "executive privilege has not often been formally asserted in foreign affairs matters."[63] During the Iran-contra committees' investigation, for example, the president did not claim executive privilege and the privilege was extensively waived during the Senate Armed Services Committee's recent study of the reinterpretation of the ABM Treaty. If anything, the experience of the select intelligence committees has revealed that the regular sharing of confidential information has advanced the development of the congressional-executive partnership.[64] Thus, like the core consultative group and the congressional legal adviser, the information-sharing proposal would promote the long-term institutional cooperation in foreign affairs decision making that the National Security Constitution seeks to foster.

Nor would such a statute necessarily put sensitive national security information at risk by exposing it to key congressional members and their staffs. Although administration members regularly deride Congress's ability to keep a secret, by any objective standard, the legislative record of keeping secrets has been commendable. President Carter's deputy secretary of state, who provided almost daily secret briefings to the Senate and House leadership during the Iranian hostage crisis from 1979 to 1981, recalled that "there was never a significant violation of the confidential relationship that was established."[65] Moreover, available data suggest that the executive branch, not Congress, has been responsible for the vast bulk of recent national security leaks.[66] To protect against inadvertent disclosures by the core consultative group, the new law could simply apply against the group's members the stringent confidentiality provisions currently found in the House and Senate Intelligence Committee rules and in the resolution establishing the Senate Iran-contra committee. It could also incorporate the current provisions of the Senate standing rules, which call for the expulsion of any senator (and dismissal and punishment for contempt of any Senate officer) who discloses without authorization documents delivered to the Senate for confidential consideration. At the same time, however, the new law could follow those same rules and empower one house, or Congress as a whole, to release classified information based on a vote concluding that the public interest would be better served by release than nondisclosure.[67] The crucial point, of course, cogently put by the former chair of the House Intelligence Committee, is that "[w]e have a government of coequal branches. Secrets are not Executive Branch secrets; they are U.S. Government secrets. Each branch must be responsible for them."[68] The concurrent constitutional authority that Congress and the president share over government information demands that a jointly enacted statute, and not presidential decision alone, should determine whether the increased risk of leaks from Congress outweighs the costs of excessive executive secrecy.[69]

Attacking the Sources of Congressional Acquiescence Congressional movement toward each of these basic institutional reforms would go a long way toward curing the four specific causes of congressional acquiescence identified in chapter 5—legislative myopia, bad drafting, ineffective tools, and political will. Creation of the core consultative group would partly redress the problem of legislative myopia. Because the group would be drawn from the congressional leadership, its members would view themselves, like the president, as representing a broad national constituency as well as other members of Congress and would thus presumably be less susceptible to particularistic interest-group influence.[70] Over time, the group and its staff would develop an overview of the foreign-policy terrain comparable to the president's, without forsaking the expertise of the existing specialized committees and committee staffs. Given that members of Congress now experience far greater longevity in office than executive branch officials, the core legislative group could very well come to gain greater perspective and expertise than its executive branch counterparts.[71] Moreover, just as earlier presidents selected secretaries of state from the Senate Foreign Relations Committee and Presidents Carter, Reagan, and Bush selected Senators Edmund Muskie and Howard Baker and Congressman Dick Cheney, respectively, to serve in the cabinet or White House, future presidents could draw upon this core group for future cabinet officers, drawing the two branches even closer together.[72]

A skilled central legal staff sensitive to the need for more carefully worded statutes would help to address Congress's second institutional problem—bad drafting.[73] For example, that staff could advise the members to amend the War Powers Resolution to include more detailed definitions of the terms "armed forces" and "hostilities." Moreover, the drafters could use the newly created core consultative group to give greater operative content to the notion that the president must genuinely consult with Congress before committing troops abroad, rather than merely brief a few selected members at the last minute. For example, Congress could require the president or his advisers to engage in full discussion with the core group (or in a true emergency, a subgroup thereof) before any decision is made to commit troops abroad. Once the staff had developed a standard definition of recurrent statutory terms, variations upon them could be inserted into the modified International Emergency Economic Powers Act, the modified Arms Export Control Act, and other statutes, depending upon the core group's assessment of the relative need for executive flexibility under each of these titles.

Even without these institutional reforms, better drafting would almost inevitably result from a congressional effort to integrate the variegated national security statutes into a single omnibus law. Congress could, for example, decide whether to subject nonuniformed operatives carrying out covert war-making operations—who are not currently regulated as "armed forces" under the War Powers Resolution—to the terms either of that resolution or of the covert operations laws. It could attempt to word its new statutory delegations more precisely and narrowly. For example, to avoid judicial manipulation of the type that occurred in *Dames & Moore,* the new legislation could declare Congress's intent to preempt presidential claims of inherent constitutional authority. To ensure that Congress withholds statutory authority from executive acts it does not wish to authorize, the law could, like the current War Powers Resolution, declare that a court may not read statutory silences or limited delegations as congressional endorsement of related presidential initiatives.[74] Finally, Congress could specifically require judicial application of the *Kent v. Dulles* "clear statement" principle when executive action taken pursuant to the statute infringes upon individual rights.

The existence of a core consultative group would also help to minimize those examples of bad drafting that result from political compromise, rather than from failures of drafting foresight. For example, the core consultative group could identify which bills overlap committee jurisdictions (and should therefore be jointly or sequentially referred to two or more committees); propose joint committee hearings on bills that are clearly related; and urge the formation of select committees when appropriate, not simply to investigate scandals, but also to propose curative legislation. Finally, the core group could agree with the president to block floor consideration of bills, resolutions, and amendments that have not been reviewed by both the group and the executive branch. By so doing, the group would consolidate and centralize the legislative consideration of a particular problem and assure the president that congressional mavericks will not disrupt painstakingly drafted interbranch compromises.[75] While none of these techniques can eliminate the political compromises that are the stuff of the legislation, they can help to rationalize the legislative process and render it more transparent.

Enhanced congressional access to better information would partially solve Congress's third problem of ineffective tools. "Congress must have the sense of our foreign policy . . . in important detail, be aware of attitudes as they are being formed and commitments as they are being made, and be able to inject influence earlier in matters on which it has constitutional responsibilities, especially those on which it will have to take formal action."[76] To ensure that Congress will have sufficient information to express its views before executive action becomes a fait accompli, the new legislation should insist that prior notice of proposed covert actions and uses of force be given in every case, rather than "in every possible instance," to afford the core group a meaningful opportunity to argue with the president before he irreversibly commits the United States to a covert or forceful course of action.

Congress can also redress the current ineffectiveness of its tools in four other ways: by developing a constitutional substitute for the legislative veto; by making more effective use of its appropriations power; by experimenting with limited application of criminal penalties for executive violations of its national security statute; and by more liberally exercising its impeachment power against executive officials. Under the legislative-veto regime, Congress delegated statutory authority to the president while retaining a right of subsequent review in particular cases. As we have seen, in 1983 the Supreme Court held legislative vetoes violative of the bicameralism and presentment clauses of the Constitution.[77] The legislative veto had numerous policy disadvantages, most prominently, the freedom it gave members to avoid visible responsibility for their actions by avoiding roll-call votes.[78] Yet despite its constitutional and policy infirmities, the legislative veto effected a crucial political compromise. While the president gained current legislative authorization for his acts, his need to return to Congress for subsequent approval provided assurances that consultation would continue while his action proceeded.

One alternative that largely preserves the veto's beneficial political compromise, without its accompanying disadvantages, is the so-called fast-track approval procedure, which has recently been employed, among other things, to ensure ongoing congressional input into the negotiation of international trade agreements. Fast-track approval is an expedited legislative procedure, found most prominently in the trade laws, whereby Congress authorizes the president to initiate a foreign-affairs action (for example, negotiation of a trade agreement), in exchange for a commitment that he will submit the product of that action back to Congress for final approval. Under modified House and Senate rules, Congress "promises" the president that it will require automatic discharge of the completed initiative from committee within a certain number of days, bar floor amendment of the submitted proposal, and limit floor debate, thereby ensuring that the package will be voted up or down within a fixed period.[79]

The fast-track procedure allows Congress to overcome both the political inertia and the procedural obstacles that most frequently prevent a controversial measure from coming to a vote at all. Furthermore, because one-fifth of the members present in each house retain constitutional power to require a roll-call vote on any matter, an individual member's vote on any particular fast-track approval resolution would almost invariably be made visible to the public.[80] If triggered by objectively determinable circumstances rather than by specific presidential acts, fast-track procedures could be used to privilege certain joint resolutions introduced by any interested member, thereby compelling Congress to vote up or down quickly on resolutions that challenge executive acts.[81]

The fast-track approval method also has the advantage of versatility, inasmuch as it can be combined with committee "gatekeeping," point-of-order, and appropriations procedures to vary the intensity of its regulation. Under a committee gatekeeping procedure, a majority vote of a single congressional committee may derail a presidential proposal from the fast track—and in many cases, effectively kill it—thereby giving the executive strong incentives to consult with the committee's members at each step of the process. Recently, such a gatekeeping procedure, the fast-track provision of the Trade and Tariff Act of 1984, afforded the House Ways and Means and Senate Finance committees extensive input into the negotiation of the United States-Canada Free Trade Agreement.[82] Similarly, when a House or Senate rule triggers a point of order in a certain circumstance, any member can raise that point of order and halt consideration of the bill until the presiding officer considers and rejects the point of order. If the president seeks to implement a program without satisfying a prior statutory requirement, such as notice or prior consultation with Congress, such rules could be used to block temporarily appropriations bills that would fund the program.[83]

In addition to incorporating such gatekeeping and point-of-order procedures, the proposed charter should also make more effective use of the appropriations process to police executive compliance with statutory terms. While members ought not use the appropriations process indiscriminately to accomplish what they cannot agree upon by legislation, Congress as a whole could properly use appropriations cutoffs to enforce other substantive provisions of the charter, for example, by tying continuation of appropriations to the president's compliance with the charter's terms. Congress could seek either to make these appropriations cutoffs self-executing, by tying them to objectively determinable facts, or judicially enforceable, through judicial review provisions.[84]

Furthermore, Congress could demand greater executive accountability at an earlier point in the appropriations process, namely, when it is authorizing those programs that will later receive appropriations. As Senator J. William Fulbright once observed with regard to foreign aid, such authorizations "provid[e] the closest thing we have to an annual occasion for a general review of American foreign policy."[85] To use this process more productively, Congress could conduct a long-term authorization review process, whereby a joint subcommittee of the foreign affairs and defense committees would regularly evaluate and review existing national security programs.[86]

Alternatively, as President Bush's March 1989 "Good Friday accords" with Congress to secure $45 million in nonlethal contra aid showed, Congress may combine its authorization and appropriations power to maintain control over executive branch spending.[87] As described in chapter 5, the president may, with clearance from the appropriate legislative committees, "reprogram" funds for different purposes within a particular appropriations account. In 1977, Congress added a provision to the Foreign Assistance Act that denied the president authority to reprogram appropriated funds unless he first notified the two authorizing committees (the foreign relations committees in each house) *and* the two appropriations committees in each house of his intent to do so and received no disapproval.[88] Although the precise details of the Good Friday accords remain secret, in March 1989, Congress apparently authorized the president to use reprogrammed funds to support the contras for seven months. In exchange, the president informally promised to return to the four authorizing committees for notice and approval as a prerequisite to tapping the last three months of reprogrammed funds.[89]

The Good Friday accords illustrate the kind of informal, nonstatutory legislative veto that has proliferated since *Chadha*. Because they are not embodied in legislation, such nonstatutory vetoes alter no legal rights or duties of persons outside the executive branch and thus do not run afoul of *Chadha*.[90] At the same time, however, they benefit both branches. The president gains assurance of continued congressional funding as long as he abides by the informal accord; Congress retains its freedom to appropriate in successive lump sums while using both its power of the purse and its expert committees to monitor executive compliance with the accord through the reprogramming process.[91]

Finally, Congress could enforce its national security charter by two other remedies: statutory criminal penalties and a more liberal use of the impeachment remedy. One of the original drafters of the 1947 National Security Act has recently proposed that criminal penalties be imposed upon any government officer or employee who knowingly and willfully violates or conspires to violate an express statutory prohibition against the expenditure of funds for a particular foreign-policy purpose.[92] Such a penalty does not seem overly harsh, given that once Congress has determined to deny appropriations to a particular activity, "the specific activity is no longer within the realm of authorized government actions."[93] At the same time, Congress could reenact the Neutrality Act—an early framework statute described in chapter 3—to provide criminal penalties for private adventurism conducted at the executive's behest. During the last session of Congress, legislation was introduced to apply the provisions of the Neutrality Act specifically to bar private assistance for paramilitary operations in contravention of statutes such as the Clark and Boland amendments, which forbid American assistance to private rebels on foreign soil.[94] To the extent that such an amended law were applied against United States government officials who order, plan, or initiate foreign activities, enforcement of all of these criminal provisions could be confided in an independent counsel, as one recent bill would have done.[95] Alternatively, Congress could authorize departmental inspectors general or an independent branch of the Justice Department analogous to the Office of Special Investigations to conduct such prosecutions.[96]

If Congress were reluctant to go this far, it could invoke one last, much-overlooked tool, namely, removal of the offending officials for violations of the substantive provisions of the charter through use of the impeachment remedy. The Constitution declares that "[t]he President, Vice President and *all civil Officers of the United States*, shall be removed from Office on Impeachment for, and Conviction of, Treason, Bribery, or other high Crimes and Misdemeanors." The House has the sole power to bring impeachments, the Senate has sole power to try them, and the president lacks constitutional power to pardon those who have been impeached.[97]

Thus, if Congress were reluctant to enforce the proposed national security charter through the courts, it could declare that certain clear violations of key charter provisions would constitute "high Crimes and Misdemeanors" warranting impeachment of the responsible officials and their removal from office. The impeachment remedy resembles criminal penalties inasmuch as it requires determination of individual responsibility. It differs, however, in the crucial respect that it was constitutionally designed to be exercised not by courts, but by Congress against precisely the kinds of violations that occurred during the Iran-contra affair, namely, executive subversion of constitutionally mandated processes. In 1974, for example, the House Committee on the Judiciary considered, but did not report to the full House, a proposed article of impeachment charging that President Nixon had engaged in unauthorized secret bombing in Cambodia, which he had concealed from both the people and Congress, thereby preventing Congress from responsibly exercising its appropriations and war powers.[98] Thus, had Oliver North and John Poindexter been holding civil office at the time of the Iran-contra hearings, Congress could have considered their removal through impeachment (rather than by attempting the inappropriate quasi-criminal prosecution described in chapter 1).

While impeachment is undeniably an extreme remedy, under these circumstances, it might well be more appropriate than criminal penalties. The impeachment remedy would not have to be enforced by a court; the charter provisions would place executive officials on clear notice regarding the acts which are prohibited; such acts would have to be proved to the satisfaction of two-thirds of the senators; and the judgment of impeachment could extend no "further than to removal from Office, and disqualification to hold and enjoy any Office of honor, Trust or Profit under the United States."[99] Thus, Congress could theoretically pursue the constitutionally authorized remedy of removal from office without prejudicing any subsequent criminal investigation or fearing that the individual removed would subsequently be pardoned by the president.

If enacted, this package of provisions would greatly alleviate Congress's fourth and most intractable problem, namely, the problem of political will. Unlike the current regime, which requires a two-thirds majority in both houses to enforce existing laws, nearly all of these proposals are designed to be enforced by a considerably lesser showing of congressional will. Many of these proposals, including the creation of the core consultative group, the congressional legal adviser, demands for executive branch legal opinions, and the long-range authorization process, could be implemented by concurrent resolution if necessary. The core consultative group and gatekeeping committees could express their will to the president even without formal votes. The fast-track, point-of-order, and confidentiality procedures could be adopted by modification of chamber rules and subsequently triggered automatically or by the action of a single interested member. The appropriations provisions could be made either self-enforcing, enforceable through impeachment, or civilly and criminally by the courts. Thus, even if Congress cannot create political will where none exists, it can modify existing institutions and procedures to give quicker and fuller expression to viewpoints that remain dispersed or submerged under Congress's current institutional structure.

Equally important, despite their ability to regulate executive conduct, none of these devices would run afoul of the Supreme Court's holding in *Chadha*. Because the fast-track procedure requires bicameral action and presentment to the president, albeit on an expedited basis, it does not constitute a legislative veto. The addition of committee gatekeeping provisions does not render such procedures unconstitutional.[100] Point-of-order procedures and impeachments exploit a different loophole in *Chadha*, which specifies that each house of Congress, acting alone, retains the power to determine its own rules and procedures.[101] The House's authority to initiate impeachments and the Senate's power to try them are similarly exempt from *Chadha*'s requirements.[102] Although the Good Friday accords gave four different congressional committees the political equivalent of a "committee veto" over contra funding, no legislative veto resulted because the interbranch accord was embodied not in legislation, but in a written gentlemen's agreement. Thus, the national security charter can employ a range of innovative procedures to revitalize Congress, while promoting the regular interbranch dialogue and power sharing essential to a scheme of balanced institutional participation.

REINVOLVING THE COURTS: DISCOURAGING ABSTENTION

Congress cannot legislate judicial courage, any more than it can legislate executive self-restraint or congressional willpower. Congress can, however, seek to stem the Supreme Court's recent migration away from the *Youngstown* vision and toward *Curtiss-Wright* by embedding in legislation the judicial role described by Justice Jackson in his *Youngstown* concurrence. With respect to the courts, Congress's central strategy should be to enact legislation that would *override the abstention doctrines* that the courts have wrapped around themselves. That legislation's broad goal should be to specify particular plaintiffs, defendants, claims, and forms of relief that would be properly subject to adjudication.

To authorize challenges to executive conduct, Congress could insert in its framework statute provisions authorizing interested citizens to act as "private attorney generals" to police violations of the charter.[103] Alternatively or cumulatively, Congress could insert a "congressional standing" provision of the type that it placed in the Gramm-Rudman-Hollings budget-balancing act, which Congressman Synar immediately invoked to bring his successful challenge to that legislation.[104] To ensure that legislators meet the constitutional as well as the statutory prerequisites for congressional standing, the Supreme Court could explicitly adopt the view of the U.S. Court of Appeals for the District of Columbia Circuit, finding congressional standing at least in those cases in which a congressional member alleges that the challenged action nullified a past or future vote.[105] To limit a dramatic influx of litigation, Congress could further require that such suits should not be brought until an individual member has fully exhausted his or her legislative remedies.

Having empowered more plaintiffs to invoke the statute, Congress might also reconsider the various immunities against money damages currently afforded to official defendants. As Justice Scalia has recently urged, Congress could amend or overrule the *Feres* doctrine, a judicially created exception to the immunity waivers in the Federal Tort Claims Act, which effectively shields the United States government from suits by servicemen.[106] Although in 1982 the Court granted the president absolute immunity and granted high executive officials qualified immunity from civil damages for actions taken within the outer perimeter of their official duties, it left ambiguous whether Congress could expressly override that immunity by statute. Thus, Congress could state exceptions to the doctrine of official immunities for particularly egregious constitutional violations.[107]

With the parties in place, Congress could create a statutory cause of action to challenge specific statutory violations by either the president or Congress. Alternatively, it could modify the relevant provisions of the

Administrative Procedure Act (APA) to afford private plaintiffs a cause of action under that statute, which arguably provides discretionary non-monetary relief against federal officials who commit unlawful actions in foreign affairs.[108] Mindful of the Supreme Court's recent declaration that the judiciary is the final authority on issues of statutory construction even in the context of foreign affairs, the statute should also include a "sense-of-Congress" resolution specifying that violations of the national security charter do not constitute nonjusticiable political questions.[109]

Finally, Congress could seek to direct the manner in which a federal court might award equitable relief against wayward executive officials, following recent decisions suggesting that the courts may entertain injunctive suits against American government officials when plaintiffs claim that they have acted in excess of their statutory or constitutional powers.[110] Even if Congress were reluctant to authorize courts to enjoin executive action before it occurs, it could perhaps specify the circumstances under which the president would be authorized to act, but would be required ex post to pay just compensation to those individuals whose private property has been taken by his or her actions.[111]

If Congress sought more extensive judicialization of the national security area, it could lay venue for all claims of statutory violation in a particular court, for example, the courts of the District of Columbia Circuit.[112] By laying statutory venue in one judicial circuit, as it has done in administrative law statutes, Congress could create a counterarena of centralized foreign-affairs expertise within the judiciary analogous to that I have encouraged it to create within itself. By inculcating expertise in a group of judges in the nation's capital who are comfortable handling cases in foreign affairs, Congress could reduce judicial deference and promote constitutional line-drawing by institutions other than the president.

One need not advocate widespread judicialization of the field of foreign affairs to accept that the courts have currently excluded themselves too thoroughly from the national security area, thereby removing themselves as a meaningful check on executive action. The courts have too readily read *Curtiss-Wright* as standing for the proposition that the executive deserves an extra, and often dispositive, measure of deference in foreign affairs above and beyond that necessary to preserve the smooth functioning of the national government. Despite protests from such unexpected sources as Judge Bork and Justice Scalia, the political question doctrine has recently become a catchall method whereby judges have avoided deciding even straightforward constitutional cases.[113] Even apart from the judicial review provisions proposed above, legislative clarification of the substantive rules of foreign-affairs law would help overcome judicial diffidence and encourage courts to speak more frequently to the merits of foreign-affairs claims. Those rules, and the judicial constructions thereof, would fill the current pressing need for clearer lines against which both congressional and executive decision makers can evaluate the legality of proposed presidential conduct.

The late Bob Cover recognized that judging is a quintessential act of violence, with violence flowing as much from a refusal to judge as from the act of judging itself. "The jurisdictional principles of deference are problematic," he declared, "precisely because, as currently articulated by the Supreme Court, they align the interpretive acts of judges with the acts and interests of those who control the means of violence."[114] Thus, the role of judges is to define the rule of law by drawing the line between illegitimate exercises of political power and legitimate exercises of legal authority. The Supreme Court drew precisely such a line in *Youngstown*. In my judgment, however, the federal judiciary failed to perform a similar task during the Vietnam War, in no small part because Congress had largely failed to make its own intentions clear.[115] By enacting national security legislation designed to encourage judicial decision making, Congress would support the judiciary in the performance of its constitutionally assigned task of line-drawing. But even without new legislation, judges retain a duty in the post-Iran-contra era to ensure that in the field of foreign affairs, legal authority does not become permanently uncoupled from legal constraint.

8 Restoring the National Security Constitution: Some Specific Proposals

Two obvious objections could be lodged against the national security charter proposed in the previous chapter: first, that Congress would never enact such ambitious legislation; and second, that we have enough laws, without adopting an even more "legalistic" approach to national security decision making. In this chapter, I consider and respond to each of these objections.

I harbor no illusions that any legislation as ambitious as I have described will soon be enacted. But I do believe that a congressional attempt to consider omnibus legislation along these lines would at least focus national attention on the right questions. What matters far more than the enactment of any particular statutory proposal is public acceptance of a *framework legislation approach* to national security reform, predicated upon principles of restraining the executive, revitalizing Congress, and reinvolving the courts. In the same way as the Gramm-Rudman-Hollings budget-balancing act and the War Powers Resolution constituted first cuts at constitutional line-drawing in their respective fields, so, too, would charter legislation based upon the principles set forth above mark an important first step toward redefining and unifying the terrain of national security law.

Though difficult to achieve, the passage of a broad new National Security Reform Act would hardly be impossible. Historians and political scientists have demonstrated that the confluence of several factors—

public awareness that something is desperately wrong with an existing system; a simple policy idea whose time has come; cooperation and competition among powerful political leaders; and activism by self-appointed "policy entrepreneurs"—can bring about sweeping legislative reform over even the severest legislative inertia.[1] For proof, one need look no further than the similar wide-ranging legislative reform efforts that Congress has enacted during the last three decades over longer odds and even greater interest-group opposition than national security reform would face: the Tax Reform Act of 1986, the deregulation and trade reform movements of the 1970s, and the environmental and civil-rights reforms of the 1960s.[2] In each of these cases, the first and most critical step toward legislative reform was increased public awareness that a problem exists. The chapters thus far have argued that the Iran-contra affair revealed a need for national security reform that is at least as pressing as any of these policy reform movements.

Mobilization of key political leaders behind a charter proposal could both spur and be spurred by heightened public awareness of the national security reform issue. In the early months of the Bush administration, both Congress and the executive branch reacted to the Iran-contra debacle by issuing widely publicized pledges to pursue a bipartisan foreign policy.[3] From a public-interest perspective, a truly bipartisan congressional-executive effort to enact charter legislation would be a logical step toward restoring the balance between executive flexibility and congressional oversight in national security matters. The Senate's swift 1988 ratification of the Intermediate-Range Nuclear Forces Treaty and the Bush administration's March 1989 Good Friday accords with Congress regarding contra aid confirmed that bipartisan agreement on foreign policy remains possible, given wide interbranch consultation and significant consensus about policy ends.

The likelihood of finding national security reform advocates does not evaporate when the self-interest of politicians is factored into the equation. For both political parties have good reason to embrace national security reform as a foreign-policy priority. President Bush could use the concept of a national security charter as a definitive way to put the Iran-contra affair behind him. The Democratic Congress could use it as a means of declaring its seriousness about foreign-policy reform. Donald Elliott, Bruce Ackerman, and John Millian have described the era of "competitive credit-claiming" between President Nixon and Senator

Muskie that ultimately contributed to the dramatic environmental reforms of the late 1960s and early 1970s.[4] As we have seen, numerous key participants in the Iran-contra drama—including the current national security assistant, defense secretary, and the Democratic leaders in both houses—have been propelled by their visibility during that episode into higher office in both the executive and legislative branches. If the president and these key cabinet and congressional leaders were to engage in a similar round of competitive credit-claiming to revamp the national security laws, there seems little reason why they, too, could not achieve the same type of aspirational lawmaking as occurred in the environmental era.

Even without strong presidential or executive branch leadership, a Congress committed to bipartisan national security reform could pass a comprehensive legislative charter. Since Vietnam, many notable reforms in foreign affairs have passed into law without significant presidential guidance or even over presidential opposition. For example, the War Powers Resolution of 1973 became law over presidential veto and the Trade Act of 1974 was enacted without significant presidential leadership. Even before the Democrats took control of the Senate in 1986, Senator Lugar, the Republican chairman of the Foreign Relations Committee, led the successful floor fight to override the veto of a South African sanctions bill that was championed by a president from his own party.[5] Making members of Congress aware that the legislative opportunity to engage in national security reform may not return until after the "next Watergate" could serve to overcome the "politician's dilemma" that would ordinarily discourage individual legislators from pursuing or supporting such an initiative.[6]

To those who say that it would be politically impossible for Congress to draft such wide-ranging legislation, let me note that there is no current shortage of legislative proposals, only of congressional will to act upon them. As recalled in chapter 2, before being shelved by then-Speaker Wright, the Cohen-Boren bill to amend the Intelligence Oversight Act passed the Senate with sufficient votes to override a presidential veto and Congressman Stokes' companion bill was reported out of the House Intelligence and Foreign Affairs committees. In each of the last two sessions of Congress, Senator Specter has proposed several bills that would have instituted important structural reforms in the intelligence area.[7] The Byrd-Nunn-Warner-Mitchell bill to amend the War Powers

Resolution is currently pending before Congress, and the concept of a core consultative group has received bipartisan support from six influential senators.[8] The Biden-Levine bill to amend the Arms Export Control Act may be reintroduced in the 101st Congress, and bills to close loopholes in the arms-export control laws are moving through both houses at this writing.[9] A weak variant of the Moynihan amendment, which would have prohibited American officials from soliciting funds from foreign countries to carry out activities for which Congress has cut off aid, recently became law as part of the 1990 foreign-aid bill. Three other bills—Congressman Conyers' bill to impose criminal penalties upon executive officials who conduct intelligence activities in violation of existing laws, Congressman Levine's bill to amend the Neutrality Act, and Senator Harkin's bill to subject the national security adviser to Senate confirmation—all remain viable proposals suitable for legislative action.[10] Moreover, virtually all of the legislative recommendations of the Iran-contra committees have yet to be acted upon, despite having won the endorsement of nine of the eleven senators on the Senate Iran-contra committee (including three Republicans). In short, nearly all of the component parts of a comprehensive national security charter already exist in an acceptable form; some pieces of this legislative jigsaw puzzle have even been subjected to hearings, committee reporting, or floor consideration and approval. All that members of Congress must now accept is the commonsense proposition that these variegated proposals should be integrated because all address different facets of the same constitutional problem—the need to restore balanced institutional participation in foreign affairs decision making.

Even if impetus for national security reform does not swiftly come from this president or congressional leadership, the time for a new national security charter will not have passed. Some of the most lasting reforms in foreign affairs of recent years—for example, the Trade Act of 1974, the 1978 Foreign Intelligence Surveillance Act, the 1978 independent counsel statute (which has played such a prominent role in the Iran-contra affair), and the 1980 Intelligence Oversight Act—became law some time after the events that originally spurred their consideration. Thus, a bipartisan effort to enact the charter I have proposed could take place any time during the next decade and could redefine the allocation of national security responsibility between the branches well into the next century.

The central problem facing the charter proposal, of course, is that it would test the political will of Congress and the president to rethink the national security problem. If President Bush should veto this statute, as President Nixon vetoed the War Powers Resolution, recent history suggests that the Democratic Congress would be less inclined than past Congresses to acquiesce in his veto. Although only nine of President Reagan's seventy-eight vetoes were overridden, Congress overrode nearly half of the vetoes that President Reagan issued after the Republicans lost the Senate in 1986.[11] But even if Congress cannot generate the political will to enact an integrated national security charter, I see no reason why it could not apply the general principles articulated in the previous chapter to amend particular statutes that are currently on the books and sorely in need of repair.

Since the Iran-contra affair, detailed and specific proposals for amending particular foreign affairs laws have proliferated, particularly with regard to the War Powers Resolution and the Intelligence Oversight Act.[12] However laudable these proposals may be in their particulars, they repeat errors of the past by treating individual areas of foreign affairs law as discrete, compartmentalized realms to be regulated by separate legislation. As I argued in chapter 7, our greater need is for a thoughtful strategy for attacking the general problems that afflict each of our foreign-policy-making institutions. Thus, rather than debate the merits of individual proposals, I will briefly sketch how Congress could apply the basic principles outlined in chapter 7 to promote useful reform in five different areas of foreign affairs law: war powers, international agreements, emergency economic powers, intelligence oversight reform, and information control.[13] Even if the president and Congress cannot enact a comprehensive national security charter in a single, concentrated effort, they could apply these guiding principles over time to reform separate statutory pieces of the national security regulatory mosaic, with an eye toward some day uniting them into a single, theoretically coherent framework statute.

WAR POWERS

The Byrd-Nunn-Warner-Mitchell proposal to amend the War Powers Resolution has already triggered extensive new commentary on the much-traversed questions as to whether that resolution is or is not constitutional and whether it should be repealed or amended.[14] Although careful consideration of that commentary could easily occupy another volume, one political scientist has sought to divide political and legal reactions to the 1973 resolution into three ideological camps: the political "conservatives," who believe the resolution is unconstitutional because it takes too much power from the president; the "radicals," who find the resolution unconstitutional because it takes too much power from Congress (by giving the president a virtual blank check to conduct war for sixty days); and the "moderates," who believe that the resolution works a constitutionally acceptable modus vivendi between the two branches.[15]

My own evaluation of the resolution's legality and wisdom spans all three camps, showing that this tripartite categorization is overly procrustean. As earlier chapters suggest, the current resolution's legislative-veto provision clearly violates the president's constitutional prerogatives, as specified in *INS v. Chadha*.[16] At the same time, however, the substantive provisions of the resolution almost certainly derogate from Congress's war-making powers by allowing the president too much freedom to make covert and short-term war and to commit military forces overseas without a clear purpose. Yet all things considered, the resolution is better than nothing. Even if its substance is defective, its form is right. For the War Powers Resolution is an attempt to define the respective roles of each political branch in a realm of shared constitutional powers not by institutional practice, but by a framework statute that aims to promote interbranch communication, consultation, and cooperation.

That the resolution has largely failed to achieve the goals of its framers has resulted partly from the president's refusal to acknowledge its legality and partly from the unwillingness of the courts to enforce it. But the resolution's greatest failing lies in a structural flaw. Its sixty-day automatic withdrawal provision would require the president to remove troops that he has already committed, without Congress ever having made a *specific judgment* that such a commitment was unwise.[17] That defect, as explained in chapter 5, can be attributed to what Professor Mayhew has called "the congressional penchant for the blunt, simple action," designed more for the last war than the next. Thus, the resolution does not directly encourage meaningful interbranch dialogue regarding the wisdom of any particular presidential commitment of troops. It promotes that end only indirectly, by threatening the president and Congress with a sixty-day statutory time limit to force them to engage in such a dialogue. Because, as explained in chapter 5, the three branches have rendered the sixty-day limit non-self-executing, that deadline has lost its power to push the president toward consultation or Congress toward voting a prompt resolution of ratification or disapproval of the president's troop commitment. Thus, the resolution has largely failed to promote just the dialogue and cooperation it was designed to produce.

Although the Byrd-Nunn-Warner-Mitchell proposal has its flaws, upon examination, that proposal at least contains the glimmerings of a legislative strategy to deal with the war powers problem. The strategy has four elements, which comport with the guiding principles for the national security charter stated in chapter 7. First, by creating core consultative groups, the bill attempts to devise centralized repositories of political expertise within Congress with continuing responsibility to deal with the war powers problem. Second, by requiring the president to consult with these groups, the bill directly fosters interbranch dialogue and attempts to equalize access to sensitive information that would otherwise lie exclusively within the president's control. In the process, the consultation requirements seek to ensure congressional involvement earlier in the decision-making process so that the president cannot simply commit troops first, then present Congress with a fait accompli. Third, the bill attempts to short-cut the problems of ineffective legislative tools and insufficient political will (identified in chapter 5) by employing various legal devices that allow Congress to declare its opposition to a presidential troop commitment by less than a two-thirds vote in each house: a fast-track procedure, an automatic appropriations cutoff device, and a judicial review provision.[18] Equally important, using the fast-track procedure to force a vote regarding each particular troop commitment forces Congress to make and announce a swift specific judgment approving or disapproving each presidential use of military force.[19] Fourth and last, by explicitly permitting "[a]ny Member of Congress [to] bring an action in the United States District Court for the District of Columbia for declaratory judgment and injunctive relief on the ground that the President or the United States Armed Forces [have] not complied with any provision," the bill not only allows individual members to seek judicial enforcement of the act, but also develops a counterarena of legal expertise in a particular federal circuit with regard to war powers issues.[20]

Each of these points suggests that Congress is finally on the right track in the war powers area. While it may take all of the political will Congress can muster simply to enact this bill, over time, Congress should consider several modifications to the basic Byrd-Nunn-Warner-Mitchell framework that would make this portion of the national security charter even more coherent. As Charles Black once pointed out, it is a peculiar war powers act indeed that defines how many months United States troops may stay abroad, but "utterly refus[es] even to begin the task of defining the conditions under which the president should not commit troops for even ten minutes—the really crucial matter."[21] The original Senate version of the War Powers Resolution set out a series of circumstances under which Congress would approve in advance the introduction of United States armed forces into actual or imminent hostilities without a declaration of war, but this provision was dropped from the final resolution in conference.[22] A core consultative group, possessing deeper familiarity with the subtleties of past cases, could work with the executive branch to refine this provision for reinsertion into future legislation. In chapter 2 I described how the War Powers Resolution, as originally enacted, took no account of either covert warfare or short-term military strikes. The core consultative group could redress that omission by treating covert war making as both a war-making and an intelligence issue to be resolved by a joint covert action subcommittee of the Armed Services and the Intelligence committees in each house. Moreover, the group could address the currently unregulated problem of short-term military strikes by expressly authorizing the president to engage in certain activities for which he currently lacks express statutory authorization as, for example, the commitment of troops overseas for such limited, short-term purposes as rescuing American citizens endangered abroad. Not only would such provisions eliminate existing ambiguities regarding the scope of the president's statutory authorities, they would render Congress's legislative package more attractive to the president by unambiguously elevating his newly authorized activities into Jackson's category one.[23]

Perhaps the most promising feature of the Byrd-Nunn-Warner-Mitchell proposal is its effort to force the courts to adjudicate cases regarding war powers. In chapter 9 I address in more general terms the case for greater judicial involvement in national security. Discussing war powers in particular, however, Professor Ely has trenchantly observed that under the current resolution, courts have inexplicably claimed separation-of-powers or judicial incompetence rationales for refusing to decide whether "hostilities" exist for the purpose of triggering the War Powers Resolution. Even so they "are routinely called upon, without incident, to decide insurance cases in which the existence or non-existence of hostilities must be judicially determined for purposes of giving effect to a war risk clause."[24] At the same time that judges have abstained from deciding whether our own government and officials have violated international law and the constitutional law of foreign affairs, they have regularly passed judgment on whether *foreign* government officials have violated international and domestic law, particularly in transnational commercial and human rights cases under the Act of State Doctrine, the Alien Tort Statute, and the Foreign Sovereign Immunities Act.[25] Even as judges have professed institutional incompetence to restrain the foreign policy branches of government with their constitutional and statutory interpretations, they have demonstrated surprising willingness and ability to employ similar interpretations to restructure schools, hospitals, prisons, and other institutions of our domestic public order.[26] Given the willingness of the courts to hear domestic institutional reform litigation, their unwillingness to review foreign policy actions that just as adversely affect individual rights seems hard to justify.[27]

INTERNATIONAL AGREEMENTS

Since the enactment of the Case-Zablocki Act, numerous reforms of the international agreement-making process have been proposed.[28] Yet the main goal of any framework statute should be to accommodate the relatively high degree of interbranch consensus that has already evolved regarding many issues in this area.

As revealed in chapters 2 and 3, constitutional text, authoritative judicial decision, framework statute, and quasi-constitutional custom have settled most constitutional questions regarding agreement making in favor of the principle of shared power. The Constitution's text expressly authorizes the president and two-thirds of the Senate together to make a treaty. Senate practice accepted by the president over time has confirmed the Senate's ability not simply to withhold consent, but also to consent while placing conditions upon its ratification. *Dames & Moore, Youngstown,* and customary practice have all authorized the president to forgo the treaty route, and to negotiate and conclude congressional-executive agreements in areas of concurrent authority pursuant to the authorization or approval of both houses of Congress. At the same time, however, the Supreme Court's decisions in *U.S. v. Belmont, U.S. v. Pink,* and executive practice endorsed by Congress (particularly from the Franklin Roosevelt presidency) have recognized the president's narrow exclusive authority to enter certain "sole" executive agreements without congressional approval (particularly when exercising his recognition and commander-in-chief powers). Similarly, executive practice repeatedly endorsed by Congress since the Washington years have confirmed the president's monopoly over diplomatic relations and negotiations leading to treaties, although particular presidents have included congressional members in negotiating delegations or shared diplomatic communications with Congress as a matter of comity. In the area of treaty breaking, the allocation of institutional responsibility emerges less clearly. After *Goldwater v. Carter,* however, both political branches appear largely to have accepted the president's power unilaterally to terminate a treaty in accordance with its terms as a matter of quasi-constitutional custom (a rule which could, however, be overridden by future framework statute or authoritative judicial decision).[29]

The prime area of substantive dispute in the treaty area thus lies in the realm of treaty bending, particularly, treaty reinterpretation. As revealed in chapter 2, the Senate recently sought to avoid future Anti-Ballistic Missile (ABM) Treaty reinterpretation disputes by advising and consenting to ratification of the Intermediate-Range Nuclear Forces Treaty with the so-called Byrd amendment, a declaration that "the United States shall interpret the Treaty in accordance with the common understanding shared by the President and Senate at the time the Senate gave its advice and consent to ratification."[30] Because that declaration expressed the view of the Senate alone and was immediately challenged by the president, Congress as a whole should enact that statement as part of its framework statute, as its considered interpretation of what the Constitution requires.

With regard to treaty procedures, a similarly high degree of interbranch consensus exists with regard to the appropriate institutional roles of each of the three branches. Existing executive branch procedures already provide a thorough process for the interagency examination of proposed agreements and thus give healthy assurance of internal accountability.[31] Both Congress and the courts have also indicated their willingness to impose external accountability upon the executive. As recounted in chapter 2, the Case-Zablocki Act requires that the executive branch report every executive agreement to Congress. Moreover, the ABM Treaty reinterpretation controversy has now set a precedent for subjecting controversial executive branch legal interpretations of treaties to the public review of the relevant congressional committees. Nor has judicial abstention posed as serious a problem in the treaty area as it has in the war powers context. Although the *Goldwater* Court abstained from examining treaty terminations, other courts have proved to be comfortable with examining executive authority to enter agreements on the merits and with interpreting the text of treaties and executive agreements. Although the courts have generally given great weight to executive branch interpretations of those documents, some courts have recently construed particular treaties by looking as well to Senate *preratification* materials, providing yet another important check against subsequent executive reinterpretation.[32]

The prime target for procedural reform in the area of international agreements is thus neither the executive nor the judicial branch, but rather, Congress. Any statutory reform effort should attempt to reconcile the Senate's desire that every major agreement be done in treaty form with the House's understandable preference for congressional-executive agreements, which now afford the House a role in agreement ratification that the Constitution's text had denied it. In some areas, particularly international trade, the Framers' method of treaty approval has almost entirely given way to fast-track approval by congressional-executive agreements; in other areas, particularly arms control and human rights, the treaty method continues to hold sway. Thus, the greatest potential for statutory improvement would lie in centralizing congressional procedures for deciding whether particular substantive agreements should be ratified by treaty or executive agreement.

Professor Henkin has suggested that Congress address this "choice-of-instruments" problem by forming a joint committee on international agreements, perhaps drawn from the two foreign-affairs committees, which would receive prior notice of the negotiation of an agreement and would advise the executive on whether the agreement should go to the Senate or both houses for consent.[33] Under my proposal, that committee could be drawn from members of the core consultative group. To address the problems of agreement bending described in chapter 2, the legislation could additionally expand the Case-Zablocki Act to require the executive branch to notify the same joint committee of all "nonagreement agreements," pending terminations and modifications of existing agreements, and "parallel unilateral policy declarations."

A generic version of a recent Senate resolution that created a congressional observer group for the nuclear and space talks in Geneva could also promote smoother ratification of pending agreements. That bipartisan group, drawn from a group very similar to the proposed core consultative group and supported by Armed Services and Foreign Relations committee staffers, was instrumental in securing the speedy ratification of the Intermediate-Range Nuclear Forces Treaty.[34] The framework statute could institutionalize this practice by directing the core consultative group to appoint such a bipartisan group for each significant international negotiation. That group could then serve as a congressional liaison with executive branch negotiators, help secure subsequent approval of the negotiated accord, and with executive permission, observe negotiations and receive information from the executive negotiators. Presidents since McKinley have followed a similar practice, which was used with particular success in the 1970s when an analogous group of committee members and staffers observed negotiations and later helped secure congressional approval of trade agreements negotiated at the Tokyo Round of the General Agreement on Tariffs and Trade (GATT) negotiations.[35] Thus, with only modest centralization within Congress, important strides could be made in easing current executive-legislative tensions in the area of international agreements.

EMERGENCY ECONOMIC POWERS

Like the War Powers Resolution, the International Emergency Economic Powers Act (IEEPA) is a statute whose possible amendment has been thoroughly vetted elsewhere.[36] Yet that law, too, could be sensibly revised in accordance with the general principles offered in chapter 7. The principles of internal and external accountability would require the president to make a more detailed showing of the "national emergency" that drove him to impose emergency sanctions, which could then be tested by interagency review at the Justice Department and adversarial congressional review (with the filing of a counterreport by the congressional legal adviser).

To promote a centralized congressional response, interbranch dialogue, and explicit power sharing, the amended bill could require the president to consult with the core consultative group before declaring such an emergency and before specifying what sanctions are to be imposed. To eliminate perpetual emergencies, the bill could further state that any declared national emergency would automatically expire within a fixed period, for example, one year, and mandate renewed face-to-face consultation between executive officials and the core group before the emergency could be extended. To ensure that Congress would expressly approve or disapprove the president's emergency actions before the emergency expired, the amendment could give fast-track legislative treatment to a joint resolution affirming the existence of the emergency and approving any executive orders issued under it. Such a joint resolution could also contain a mandatory sunset provision of perhaps two years. This revision would allow the president to conduct his emergency actions pursuant to express congressional approval at all times, but would require him to return to Congress periodically for extension of his emergency authority.

As the discussion of *Dames & Moore* and *Regan v. Wald* in chapter 6 revealed, the courts have generally been willing to decide challenges to the president's exercise of his statutory authorities under IEEPA. Nevertheless, to ensure that courts quickly dispel any doubts regarding the validity of the president's actions, the amended bill could contain procedures for expedited judicial review of any national emergency declaration and sanctions order (similar to the expedited review provisions found in the Byrd-Nunn-Warner-Mitchell bill). Moreover, because any challenge to the president's IEEPA authority would involve statutory interpretation, the political question doctrine should not bar judicial review of the question.[37]

In connection with these amendments, Congress could follow the recommendation of the Iran-contra committees and amend or repeal the so-called Hostage Act of 1868, an obscure statutory provision which Oliver North claimed provided the executive branch with "the authority to do whatever [was] necessary" during the Iran-contra affair.[38] Despite powerful arguments that the Congress of 1868 had never intended that law to be a blank check authorizing all future presidents to use any means to rescue hostages, President Carter regularly invoked that statute, along with IEEPA, as legislative authorization for virtually all of his actions during the Iranian hostage crisis. In *Dames & Moore*, the Court did not expressly rely upon the act as a source of presidential authority, but treated it as "highly relevant in the looser sense of indicating congressional acceptance of a broad scope of executive action in circumstances such as those presented in this case."[39] If Congress wishes prospectively to authorize the president to exercise such sweeping powers to rescue hostages, it need not retain the Hostage Act. Instead, it should simply redefine the term "national emergency" in IEEPA, specifying that the taking of American hostages is a factual trigger justifying the president's exercise of extraordinary statutory emergency powers.

INTELLIGENCE OVERSIGHT REFORM

In chapter 2 I recounted how Congress's intelligence oversight reform efforts have thus far centered almost exclusively on the so-called forty-eight-hour covert action reporting bill (what one former CIA general counsel has dubbed "a spate of legislative activity designed to lock the particular barn door in the Iran-Contra Affair").[40] Virtually overlooked have been the issues that should be Congress's primary focus, namely, strengthening the internal and external accountability mechanisms for the oversight of intelligence activities.

To begin with, the three internal agency control principles and the due process principles of foreign policy administration set forth in chapters 2 and 4 should be formally embodied either in the framework statute or the president's Executive Order on intelligence. Any oversight statute should then address the problem of internal agency oversight by recognizing that the general counsel and inspector general of the Central Intelligence Agency (CIA) lack the independence exercised by their counterparts in other agencies. In most cabinet departments and agencies, the general counsel evaluates the legality of agency operations by construing the agency's organic laws, while the inspector general polices internal practices by investigating allegedly illegal acts by agency employees. Both tasks would seem to require independence from the agency head, yet the CIA general counsel and inspector general both serve at the pleasure of the director of central intelligence, which leaves the director free to simply deny them access to information about proposed agency actions. To redress this defect and promote greater independence for these officials, Congress should adopt two valuable structural reforms proposed by the Iran-contra committees: the creation of an independent CIA inspector general and Senate confirmation of the CIA's general counsel.[41]

To enhance oversight of the intelligence agencies within the executive branch, the Iran-contra committees also suggested the revitalization and strengthening of the president's Intelligence Oversight Board, a thinly staffed group of private citizens which investigates and receives reports from intelligence agency general counsels and inspectors general regarding possibly unlawful agency conduct.[42] An expert working group on intelligence oversight made that proposal more concrete, by proposing that Congress create an entirely new, bipartisan national intelligence board that would oversee and review the performance of the intelligence agencies for purposes of regular reporting and recommendation to the president. The board's membership would be drawn from outside the intelligence community, serve on a full-time, compensated basis for periods overlapping presidential administrations, and be granted statutory access to information under agency control as well as a sufficient budget to maintain a qualified professional staff.[43] Congress could also assign greater oversight responsibilities within the executive branch to the Office of Intelligence Policy within the Justice Department, which assists the attorney general in reviewing the implementation of executive orders by intelligence agencies and carries out the attorney general's functions under the Foreign Intelligence Surveillance Act.[44] To enhance the external accountability of the director of central intelligence, new legislation could adapt one of Senator Specter's proposals to mandate that the director and his deputy be political appointees, to be nominated and reconfirmed with each presidential term.[45]

Unlike the area of international agreements, where considerable room remains for further centralization of congressional expertise, little need exists for additional centralization within Congress in the intelligence area. The role of the two select intelligence committees is well established and extensive information sharing already occurs between the committees and the executive branch. Information sharing could undeniably be enhanced by tightening the intelligence finding requirements as described in chapter 7. The proposal of the minority members of the Iran-contra committees to combine the House and Senate intelligence committees into a single joint committee, however, would take centralization too far, inviting committee capture of the kind that occurred with Congress's Joint Committee on Atomic Energy. Congress could achieve more central coordination of its oversight function without risking such capture simply by mandating periodic joint hearings between the two committees and the intelligence agencies.[46]

To enforce its regulation of intelligence, Congress could supplement its reform legislation with an appropriations cutoff device, which would automatically terminate the expenditure of funds for any covert activity with respect to which the president had failed to notify the committees with a signed finding.[47] Along with the various proposals for imposing criminal penalties on wayward intelligence agents described in chapter 7, violations of such appropriations restrictions could be evaluated by the courts, thus subjecting intelligence activities to the occasional salutary influence of judicial examination.[48] Alternatively, Congress could choose to use this arena for applying the impeachment remedy that has been discussed in the previous chapter.

If Congress considered judicial oversight a more effective check on executive conduct than either committee oversight or impeachment, it could adopt a more radical form of judicialization, namely, the creation of a secret court along the lines of the one devised by the Foreign Intelligence Surveillance Act. Congress could require intelligence officials to make an ex parte, in camera submission to the court of their evidence and justifications for *not* informing the congressional committees of a particular covert action, with the court having discretion to deny that submission and order the release of the classified information to the committees.[49] Over time, such a court could become an expert referee between the intelligence agencies and the committees, while reducing the likelihood of leaks and offering greater protection of classified information.

INFORMATION CONTROL

One final area in which Congress could usefully apply the general principles stated in chapter 7 is with regard to information control. Although few would deny the executive's legitimate need to deny sensitive national security information to foreign powers or domestic subversive elements, since Vietnam the question has persistently arisen "whether the public and Congress receive enough information about defense and foreign policy matters to be able to influence policy decisions and to exercise an effective external check on the power of the executive."[50] The recent revelations of overclassification from the Oliver North trial are only the latest tales in a long, documented history of executive overclassification. During the Vietnam War, for example, former Supreme Court Justice and United Nations Ambassador Arthur

Goldberg testified to Congress, "In my experience, 75 percent of [the classified] documents [I have read] should never have been classified in the first place; another 15 percent quickly outlived the need for secrecy; and only about 10 percent genuinely required restricted access over any significant period of time."[51]

If anything, public reaction to this feature of the Iran-contra affair was intensified by the perception that the Reagan administration had applied a wide range of information control techniques to shape or limit the kinds of information reaching the public regarding foreign policy issues. Like previous administrations, the Reagan administration denied visas and permanent residence status to foreigners with views critical of American foreign policy.[52] It followed earlier administrations in employing statutory and constitutional devices to restrict the travel of Americans abroad.[53] It labeled imported foreign films as political propaganda, refused to certify disfavored domestic films as educational materials qualified for duty-free export, and closed foreign information offices in the United States.[54] Moreover, the administration supplemented these statutory devices with new regulations narrowing the access of journalists to events occurring abroad.[55] Through polygraph tests, secrecy pledges, and prosecutions brought under the espionage statutes, it sought to restrain leaks by government employees.[56] By the admission of its own officials, the Reagan administration spread "disinformation" abroad and conducted "spin control" at home.[57]

The measures that Congress could take to ensure its own access to confidential information have been described in chapter 7. But as suggested in chapter 4, the National Security Constitution requires that the public, as well as Congress, receive as much information as is necessary to evaluate the wisdom and legality of executive conduct. One area of legislative reform could focus upon amending IEEPA to bar its restriction of "travel transactions" (that is, financial transactions incident to foreign travel) to particular countries.[58] A second reform target would be the Freedom of Information Act (FOIA). This act exemplifies yet another far-reaching post-Vietnam framework statute that has gradually been weakened by executive initiative, congressional acquiescence, and judicial tolerance. As originally drafted, the act specified a role for Congress, the executive, the courts, and private individuals in the public release of government information. It requires every government agency to disclose documents requested by the public, but its "national security" exemption specifically exempts from disclosure "matters that are . . . established by an Executive order to be kept secret in the interest of national defense or foreign policy and . . . are in fact properly classified pursuant to such Executive order."[59] To preserve external accountability, the act empowers the district courts to review an agency's refusal to release requested records and, if necessary, to review de novo a decision to withhold information, with the agency bearing the burden to show proper classification.[60] Predictably, however, executive officials have exercised their statutory discretion broadly to withhold documents. The Reagan administration revised the Carter administration's executive order regarding classification to enhance that discretion further.[61] The courts have proved reluctant to exercise searching review and have often withheld requested information based on wide deference to executive classification decisions.[62] Congress has acquiesced in these trends by failing to amend the act to preserve its original intent.

The Iran-contra affair starkly testified to the wages of concealing information from Congress and the public. Professor Rostow, a strong advocate of executive power, has nevertheless observed that "[i]f the President and the executive branch cannot persuade Congress and the public that a policy is wise, it should not be pursued."[63] To enhance the flow of information to the public and to further the executive branch's external accountability, Congress could now amend FOIA to mandate periodic declassification of information that was originally classified under an executive order, unless the executive agency chooses specifically to reinstate that classification. A less sweeping measure would be a FOIA amendment revising the national security exemption to require the agency first to identify the damage to national security likely to result from the release of a particular document and second, to find specifically that the agency's need to protect the information outweighs the public interest in disclosure.[64] The latter amendment would not drastically change classification law, but would merely restore by statute the rules regarding disclosure that were applied before the Reagan administration under President Carter's classification executive order.[65] Moreover, Congress could amend FOIA to clarify how far courts should defer to agency affidavits concerning how disputed records were classified in order to ensure that courts do not wholly abdicate the checking function that FOIA originally intended for them.[66]

DO WE HAVE ENOUGH LAWS?

Assuming that Congress could enact any or all of the specific reform proposals outlined here, one likely objection would be that they are too "legalistic." Under this view, one can no more solve the problems unveiled by the Iran-contra affair by passing new laws than one can solve the problems of the welfare state by throwing money at them. Two quite different versions of this claim have been heard from opposing ends of the political spectrum.

From the left, some commentators have argued that the problem un-covered by the Iran-contra affair was one of politics and not law.[67] Under their view, enacting new laws should be given lower national priority than enforcing the ones we have. In Professor Kenneth Sharpe's words, "the abuses of the Reagan administration show that new laws are insufficient if the political will to enforce them is lacking."[68] From the right, defenders of presidential power have argued not that our current laws are underen-forced, but that we already have too many laws that unwisely fetter the president. Robert Bork, a prominent advocate of this position, has charged that "what Congress has been attempting to do with the presi-dent's powers under the Constitution . . . [is] 'to change, entirely, the character of the instrument, and give it the properties of a legal code.' . . . [T]he War Powers Act . . . serves no useful purpose . . . [except to] weaken the presidency and divert the public debate from the substance of policy to legalisms."[69]

I would be the last one to champion passing new laws for their own sake.[70] But my response to both criticisms is the same. Even if we have enough (or too many) of the wrong kind of laws in the national security area, we still have too few of the right kind. Many of our current national security laws are predicated on assumptions that our national institutions behave in ways in which they do not in fact behave. For example, to pretend that the president will always obey a new forty-eight-hour notice requirement for covert actions when he did not always obey the "timely notice" requirement in the current law betrays an optimism that recalls Yogi Berra's famous remark: "We could eliminate all those close plays at first base if we could only move the bag one foot further from home plate."[71] In this sense, the critics from the left are surely correct that we accomplish little by enacting new piecemeal national security legislation, as long as Congress lacks the political will to challenge and the courts lack the judicial will to adjudicate executive violations of those statutes that already exist.

But my recommendation, unlike Yogi Berra's, is not simply to move first base. Rather, it is a legal strategy to *reinvolve the first baseman and the umpire in the game*. The new laws that I have proposed are designed not to clutter the decision-making arena or to hamstring the presidency, but to restore the constitutional roles of both Congress and the courts as active players in a system of balanced institutional participation. The proposals seek to accomplish that end not by ignoring, but by accounting for and revising, the incentives of the regulated institutions.

As demonstrated in chapters 5 and 6, the executive branch has an institutional incentive to concentrate operational power within subexecutive entities that can move swiftly, secretly, and without accountability to Congress or other parts of the executive branch. The laws proposed to promote internal accountability are designed to counteract that incentive by making those subexecutive entities accountable to the president, the cabinet, and the government attorneys who are charged with ensuring executive fidelity to the rule of law. Similarly, the parallel laws to effectuate external accountability are designed to make executive entities directly answerable not just to their superiors, but also to Congress and the courts for their actions.

Similarly, I have argued that Congress has institutional incentives to acquiesce in presidential judgments. To say this is not to charge that individual members of Congress have been doing nothing. To the contrary, the post-Vietnam period has marked an era of almost unprecedented congressional activity. But because Congress's legislative structure is so decentralized, its receipt of legal advice so fragmented, and its access to national security information so irregular, Congress's constant activity has only rarely inserted it beneficially into the process of foreign-policy decision making.[72] Both the laws and institutional changes that I have proposed for Congress aim at these structural sources of congressional acquiescence by creating new response centers and increasing information flows to and from them.

Third and last, I have argued that the courts are uniquely positioned and structured to police the boundaries of congressional-executive authority in national security matters.[73] Yet particularly since the Vietnam era, courts have abandoned that function in favor of a broad deference to the executive in foreign affairs, a deference that arises as much from a complex admixture of confusion and cowardice as from legitimate concerns about competence and the Constitution. In part, that deference reflects the generally relaxed attitude toward the judicial review of executive action that has recently dominated domestic administrative law.[74] In some contexts, particularly in immigration cases, concerns about national sovereignty enhance the judicial drive to abstain.[75] Some federal judges may also betray proexecutive bias because of past service in the executive branch.[76]

As clarified in chapter 9, I do not deny that judicial deference also reflects valid concerns about the separation of powers and judicial incompetence in deciding particular foreign-affairs cases.[77] In recent times, however, courts have deferred far beyond the extent necessary to protect these bona fide concerns in circumstances under which they had historically never hesitated to adjudicate. As described in chapter 6, judges have invalidated legislative restraints on presidential conduct and inferred legislative "approval" for presidential measures from congressional silence, thereby encouraging executive activism and condoning legislative inaction during times that have demanded collective decision making. The laws I propose for the courts are designed to counteract this judicial tendency to abstain for unwarranted "prudential" reasons. My proposals are designed to override these concerns to encourage the judiciary to referee recurrent interbranch disputes over allocations of authority in foreign affairs.

If these proposals sought to modify institutional behavior by piecemeal legislation that took no account of political realities, they would deserve the pejorative "legalistic" label. But their goal is not simply to add to our store of rules, but to restore a *constitutional process* of national security decision making. Such a legal-process approach to national security reform aims to create a legal structure within which the political system of checks and balances may operate. It tries to modify the current, ineffective legal structure with one more conducive to encouraging dialogue, interaction, and political cooperation among the branches.

As one scholar has noted, such a strategy drove the Federalists to create the two great structural principles of the Constitution, separation of powers and federalism: "Vest power in different sets of agents who will have personal incentives to monitor and enforce limitations on each other's power."[78] As Justice Brandeis recognized, the purpose of separation of powers is "not to avoid friction, but, by means of the inevitable friction incident to the distribution of the governmental powers among the departments, to save the people from autocracy."[79] The statutory reforms proposed here similarly seek to harness this inevitable friction between the branches. Far from denying the institutional incentives and political attributes of each branch, these proposals acknowledge those incentives and pit them against one another. They discourage overreaching by any one branch by encouraging participation and checking behavior by the other two.

Nor do these proposals assume that Congress and the courts are somehow better qualified than the president to make foreign policy. On the contrary, the approach seeks to preserve the respective roles of the three branches under our National Security Constitution with the president in the lead, Congress in a participating, partnership role, and the courts as crucial arbiters of a lawful foreign policy. They seek to limit the president only to the extent that his conduct threatens to disrupt constitutional equilibrium. At the same time, however, they preserve that equilibrium by promoting formal institutional procedures for informed interbranch dialogue and power sharing.

Some antilegalists suggest that such dialogue should be produced through informal accords and interbranch accommodations, not changes in formal legal structures.[80] But as has been suggested in chapter 2, over time, such informal accords display too many disadvantages. They may be concluded in secret and are rarely formally legitimated by the entire Congress and presidency. Thus, they provide little clarity to the parties, the public, our allies, or our adversaries as to whether institutions are complying with enduring constitutional norms or acting out of transitory political convenience. Informal accords are generally ad hoc in scope, designed to solve one transient piece of a larger national security problem. Their instant mutability gives little assurance of sustained voluntary compliance. Because successive presidents or Congresses may unilaterally breach or ignore previous accords, informal accords offer insufficient protection to settled expectations. When understandings are wholly informal, each political branch may construe and alter them as exigencies demand, with enforcement depending solely upon the retaliatory political power of the other branch. When one branch has confidence that the other will not (or cannot effectively) retaliate, it can break the informal accord without discussion. Thus, informal accords fail to promote interbranch dialogue at precisely the moment when they are most needed—when the more powerful party is contemplating deviation.

Formal framework legislation, by contrast, has none of these disadvantages. It would be a public act, jointly legitimated by Congress and the president, comprehensive in scope, and not subject to momentary abandonment.[81] Framework legislation would inform all observers of the institutional and constitutional allocation of decision-making responsibility and would protect settled expectations by providing higher assurance of mutual compliance. When Congress and the president embody their understandings in a framework statute, all three branches may construe that statute and the courts can authoritatively decide whether particular conduct comports with those formal understandings. While the more powerful political branch is deciding whether to violate that accord, the threat of being held in violation of law will drive it toward interbranch dialogue as a means of averting confrontation. Once the court rules, more dialogue will be required to bring the conduct of the branches into compliance with the judicial decision.

To reap these advantages, the framework legislation that I propose would not need to incorporate all, or even most, of the specific provisions I have proposed. More important than any particular proposal is that the charter formally reassert the principles of shared power and balanced institutional participation in national security decision making as norms, not merely of political prudence, but of constitutional stature. By so saying, the charter would reaffirm that the goal of legal reform in this area is not simply to exalt legalism, but to ensure that foreign, like domestic, affairs are conducted under the rule of law.

9 A National Security Constitution for the Posthegemonic Age

The journey thus far has taught us that we must learn enduring, not transient, lessons from the Iran-contra affair. If we recognize its precedent as Vietnam, not Watergate, we learn that the affair represented yet another challenge by the advocates of executive discretion to the constitutional principle of shared power. If we view the problem as institutional incentives, not evil people, we learn that our national institutions have not voluntarily preserved balanced institutional participation in foreign affairs. If we view the prescription as the enactment of a national security charter, not passivity, we learn that the major political challenge of the affair lies not behind us, but ahead.

To this analysis, one persistent objection has been made: However appropriate a National Security Constitution based on active congressional and judicial participation may have been for an earlier age, it is totally inappropriate for the world in which we now live. This view posits that the proposed charter would unwisely weaken the presidency at a time when our world situation demands an even stronger president than we already have. According to this claim, new national security legislation would invite both the congressional micromanagement of foreign affairs and inappropriate judicial involvement in political decisions, draining the presidential energy needed to maintain our precarious position in world affairs.

Although this alternative view has been urged most vociferously by defenders of the Iran-contra affair, in recent years it has struck chords with commentators of all political stripes. Their arguments raise a common theme—that the affair derived ultimately not from bad people or bad laws, but from America's geopolitical situation. What the affair confirmed, these commentators say, is that over time, America's constitutionalism has grown increasingly incompatible with its globalism.

Writing shortly after the Iran-contra affair first came to light, Charles Krauthammer observed: "This affair is not a Reagan crisis nor a presidential crisis, but a recurring American crisis, rooted ultimately in the tension between America's need to act like a great power and its unwillingness to do so. . . . [T]he presidency finds itself in the permanent bind: to fulfill its obligations as leader of a superpower or to fulfill its obligations as leader of a democracy."[1] Those who believe and those who deny that America is in decline accept that America's eighteenth-century constitutional regime poorly suits the prevailing international regime of the late twentieth century. In the final chapter of his celebrated *The Rise and Fall of the Great Powers,* Paul Kennedy cautions that the United States "may not always be assisted by its division of constitutional and decision-making powers, deliberately created when it was geographically and strategically isolated from the rest of the world two centuries ago . . . but which may be harder to operate when it has become a global superpower, often called upon to make swift decisions vis-à-vis countries which enjoy far fewer constraints."[2]

If America's constitutionalism cannot sustain its globalism, the question becomes, which must give way? Critics of American interventionism, on the one hand, argue that America must surrender its imperial ambitions if it hopes to sustain its constitutional democracy.[3] Advocates of presidential power, on the other hand, aver that the exigencies of a posthegemonic age require America to reform its Constitution to give the president broader discretion.[4]

Some commentators have expressly called for a constitutional amendment to enhance the president's discretion in foreign affairs.[5] Others have asserted that under *Curtiss-Wright,* the Constitution should already be read to afford the president that greater freedom of action. Oliver North himself made this claim most baldly during the Iran-contra hearings when he cited *Curtiss-Wright* and declared that "this nation is at risk in a dangerous world. . . . [W]e all ha[ve] to weigh . . . the difference between lies and lives."[6] President Reagan's tragic remark—that "the American people will never forgive me if I fail to get these hostages out over this legal question"—suggests his apparent agreement that in times of crisis, the Constitution must give way to the press of external events.[7]

In short, we have come full circle from Woodrow Wilson's day. Rather than asking whether America should make the world safe for democracy, we are now asked whether the world is too unsafe for traditional constitutional democracy in the conduct of American foreign affairs. I would answer that question in the negative, but to do so, I must first anticipate and address both the constitutional and the policy objections to the analysis thus far. As a matter of constitutional law, some critics may argue that the charter proposal is unconstitutional. Under this view, external events have *already* effectively amended the National Security Constitution to establish *Curtiss-Wright,* not *Youngstown,* as the dominant constitutional vision in foreign policy decision making. As a matter of policy, other critics may attack the charter proposal as unworkable. Under this view, a framework statute promoting greater involvement by Congress and the courts would sap presidential energy and thereby harm the national interest. In this last chapter, I rebut both objections and consider finally whether our constitutionalism and globalism can, in fact, be reconciled.

THE CONSTITUTIONAL OBJECTION

The lesson of chapter 3 should be that the first, constitutional objection to the argument here is not a novel one. Rather, legal claims of unfettered executive authority in foreign affairs have been heard throughout our constitutional history. In each succeeding historical era, critics have challenged the existing constitutional structure of foreign policy making as inadequate to cope with rapidly changing external events. Over the years, Alexander Hamilton, Theodore Roosevelt, and Woodrow Wilson were all heard to make that claim. In *Durand v. Hollins, The Prize Cases, In re Neagle,* and culminating with *Curtiss-Wright,* the courts occasionally echoed it in dicta. In 1948, Professor Rossiter speculated that the cold war had made a constitutional dictatorship necessary.[8] Shortly after the Korean War began, Arthur Schlesinger, who would later write *The Imperial Presidency,* invoked an expansive view of executive power to defend the president's constitutional prerogative as commander-in-chief to commit troops without a declaration of war.[9] Even Senator Fulbright, later the strongest congressional opponent of the Vietnam War, argued in 1961 that "for the existing requirements of American foreign policy we have hobbled the President by too niggardly a grant of power."[10]

That both Schlesinger and Fulbright had completely changed their tune by the end of the Vietnam War suggests that we need a more thoughtful understanding of the interrelationship between America's constitutional regimes and its changing role in international regimes. As demonstrated in chapter 3, the claim that the world is too unsafe for constitutional democracy was heard at times even more precarious than these—during America's infancy, when the nation was at its most vulnerable; during our adolescence and adulthood, when America first aggressively stepped into the world arena; and during the height of the cold war, when the threat of nuclear destruction became a feature of everyday life.

At the Republic's birth, the Framers deliberately drafted a Constitution of shared powers and balanced institutional participation, fully aware of the risks that arrangement posed to the nation's international well-being. By mandating that separated institutions share powers in foreign as well as in domestic affairs, the Framers determined that we must sacrifice some short-term gains from speed, secrecy, and efficiency in favor of the longer-term consensus that derives from reasoned interbranch consultation and participatory decision making. Although in the early years of the Republic, all three branches condoned a de facto transformation of the original National Security Constitution from a scheme of congressional primacy to one of executive primacy, they never rejected the concepts of power sharing and institutional participation. Until the 1930s and the rise of the personalized, institutional presidency, the political branches traded the upper hand back and forth, but without fundamental alteration of the underlying constitutional scheme. Framework statutes, judicial decisions, and institutional practice helped clarify particular zones of shared and exclusive constitutional responsibility, but never established foreign affairs as a realm apart, from which the courts were excluded and checks and balances did not apply.

In 1936, *Curtiss-Wright*'s dicta boldly asserted the alternative vision of unfettered presidential management. But even as the cold war raged, the 1947 National Security Act, *Youngstown,* and finally the post-Vietnam era framework statutes definitively rejected that vision as America's constitutional model for dealing with the outside world. Vietnam (and

Watergate as well, to the extent that it arose from Vietnam) then taught that even in a nuclear age, America would not conduct globalism at the price of constitutionalism. It is therefore ironic that the *Curtiss-Wright* model should now resurface at a historical moment when many commentators assert that we are emerging from the cold war and thus should be at greater liberty than ever to conduct our foreign affairs according to democratic processes.[11]

To this, critics may respond that post-Vietnam patterns of executive dominance and judicial deference (recounted in chapters 2 and 6) have finally rendered *Youngstown* a relic. Since the early 1970s, this view would assert, Congress and the courts have allowed de facto reformation of the National Security Constitution in *Curtiss-Wright*'s image by acquiescing in executive dominance across the spectrum of foreign policy making. But as I have argued in chapter 3, even two decades of informal accommodations by the three branches can only generate new pockets of customary constitutional law on particular matters of foreign policy. They cannot permanently amend the National Security Constitution unless additionally blessed by authoritative judicial decision, framework statute, or constitutional amendment.

None of these transformative events, I would argue, has yet occurred. The Burger and Rehnquist Courts may have trumpeted executive discretion in foreign affairs with broad dicta, but they have supported that language with relatively narrow holdings. More frequently, as was shown in chapter 6, judicial "endorsement" of executive discretion has resulted from abstention rather than adjudication. Congress has not repealed its framework legislation of the 1970s; no constitutional amendment formally increasing the president's power has been adopted, nor is one pending. As a strict matter of constitutional law, then, *Curtiss-Wright* has only challenged, not displaced, the prevailing constitutional vision of a shared power in foreign affairs. *Youngstown* remains the controlling vision of the National Security Constitution, although only time will tell whether the future will reinforce it by new framework legislation or erode it with further institutional practice.

THE POLICY OBJECTION

To make the lawyer's argument that balanced institutional participation remains the prevailing constitutional vision in foreign affairs does not answer the various policy objections that could be lodged against a national security charter. Most of these center on the claim that a national security charter would harm the national interest by fostering three forms of executive weakness: by effectively forcing executive decision making in foreign affairs out of the White House and into an outmoded bureaucratic system of cabinet government ill-suited for a nuclear age; by encouraging Congress to interfere improvidently in the details of executive foreign policy making; and by thrusting the courts into political disputes that they are neither competent nor constitutionally qualified to resolve.[12] Although each of these objections deserves serious discussion, I find none of them ultimately persuasive.

The first objection argues that the principles of internal and external executive branch accountability stated in chapter 7 would unwisely freeze into law an outmoded picture of executive decision making. That picture, born in the 1947 National Security Act, assumes that the cabinet departments should play the primary role and the National Security Council (NSC) and the Central Intelligence Agency (CIA) the secondary role in the foreign policy process. In fact—the contrary view would maintain—policy makers and political scientists alike have criticized the bureaucratic ineffectiveness of the State and Defense departments and have found the reallocation of foreign policy powers to agencies closer to the President, such as the NSC, to be necessary or salutary developments.[13]

While I recognize and accept many of the insights of this political science literature, they do not, to my mind, undercut the need for the legal principles that I have proposed. In my judgment, how each president chooses to organize his foreign-policy-making apparatus is a matter largely within his own discretion and is rarely a subject of constitutional concern. But the president's power to govern, even within his own branch, derives from and is ultimately limited by the terms of the Constitution.[14] As I have argued in chapter 4, certain principles are so central to our notions of constitutional government that no president should knowingly violate them, even in the pursuit of the most efficient and effective foreign-policy-making mechanism. Thus, the president would violate his oath to "preserve, protect and defend the Constitution" and his duty to "take Care that the Laws be faithfully executed" if he were knowingly to flout the principles of civilian control of the military, nondelegation of government authority to private parties, and presidential supervision and responsibility for official acts carried on in his or her name. Apart from articulating these core principles of "due process of foreign policymaking," the national security charter would not impinge upon the president's policy choices regarding the distribution of intraexecutive branch decision-making authority. Instead, the charter would aim to promote greater official sensitivity to the potential illegality of proposed executive branch decisions wherever those decisions might be made.

The Iran-contra affair illustrated that many parts of the executive branch's national security decision-making structure have grown in recent years extraordinarily isolated from external checks and balances. That reality makes particularly crucial the creation of an *internal* system of checks and balances within the executive branch capable of adversarially testing the wisdom and legality of proposed executive initiatives.[15] The charter proposal would create such a check by mandating a branchwide, rather than simply agencywide, legal review of executive action.

I reject the notion that more intense legal scrutiny of executive decisions would necessarily foster presidential paralysis when world events demand a prompt response. Most foreign-policy decisions are implemented over the course of months and years, not moments. Excepting, perhaps, a response to a nuclear strike, the occasions are exceedingly rare when the president would jeopardize the nation by considering legality before committing the nation to a course of international action. Nor can I accept that requiring the president to act lawfully would confine him or her to conducting foreign policy through inefficient, existing cabinet bureaucracies. As the Cuban missile and the Iranian hostage crises illustrated, presidents can quickly respond to pressing international crises, even through ad hoc nonbureaucratic channels, without offending core constitutional principles or forgoing the expert advice of legal counsel.[16]

To say this is not to deny that the legal restraints I would propose for executive branch decision making would impose administrative costs and slow response times. But recent diplomatic history, from the Tonkin Gulf Resolution to the Iran-contra affair, have taught that speed and efficiency are not our only foreign-policy values. In the end, I believe that the costs of a system of greater accountability would be more than outweighed by the benefits gained in more lawful policies and the avoidance of the occasional Iran-contra fiasco.

A similar answer can be given to the second policy argument: that a national security charter would weaken the presidency by thrusting Congress too deep into the details of foreign policy making. That argument assumes that presidential strength is the principal element in a successful American foreign policy and that greater congressional participation in foreign affairs would necessarily diminish that strength.[17] To my mind, this argument confuses the desirable notion of presidential strength with the less crucial concept of presidential autonomy. I fully agree that presidential strength is critical to a successful foreign policy. I also concede that greater congressional participation in foreign affairs is likely to diminish presidential autonomy. I do not agree, however, that the president's freedom to act alone is the best measure of presidential strength.

On the contrary, as the discussion in chapter 4 revealed, Justice Jackson's concurring opinion in *Youngstown* made precisely the opposite point. The president's constitutional strength in foreign affairs is at its peak when he acts *with the authorization and approval of Congress*. It is qualitatively weaker when he acts alone in the face of congressional silence. "When the President takes measures incompatible with the express or implied will of Congress, his power is at its lowest ebb, for then he can rely only upon his own constitutional powers minus any constitutional powers of Congress over the matter."[18]

Jackson's reasoning makes good policy as well as constitutional sense. The guiding principles for congressional reform outlined in chapter 7— centralizing congressional decision making, centralizing congressional legal advice, and promoting information sharing—and the particular techniques suggested to accomplish those reforms—for example, the filing of counterreports, consolidation of committees, use of the fast-track approval device—are designed to promote two ends. They aim first to force the president to consult with Congress *before* he acts, and second, to force Congress to declare approval or opposition to his action promptly *after* it happens. These reforms seek to involve Congress in the decision-making process earlier, to make that participation more useful and informed, and to avoid the mistrust and confrontation that almost inevitably follow when the president presents Congress with a fait accompli.

Even if the short-term result of such reforms is a reduction in presidential autonomy, the long-term intent is to enhance presidential strength. As Professor Schlesinger warned in the waning days of Vietnam, we need "to devise means of reconciling a strong and purposeful

Presidency with equally strong and purposeful forms of democratic control. . . . [W]e need a strong Presidency—but a strong Presidency *within the Constitution.*"[19]

As chronicled in chapter 2, our experience in the post-Vietnam years has evinced the nation's failure to heed that warning. During the post-Vietnam years, both the economic and the political dimensions of our foreign policy have been nominally predicated upon the international ideal of multilateral cooperation and the domestic ideal of congressional-executive partnership. In international trade and monetary affairs, successive administrations have consistently declared that world economic interdependence requires bipartisan domestic commitment to the multilateral trading system in order to mitigate self-destructive cycles of trade retaliation and to promote economic efficiency, trade expansion, and world welfare. In the political and military realm, nearly every postwar president has taken office by announcing a similar intent to consult and closely cooperate with Congress and our allies.

As revealed in chapter 5, the bane of both of these ideals has proved to be unilateralism—unilateral American action on the international level and unilateral presidential action on the domestic level. At the same time as the United States has pulled back from numerous multilateral commitments in the international arena, four of our last six presidents—Johnson, Nixon, Carter, and Reagan—increasingly resorted to unilateral domestic decision making in the conduct of foreign policy. Not surprising is that Congress reacted against this unilateralism, leaving all four presidencies embattled by Congress, foreign policy, or both. Although it is too early to tell whether the Bush presidency will repeat this cycle, interbranch relations began with optimistic bipartisan noises but quickly clouded with battles over key foreign affairs appointees, the Moynihan amendment, and a failed coup attempt in Panama.[20] By 1990, President Bush had invaded Panama and issued three foreign policy vetoes, declaring that in foreign negotiations "it is imperative that the United States speak with one voice. The Constitution provides that that one voice is the President's. . . . I cannot accept binding provisions . . . that would tie my hands in the exercise of my constitutional responsibilities."[21]

Of course, some level of congressional-executive conflict in foreign affairs is unavoidable, particularly when the president and the congressional majority hale from different political parties. But I would argue that the more recent cyclical pattern of conflict and stalemate among the political branches has been highly destructive of presidential strength as well as of a coherent foreign policy.[22] As the Iran-contra affair revealed, when the president bears nearly exclusive obligation to respond to all external threats, it is only a matter of time before he or she will stop seeking Congress's advice before responding. By the same token, when the president regularly diminishes Congress's role from the constitutional function of "advise and consent" to one of perfunctory ratification of faits accomplis, it becomes almost inevitable that Congress will reassert its prerogative directly and intransigently. Unfortunately, the most opportune moments for such intransigence arise when the president is particularly weak or in need of congressional support, fostering the impression of a Congress myopically pursuing partisan politics while the president is seeking bipartisan consensus.[23] As I argued in chapter 7, the principle of unchecked executive discretion engenders these cycles of conflict by trading short-term presidential autonomy and "victories" for long-term interbranch strife. In contrast, a national security charter based on principles of balanced institutional participation would foster a long-term, bounded equilibrium among the branches to mitigate interbranch conflict and enhance presidential strength (in the Jacksonian sense). For proof of this principle, one need look no farther than the last administration. President Reagan was at his strongest in foreign affairs when he negotiated and concluded the Intermediate-Range Nuclear Forces Treaty with prior congressional consultation, involvement, and support; he was at his weakest after the Iran-contra affair when he sought and obtained none of these.

I do not deny that Congress's increased role under the charter proposal would inconvenience the president. A loss of autonomy generally does. Executive energies will doubtless be diverted to testifying to Congress, supplying information, preparing reports, and meeting with the core consultative group. While steps can and should be taken to reduce repetitive or perfunctory consultations, over time the benefits of these enforced dialogues will far exceed the costs of doing without them. The price in terms of leaked information seems vastly overstated. As we saw in chapter 7, the empirical evidence regarding congressional leaks is weak and national security information does not, in any event, belong solely to the executive branch.[24] More serious are the concerns that congressional mavericks will disrupt reasonable executive initiatives by too readily bringing lawsuits or by indiscriminately triggering point-of-order and committee gatekeeping procedures, and that threats of civil and criminal penalties or impeachment will unduly chill executive officials in the performance of their duties. Only experimentation with these remedies can reveal how likely these scenarios are; careful drafting should forestall the most foreseeable abuses. Such remedies should therefore be incorporated in the charter with sunset provisions and be modified or eliminated if they proved to be superfluous or counterproductive.

Of course, in one clear case the charter proposal, if adopted, would undeniably diminish the president's strength—if he chose to act in foreign affairs over Congress's clear and unambiguous opposition. Under the *Curtiss-Wright* view, the president would have the freedom to take such an action. Under the *Youngstown* view of the National Security Constitution, such a situation would place the president in Jackson's category three dilemma: to refrain from an action that the president might deem vitally necessary to respond to world events or to proceed unilaterally on the belief that he or she is lawfully acting within an area of exclusive constitutional authority. While these are difficult choices, they are just the ones we elect our president to make. President Truman made precisely such a decision in 1952 when he unsuccessfully seized the steel mills, as did President Carter in 1979 when he successfully terminated our mutual defense treaty with Taiwan.[25] With regard to such choices, the crucial point is that the proposed national security charter would not deny the president's power to act in such circumstances; it would only force him to act openly, knowing that he would later have to defend the legality of his act in court (and withdraw it if the court found it illegal). While in such cases the charter proposal would clearly restrain presidential autonomy, such a restraint—as the Iran-contra affair showed— would probably be a good thing. To the extent that these reform proposals are designed, however, to authorize certain presidential activities, clarify zones of constitutional responsibility, promote interbranch dialogue and cooperation, and avert cyclical interbranch conflict, they should ultimately strengthen, not weaken, the president's hand vis-à-vis the outside world.[26]

The third and most serious objection to the charter proposal is that it would improperly intrude the courts into the foreign policy decision-making process. Over the years, many thoughtful constitutional analysts, including Alexander Bickel, Herbert Wechsler, and Jesse Choper, have articulated theories arguing against such a judicial role. Professor Bickel articulated a philosophy of prudence, felicitously called the "passive virtues," under which the Supreme Court should be allowed to withhold constitutional judgment in cases raising concerns over separation of powers. Dean Choper reached the same conclusion by a different, "functional" rationale. He reasoned that the branches of government possess adequate political weapons to protect their interests against one another and that the courts should thus refrain from reviewing interbranch controversies involving separation of powers to husband their resources for individual rights cases. Professor Wechsler posited the narrowest judicial avoidance rationale, based on *Marbury v. Madison* whereby the courts may not broadly abstain, but may be "called upon to judge whether the Constitution has committed to another agency of government the autonomous determination of the issue raised."[27]

The judicial decisions chronicled in chapter 6 demonstrate that these three rationales have found expression in a wide array of justiciability doctrines, regarding private and congressional standing, the immunity of defendants, nonripeness or mootness, equitable discretion, and prudential decisions to decide cases narrowly to avoid reaching constitutional questions. The most indiscriminately invoked of these doctrines has been the "political question" doctrine, in the words of one court: "a tempting refuge from the adjudication of difficult constitutional claims [whose] shifting contours and uncertain underpinnings make it susceptible to indiscriminate and overbroad application to claims properly before the federal courts."[28] Shortly after the Vietnam War, Professor Henkin argued that the doctrine does not exist, reflecting that virtually all of the cases on foreign affairs allegedly decided under the "doctrine" actually involved judicial determinations upholding executive decisions on the merits.[29] Other commentators have argued persuasively that the political question doctrine does exist, but that it should play little or no role in the exercise of judicial review.[30]

In my judgment, there *is* a political question doctrine, and a strict reading of Professor Wechsler's view best captures its constitutional core.[31] The doctrine grows not from judicial deference, but from judicial interpretation. As the discussion in the foregoing chapters suggests, when the Supreme Court has applied the doctrine in the foreign affairs context, it has not abdicated its power to interpret the Constitution altogether. Rather, it has read the Constitution and found conclusive direction there committing the foreign-affairs decision under challenge to one of the other two branches.[32] The Supreme Court's fullest expression of the doctrine—which came less than thirty years ago in the context of legislative apportionment and not foreign affairs—bears out this reading. In *Baker v. Carr,* the Court carefully emphasized that the doctrine is one "of 'political questions,' not one of 'political cases,' " calling "it . . . error to suppose that every case or controversy that touches foreign relations lies beyond judicial cognizance." Reviewing the same history of judicial precedent recounted in chapter 3, Justice Brennan concluded: "Our cases in this field seem invariably to show a discriminating analysis of the particular question posed, in terms of the history of its management by the political branches, of its susceptibility to judicial handling in the light of its nature and posture in the specific case, and of the possible consequences of judicial action." Applying those standards to decided cases, Brennan uncovered a rich historical tradition of judicial decision making in foreign affairs.[33]

The evidence in chapter 3 confirms Justice Brennan's findings. Since the beginning of the Republic, federal judges have issued rulings that span the foreign policy spectrum and involve interpretation of virtually all bodies of law. They have reviewed the legality of military seizures, presidential orders in wartime, retaliatory strikes, covert actions, executive agreements, and treaty interpretation. They have reviewed and rejected defenses of executive privilege, superior orders, and inherent presidential powers. As *Youngstown* made clear, courts have reviewed the legality of executive action that relies upon unenumerated presidential powers shared with Congress. As *Curtiss-Wright* suggested, courts may also evaluate whether the president is validly exercising his unenumerated "sole organ" power. The Court's decisions of the early 1800s, coupled with its "recognition" decisions earlier in this century, establish that a president's exercise of his or her textually enumerated authorities—for example, the commander-in-chief and recognition powers—are not immune from judicial review (although the court may construe those powers generously). Nor does any impediment to judicial review arise when the president construes an executive agreement, treaty, or customary international law.[34] The political question doctrine plainly does not bar review when executive conduct is directly contested by Congress acting as a whole.[35] Perhaps most important of all, as even Dean Choper would concede, the courts have a special duty to look closely when executive conduct in foreign affairs infringes directly upon individual rights.[36]

Whatever the general vitality of the political question doctrine in constitutional cases, the crucial point for present purposes is that it would not apply if Congress were expressly to override its application in a national security framework statute. Justice White put the point bluntly in the *Japan Whaling* case: "Under the Constitution, one of the judiciary's characteristic roles is to interpret statutes, and we cannot shirk this responsibility merely because our decision may have significant political overtones."[37] As recently as 1988, the Court held that the National Security Act of 1947—the predecessor to the charter that I have proposed—was not intended to preclude judicial review of a constitutional challenge to an executive decision made under that framework law.[38] Similarly, in *Curtiss-Wright* and *Dames & Moore*, the two cases most frequently cited by executive-power advocates, the Court reviewed on the merits the president's conduct under foreign affairs statutes. If Congress were to enact a framework statute, but left unclear whether it authorized any given executive act, the courts could remand a challenge to that action to the relevant agency to determine whether the challenged act was consistent with past agency practice.[39]

As a matter of law and history, there is equally little doubt that a framework statute could recognize private and congressional standing, override official immunities, and eliminate the courts' equitable discretion to refrain from issuing particular remedies.[40] As a policy matter, however, the questions remain whether the courts would be competent to rule in such cases (even if they were not constitutionally barred from doing so) and whether judicial intervention would unwisely weaken the president's hand at crucial moments.

Opponents of judicial review have enumerated several "prudential" reasons why courts should not resolve questions of foreign affairs: that courts could not derive principled standards by which to decide such cases; that courts would lack the necessary institutional capacities to make delicate national security determinations and to supervise any relief they might order; that judges should not adjudicate for fear that their judgments will be ignored; and that the judiciary could not rule against the executive without "embarrassing" the president and confusing the rest of the world as to who is in charge of our foreign policy.[41] In my judgment, each of these policy arguments against adjudication lacks merit. The notion that the courts could not derive principled standards to adjudicate in this area is belied by their demonstrated ability in domestic cases to derive workable standards from even the vaguest constitutional provisions. If the Court can derive detailed rules of criminal procedure from the Fifth Amendment and elaborate standards of personal jurisdiction from the due process clause of the Fourteenth Amendment, then surely it can construe the terms of even the most broadly worded framework statute. Similarly, the claim that the courts lack the expertise and information to conduct a national security review function is totally self-fulfilling. Under the statute I have described, such reviews would be concentrated in an expert court and the parties would be required to provide the information (*in camera*, if necessary) for the court to make its adjudication. One need look no further than Judge Gesell's adept handling of the Oliver North trial to determine that even cases involving massive amounts of classified information can be fairly adjudicated by a competent and conscientious judge. Equally self-defeating is the charge that the courts should not rule for fear that the political branches will ignore their judgments. Presidential compliance in *Youngstown* and the *Nixon Tapes* case has largely put that fear to rest. The claim that the court would lack the resources to supervise its relief likewise seems wholly insubstantial. The power and ability of courts not simply to review the action of the political branches but also to order coercive remedies against proper executive branch representatives has been settled at least since *Marbury v. Madison.* Moreover, as the U.S. Court of Appeals for the D.C. Circuit noted in *Ramirez v. Weinberger,* while enjoining American military movements in Honduras, "[i]t must be presumed that the defendants, all officials of the United States government present in Washington, D.C., will obey an order of the district court."[42]

The final policy argument—that the judiciary could not rule against the executive without embarrassing the president and confusing our allies—points to the effect of judicial intervention not on the courts but on the president. If this claim rests on foreign confusion, it denigrates our allies' intelligence and assumes that they cannot comprehend a constitutional system of shared powers. As Professor Redish notes, even when the Senate refuses to ratify a treaty that the president has negotiated, "other nations are [also] asked to understand our complex constitutional system of checks and balances, and we somehow manage to survive as a nation."[43] Nor does it make sense to condone illegal executive conduct simply to avoid embarrassing the president, particularly if the unlawfully acting party should be embarrassed. As the Iran-contra affair revealed, embarrassing information will emerge anyway during subsequent executive, legislative, and criminal investigations. To bar civil adjudication on this ground while the illegal conduct takes place runs the risk—realized during the Iran-contra affair—that the unscrutinized conduct will later cause even greater embarrassment for the country.

I do not doubt that my statutory proposals would, at least in the short run, increase the number of federal court suits involving foreign affairs filed against the government and its officials. But I do not see that result as permanently disrupting or impairing the operation of the executive branch. As in the case of the Federal Election Campaign Act or the Gramm-Rudman-Hollings budget-balancing act, the first suits might seek to declare portions of the framework statute unconstitutional as usurpations of executive or congressional power.[44] Even if such litigation were to ensue, however, judicial resolution of those disputes would help to clarify currently ambiguous boundaries of constitutional responsibility. In such cases, the Court could either sustain the statute as written or follow past practice and strike the statute's unconstitutional parts, while staying its judgment pending congressional modification of the law to comply with the Court's constitutional interpretation.[45] Once the Court had resolved such initial disputes, an interbranch modus vivendi under the act could ensue, now guided by clearer judicial statements regarding which presidential actions are or are not legislatively or constitutionally authorized. Because a framework statute could not, by definition, override the Constitution, the new charter could not require federal judges to surrender their discretion to dismiss those suits in which concerns about separation of powers proved particularly intense, for example, suits brought by constitutionally inappropriate plaintiffs or against constitutionally immunized defendants. Moreover, well-established procedural doctrines requiring that administrative remedies be exhausted, that the forum be convenient, and that insubstantial claims be dismissed before discovery or on summary judgment would remain available to spare government officials the burden of unwarranted trials.[46] In the long term, the likelihood that executive officials would win most suits brought against them on the merits would dampen litigant incentives to bring frivolous statutory claims.

In short, however different foreign affairs might be from domestic affairs, that difference does not exempt them from our constitutional system of checks and balances, particularly the check of judicial review. If anything, meaningful judicial review is even more constitutionally necessary in foreign affairs than in domestic affairs. By rendering the federal government supreme to the states in international matters, the Framers deliberately removed state prerogatives—ordinarily a potent domestic force—as a political check against presidential action. Furthermore, as I demonstrated in chapter 5, the institutional structure of Congress makes some measure of congressional acquiescence virtually inevitable. The reduced effectiveness of these other political checks in foreign affairs enhances the need for judicial review of presidential actions, particularly when those actions impinge upon individual rights.

As demonstrated in chapter 3, the Framers designed our constitutional system with foreign affairs—and judicial review of foreign affairs—firmly in mind. When the courts systematically remove themselves from independent review of executive action, it is only a matter of time before clear lines of legality fade from the landscape of American foreign affairs.[47] Left behind are temporary lines in the sand drawn by the latest interbranch turf battle, only to be redrawn by the next powerful president or the next powerful Congress. The federal judge who said during the Iranian hostage crisis that "it is not the business of courts to pass judgment on the decisions of the President in the field of foreign policy" was simply wrong.[48] Precisely *because* federal judges enjoy life tenure and salary independence and owe nothing to those who appointed them, it is their business to say what the law is in foreign affairs. In *Ramirez v. Weinberger,* then-Judge Scalia protested a federal court decision restraining American military activities in Honduras. No "special charter," he argued, authorizes judges to keep the executive in line in foreign affairs.[49] Judge Malcolm Wilkey, a once and future executive branch official, answered that "the Judiciary does operate under a '*special* charter' to help preserve the fundamental rights of this nation's citizens. That charter is commonly known as the United States Constitution."[50]

GLOBALISM AND CONSTITUTIONALISM

In closing, we must answer one final question: Can America's globalism and constitutionalism be reconciled? On this point, commentators again align on the left and the right. Leftist critics of the Iran-contra affair, typified by Professor Jules Lobel, argue that our constitutional scheme is inconsistent with aggressive American assertions of international power. To save our constitutionalism, they aver, we must abandon a foreign policy of activist interventionism and scale back expectations that America can function as a dominant world power in a posthegemonic age.[51] Critics on the right, in contrast, argue that to preserve our activist foreign policy, we must revise constitutionalism, abandoning the *Youngstown* vision in favor of *Curtiss-Wright*.[52] Yet because many of these same critics also espouse the constitutional jurisprudence of original intent, they are forced to engage in revisionist history to contend that the Framers did not originally draft the Constitution to promote *congressional* dominance in foreign affairs.[53]

In short, critics on the left declare that the world is not too unsafe for constitutional democracy, but only as long as we renounce our desires to control the world. Critics on the right agree that constitutional democracy can survive in a dangerous world, but only as long as "democracy" is redefined to mean government by the president.[54] The underlying unity between these views rests in a mutual desire to impose a substantive vision upon either constitutionalism or globalism. Those on the left would resolve the tension between the two by imposing their substantive foreign-policy views on global strategy; those on the right would resolve the dilemma by imposing their substantive political views upon constitutional interpretation.

Both of these approaches, I would argue, are doomed to failure. Although the proponents of each view claim to be sensitive to underlying political realities, both groups acknowledge only the political realities that appeal to them. Those on the left ignore the international political realities that drive America to adopt activist positions even in a posthegemonic age. As argued in chapter 5, the United States cannot simply renounce activism in an international regime in which it is an engaged (and in nearly all senses, the leading) global participant. Similarly, those on the right ignore the domestic political realities that make Congress a political partner in nearly all phases of foreign-policy making. As we have seen, the president may hope to run foreign policy by himself. But sooner or later, Congress's power over the purse, its textual role in treaty making and appointments, and its constitutional authority over the military and commerce, will compel its inclusion in the decision-making process.

Moreover, those on the right err when they conclude that in the late twentieth century, an executive monopoly would somehow render our foreign policy more democratic than a policy made through the traditional decision-making process of balanced institutional participation.

Although the president and vice-president are now essentially popularly elected, they are the only two members of the executive branch who are, and even they do not face reelection during their second terms. Members of Congress, by contrast, are perennially subject to reelection and are at least as responsive to the popular will. Since the framing of the Constitution, dramatic expansions of the right to suffrage, the direct election of senators, and the diminution of the electoral college have combined to make our republic more, not less, democratic.[55] At this moment of greatest public participation in the political process, it would be ironic if advocates of *Curtiss-Wright* could use arguments about democracy to justify further concentrating the nation's powers in foreign affairs in the hands of a single individual.

If these substantive approaches cannot succeed in reconciling constitutionalism and globalism, why should a national security charter succeed? The answer, I would argue, is that it imposes no substantive view, but rather embodies a *procedural* notion that already lies at the heart of our National Security Constitution—the principle of balanced institutional participation. That principle leaves it not to the president or Congress alone, but to the three branches acting together to construct a lawful global strategy for the posthegemonic age.

What the Iran-contra affair revealed are defects in our *process* of national security decision making. In too many instances, that process has degenerated into one in which the president (or his people) acts, Congress reacts belatedly (if at all), and the courts validate or defer. Had we any assurance that our presidents would always be omniscient, such a system might form the optimal decision-making structure for American foreign policy. However, as both Vietnam and the Iran-contra affair have so starkly taught us, the president is too rarely omniscient. It was precisely to avoid entrusting too much power to the president that the Framers chose not to vest all decision-making power in a single branch. In both foreign and domestic affairs, they created the same constitutional process based on separated institutions sharing powers.

In constructing this process, the Framers willingly sacrificed speed, secrecy, and efficiency. But as Justice Brandeis explained, "[t]he doctrine of separation of powers was adopted by the Convention of 1787, not to promote efficiency but to preclude the exercise of arbitrary power."[56] By knowingly trading losses in efficiency, the Framers opted for gains in interbranch consultation, participatory decision making, and protection against presidents who are not omniscient, but evil, foolish, or inattentive.

To preserve a constitutional process of national security decision making in the years ahead, I have argued that we should continue to preserve the original concept of shared power that underlies the National Security Constitution. Staying true to that concept need not, however, require that we remain wedded to any particular conception of it.[57] On the contrary, what history reveals is that we need a better process for *incrementally amending* the National Security Constitution that remains faithful to its original concept, yet flexible enough to respond to fast-moving times. That external events may require us to reform the National Security Constitution nowhere entails that that Constitution be reformed solely in accordance with executive practice, for that process inevitably places the job of rewriting the Constitution in the president's hands alone. I have argued that a more wise and enduring method of constitutional reform would be to grant that task to all three branches working together—to a Congress that enacts framework statutes in realms of constitutionally shared powers; to a president who construes those statutes by executing (or challenging) them; and to a judiciary that interprets those statutes by determining their constitutionality, ratifying some executive actions taken under them, and questioning others.

The Framers never purported to resolve all questions of constitutional responsibility in foreign affairs. Certainly, they did not consider how institutional authority would be specifically allocated in a nuclear age. If, as some have argued, a National Security Constitution based on the principle of checks and balances is truly unworkable in a nuclear age, they are welcome to propose its formal amendment.[58] But were we to undertake such a prodigious task, we would soon discover the impossibility of resolving for all time how zones of substantive responsibility for foreign affairs should be allocated among the branches. Given the difficulties of obtaining formal constitutional amendment, our more modest goal should not be to freeze any particular allocation of institutional power into a statute, but rather, to create a dynamic legal process that will allow our postimperial National Security Constitution to evolve over time. By supplementing executive action with both congressional role delineation and judicial guidance, that process would be flexible enough to respond to unforeseen world events while remaining true to the Founders' constitutional concept of balanced institutional participation.

Such a process would accept many political, ideological, and economic views of what our foreign policy should be. It would operate equally well with a Republican Congress and a Democratic president, an interventionist president and an isolationist Congress, a free-trading president and a protectionist Congress as with any other combination. In short, our National Security Constitution, freshly embodied in a national security charter, could accommodate many policy visions within a single constitutional framework that viewed the foreign affairs power as a power shared.

As one appellate court recently recognized, "[t]he world has changed since 1787. It is smaller than it once was. . . . Yet, the world has not changed so dramatically that we can no longer abide by the provisions of our Constitution."[59] The release of the Iran-contra committees' report should have marked the beginning, not the end, of Congress's efforts to deal with the constitutional crisis exposed by the Iran-contra affair. As Justice Jackson suggested in his concurring opinion in *Youngstown,* "[a] crisis that challenges the President equally, or perhaps primarily, challenges Congress. . . . We may say that power to legislate . . . belongs in the hands of Congress, but only Congress itself can prevent power from slipping through its fingers."[60]

The Iran-contra affair has started the pendulum of foreign-policy-making power swinging back to Congress for the first time since Vietnam. By so doing, it has brought the National Security Constitution to yet another turning point in its remarkable two-hundred-year history. Neither Congress nor the president should miss this rare opportunity to consider broadly how to remake our National Security Constitution for the posthegemonic age. The undertaking is formidable and the time already late. But if we do not learn the lessons of the Iran-contra affair, surely we will be condemned to relive it.

Notes

INTRODUCTION

1. Roberts, "Washington in Transition; Reagan's Final Rating Is Best of any President Since 40's," N.Y. Times, Jan. 18, 1989, at A1, col. 4. North received a three-year suspended sentence, two years of probation, $150,000 in fines, and an order to perform hundreds of hours of community service, but was spared prison. See Johnston, "North, Spared Prison, Gets $150,000 Fine and Probation for His Iran-Contra Crimes," N.Y. Times, July 6, 1989, at A1, col. 6.
2. Other Iran-contra investigators were narrowly denied key posts in the new foreign-policy-making order. Although President Bush originally nominated Tower commission chairman John Tower as secretary of defense, Tower was denied confirmation by Senate opposition led by Sam Nunn of Georgia, another prominent Senate Iran-Contra Committee member. Senator Mitchell won the majority leadership by defeating a field that included Senator Inouye, the chairman of the Senate's Iran-contra committee.
3. "It is the conclusion of these Committees that the Iran-Contra Affair resulted from the failure of *individuals* to observe the law, not from deficiencies in existing law or in our system of governance" (emphasis added). House Select Comm. to Investigate Covert Arms Transactions with Iran and Senate Select Comm. on Secret Military Assistance to Iran and the Nicaraguan Opposition, *Report of the Congressional Comms. Investigating the Iran-Contra Affair,* 100th Cong., 1st Sess., S. Rept. 216, H. Rept. 433, 423 (1987) [hereinafter *Iran-Contra Report*]. See, also, President's Special Review Board, *The Tower Commission Report* 4 (N.Y. Times ed. 1987) [hereinafter *Tower Report*] ("The problems we examined in the case of Iran/Contra caused us deep concern. But their solution does not lie in revamping the National Security Council system").
4. See, *e.g.,* the remarks of Arthur Liman, chief counsel of the Senate Iran-Contra Committee: "I saw these hearings, in a way, as a birthday present for the Constitution . . . the Constitution has built into it a kind of immune system like that of the

human body. When an alien concept enters, we expel it. The Iran-contra hearings were part of the process of disgorging this alien concept." Liman, "The Iran-Contra Hearings: From the Inside," *Yale Law Report* (Fall 1987):72.

5. *Iran-Contra Report, supra* note 3, at 423.

6. See, *e.g., Iran-Contra Report, supra* note 3, at 665 (supplemental views of Senator Hatch). The minority conceded that mistakes had been made during the affair, but concluded "that the underlying cause of the Iran-Contra Affair had to do with people rather than with laws." *Id.* at 583 (minority report).

7. See, *e.g.,* O. North, *Taking the Stand: The Testimony of Lieutenant Colonel Oliver L. North* 266 (1987); editorial, "The $12 Million Misunderstanding," Wall St. J., Jan. 6, 1989, at A10, col. 1.

8. *Iran-Contra Report, supra* note 3, at 583 (minority report).

9. The first generation of Iran-contra pathologies, falling (in Theodore Draper's words) "somewhere between news and history," include W. Cohen & G. Mitchell, *Men of Zeal: A Candid Inside Story of the Iran-Contra Hearings* (1988); B. Bradlee, *Guts and Glory: The Rise and Fall of Oliver North* (1988); M. Ledeen, *Perilous Statecraft: An Insider's Account of the Iran-Contra Affair* (1988); J. Mayer & D. McManus, *Landslide: The Unmaking of the President, 1984–1988* (1988); C. Menges, *Inside the National Security Council: The True Story of the Making and Unmaking of Reagan's Foreign Policy* (1988); H. Smith, *The Power Game: How Washington Works* 616–37 (1988); S. Segev, *The Iranian Triangle: The Untold Story of Israel's Role in the Iran-Contra Affair* (1988). For a cogent review of many of these, see Draper, "Rewriting the Iran-Contra Story," *N.Y. Rev. Bks.* (Jan. 19, 1989):38–45.

10. The phrase is Richard Neustadt's. See R. Neustadt, *Presidential Power: The Politics of Leadership with Reflections on Johnson and Nixon* 101 (rev. ed. 1976). As I argue in chapter 3, however, the idea dates back to Alexander Hamilton. See *The Federalist* No. 75, at 488 (A. Hamilton) (Modern Library ed. 1937) ("It must indeed be clear to a demonstration that the joint possession of the [treaty] power . . . by the President and Senate, would afford a greater prospect of security, than the separate possession of it by either of them").

11. Casper, "Constitutional Constraints on the Conduct of Foreign and Defense Policy: A Nonjudicial Model," 43 *U. Chi. L. Rev.* 463, 482 (1976).

12. 50 U.S.C. §§ 401–405 (1982).

13. Youngstown Sheet & Tube Co. v. Sawyer, 343 U.S. 579, 635 (1952) (Jackson, J., concurring).

14. See Destler, "The Presidency: The Autonomy Problem," in *Mr. Madison's Constitution and the Twenty-first Century: A Report from the Williamsburg Conference 1988* 30 (1988) (national security laws should "not seek to establish Congressional control over presidents, but rather to institutionalize the dialectic between presidential policy purpose and democratic process"); *id.* at 33 (We must "begin to think of presidential autonomy as a central constitutional problem").

15. Morgenthau, "Conduct of American Foreign Policy," in *The President: Roles and Powers* 314, 319 (D. Haight & L. Johnston eds. 1965).

16. "Remarks and a Question-and-Answer Session with Students and Guests of the University of Virginia in Charlottesville, Virginia," 24 *Weekly Comp. Pres. Doc.* 1628, 1634 (Dec. 16, 1988).
17. Myers v. United States, 272 U.S. 52, 293 (1926) (Brandeis, J., dissenting).

CHAPTER I: HOW THE IRAN-CONTRA INVESTIGATORS FAILED

1. "[T]he ultimate responsibility for the events in the Iran-Contra Affair must rest with the President." House Select Comm. to Investigate Covert Arms Transactions with Iran and Senate Select Comm. on Secret Military Assistance to Iran and the Nicaraguan Opposition, *Report of the Congressional Comms. Investigating the Iran-Contra Affair,* 100th Cong., 1st Sess., S. Rept. 216, H. Rept. 433, 21 (1987) [hereinafter *Iran-Contra Report*].
2. See editorial, "This Is Watergate," *New Republic* (Mar. 16, 1987): 7; Kurland, "Comment on Schlesinger," 47 *Md. L. Rev.* 75, 81 (1987) ("the constitutional problem in the Iran-Contra fiasco is essentially not different from the Watergate fiasco"); Sharpe, "The Real Cause of Irangate," 68 *Foreign Pol'y* 19, 24 (1987) (Watergate arose from Nixon White House efforts to keep the bombing of Cambodia secret from the public, Congress, and other parts of executive branch). For a popular historical account of Watergate, see, generally, B. Woodward & C. Bernstein, *All the President's Men* (1974). For a factual account of Contragate, see, generally, *Iran-Contra Report, supra* note 1, at 3–22.
3. See, *e.g., Testimony of Richard V. Secord: Joint Hearings before the House Select Comm. to Investigate Covert Arms Transactions with Iran and the Senate Select Comm. on Secret Military Assistance to Iran and the Nicaraguan Opposition,* 100th Cong., 1st Sess. 21 (1987) (Statement of Rep. Peter W. Rodino, Jr.) [hereinafter *Iran-Contra Hearings*] ("The question which has been asked most frequently since the November disclosures of the Iran-Contra affair has been is this another Watergate").
4. See *Iran-Contra Report, supra* note 1, at 387–88 (statements of witnesses Poindexter and North).
5. In addition to the three investigative bodies discussed in text, three other legislative bodies conducted avowedly preliminary inquiries into the affair. The House and Senate Select Committees on Intelligence separately investigated the affair in November 1986, but only the Senate committee made its report public. See Senate Select Comm. on Intelligence, *Preliminary Inquiry into the Sale of Arms to Iran and Possible Diversion of Funds to the Nicaraguan Resistance,* 100th Cong., 1st Sess., S. Rept. 7 (1987). The House Foreign Affairs Committee contemporaneously held both closed and open hearings on the matter. See *The Foreign Policy Implications of Arms Sales to Iran and the Contra Connection: Hearings before the House Comm. on Foreign Affairs,* 99th Cong., 2d Sess. (1986).
6. For the executive order creating the Tower commission, see § 2, Exec. Order No. 12,575, 51 Fed. Reg. 43,718 (1986). The commission was chaired by former senator John Tower and included former senator and Secretary of State Edmund

Muskie and former (and now current) National Security Assistant Brent Scowcroft. For the resolutions creating the House and Senate select committees, see H.R. Res. 12, 100th Cong., 1st Sess. (1987), *reprinted in Iran-Contra Hearings, supra* note 3, at 607; S. Res. 23, 100th Cong., 1st Sess., 133 *Cong. Rec.* S89 (daily ed. Jan. 6, 1987), *reprinted in Iran-Contra Hearings, supra* note 3, at 619. Former American Bar Association president and Judge Lawrence Walsh was appointed independent counsel by the United States Court of Appeals for the District of Columbia Circuit, Independent Counsel Division, pursuant to the independent counsel provisions of the Ethics in Government Act, 28 U.S.C. § 592(c)(1) (1982) and based upon the statutory application of Attorney General Edwin Meese. See Lardner & Kurtz, "Iran Inquiry Counsel Selected," Wash. Post, Dec. 20, 1986, at A1, col. 4.

7. See Freiwald, "Iran-Contra: Costs and Questions: Probe Tab $40 Million . . . and Rising," Legal Times, Feb. 20, 1989, at 1 ("conservatively" estimating costs to date of Iran-contra investigations at $42.487 million); "Iran-Contra probe cost soars past $47 million," New Haven Reg., Nov. 3, 1989, at 59, col. 3 ("47.5 million and still rising").

8. The commission was originally directed to submit its report by Feb. 1, 1987, but received two extensions of time to complete its work, one simply to digest newly discovered notes from the NSC's computer system. See "Excerpts from the Tower Commission's News Conference Opening Statements," N.Y. Times, Feb. 27, 1987, at A8, col. 2 (statement by Edmund Muskie); J. Mayer & D. McManus, *Landslide: The Unmaking of the President, 1984-1988* 377 (1988).

9. See "Cover Letter from President's Special Review Board to The Honorable Ronald W. Reagan," in President's Special Review Board, *The Tower Commission Report* i (N.Y. Times ed. 1987) [hereinafter *Tower Report*]; Apple, "Introduction," *id.* at xi–xii. The commission had a staff of 23, including six attorneys. See *id.* at 521; Rasky, "Those Who Labored on the Report," N.Y. Times, Mar. 3, 1987, at A20, col. 4.

10. See Rasky, "How the Tower Inquiry Stumbled on Aid Effort," N.Y. Times, Feb. 27, 1987, at A11, col. 1 (statement of John Tower).

11. Walcott & Pasztor, "Tower Panel Blames Iran-Contra Debacles on Reagan, Cites Forgotten Decisions, Ignorance of Aides' Actions," Wall St. J., Feb. 27, 1987, at 3, col. 3; M. Ledeen, *Perilous Statecraft: An Insider's Account of the Iran-Contra Affair* 278–79 (1988) (charging that the report was skewed in favor of former National Security Assistant Robert McFarlane).

12. Exec. Order No. 12,575, 51 Fed. Reg. 43,718, § 2(a) (1986) (emphasis added).

13. See "Cover Letter from President's Special Review Board to The Honorable Ronald W. Reagan," *Tower Report, supra* note 9, at i; Rosenbaum, "Panel's Plans: Subpoenas and Immunity Will Be Used to Invigorate Inquiry," N.Y. Times, Feb. 27, 1987, at A12, col. 5 (statement by Arthur L. Liman, Senate Iran-Contra Committee counsel, that the congressional committees "intended to use the Tower commission's work in much the same way a prosecutor uses a pre-trial

examination, as the foundation for further inquiry"); "Excerpts from the Tower Commission's News Conference, Opening Statements," N.Y. Times, Feb. 27, 1987, at A8, col. 1 (statement of John Tower) ("I emphasize that it was not our function to make judgments on criminal culpability").

14. "Excerpts from the Tower Commission's News Conference, Opening Statements," N.Y. Times, Feb. 27, 1987, at A8, col. 1 (statement of John Tower); *id.* at col. 4 ("This was an aberration, the Iran-contra affair").

15. *Id.* at col. 2 (statement of Brent Scowcroft) ("It was not that the structure was faulty. It is that the structure was not used").

16. *Tower Report, supra* note 9, at 98–99 (emphasis added); *id.* at 94 (refusing to endorse "the inflexibility of a legislative restriction").

17. *Id.* at 98 (emphasis added).

18. See *id.* at 94–95. The commission reasoned that "if the National Security Advisor were to become a position subject to confirmation, it could induce the President to turn to other internal staff or to people outside government to play that role." *Id.* at 95.

19. *Compare Iran-Contra Report, supra* note 1, at 427 (majority report) *with Tower Report, supra* note 9, at 97–98. For a discussion of the value of interagency review, see chapter 7, *infra.* For further criticism of the joint intelligence committee proposal, see Johnson & Glennon, "Combining House, Senate intelligence committees a simple-minded idea," Atlanta Constitution, Oct. 21, 1987. But see "Iran Arms and *Contra* Aid Controversy: Statement by the Assistant to the President for Press Relations on the Report of the Congressional Investigating Committees," 23 *Weekly Comp. Pres. Doc.* 1344 (Nov. 18, 1987); *Iran-Contra Report, supra* note 1, at 583 (minority report) (both supporting the single committee proposal).

20. See *Tower Report, supra* note 9, at xviii ("The N.S.C. system will not work unless the President makes it work"); *id.* at 28–29 (President claimed first that he had approved August 1985 arms sale to Israel, then that he had not, and finally that he could not remember).

21. M. Ledeen, *supra* note 11, at 277.

22. R. Falk, *Revolutionaries and Functionaries: The Dual Face of Terrorism* 128 (1988). See, also, editorial, "Government by Black Boxes," N.Y. Times, Feb. 13, 1989, at A20, col. 1 (criticizing presidential commission process).

23. See, *e.g.,* Tower, "Congress versus the President: The Formulation and Implementation of American Foreign Policy," 60 *Foreign Aff.* 229 (1981/82) (criticizing congressional intervention in foreign policy making).

24. *Compare Tower Report, supra* note 9, at 95 *with* Weinraub, "Bush Backs Plan to Enhance Role of Security Staff," N.Y. Times, Feb. 2, 1989, at A1, col. 4; "NSC change," *Economist* (Feb. 11, 1989): 21 (announcing President Bush's directive that Scowcroft would chair a foreign policy committee of cabinet members, including the secretaries of state and defense and that his deputy would chair a "deputies committee," including the vice chairman of the Joint Chiefs of Staff and the deputy director of the CIA).

25. Speech by John Nields, Jr., chief counsel, House Select Committee, Iran-Contra Hearings, at Yale Law School (April 7, 1988) (on file with author). For accounts of the public value of the hearings, as seen by its key participants, see W. Cohen & G. Mitchell, *Men of Zeal: A Candid Inside Story of the Iran-Contra Hearings* (1988) and the remarks of Arthur L. Liman, the chief counsel of the Senate Iran-Contra Committee, in "The Iran-Contra Hearings: From the Inside," *Yale Law Report* (Fall 1987):70.

26. *Compare Iran-Contra Report, supra* note 1, at 20–22 ("Who was responsible for the Iran-Contra Affair?") *with id.* at 423–27 (majority report); *id.* at 583–85 (minority report) (legislative recommendations).

27. See, generally, K. Shepsle, *The Giant Jigsaw Puzzle: Democratic Committee Assignments in the Modern House* (1978); Denzau & Mackay, "Gatekeeping and Monopoly Power of Committees: An Analysis of Sincere and Sophisticated Behavior," 27 *Am. J. Pol. Sci.* 740 (1983). *Cf.* Weingast & Marshall, "The Industrial Organization of Congress; or, Why Legislatures, Like Firms, Are Not Organized as Markets," 96 *J. Pol. Econ.* 132, 143–48 (1988) (permanent committee system restricts ability of legislators to form coalitions on issues that transcend committee boundaries).

28. "Much Ado About Not Much: An Inquiry out of Questions," *Insight* (Aug. 10, 1987):14.

29. See Madison, "Turf Wars, Long Waits May Defuse Iran Probe," 19 *Nat'l J.* 29, 30 (1987) (committee included chairs of the House Armed Services, Foreign Affairs, Government Operations, Intelligence, and Judiciary committees); see, also, speech by John Nields, Jr., *supra* note 25.

30. See Engelberg & Rosenbaum, "What the Iran-Contra Committees Wish They Had Done Differently," N.Y. Times, Nov. 20, 1987, at A1, col. 3 & A6, col. 1; J. Grabow, *Congressional Investigations: Law and Practice* 56–57 (1988).

31. See Madison, "Iran: Act Two," 19 *Nat'l J.* 1050, 1053–54 (1987). See the Maui News, Feb. 19, 1988, at A1, cols. 4–5 (interview with Arthur Liman, chief counsel of Senate Select Committee) (explaining why Liman led questioning of Vice Adm. John Poindexter, while John Nields, chief counsel of House Select Committee, questioned Lt. Col. Oliver North). *Compare* O. North, *Taking the Stand: The Testimony of Lieutenant Colonel Oliver L. North* 10–260 (1987) (aggressive cross-examination of North by chief House counsel) *with* Liman, *supra* note 25, at 70 ("[M]y role [in cross-examining North] was very different from the one I was accustomed to as a trial lawyer. . . . My role, as I saw it, was . . . to try to avoid . . . mak[ing] this into a classic case of lawyer versus hostile witness").

32. *Compare* D. Mayhew, *Congress: The Electoral Connection* 52–61 (1974) (defining credit-claiming as a prime congressional incentive) *with Iran-Contra Report, supra* note 1, at 438 (minority report) (decrying "'j'accuse' atmosphere with which witnesses were confronted . . . as Members used the witnesses as objects for lecturing the cameras").

33. See the Maui News, *supra* note 31, at A1, col. 4 (interview with Arthur Liman, chief counsel of Senate Select Committee) ("Members of Congress got so jumpy during Olliemania, Liman said, that Liman's questioning of North was cut short by several days").

34. See, *e.g.*, O. North, *supra* note 31, at 7–10 (Senate committee chairman's compulsion of testimony pursuant to committee subpoenas over North's Fifth Amendment objection). *Cf.* J. Grabow, *supra* note 30, at 262–63 (1988) (House chairman overruling witness's evidentiary objection on the ground that the question goes to a legislative and not a prosecutorial purpose).

35. O. North, *supra* note 31, at 264. For a description of North's testimonial success, see Hunt, "Beyond the Ollie Show," Wall St. J., July 15, 1987, at 28, col. 3.

36. R. Keeton, *Trial Tactics and Methods* 95 (2d ed. 1973).

37. J. Grabow, *supra* note 30, at 62 n.45. The congressional use immunity statute, 18 U.S.C. § 6002 (1982), authorizes Congress to compel a witness's testimony at a "proceeding before . . . either House of Congress . . . or a committee . . . of either House." Because it was ambiguous whether congressional depositions such as North's would constitute a "proceeding" if conducted by staff, the committees required a quorum of two members to be present at most key depositions. See J. Grabow, *supra* note 30, at 109–10 n.143. The committees' final report recommended that the immunity statute be amended to repair this ambiguity. See *Iran-Contra Report, supra* note 1, at 426.

38. J. Grabow, *supra* note 30, at 62; see, also, 28 U.S.C.A. § 1365(a) (1989) (civil contempt in Senate actions) ("This section shall not apply to an action . . . to prevent a threatened refusal to comply with, any . . . order issued to an officer or employee of the Federal Government acting within his official capacity").

39. J. Grabow, *supra* note 30, at 62; *Iran-Contra Report, supra* note 1, at 687–88.

40. See, *e.g.*, *Iran-Contra Hearings, supra* note 3, at 6 (introductory statement of Rep. Lee H. Hamilton) ("What was the extent of the President's knowledge and involvement?"); *id.* at 29 (introductory statement of Sen. Orrin G. Hatch) ("In my mind, there are two questions for us to try to answer: What did the President know? And where did the money go? Almost everything else centers on those two questions").

41. See, *e.g.*, *Iran-Contra Report, supra* note 1, at 659 (supplemental views of Sen. James A. McClure); *id.* at 661 (additional views of Rep. William S. Broomfield).

42. See *Iran-Contra Report, supra* note 1, at 437 (minority report).

43. See Liman, *supra* note 25, at 70 ("The only issue in Watergate . . . was, who was involved? In particular, what was the president's involvement? No one tried to justify the burglary. It was accepted that it was wrong and that if the president or anyone else participated . . . they would have to bear the consequences").

44. Elliott, "Regulating the Deficit After *Bowsher v. Synar,*" 4 *Yale J. on Reg.* 317, 350 (1987) (discussing Bruce Ackerman's theory of "constitutional moments").

45. *Compare Iran-Contra Report, supra* note 1, at 388, 391 (majority report) *with id.* at 437, 450 (minority report).
46. *Iran-Contra Report, supra* note 1, at 423–27 (listing twenty-seven recommendations). In my judgment, many of the legislative proposals contained in the Iran-contra committees' majority report are worthwhile. Chapter 7 suggests how some of those recommendations may be incorporated into the legislative package that I would propose.
47. *Iran-Contra Report, supra* note 1, at 423 (majority report).
48. See *id.* at 583–85 (minority report).
49. *Compare Iran-Contra Report, supra* note 1, at 426 *with* Johnson, "Mentors Help to Shape General Powell's Career," N.Y. Times, Sept. 16, 1988, at A20, col. 1.
50. See, generally, *Congress Investigates: 1792–1974* (A. Schlesinger & R. Bruns, eds. 1975) (giving examples of similar investigations).
51. See, *e.g.*, Madison, "A Puzzle That's Missing Some Pieces," 19 *Nat'l J.* 2982, 2983 (1987) (remarks of Senator Inouye) (it is "time to put the Iran-contra affair behind us"); New Haven Reg., Mar. 3, 1988, at 2, cols. 4–5 (remarks of Chief Counsel of Senate Iran-Contra Committee Arthur Liman) ("We can't be preoccupied with one scandal for the rest of our lives").
52. United States v. Poindexter, 109 S. Ct. 1638 (1989); Thornburgh v. Walsh, No. A-643 (vacated and dismissed Feb. 16, 1989); North v. Walsh, 108 S. Ct. 753 (1988).
53. "Iran Arms and Contra Aid Controversy: Statement by the President on the Appointment of an Independent Counsel," 22 *Weekly Comp. Pres. Doc.* 1658 (1986) (remarks of President Reagan) ("Mr. Walsh has my promise of complete cooperation").
54. See Brief on Behalf of Amicus Curiae United States in Nos. 87-5261, 87-5264, and 87-5265, In re Sealed Case (Morrison v. Olson), 838 F.2d 476 (D.C. Cir. 1987), *rev'd,* 108 S. Ct. 2597 (1988).
55. See Morrison v. Olson, 108 S. Ct. 2597 (1988) (upholding statute); In re Sealed Case (North), 829 F.2d 50 (D.C. Cir. 1987), *cert. denied sub nom.* North v. Walsh, 108 S. Ct. 753 (1988) (upholding parallel appointment). The Justice Department offered parallel appointments to all four independent counsels who were contemporaneously conducting investigations. Along with Walsh, James McKay, who was investigating the conduct of former Attorney General Meese and former Reagan adviser Lyn Nofziger in the Wedtech affair, accepted a parallel appointment. Alexia Morrison and Whitney North Seymour, who were investigating Theodore Olson and Michael Deaver, respectively, declined the appointments. It was thus in the context of Olson's case, rather than North's, that the constitutionality of the independent counsel statute was ultimately resolved.
56. See Pelham, "North Jury Search Raises Question of 'Triability,'" Legal Times, Feb. 6, 1989, at 6, col. 4; *Iran-Contra Report, supra* note 1, at 687 (describing Walsh's opposition to immunity grant for North). Immunity problems had forced the Watergate special prosecutors to drop the prosecution of one congressionally

immunized witness, Gordon Strachan. John Dean, another immunized witness, pleaded guilty. See Strachan, "Self-Incrimination, Immunity, and Watergate," 56 *Tex. L. Rev.* 791 (1978).

57. See United States v. Poindexter, 698 F. Supp. 300, 312–13 (D.D.C. 1988) ("Prosecuting personnel were sealed off from exposure to the immunized testimony itself and publicity concerning it. Daily newspaper clippings and transcripts of testimony before the Select Committees were redacted by nonprosecuting 'tainted' personnel to avoid direct and explicit references to immunized testimony. Prosecutors, and those immediately associated with them, were confined to reading these redacted materials. In addition, they were instructed to shut off television or radio broadcasts that even approached discussion of the immunized testimony"); see, also, Rosenbaum, "Immunity Decision: A Prosecutor's Nightmare," N.Y. Times, June 20, 1988, at B6, col. 3 (recounting other costs to prosecution of congressionally granted immunity).

58. Nearly all of the witnesses who testified before the grand jury had been exposed to the defendants' compelled congressional testimony and potentially altered their own testimony in light of it. The ACLU argued that the effect was equivalent to a prosecutor calling a defendant to the witness stand at the start of trial and forcing him to testify about alleged criminal events with all of the prosecution witnesses present. See Halperin, "Why the ACLU is Defending North," *First Principles* (Sept. 1988):11.

59. See United States v. Poindexter, 859 F.2d 216, 219 (D.C. Cir. 1988) (per curiam) (denying interlocutory appeal but noting that defendants "may ultimately be correct in their assertion that if the grand jury's probable cause determination was 'tainted' by the use of immunized testimony, dismissal of the indictment will be required to remedy the harm"), *cert. denied,* 109 S. Ct. 1638 (1989).

60. United States v. Poindexter, et al., No. 88-0080, Order (D.D.C. June 8, 1988).

61. See Pasztor, "Federal Judge Orders Separate Trials for Four Charged in Iran-Contra Case," Wall St. J., June 9, 1988, at 22, col. 4 (remarks of former senior Justice Department prosecutor).

62. Wines, "Defense Tactics Hinted in North Jury Selection," N.Y. Times, Feb. 6, 1989, at A13, col. 5; "Judge Rules North Jury Will Not be Sequestered," New Haven Reg., Feb. 7, 1989, at 24, col. 2 (statement of Judge Gesell to North's attorney) ("I understand your position—everybody is disqualified").

63. Wines, "Selection of Jury Begins for North," N.Y. Times, Feb. 1, 1989, at A12, col.1; "North Judge Questions if Impartial Jury Possible," New Haven Reg., Feb. 1, 1989, at 1, col. 6.

64. See, *e.g.,* Dellinger, "Case Closed," *New Republic* (Jan. 9 & 16, 1989):15 ("At its core, *United States* v. *North* is an embezzlement case").

65. See Indictment, United States v. Poindexter, No. 88-0080 (D.D.C. returned by grand jury Mar. 16, 1988), Count 1 (conspiracy to defraud the United States); *id.,* Count 2 (unauthorized embezzlement and conversion of valuable items belonging to the United States) [hereinafter Indictment]; Record at 61, United States v.

Poindexter, No. 88-0080 (D.D.C. June 8, 1988) (argument of Independent Counsel Walsh) (the conspiracy count of the indictment "really comes down to this illegal use of government personnel and assets after Congress has told [the co-conspirators] not to").

66. See Indictment, *supra* note 65, Counts 4, 9, 13 (obstruction of Congress by North), Counts 5–7 (false statements to Congress by North), Counts 8, 10 (obstruction of Congress by Poindexter), Counts 11–12 (false statements to Congress by Poindexter); Counts 14–16 (charging North with obstruction, false statements, and document alteration during attorney general's inquiry); Counts 17–20 (receipt, offer, payment, and conspiracy by Secord and Hakim to pay North illegal gratuity), Count 21 (obstruction of justice by North regarding security system), Count 22 (conversion of travelers' checks by North), Count 23 (conspiracy to defraud United States, Treasury, and IRS).

67. See United States v. North, 698 F. Supp. 322, 324 (D.D.C. 1988). Some of North's defenders, including President Reagan, also suggested that no theft had occurred because the United States government had received the full, legally required payment for the arms. See, *e.g.*, Shenon, "North, Poindexter and Two Others Indicted on Iran-Contra Fraud and Theft Charges," N.Y. Times, Mar. 17, 1988, at D27, col. 5 (remarks of President Reagan). This defense misses the point, however. An employee who sells his boss's property worth $100 for $500 is still guilty of embezzlement even if he repays his boss the full $100 and gives the balance to charity. In the same way, the profits of the Iranian arms transaction belonged to the Treasury; North possessed no legal authority to divert them to other unauthorized uses.

68. See Defendant's Pretrial Motion No. 40, United States v. North, No. 88-0080-02 (D.D.C. filed Oct. 11, 1988).

69. See Defendant's Pretrial Motion No. 39, United States v. North, No. 88-0080-02 (D.D.C. filed Oct. 11, 1988). For the text of the Boland amendments, see 133 *Cong. Rec.* H4982-87 (daily ed. June 15, 1987).

70. See O. North, *supra* note 31, at 256. North's defenders echoed this justification. See, *e.g., Iran-Contra Report, supra* note 1, at 659 (remarks of Sen. James A. McClure)("Would you lie to save the life of your wife or child?").

71. See Memorandum and Order re Defendant North's Motions to Dismiss Nos. 39–42, 44–46, 49, at 8, 1988 U.S. Dist. LEXIS 16,024, at 9 (D.D.C. Nov. 29, 1988) ("Not every matter touching on foreign affairs is barred [from judicial examination] by the political question doctrine"); United States v. Poindexter, 1989 U.S. Dist. LEXIS 12,572, 16–19 (D.D.C. Oct. 24, 1989).

72. 1988 U.S. Dist. LEXIS 16,024, 10–12.

73. See Memorandum and Order re Defendant North's Motions to Dismiss Counts 5, 6, and 7, Charging North with Making False Statements to Congress 4, nn.3 & 6, 1988 U.S. Dist. LEXIS 16,023, 4–6 (D.D.C. Nov. 29, 1988) (emphasis added).

74. See Memorandum of Law of the United States Filed by the Department of Justice as *Amicus Curiae* with respect to the Independent Counsel's Opposition to the

Defendant's Motions to Dismiss or Limit Count One at 6, United States v. North, No. 88-0080-02 (D.D.C. filed Nov. 18, 1988) [hereinafter Justice Department Memorandum).

75. *Id.* at 4–6, 12, 18–19 (citations omitted).

76. See Independent Counsel's Memorandum of Points and Authorities in response to the Memorandum of Law Filed by the Department of Justice as *Amicus Curiae* with respect to the Independent Counsel's Opposition to the Defendant's Motion to Dismiss or Limit Count One at 4, 9, United States v. North, No. 88-0080-02 (D.D.C. filed Nov. 21, 1988) (emphasis added).

77. See Goldstein, "Conspiracy to Defraud the United States," 68 *Yale L.J.* 405 (1959).

78. See *Report of the Senate Committee on the Judiciary on the Classified Information Procedures Act,* 96th Cong., 2d Sess., S. Rept. 823, 4, *reprinted in* 1980 U.S. Code Cong. & Admin. News 4294, 4297 (statement of Philip Heymann, Assistant Attorney General, Criminal Division, U.S. Department of Justice).

79. Pub. L. No. 96-456, 94 Stat. 2025 (codified at 18 U.S.C. app. §§ 1–16 [1982]). For commentary on CIPA, see, generally, Note, "Government Secrets, Fair Trials, and the Classified Information Procedures Act," 98 *Yale L.J.* 427 (1988); Note, "Graymail: The Disclose or Dismiss Dilemma in Criminal Prosecutions," 31 *Case W. Res. L. Rev.* 84 (1980).

80. See, generally, Tamanaha, "A Critical Review of the Classified Information Procedures Act," 13 *Am. J. Crim. L.* 277 (1986).

81. See *Graymail Legislation, 1979: Hearings on H. 4736 before the Subcomm. on Legislation of the Permanent Select Comm. on Intelligence,* 96th Cong., 1st Sess. 106–07 (1979) (statement of Watergate Special Prosecutor Philip Lacovara) (arguing that prosecutors should resist such pressures because "on close examination much or most classified information is overclassified" and "its disclosure at trial, if necessary, would not present truly grave risks of jeopardizing our military security").

82. See CIPA § 5 Preclusion Memorandum and Order, 1988 U.S. Dist. LEXIS 16,022 (D.D.C. Dec. 12, 1988).

83. See Johnston, "U.S. Drops Part of Its Case Against Iran-Contra Figures," N.Y. Times, June 17, 1989, at A7, col. 4 (Poindexter and Secord); Johnston, "Case Dismissed in Contra Affair, Clearing Agent," N.Y. Times, Nov. 25, 1989, at A1, col. 1 (Joseph Fernandez case). See *infra* notes 86 & 107.

84. See Sealed Memorandum and Order re North's CIPA § 5 Notices (D.D.C. Jan. 19, 1989).

85. See Johnston, "Trial of North Stalled Again; Defense Moves for Dismissal," N.Y. Times, Mar. 1, 1989, at A1, col. 4 & A20, col. 1.

86. Memorandum and Order re Motion of Defendant North to Dismiss the Indictment for Prosecutorial Misconduct at 5 (D.D.C. Mar. 6, 1989). A similar situation later arose during Walsh's prosecution of former CIA station chief Joseph Fernandez. There, the Justice Department again blocked disclosure of classified information

regarding the location of CIA stations that had already been widely reported in the press, forcing dismissal of the case. See Pelham, "Walsh Clashes with Justice Department over Secrets," Legal Times, July 31, 1989, at 2, col. 1. See, also, Johnston, "Case Dismissed," *supra* note 83.

87. One cannot automatically infer from Walsh and Gesell's acquiescence, however, that the information was properly withheld. Walsh's options were limited even if he strongly disagreed with the president's decision to withhold disclosure. Had he either publicly challenged the president's decision or threatened to resign, he would have acted inconsistently with his statutory and judicial mandate to try the case to judgment. Similarly, Judge Gesell never heard argument on whether the withheld information was properly classified, reasoning that the forum for challenging such classification decisions should not be a criminal trial but a civil action under the Freedom of Information Act.

88. See Remarks of Attorney General Dick Thornburgh, *This Week with David Brinkley* (Jan. 8, 1989); Liman & Belnick, "Reagan, North and the Truth," N.Y. Times, Jan. 10, 1989, at A23, col. 4 ("A trial on the conspiracy and theft charges would be unlikely to add anything to the record established by the [Tower] commission . . . and the Congressional committees").

89. An inquisitorial congressional investigation is designed to unearth facts and to recommend legislation to ensure that past wrongs will not recur. A criminal trial asks the complementary question whether individuals who have participated in past wrongs should be punished because they have been proven guilty beyond a reasonable doubt. See *Iran-Contra Report, supra* note 1, at 19 ("The Committees make no determination as to whether any particular individual involved in the Iran-Contra Affair acted with criminal intent or was guilty of any crime. That is a matter for the Independent Counsel and the courts").

90. Memorandum of Points and Authorities in Support of the Motion of the President and the President-Elect to Quash the Defendant's Subpoenas, United States v. North, No. 88-0080-02, at 18, 22, 23 (D.D.C. filed Jan. 18, 1989). But see Rotunda, "Presidents and Ex-Presidents as Witnesses: A Brief Historical Footnote," 1975 *U. Ill. L.F.* 1, 9–10 ("The historical evidence shows that voluntary or involuntary submission to interrogation by a former President will not offend the separation of powers doctrine nor do lasting damage to the Office of the Presidency—even if the ex-President undergoes vigorous or hostile cross-examination. . . . When a President or ex-President had knowledge relating to colorable charges of executive misconduct, he has made his testimony available").

91. See Memorandum and Order re Motion of President Reagan to Quash the Defendant's subpoena ad testificandum, United States v. North, No. 88-0080-02, 1989 U.S. Dist. LEXIS 2903, 1 (D.D.C. Mar. 31, 1989); Order re Motion of the President and the President-Elect to Quash the Defendant's Subpoena, slip op. at 1–2 (D.D.C. Jan. 30, 1989) (quashing testimonial subpoena directed against President Bush for insufficient showing that he had specific information relevant and material to the charges and holding that "President Reagan shall remain subject to call on the [testimonial] subpoena previously

served"); *cf.* United States v. Poindexter, 1989 U.S. Dist. LEXIS 12,572 at 35–43 (D.D.C. Oct. 24, 1989) (holding that Poindexter would be entitled to "specific, relevant" documents within Reagan's custody because Poindexter, unlike North, met with Reagan "daily, frequently alone").

92. Motion of the Attorney General's Classified Information Procedures Act (CIPA) Designate to Compel Adherence to CIPA Procedures, United States v. North, No. 88-0080-02 (D.D.C. filed Feb. 8, 1989).

93. See Order Denying Stay at 2 (D.D.C. Feb. 9, 1989) ("The Attorney General's attempt to appeal is . . . frivolous"); United States v. North, No. 89-3021 (D.C. Cir. Feb. 9, 1989) (per curiam); United States v. North, No. 89-3021 (D.C. Cir. Feb. 10, 1989) (per curiam) (order denying emergency motion for reconsideration of motion for stay); Thornburgh v. Walsh, No. A-643 (Rehnquist, C.J.) (Feb. 12, 1989) (staying trial pending full Supreme Court consideration of motion); Thornburgh v. Walsh, No. A-643 (Rehnquist, C.J.) (Feb. 16, 1989) (vacating stay and dismissing application). Seven months later, the Fourth Circuit followed suit, ruling that the independent counsel, and not the attorney general, had exclusive authority to appeal from a CIPA ruling made before the trial of former CIA station chief Joseph Fernandez. See United States, United States v. Fernandez, 1989 U.S. App. LEXIS 15,037 (4th Cir. Sept. 29, 1989). See, also, *infra* note 107.

94. Memorandum for Lawrence E. Walsh, Independent Counsel, in Opposition, Thornburgh v. Walsh, No. A-643 (U.S. S. Ct. filed Feb. 11, 1989).

95. See Memorandum and Preliminary Order re CIPA at 8 (D.D.C. June 22, 1988).

96. For example, Judge Gesell's shrewd pretrial ruling placing President Reagan "on call" to testify, but specifying that he would not be required to do so except by future court order, created no issue appealable before trial. Had the judge granted President Reagan's motion to quash outright, North could have appealed it immediately. Had he denied the motion and ordered President Reagan to testify, the president's lawyers would have appealed it immediately.

97. Barrett, "North Trial Starts as Prosecutor Focuses on His Actions, not White House Policy," Wall St. J., Feb. 22, 1989, at A9, col. 4.

98. By taking the stand in his own defense and testifying at length, North drastically limited his own freedom to plead the Fifth Amendment privilege against self-incrimination (for fear of making a negative impression upon the jury) and weakened his claim on appeal that the trial had been irreversibly tainted by the prior exposure of witnesses to his immunized congressional testimony. See *supra* note 58.

99. See "North Ends Six Days on Stand as Lawyers near Wrap-Up," 47 *Cong. Q.* 843 (Apr. 15, 1989) (during cross-examination, the judge regularly "interrupted to direct North to answer the question forthrightly," preventing North from dominating "the colloquy with the long, sometimes rambling answers he effectively used to parry congressional questioners in 1987").

100. See "Ollie's Tarnished Image," *Newsweek* (Apr. 24, 1989): 38; Rowley,

"North's Defense may have hurt him," New Haven Reg., Apr. 16, 1989, at A13, col. 1 (statement of John Nields, Jr., chief counsel of House Iran-Contra Committee) ("The most damaging thing that happened to [North] during the trial was the cross-examination on [his private use of] the money. That was just devastating").

101. See Boyd, "North Trial Reveals a Wider Role for Bush in Aiding Contras in '85," N.Y. Times, Apr. 13, 1989, at A1, col. 4; Engelberg, "North Trial Casts Light on Reagan and Raises New Shadow for Bush," N.Y. Times, Apr. 9, 1989, at A1, col. 1. At the request of Senate leaders, the Senate Select Committee on Intelligence conducted an investigation into why the seven newly discovered documents had escaped the notice of the Iran-contra committees but found no evidence that the Reagan administration had made a deliberate and systematic effort to withhold them. The Intelligence Committee warned, however, that it could not "absolutely rule out the possibility that selective efforts could have been made by an unknown person or persons to remove certain copies of the documents in question from certain files." Senate Select Comm. on Intelligence, "Were Relevant Documents Withheld from the Congressional Committees Investigating the Iran-Contra Affair?" 11 (June, 1989) (emphasis omitted) (copy on file with author).

102. The administration charged that North's attorneys had drafted the stipulation and that Walsh had accepted it only to ensure that his prosecution could proceed. Engelberg, "North Trial Document Called Faulty," N.Y. Times, Apr. 26, 1989, at A19, cols. 1–2 (statement of Michael G. Kozak, acting assistant secretary of state for Inter-American Affairs).

103. Jury Instruction on Specific Intent at 6 (D.D.C. Apr. 21, 1989). See, also, *id.* ("The conduct of others working with the defendant is not, standing alone, any justification for the defendant's conduct nor is the intent of others necessarily his. You are not to judge defendant's guilt or innocence based solely on the actions of others").

104. The jury also acquitted on one count of illegal conversion of travelers' checks and one count of illegal use of a tax-exempt organization. "North Verdict Ends Chapter, but Story Continues On," 47 *Cong. Q.* 1055 (May 6, 1989).

105. The *Federal Sentencing Reporter* has calculated that under federal sentencing guidelines now in force, North's actions would have warranted a recommended "sentence range of 21–27 months in prison on the low end, and a range of 46–57 months in prison on the high end." "Editors' Observations," 2 *Fed. Sent. R.* 64 (1989). The sentencing guidelines pertain only to federal crimes committed after November 1, 1987, however, and thus did not apply to North's case. Furthermore, even if the guidelines had applied, Judge Gesell would have had substantial discretion to depart from their recommendations.

106. "North Depicted as Liar, Patriot as Trial Gets Under Way," 47 *Cong. Q.* 407, 409 (Feb. 25, 1989); "Members Request Hill Inquiry on North Trial Documents," 47 *Cong. Q.* 986 (Apr. 29, 1989); "Iran-Contra Revisited," 21 *Nat'l J.* 1298 (1989).

107. For an account of these struggles in the Poindexter and Secord cases, see Johnston, "U.S. Drops," *supra* note 83. Similar pretrial disputes ultimately caused dismissal of the trial of former CIA station chief Joseph Fernandez. See *supra* notes 86, 91 & 93. In November 1989, while Poindexter was awaiting trial, Secord, Hakim, and a corporation owned by Hakim all pleaded guilty to relatively minor counts. See Johnston, "Secord Is Guilty of One Charge in Contra Affair," N.Y. Times, Nov. 9, 1989, at A24, col. 1; Johnston, "Albert Hakim, Iran-Contra Figure, Pleads Guilty to One Misdemeanor," N.Y. Times, Nov. 22, 1989, at A18, col. 4. See Johnston, "Case Dismissed," *supra* note 83; Pelham, *supra* note 86.

108. See 28 U.S.C. § 595 (a)(2) (1982) ("An independent counsel . . . shall submit to the Congress such statements or reports . . . as the independent counsel considers appropriate").

109. Wines, "Judge in North Trial Rejects U.S. Effort to Censor Testimony," N.Y. Times, Feb. 9, 1989, at A1, col. 1.

CHAPTER 2: RECOGNIZING THE PATTERN OF HISTORY

1. Joint Resolution of August 10, 1964, H.R.J. Res. 1145, 88th Cong., 2d Sess., 78 Stat. 384, *repealed by* Act of Jan. 12, 1971, Pub. L. No. 91-672, § 12, 84 Stat. 2053. See, also, Department of State, Office of the Legal Adviser, "The Legality of United States Participation in the Defense of Viet Nam," 75 *Yale L.J.* 1085, 1102–06 (1966). On the Tonkin Gulf incident, see D. Halberstam, *The Best and The Brightest* 411–14 (1972); W. LaFeber, *The American Age: United States Foreign Policy at Home and Abroad Since 1750* 574 (1989); D. Kearns, *Lyndon Johnson and the American Dream* 198–99 (1976). For further discussion of Johnson's decision to escalate the war, see Barrett, "The Mythology Surrounding Lyndon Johnson, His Advisers, and the 1965 Decision to Escalate the Vietnam War," 103 *Pol. Sci. Q.* 637 (1988).

2. Pub. L. No. 93-148, 87 Stat. 555 (codified at 50 U.S.C. §§ 1541–1548 [1982]).

3. *Compare* 50 U.S.C. §§ 1542–1543 (1982) *with* House Select Comm. to Investigate Covert Arms Transactions with Iran and Senate Select Comm. on Secret Military Assistance to Iran and the Nicaraguan Opposition, *Report of the Congressional Comms. Investigating the Iran-Contra Affair,* 100th Cong., 1st Sess., S. Rept. 216, H. Rept. 433, 144–47, 287–88 (1987) (describing Hasenfus affair) [hereinafter *Iran-Contra Report*].

4. On President Ford's actions, see Letter to the Speaker of the House and the President Pro Tempore of the Senate Reporting on United States Actions in the Recovery of the SS Mayaguez, *Pub. Papers of the Presidents: Gerald Ford,* 669 (1975) ("taking note of" rather than complying with the terms of the resolution); *War Powers: A Test of Compliance—Relative to the Danang Sealift, the Evacuation of Phnom Penh, the Evacuation of Saigon, and the Mayaguez Incident: Hearings before the House Comm. on Int'l Rel.,* 94th Cong., 1st Sess. 61 (1975). On President Carter's Iranian operation, see Letter to the Speaker of the House

and the President Pro Tempore of the Senate Reporting on the Operation, *Pub. Papers of the Presidents: Jimmy Carter*, 777 (1980–81); Legal Opinion of Lloyd Cutler, President's Counsel, on War Powers Consultation Relative to the Iran Rescue Mission (May 9, 1980), Subcomm. on Int'l Security and Scientific Affairs of the House Comm. on Foreign Affairs, *War Powers Resolution: Relevant Documents, Correspondence, Reports,* 98th Cong., 1st Sess. 50 (1983). On President Reagan's actions, see 129 *Cong. Rec.* 14,610 (Oct. 26, 1983); Rubner, "The Reagan Administration, the 1973 War Powers Resolution, and the Invasion of Grenada," 100 *Poli. Sci. Q.* 627 (Winter 1985–86); Torricelli, "The War Powers Resolution After the Libya Crisis," 7 *Pace L. Rev.* 661 (1987); R. Lugar, *Letters to the Next President* 47–48 (1988) (consultation on Libyan strike ended twenty-seven minutes before air strike began); Note, "The War Powers Resolution: An Act Facing 'Imminent Hostilities' A Decade Later," 16 *Vand. J. Transnat'l L.* 915, 964–1013 (1983); Lowry v. Reagan, 676 F. Supp. 333, 336–37 (summarizing Persian Gulf notices). On President Bush's actions, see Dowd, "George Bush, First Year: Likes, Dislikes, Surprises," N.Y. Times, Dec. 31, 1989, at A21, col. 3.

5. See Multinational Force in Lebanon Resolution, Pub. L. No. 98-119, 97 Stat. 805 (1983) (codified at 50 U.S.C. §§ 1541–1544 [Supp. 2 1987]). For an account of the Lebanon experience, see Vance, "Striking the Balance: Congress and the President under the War Powers Resolution," 133 *U. Pa. L. Rev.* 79, 94–95 (1984).

6. See War Powers Act Compliance Resolution, S.J. Res. 194, 133 *Cong. Rec.* S14,630 (daily ed. Oct. 21, 1987).

7. See Lowry v. Reagan, 676 F. Supp. 333 (D.D.C. 1987), *appeal dismissed* No. 87-5426 (D.C.Cir. Oct. 17, 1988) (per curiam); "Statement on the Downing of an Iranian Jetliner by the United States Navy in the Persian Gulf," 24 *Weekly Comp. Pres. Doc.* 896 (July 3, 1988).

8. See, *e.g.,* S.J. Res. 323, 100th Cong., 2d Sess., 134 *Cong. Rec.* S6239 (daily ed. May 19, 1988) (Byrd-Nunn-Warner-Mitchell proposal); Ely, "Suppose Congress Wanted a War Powers Act that Worked," 88 *Colum. L. Rev.* 1379 (1988); Halperin & Stern, "Lawful Wars," 72 *Foreign Pol'y* 173 (1988); Committee on Federal Legislation, "The War Powers Resolution," 44 *Rec. of Ass'n of the Bar of the City of New York* 106 (1989).

9. For further explication of these categories, see Koh, "The Treaty Power," 43 *U. Miami L. Rev.* 106 (1988), from which much of this section derives.

10. See U.S. Const. art. I, § 10, cls. 1, 3; art. II, § 2; Art. VI, § 2.

11. For historical treatments, see Bestor, "Respective Roles of Senate and President in the Making and Abrogation of Treaties—The Original Intent of the Framers of the Constitution Historically Examined," 55 *Geo. Wash. L. Rev.* 1, 135 (1979) ("treatymaking was to be a cooperative venture from the beginning to the end of the entire process"); Rakove, "Solving a Constitutional Puzzle: The Treatymaking Clause as a Case Study," 1 *Perspectives in American History: New Series* 233 (B. Bailyn, D. Fleming, & S. Thernstrom eds. 1984).

12. *The Federalist* No. 75 (A. Hamilton) (Modern Library ed. 1937); 2 *The Debates in the Several State Conventions on the Adoption of the Federal Constitution* 507 (J. Elliot ed. 1896) (statement of James Wilson) ("Neither the President nor the Senate, solely, can complete a treaty; they are checks upon each other, and are so balanced as to produce security to the people"); L. Levy, *Original Intent and the Framers' Constitution* 49 (1988) ("the records of the Convention show that only one delegate . . ., Butler of South Carolina, proposed that the President should possess the treaty power exclusively; the records show, too, that no delegate preferred a more important role for the President in foreign affairs than for the Senate"). See, generally, Koh, *supra* note 9, at 107–09.

13. *The Federalist, supra* note 12, No. 64, at 420 (J. Jay) (This collaboration "provides . . . our negotiations for treaties [with] every advantage which can be derived from talents, information, integrity, and deliberate investigations [of the Senate], on the one hand, and from secrecy and despatch [secured by presidential action] on the other").

14. See Missouri v. Holland, 252 U.S. 416, 432 (1920); United States v. Belmont, 301 U.S. 324, 331 (1937); United States v. Pink, 315 U.S. 203, 230–31 (1942).

15. See Borchard, "The Attorney General's Opinion on the Exchange of Destroyers For Naval Bases," 34 *Am. J. Int'l L.* 690, 690 (1940). See, generally, T. Franck & M. Glennon, *Foreign Relations and National Security Law* 379–86 (1987). In concluding the destroyers-for-bases deal, Roosevelt expressly relied upon a controversial opinion by then–Attorney General Robert Jackson, which found the transfer supported by two statutes as well as the president's constitutional powers. See 39 Op. Att'y Gen. 484 (1940). See, also, A. Schlesinger, *The Imperial Presidency* 110–13 (1973) (describing 1941 executive agreements).

16. See, *e.g.*, McDougal & Lans, "Treaties and Congressional-Executive or Presidential Agreements: Interchangeable Instruments of National Policy," 54 *Yale L.J.* 181, 186 (1945).

17. L. Margolis, *Executive Agreements and Presidential Power in Foreign Policy* 30, 101–39 (1986) (listing executive agreements).

18. See Dames & Moore v. Regan, 453 U.S. 654 (1981) (upholding Iranian Hostages Agreement); United States v. Pink, 315 U.S. 203 (1942) (upholding Litvinov Assignment); United States v. Belmont, 301 U.S. 324 (1937) (upholding Litvinov Assignment). See, also, Jackson, "The General Agreement on Tariffs and Trade in United States Domestic Law," 66 *Mich. L. Rev.* 250, 253 (1967) (describing use of executive agreement by United States to accept the General Agreement on Tariffs and Trade). The most significant congressional-executive disputes over international agreements in the 1950s and 1960s revolved around the so-called Bricker amendment and international trade agreements. See, generally, D. Tananbaum, *The Bricker Amendment Controversy: A Test of Eisenhower's Political Leadership* (1988); Koh, "Congressional Controls on Presidential Trade Policymaking After *I.N.S. v. Chadha*," 18 *N.Y.U. J. Int'l L. & Pol.* 1191, 1197–1200 (1986); Lowenfeld, "Roles of the President and Congress," *Yale L. & Pol'y Rev.* 71 (Special Issue No. 1) (1988).

19. S. Res. 85, 91st Cong., 1st Sess., 115 *Cong. Rec.* 3603, 17,245 (1969). The House of Representatives never acted on the measure. L. Henkin, *Foreign Affairs and the Constitution* 348 n.34 (1972). For the mood of the era, see H. Steiner & D. Vagts, *Transnational Legal Problems* 607 (2d ed. 1976).

20. See, generally, *Congressional Oversight of Executive Agreements: Hearings on S. 3475 before the Subcomm. on Separation of Powers of the Senate Comm. on the Judiciary,* 92d Cong., 2d Sess. (1972).

21. See Transmittal Act, Pub. L. No. 94-303, 86 Stat. 619 (1972) (codified at 1 U.S.C. § 112b [1982]) (requiring secretary of state to transmit to Congress any international agreement other than a treaty as soon as practicable after its entry into force with respect to the United States). For examples of congressional oversight legislation introduced but not enacted in the years after Case-Zablocki, see the Morgan-Zablocki Bill, H.R. 4438, 94th Cong., 1st Sess. (1976); S. 1251, S. 632, 94th Cong., 1st Sess. (1975); S. 1286, 93d Cong., 2d Sess. (1974).

22. See, *e.g.,* Consumers Union v. Kissinger, 506 F.2d 136 (D.C. Cir. 1974), *cert. denied,* 421 U.S. 1004 (1975) (upholding President Nixon's voluntary restraint agreement with Japan on steel); J. Jackson & W. Davey, *Legal Problems of International Economic Relations* 617–22 (2d ed. 1986) (similar Japanese restraints on auto exports); "Administration Announces Import Restraints, Other Measures to Aid Machine Tool Industry," 3 *Int'l Trade Rep.* (BNA) 1537 (Dec. 24, 1986) (Japanese and Taiwanese restraints on machine tools); 25 I.L.M. 1408 (1986) (similar "arrangement" with Japan regarding semiconductors). Congress received no formal notice of the steel voluntary restraint agreements entered between 1969 and 1974 or the auto agreement entered in 1981, all of which took the form of unilateral letters written to U.S. government officials by the industries involved. The remaining Reagan voluntary restraint agreements were all formal, jointly signed documents, but only the 1982 steel accord with the European Community was formally notified to Congress in compliance with the Case-Zablocki Act. For a critique of executive conduct in concluding such agreements, see Kennedy, "Voluntary Restraint Agreements: A Threat to Representative Democracy," 11 *Hastings Int'l & Comp. L. Rev.* 1 (1987).

23. See "Unilateral Policy Declaration by the United States with respect to the SALT II Treaty," *reported in* 123 *Cong. Rec.* S31,901 (daily ed. Oct. 3, 1977) (letter from Secretary of State Cyrus Vance to Sen. John Sparkman, chairman, Senate Foreign Relations Committee, dated Sept. 21, 1977).

24. See "Over the Top," *Time* (Dec. 8, 1986):43; Reisman, "The Cult of Custom in the Late Twentieth Century," 17 *Cal. Western Int'l L.J.* 133, 142 (1987) (SALT II exemplified a "new type of executive agreement . . . in which Congress indicates disapproval, but which the Executive respects 'as if' there were an agreement on the condition that the other negotiating state lives up to the terms of the unratified treaty").

25. See "United States Ocean Policy," 19 *Weekly Comp. Pres. Doc.* 383 (1983), *reprinted in* 22 I.L.M. 464 (1983); Proclamation No. 5030 of March 10, 1983, 3

C.F.R. 22–23 (1984). See, also, Presidential Proclamation No. 5928 of Dec. 27, 1988, 54 Fed. Reg. 777 (1989) (announcing that the United States would henceforth recognize a territorial sea of twelve nautical miles pursuant to customary international law).

26. Reisman, *supra* note 24, at 134; Letter of Transmittal from President Ronald Reagan, Protocol II Additional to the 1949 Geneva Conventions of 12 August 1949, and Relating to the Protection of Victims of Noninternational Armed Conflicts, S. Treaty Doc. No. 2, 100th Cong., 1st Sess. III (1987), *reprinted in* 81 *Am. J. Int'l L.* 910 (1987) (refusing to submit Protocol I of Geneva Convention, which the United States had previously signed, for advice and consent, but accepting some of its provisions as customary international law). For critiques of that decision, see R. Falk, *Revolutionaries and Functionaries: The Dual Faces of Terrorism* 155–61 (1988); Gasser, "An Appeal for Ratification by the United States," 81 *Am. J. Int'l L.* 912 (1987).

27. See National Defense Authorization Act for Fiscal Years 1988 and 1989, Pub. L. No. 100-180, § 225(a)(2), 101 Stat. 1019, 1056 (1987); H. Rept. 446, 100th Cong., 1st Sess., 594 (1987); S. Res. 167, 100th Cong., 1st Sess., 133 *Cong. Rec.* S12,498 (daily ed. Sept. 22, 1987); Senate Comm. on Foreign Relations, *The* ABM *Treaty Interpretation Resolution,* S. Rept. 164, 100th Cong., 1st Sess. (1987); "Senate's Condition to Treaty," N.Y. Times, May 28, 1988, at A4, cols. 5–6 (noting exception to Byrd amendment in cases where the Senate has consented to the new interpretation by subsequent treaty or protocol or through legislative enactment). For accounts of the controversy, see, generally, R. Garthoff, *Policy versus the Law: The Reinterpretation of the ABM Treaty* (1987); Koplow, "Constitutional Bait and Switch: Executive Reinterpretation of Arms Control Treaties," 137 *U. Pa. L. Rev.* 1353 (1989); Chayes & Chayes, "Testing and Development of 'Exotic' Systems under the ABM Treaty: The Great Reinterpretation Caper," 99 *Harv. L. Rev.* 1956 (1986); Nunn, "The ABM Reinterpretation Issue," 10 *Wash. Q.* 45 (Autumn 1987). For a defense of the administration's position, see Sofaer, "The ABM Treaty: Legal Analysis in the Political Cauldron," 10 *Wash. Q.* 59 (Autumn 1987).

28. See "Message to the Senate on the Soviet-United States Intermediate-Range Nuclear Force Treaty," 24 *Weekly Comp. Pres. Doc.* 779, 780 (June 10, 1988).

29. Goldwater v. Carter, 444 U.S. 996, 1006 (1979) (Brennan, J., concurring) (citing president's power under Article II, § 3 of the Constitution to "receive Ambassadors").

30. See Beacon Prods. Corp. v. Reagan, 633 F. Supp. 1191, 1199 (D. Mass. 1986), *aff'd,* 841 F.2d 1 (1st Cir. 1987) (dismissing private challenge to State Department's notice of termination of bilateral U.S. Friendship, Commerce, and Navigation Treaty with Nicaragua); Letter from Secretary of State George P. Shultz to Secretary-General of the United Nations Javier Perez de Cuellar (Oct. 7, 1985), *reprinted in* 24 I.L.M. 1742 (1985) (terminating U.S. acceptance of compulsory jurisdiction of International Court of Justice); "Science and Technology," 21

Weekly Comp. Pres. Doc. 336, 338 (Mar. 20, 1985) (announcing U.S. withdrawal from UNESCO).

31. See Letter from Secretary of State George P. Shultz to Secretary-General of the United Nations Javier Perez de Cuellar (Apr. 6, 1984), *reprinted in* 23 I.L.M. 670 (1984) (immediately and temporarily "modifying" the 1946 acceptance by the United States of International Court of Justice's compulsory jurisdiction, notwithstanding treaty provision requiring six months' notice of termination).

32. For example, the Reagan administration offered the Genocide Convention to the Senate for advice and consent to ratification with more conditions than had been offered by any prior administration. See Leich, "Contemporary Practice of the United States Relating to International Law," 80 *Am. J. Int'l L.* 612–22 (1986). See, also, "Message to the Senate Transmitting the Convention Against Torture and Other Inhuman Treatment or Punishment," 24 *Weekly Comp. Pres. Doc.* 642 (May 20, 1988); Letter of May 10, 1988 from Secretary of State George P. Shultz to President Ronald Reagan regarding the Convention Against Torture and Other Cruel, Inhuman or Degrading Treatment or Punishment (copy on file with author) (advising transmittal of that convention to Senate with seventeen reservations, understandings, and declarations).

33. See, *e.g.,* Japan Whaling Ass'n v. American Cetacean Soc'y, 478 U.S. 221 (1986) (upholding commerce secretary's refusal to certify that new executive agreement "diminishes the effectiveness" of the international whaling convention).

34. Garcia-Mir v. Meese, 788 F.2d 1446, 1455 (11th Cir.), *cert. denied,* 107 S. Ct. 289 (1986). As Professor Henkin has noted, the Eleventh Circuit's dicta could be read to support an "assertion that . . . the President and lesser executive officials may disregard a treaty or a rule of international law." See Henkin, "The Constitution and United States Sovereignty: A Century of *Chinese Exclusion* and Its Progeny," 100 *Harv. L. Rev.* 853, 864 (1987). See, generally, "Agora: May the President Violate Customary International Law?" 80 *Am. J. Int'l L.* 913 (1986); "Agora: May the President Violate Customary International Law? (Cont'd)," 81 *Am. J. Int'l L.* 371 (1987); Malawer, "Reagan's Law and Foreign Policy, 1981–1987: The 'Reagan Corollary' of International Law," 29 *Harv. Int'l L.J.* 85 (1988) (enumerating Reagan administration foreign policy decisions that have modified or deviated from preexisting international legal rules).

35. Rainbow Navigation, Inc. v. Dep't of the Navy, 699 F. Supp. 339, 349 (D.D.C. 1988) (Greene, J.); see, also, Rainbow Navigation, Inc. v. Dep't of the Navy, 686 F. Supp. 354 (D.D.C. 1988). Mindful of the ABM Treaty controversy, the district judge in *Rainbow Navigation* declared as a matter of domestic constitutional law, that the executive branch was bound by authoritative representations that it had made to the Senate regarding the meaning of the agreement in order to secure advice and consent. 699 F. Supp. at 343. But see United States v. Stuart, 109 S. Ct. 1183, 1195–97 (1989) (Scalia, J., concurring in the judgment) (questioning this ruling).

36. For discussion of these trends, see, generally, Ornstein, "The House and the Senate in a New Congress," in *The New Congress* 363 (T. Mann & N. Ornstein eds. 1981); Ornstein, "Interest Groups, Congress and American Foreign Policy," in *American Foreign Policy in an Uncertain World* 49, 54 (D. Forsythe ed. 1984); T. Franck & E. Weisband, *Foreign Policy by Congress* 228, 242–45 (1979) (discussing S. Res. 4 staffers and creation of the Congressional Research Service, the General Accounting Office, the Congressional Budget Office, and the Office of Technology Assessment).

37. See, *e.g.*, International Emergency Economic Powers Act, 50 U.S.C. §§ 1701–1706 (1982); National Emergencies Act, 50 U.S.C. §§ 1601–1651 (1982); Trade Act of 1974, 19 U.S.C. §§ 2101–2487 (1982); Export Administration Act of 1979, 50 U.S.C. §§ 2401–2413 (1982); Foreign Intelligence Surveillance Act, 50 U.S.C. §§ 1801–1811 (1982); International Development and Food Assistance Act of 1975, Pub. L. No. 94-161, 89 Stat. 849 (codified as amended in scattered sections of 7 and 22 U.S.C.); Hughes-Ryan Amendment to the Foreign Assistance Act, 22 U.S.C. § 2422 (1982) (intelligence oversight); International Security Assistance and Arms Export Control Act of 1976, 22 U.S.C. §§ 2751–2796 (1982); Section 502B of the Foreign Assistance Act of 1961, 22 U.S.C. § 2304 (1982); and the Nuclear Non-Proliferation Act of 1978, Pub. L. No. 95-242, 92 Stat. 120 (codified as amended in scattered sections of 22 and 42 U.S.C.). For descriptions of this intense period of legislative activity, see, generally, T. Franck & E. Weisband, *supra* note 36; *The Tethered Presidency: Congressional Restraints on Executive Power* (T. Franck ed. 1981).

38. For descriptions of the typical post-Vietnam legislative package, see, generally, Koh, *supra* note 18, at 1204–08; Franck & Bob, "The Return of Humpty-Dumpty: Foreign Relations Law After the Chadha Case," 79 *Am. J. Int'l L.* 912 (1985). One statute which expressly denied the president new delegated authority, however, was the War Powers Resolution. See 50 U.S.C. § 1547(d)(2) (1982) ("[n]othing in this [joint resolution] . . . shall be construed as granting any authority to the President with respect to the introduction of United States Armed Forces"). But see *supra* text accompanying notes 3–4 (describing how executive branch has treated resolution's time limits as de facto congressional permission to commit troops abroad for up to sixty days).

39. 50 U.S.C. §§ 1701–1706 (1982).

40. 50 U.S.C. app. §§ 1–6, 7–39, 41–44 (1982). For legislative histories of IEEPA, see A. Lowenfeld, *Trade Controls for Political Ends* 545–46 (2d ed. 1983); *Emergency Controls on International Economic Transactions: Hearings before the Subcomm. on International Economic Policy and Trade of the House Comm. on International Relations*, 95th Cong., 1st Sess., 110 (1977) (remarks of Rep. Bingham); Note, "The International Emergency Economic Powers Act: A Congressional Attempt to Control Presidential Emergency Power," 96 *Harv. L. Rev.* 1102, 1104 (1983).

41. Regan v. Wald, 468 U.S. 222, 245 (1984) (Blackmun, J., dissenting) (noting that

in 1977, states of emergency originally declared in 1933, 1950, 1970, and 1971 were still in effect).

42. See Dames & Moore v. Regan, 453 U.S. 654 (1981); INS v. Chadha, 462 U.S. 919 (1983) (invalidating legislative-veto provision in National Emergencies Act of 1976 that permitted Congress to terminate presidentially declared IEEPA emergencies, 50 U.S.C. § 1622(a)(1)); Regan v. Wald, 468 U.S. 222 (1984). For further discussion of the Court's technique of statutory interpretation in these cases, see *infra* chapter 6.

43. See Exec. Order No. 12,170, 44 Fed. Reg. 65,729 (1979) and Exec. Order No. 12,205, 45 Fed. Reg. 24,099 (1980) (Iran); Exec. Order No. 12,513, 50 Fed. Reg. 18,629 (1985) (Nicaragua); Exec. Order No. 12,543, 51 Fed. Reg. 875 (1986) and Exec. Order No. 12,544, 51 Fed. Reg. 1235 (1986) (Libya); Exec. Order No. 12,532, 50 Fed Reg. 36,861 (1985) (South Africa); Exec. Order No. 12,635, 50 Fed. Reg. 12,134 (1988) (Panama). See, generally, B. Carter, *International Economic Sanctions: Improving the Haphazard U.S. Legal Regime* 191–96 (1988).

44. See House Comm. on International Relations, *Trading with the Enemy Act Reform Legislation,* 95th Cong., 1st Sess., H. Rept. 459, 10 (1977).

45. See Lobel, "Emergency Power and the Decline of Liberalism," 98 *Yale L.J.* 1385, 1415 (1989); B. Carter, *supra* note 43, at 197–203; Note, *supra* note 40, at 1115 ("given the infinite variety of human events, almost any major event in the future course of the nation's history could be described as 'unusual and extraordinary' ").

46. See Beacon Prods. Corp. v. Reagan, 633 F. Supp. 1191 (D. Mass. 1986), *aff'd,* 841 F.2d 1 (1st Cir. 1987) (Nicaragua); Chang v. United States, 859 F.2d 893, 896 n.3 (Fed. Cir. 1988) (Libya).

47. See Exec. Order No. 12,444, 3 C.F.R. 168 (1984); Exec. Order No. 12,470, 3 C.F.R. 168 (1985); Harris & Bialos, "The Strange New World of United States Export Controls under the International Emergency Economic Powers Act," 18 *Vand. J. Transnat'l L.* 71 (1985).

48. B. Carter, *supra* note 43, at 199; see Beacon Prods. Corp. v. Reagan, 633 F. Supp. 1191 (D. Mass. 1986), *aff'd,* 841 F.2d 1 (1st Cir. 1987) (whether a particular country poses sufficient threat to trigger IEEPA declaration of national emergency constitutes nonjusticiable political question).

49. Exec. Order No. 12,532, 50 Fed. Reg. 36,861 (1985); R. Lugar, *supra* note 4, at 221 ("The Secretary [of state] said [to the Senate sponsor of the bill], 'This is your bill in executive-order form' "); B. Carter, *supra* note 43, at 201 ("It was not clear . . . why the threat was so 'unusual and extraordinary' that it was necessary to declare a national emergency, especially since legislation to impose sanctions was already far along in Congress").

50. See "Trade Policy: Administration Weighing Emergency Powers Act Changes, State Department Official Says," 4 *Int'l Trade Rep.* (BNA) 1300, 1300 (Oct. 21, 1987) (statement of Ambassador-at-Large L. Paul Bremer III).

51. See Robinson, "The Routinization of Crisis Government," 63 *Yale Rev.* 161 (1973). See, also, Lobel, *supra* note 45, at 1408 (Congress has enacted nearly 470 statutes delegating broad emergency powers to the executive).

52. See Madison, "The Arms Sale Say-So," 19 *Nat'l J.* 667, 668–69 (1987); H. Kissinger, *White House Years* 1264 (1979); G. Sick, *All Fall Down: America's Tragic Encounter with Iran* 16 (1986) ("Significantly . . . it was the Department of Defense that objected vigorously to the notion of selling the shah everything he wanted").

53. See Pub. L. No. 90-629, 82 Stat. 1320 (codified as amended at 22 U.S.C. §§ 2751–2796 [1982 & Supp. IV 1986]). See Note, "The United States Is Moving Further from Fostering Multilateral Restraint of Conventional Arms Sales," 6 *Dick. J. Int'l L.* 343, 346–49 (1988) [hereinafter Dickinson Note]; R. Labrie, J. Hutchins, E. Peura, & D. Richman, *U.S. Arms Sales Policy: Background and Issues* 6–7 (1982); T. Franck & E. Weisband, *supra* note 36, at 98 ("Where once the export of arms had been a high-minded part of a global strategy to make the world safe for democracy, now the U.S. appeared to be willing to supply any regime, no matter how unsavory, so long as the customer professed anti-communism and could pay cash").

54. See Dickinson Note, *supra* note 53, at 349.

55. G. Sick, *supra* note 52, at 17. *Compare id.* (quoting Henry Kissinger's memorandum to the president) ("we adopted a policy which provides, in effect, that we will accede to any of the Shah's requests for arms purchases from us") *with* W. Shawcross, *The Shah's Last Ride: The Fate of an Ally* 168 (1988) ("Never before in American history had the president ordered the national security bureaucracy to accept the demands and judgment of a foreign leader on arms transfers").

56. See Nelson-Bingham Amendment to the Foreign Assistance Act of 1974, Pub. L. No. 93-559, 88 Stat. 1795, 1814 (codified as amended at 22 U.S.C. § 2776 [1982]); T. Franck & E. Weisband, *supra* note 36, at 98–111 (describing enactment of amendment). See, also, 120 *Cong. Rec.* 38,073 (1974) (remarks of Sen. Gaylord Nelson) ("The executive branch of this Nation involves the United States in military situations throughout the world without congressional and public debate, discussions, or deliberations").

57. See Pub. L. No. 94-329, 90 Stat. 729 (codified as amended at 22 U.S.C. § 2318 [1982 & Supp. IV 1986]). The law subjected intergovernmental arms sales to two-house disapproval only if they exceeded particular dollar thresholds: $14 million for sophisticated weaponry, called "major defense equipment," and $50 million for defense articles or services. See 22 U.S.C. § 2753(d) (1982).

58. *Legislative Veto: Arms Export Control Act: Hearing on S. 1050 Before the Senate Comm. on Foreign Relations,* 98th Cong., 1st Sess. 40 (1983) (Statement of Hon. Matthew Nimetz, former undersecretary of state for Security Assistance, Science, and Technology).

59. See INS v. Chadha, 462 U.S. 919 (1983).

60. See Arms Export Control Act, Legislative Veto, Pub. L. No. 99-247, 100 Stat. 9 (1986); Note, "Congress and Arms Sales: Tapping the Potential of the Fast-Track Guarantee Procedure," 97 *Yale L.J.* 1439, 1447–49 (1988) (describing events leading to congressional amendment). The Supreme Court had long validated such report-and-wait provisions. See INS v. Chadha, 462 U.S. 919, 935 n.9 (1983); Sibbach v. Wilson, 312 U.S. 1, 14–15 (1941).

61. See 22 U.S.C. § 2753(d)(2) (Supp. III 1985); see, generally, Scheffer, "U.S. Law and the Iran-Contra Affair," 81 *Am. J. Int'l L.* 696, 698 ("The Reagan administration's covert sale of military arms to Iran falls into a legal quagmire because of the conflict between the laws governing the export of military arms and the laws governing covert activities by the United States Government"); *Iran-Contra Report, supra* note 3, at 451, 539–46 (minority report) (arguing that covert transfers under National Security Act and Economy Act can substitute for transfers under Arms Export Control Act). But see *id.* at 418–19 (majority report) (disputing minority's conclusion).

62. Madison, *supra* note 52, at 669. Congress originally supported the joint resolution of disapproval by votes of 356–62 in the House and 73–22 in the Senate. See Roberts, "Senate Upholds Arms for Saudis, Backing Reagan," N.Y. Times, June 6, 1986, at A1, col. 6.

63. See Felton, "Rare Aid Funding Bill Comes down to the Wire," 46 *Cong. Q.* 2731 (Oct. 1, 1988); Yang, "Reagan Plan to Sell Arms to Kuwait Barred by Senate," Wall St. J., July 8, 1988, at 38, col. 3.

64. See Letter from Senator Joseph R. Biden, Jr. and Representative Mel Levine, N.Y. Times, Apr. 2, 1987, at A30, col. 4 (supporting S. 419 and H.R. 898, their bills to amend Arms Export Control Act). Both bills died in the 100th Congress.

65. See Pear, "Saudis Seen as Top Mideast Buyer of U.S. Arms," N.Y. Times, Feb. 3, 1989, at A3, col. 1.

66. See, generally, *Iran-Contra Report, supra* note 3, at 395–407; Note, "The Boland Amendments and Foreign Affairs Deference," 88 *Colum. L. Rev.* 1535, 1567–70 (1988) (describing history of amendments). For the text of the various amendments, see 133 *Cong. Rec.* H4982-87 (daily ed. June 15, 1987).

67. *Compare* S. Rept. 431, 92d Cong., 2d Sess. 13 (1972) *with Iran-Contra Report, supra* note 3, at 185–86; Victor, "CIA Counsel's Role Questioned," *Nat'l L.J.*, Feb. 2, 1987, at 3, col. 1 (describing retroactive finding in Iran-contra affair). See, generally, Meyer, "Congressional Control of Foreign Assistance," 13 *Yale J. Int'l L.* 69, 73–76 (1988) (chronicling presidential abuses of military-aid process from 1961 to 1972).

68. Constitutional Symposium on Indochina War, 116 *Cong. Rec.* 17,387, 17,392 (May 28, 1970) (remarks of Alexander Bickel). For the text of the Cooper-Church amendment, see S. Rept. 865, 91st Cong., 2d Sess. 15 (1970), *reprinted in* Mikva & Lundy, "The 91st Congress and the Constitution," 38 *U. Chi. L. Rev.* 449, 486 n.107 (1971). For the text of the Hatfield-McGovern amendment, see S. Amend.

609, 91st Cong., 2d Sess. (1970), *cited in* Note, "The Appropriations Power as a Tool of Congressional Foreign Policy Making," 50 *B.U. L. Rev.* (Special Issue) 34, 49 n.107 (1970).

69. See Section 30 of the Foreign Assistance Act of 1973, 22 U.S.C. § 2151, 87 Stat. 732, *as amended by* Foreign Assistance Act of 1973, Pub. L. No. 93-189, § 30, 80 Stat. 714 ("[n]o funds authorized or appropriated under this or any other law may be expended to finance military or paramilitary operations by the United States in or over Vietnam, Laos, or Cambodia"); Department of Defense Appropriations Act of 1975, Pub. L. No. 93-437, § 839, 88 Stat. 1212, 1231; Department of Defense Appropriations Act of 1974, Pub. L. No. 93-238, 87 Stat. 1026 (1973); Department of Defense Appropriations Authorization Act of 1974, Pub. L. No. 93-55, § 806, 87 Stat. 615 (1973); Department of State Appropriations Authorization Act of 1973, Pub. L. No. 93-126, § 13, 87 Stat. 454 (1973); Continuing Appropriations Resolution of 1974, Pub. L. No. 93-52, § 108, 87 Stat. 130 (1973); Fulbright Amendment to Second Supplemental Appropriations Act of 1973, Pub. L. No. 93-50, § 307, 87 Stat. 129 (1973).

70. Pub. L. No. 93-559, § 32, 88 Stat. 1795, 1804–05 (1974) (codified at 22 U.S.C. § 2422 [1982]).

71. *Compare* Glennon, "Strengthening the War Powers Resolution: The Case for Purse-Strings Restrictions," 60 *Minn. L. Rev.* 1, 21–23 (1975) (objecting to those actions) *with War Powers: A Test of Compliance Relative to the Danang Sealift, the Evacuation of Phnom Penh, the Evacuation of Saigon, and the Mayaguez Incident: Hearings Before the Subcomm. on International Security and Scientific Affairs of the House Comm. on International Relations,* 94th Cong., 1st Sess. 16–17, 88–89 (1975) (testimony of State Department Legal Adviser Monroe Leigh) (arguing that Congress did not intend those statutory funding prohibitions to curtail presidential efforts to evacuate Americans).

72. Pub. L. No. 94-329, § 404, 90 Stat. 729, 757–58 (1976), *as amended by* Pub. L. No. 96-533, tit. I, § 118(a)–(d), 94 Stat. 3141 (codified as amended at 22 U.S.C. § 2293 note [1980]); C. Meyer, *Facing Reality: From World Federalism to the CIA* 258 (1980).

73. See G. Treverton, *Covert Action: The Limits of Intervention in the Postwar World* 220 (1987).

74. J. Prados, *Presidents' Secret Wars: CIA and Pentagon Covert Operations from World War II through Iranscam* 347–48 (rev. ed. 1988).

75. Ungar & Kohen, "An Angola Angle to the Scandal?" N.Y. Times, Jan. 20, 1987, at A25, col. 2 (North introduced himself to others as a marine officer who had participated in two American wars: Vietnam and Angola); Maren, "What Congress Didn't Ask," N.Y. Times, Nov. 23, 1987, at A23, col. 1.

76. O. North, *Taking the Stand: The Testimony of Lieutenant Colonel Oliver L. North* 270 (1987). See, also, *id.* at 269–71, 512.

77. See O. North, *supra* note 76, at 284–85, 369, 387; Maren, *supra* note 75, at cols. 1–2 ("Though elements of the Africa connection surfaced on a few occasions

during testimony, committee members never pursued the angle, never asked a single question or subpoenaed a single document relating to charges that the Federal Government was arming Unita").

78. See H. Kissinger, *supra* note 52, at 698–763.

79. 50 U.S.C. § 402(a) (1982) (emphasis added). See J. Bock, *The White House Staff and the National Security Assistant: Friendship and Friction at the Water's Edge* 12 (1987) (the act's drafters "worked . . . to limit the authority of the NSC . . . by making it an *advisory* rather than policy-*enforcing* body") (emphasis in original).

80. See President's Special Review Board, *The Tower Commission Report* 6 (N.Y. Times ed. 1987) [hereinafter *Tower Report*].

81. Truman personally attended less than 25 percent of the meetings of the council. See Hamby, "Harry S. Truman: Insecurity and Responsibility," in *Leadership in the Modern Presidency* 41, 61 (F. Greenstein ed. 1988) [hereinafter F. Greenstein]; Institute for Defense Analyses, *The President and the Management of National Security* 58–59 (K. Clark & L. Legere eds. 1969) [hereinafter Clark & Legere].

82. See Franck, "The Constitutional and Legal Position of the National Security Adviser and Deputy Adviser," 74 *Am. J. Int'l L.* 634, 635 (1980). The only statutory authority given the "Executive Secretary" was the power to appoint and fix the compensation of the tiny NSC staff. J. Bock, *supra* note 79, at 12.

83. 3 U.S.C. § 105(a)(1) (1982); P. Henderson, *Managing the Presidency: The Eisenhower Legacy—From Kennedy to Reagan* 74 (1988).

84. P. Henderson, *supra* note 83, at 81, 85–90 (Eisenhower presided over nearly 90 percent of the 366 NSC meetings held during his tenure); D. Acheson, *This Vast External Realm* 195 (1973) ("The NSC decides nothing. It is merely a mechanism for preparing and presenting matters for the President's decision").

85. See 50 U.S.C. § 403(d)(5) (emphasis added). For detailed histories of the CIA, see, generally, R. Jeffreys-Jones, *The CIA and American Democracy* (1989); J. Prados, *supra* note 74; G. Treverton, *supra* note 73. For a description of the CIA's place amid other intelligence agencies, see J. Richelson, *The U.S. Intelligence Community* 20–34 (1985).

86. 50 U.S.C. § 403(d)(3) (1982).

87. See A. Whiting, *Covert Operations and the Democratic Process: The Implications of the Iran/Contra Affair* 8–36, 41–55 (1987).

88. See Sorenson, "The President and the Secretary of State," 66 *Foreign Aff.* 231, 233 (1987–88); J. Bock, *supra* note 79, at 52; P. Henderson, *supra* note 83, at 127–32; Clark & Legere, *supra* note 81, at 70–98; I. Destler, *Presidents, Bureaucrats and Foreign Policy: The Politics of Organizational Reform* 109–12 (1972); D. Kearns, *supra* note 1, at 319–22.

89. See T. Schoenbaum, *Waging Peace and War: Dean Rusk in the Truman, Kennedy & Johnson Years* 284 (1988); U.S. Const. art. II, § 2, cl. 2.

90. See Franck, *supra* note 82, at 634–39.

91. H. Kissinger, *supra* note 52, at 38.

92. Brzezinski, "The NSC's Midlife Crisis," 69 *Foreign Pol'y* 80, 86–7 (1987) (emphasis added).
93. C. Lord, *The Presidency and the Management of National Security* 73–74 (1988); Hoff-Wilson, "Richard M. Nixon: The Corporate Presidency," in F. Greenstein, *supra* note 81, at 164, 185 (Nixon would point in the direction of the Oval Office and say, "There's the State Department"); P. Henderson, *supra* note 83, at 135; J. Bock, *supra* note 79, at 83–100; I. Destler, *supra* note 88, at 118–32.
94. See, generally, H. Kissinger, *supra* note 52, at 277–82, 733–87, 823–33, 1124–64; R. Morris, *Uncertain Greatness: Henry Kissinger and American Foreign Policy* 245–49 (1977); C. Kegley & E. Wittkopf, *American Foreign Policy: Pattern and Process* 242–54, 352 (3d ed. 1987); Sharpe, "The Real Cause of Irangate," 68 *Foreign Pol'y* 19, 24 (1987) (Kissinger created an elaborate covert network to keep Cambodian bombing secret even from Strategic Air Command); Hoff-Wilson, *supra* note 93, at 185–86.
95. See J. Bill, *The Eagle and the Lion: The Tragedy of American-Iranian Relations* 86–94 (1988); W. Shawcross, *supra* note 55, at 65–71; R. Falk, *supra* note 26, at 114–22 (detailing CIA's actions in Iran); J. Prados, *supra* note 74, at 30–238 (detailing agency's pre-Vietnam activities); R. Jeffreys-Jones, *supra* note 85, at 90–99 (describing Dominican Republic, Guatemalan, and Cuban activities); *id.* at 118–38 (describing Bay of Pigs fiasco); G. Treverton, *supra* note 73, at 84–98 (same).
96. R. Jeffreys-Jones, *supra* note 85, at 143; J. Prados, *supra* note 74, at 247–50; D. Halberstam, *supra* note 1, at 411–14. It does not appear, however, that that surveillance unit was under the direction of the CIA.
97. See, generally, M. Halperin, J. Berman, R. Borosage, & C. Marwick, *The Lawless State: The Crimes of the U.S. Intelligence Agencies* 15–57, 135–54 (1976); R. Jeffreys-Jones, *supra* note 85, at 167; J. Prados, *supra* note 74, at 171–296; Bernstein, "The Road to Watergate and Beyond: The Growth and Abuse of Executive Authority Since 1940," 40 *Law & Contemp. Probs.*, Spring 1976, at 58, 81–84.
98. J. Prados, *supra* note 74, at 239–312. Indeed, Cambodia's exiled Prince Norodom Sihanouk entitled his 1973 book *My War with the CIA.* R. Jeffreys-Jones, *supra* note 85, at 182.
99. See P. Shane & H. Bruff, *The Law of Presidential Power, Cases and Materials* 137–38 (1988); R. Jeffreys-Jones, *supra* note 85, at 184–85.
100. A. Haig, *Caveat: Realism, Reagan, and Foreign Policy* 141–42, 306–16 (1984); R. Jeffreys-Jones, *supra* note 85, at 235–51; C. Lord, *supra* note 93, at 79; J. Bock, *supra* note 79, at 159–64; J. Prados, *supra* note 74, at 396–418. For recent journalistic accounts of Casey's role in formulating Central American policy, see B. Woodward, *Veil: The Secret Wars of the CIA 1981–1987* (1987); R. Gutman, *Banana Diplomacy: The Making of American Policy in Nicaragua: 1981–1987* 29–30 (1988).
101. C. Lord, *supra* note 93, at 81. During his congressional testimony, Oliver North

acknowledged that his duties as deputy director for Political-Military Affairs of the NSC had included not merely the coordination of national security policy but "the rescue of American students in Grenada . . . and the US raid in Libya in response to their terrorist attacks." O. North, *supra* note 76, at 264, 657–58. See, also, C. Menges, *Inside the National Security Council: The True Story of the Making and Unmaking of Reagan's Foreign Policy* 54–90, 250–76 (1988) (describing and defending NSC's role in these incidents).

102. See J. Bill, *supra* note 95, at 409–15.

103. See Commission on CIA Activities within the United States, *Report to the President* (1975) (Rockefeller commission); J. Prados, *supra* note 74, at 333.

104. See 22 U.S.C. § 2422 (1982) (requiring president to report "in a timely fashion, a description and scope of such operation" to the appropriate congressional committees).

105. See, generally, L. Johnson, *A Season of Inquiry* (1985) (describing investigations of the most famous of these, the Senate Select Committee to Study Governmental Operations with respect to Intelligence Activities [the "Church Committee"]).

106. Pub. L. No. 96-450, 94 Stat. 1981 (1980) (codified at 50 U.S.C. § 413 [1982]), *described in* Paterson, "Oversight or Afterview?: Congress, the CIA, and Covert Actions Since 1947," in *Congress and United States Foreign Policy: Controlling the Use of Force in the Nuclear Age* 164–65 (M. Barnhart ed. 1987).

107. 50 U.S.C. § 413 (a)(1) (1982). See, also, A. Whiting, *supra* note 87, at 36–41.

108. 50 U.S.C. § 413(b). The eight members to be notified are comprised of the chairmen and ranking minority members of both intelligence committees, the majority and minority leaders of the Senate, and the Speaker and minority leader of the House. *Id.* § 413(a)(1)(B).

109. Paterson, *supra* note 106, at 165.

110. *Compare* § 3–4 of Exec. Order No. 12,036, 43 Fed. Reg. 3674 (1978), *as amended by* Exec. Order No. 12,139, 44 Fed. Reg. 30,311 (1979) *with* 50 U.S.C. § 413(a) (1982). See, also, 126 *Cong. Rec.* S13,106 (daily ed. June 3, 1980) (remarks of Senator Moynihan) ("[W]hat we have here is a codification in law of the practice our committee has followed with the administration for the past $3\frac{1}{2}$ years").

111. Note, "Policing Executive Adventurism: Congressional Oversight of Military and Paramilitary Operations," 19 *Harv. J. on Legis.* 327, 357 (1982).

112. See Goodman, "Reforming U.S. Intelligence," 67 *Foreign Pol'y* 121, 123–24 (1987).

113. *Compare* Exec. Order No. 12,036, 43 Fed. Reg. 3674, 3692 (1978) (emphasis added) *with* Exec. Order No. 12,333, 46 Fed. Reg. 59,941 (1981), *reprinted in* 50 U.S.C. § 401 (1982).

114. See Memorandum from Assistant Attorney General Charles J. Cooper for the Attorney General, "Legal Authority for Covert Arms Transactions to Iran," Dec. 17, 1986, at 14, *cited in Iran-Contra Report, supra* note 3, at 542 n.**

(minority report) ("Activities authorized by the President cannot 'violate' an executive order in any legally meaningful sense").

115. See Fiorina, "Congressional Control of the Bureaucracy," in *Congress Reconsidered* 332, 337 (L. Dodd & B. Oppenheimer eds. 2d ed. 1981). During the 1960s and 1970s, numerous economists and political scientists advanced the notion that regulated entities "capture" the governmental bodies that regulate them. See, generally, Posner, "Theories of Economic Regulation," 5 *Bell J. Econ. & Mgmt. Sci.* 335, 341–44 (1974). Although most versions of the capture theory address cases where private interests capture their agency regulators, Professor Niskanen has described situations in which a government "bureau and [its congressional] review committee [are] 'in bed with each other.' " See W. Niskanen, *Bureaucracy and Representative Government* 148 (1971).

116. See Gelb, "Overseeing of C.I.A. by Congress Has Produced Decade of Support," N.Y. Times, July 7, 1986, at A1, col. 1 (remarks of Senator Moynihan). See, also, T. Franck & E. Weisband, *supra* note 36, at 132 ("Senate committees face an unenviable dilemma when they attempt to oversee government secrets. If they expect to get data, the Agencies will expect discretion in return").

117. Two years later, the International Court of Justice decided that case in Nicaragua's favor. See Case Concerning Military and Paramilitary Activities in and against Nicaragua (Nicar. v. U.S.), 1986 I.C.J. 14 (Judgment of June 27, 1986). See, generally, "Appraisals of the icj's Decision: Nicaragua v. United States (Merits), 81 *Am. J. Int'l L.* 77 (1987). For a critique of the U.S. legal position in the case, see Kahn, "From Nuremberg to The Hague: The United States Position in *Nicaragua v. United States* and the Development of International Law," 12 *Yale J. Int'l L.* 1 (1987).

118. While the Senate committee vice-chair claimed he had never been informed, other senators recalled a grudging consultation. See R. Lugar, *supra* note 4, at 183 ("My own recollection is that Casey did include mention of the general subject deep in a report which he read in a sometimes inaudible briefing style. While thus fulfilling the bare letter of consultation, he . . . adopted an approach which suggested that if a committee member did not think of the right questions to ask or phrase them in such a way as to dredge up important information, that was his own tough luck").

119. See Scheffer, *supra* note 61, at 722; B. Woodward, *supra* note 100, at 325; Goodman, *supra* note 112, at 125–26.

120. For a discussion of these events, see *Iran-Contra Report, supra* note 3, at 37, 167–68, 271–73; *id.* at 20; *id.* at 208.

121. See H.R. 3822, 100th Cong., 1st Sess., 133 *Cong. Rec.* H11,866 (daily ed. Dec. 18, 1987) (introduced by Congressman Stokes); S. 1721, 100th Cong., 1st Sess., 133 *Cong. Rec.* S12,852 (daily ed. Sept. 25, 1987) (introduced by Senator Cohen). The Senate bill stated, "Each finding shall be in writing, unless immediate action by the United States is required and time does not permit the preparation of a written finding, in which case a written record of the President's

decision shall be contemporaneously made and shall be reduced to a written finding as soon as possible but in no event more than forty-eight (48) hours after the decision is made." *Id.* at S12,853. If, however, the president should determine that "it is essential to limit access to the finding to meet extraordinary circumstances affecting vital interests of the United States," the bill authorized the president to report that finding to the "Gang of Eight" described in the text.

122. See "The Director: 'We're Not out of Business,'" *Newsweek* (Oct. 12, 1987): 30 (remarks of CIA Director William Webster) ("As far as covert action [is concerned] . . . the procedures are already there. We need only people who will follow the procedures").

123. See Morrison, "An Eye on the CIA," 20 *Nat'l J.* 1009, 1010 (1988); Testimony of Charles J. Cooper, Assistant Attorney General, Office of Legal Counsel, Before the Senate Select Committee on Intelligence, on S. 1721, at 3 (on file with author) ("We believe . . . that by purporting to oblige the President, under *any and all circumstances,* to notify Congress of a covert action within a fixed period of time, S. 1721 infringes on [a] constitutional prerogative of the President") (emphasis in original).

124. *Cf.* Engelberg, "Covert Intelligence: New Glitches and New Eyebrows," N.Y. Times, Dec. 15, 1987, at B12, col. 1 (president's directive to attorney general not to implement provision in annual spending bill for intelligence agencies which required annual report to Congress on certain movements of Soviet diplomats). Members of Congress or private citizens could not have challenged such an action in court without overcoming the numerous obstacles to justiciability described in chapter 6.

125. See "Covert Action Programs, Letter to the Chairman and Vice Chairman of the Senate Select Committee on Intelligence Regarding Procedures for Presidential Approval and Notification of Congress," 23 *Weekly Comp. Pres. Doc.* 910 (Aug. 7, 1987) (remarks of President Reagan); Seib, "New Rules for Reporting Covert Actions to Congress Are Announced by Reagan," Wall St. J., Aug. 10, 1987, at 10, col. 1.

126. See Engelberg, "3 in CIA Expected to Appeal on Jobs," N.Y. Times, Dec. 25, 1987, at A19, col. 1 (announcing disciplinary actions).

127. The Senate bill passed by a vote of seventy-one to nineteen. "Senate Votes Bill on Covert Action," N.Y. Times, Mar. 16, 1988, at A8, col. 4. After being jointly referred to both the House Intelligence and Foreign Affairs committees, the House bill was marked up and reported out of both. See 100th Cong., 2d Sess., H. Rept. 705, pt. I (1988) (Intelligence Committee); pt. 2 (1988) (Foreign Affairs Committee).

128. Pear, "Wright Disclosure Termed Accurate," N.Y. Times, Sept. 25, 1988, at A15, col. 1.

129. See, generally, *id.*; Johnson, "White House Chides Wright over C.I.A. Comments," N.Y. Times, Sept. 22, 1988, at A15, col. 1; "Wright Formally Denies Breach on Nicaragua," N.Y. Times, Oct. 6, 1988, at A5, col. 1; Stern, "'Iran-Contra' Fades from Center Stage," *First Principles* (Dec. 1988): 9, col. 3.

Subsequently, of course, Congressman Wright left the House over unrelated charges of ethical violations.

130. See Oreskes, "Wright, in Gesture to Bush, Shelves Bill on Covert Acts," N.Y. Times, Feb. 1, 1989, at A12, col. 5; Engelberg, "Bush to Tell Congress of Covert Plans," N.Y. Times, Oct. 28, 1989, at A3, col. 1 (Bush agrees to notify Congress of most, but not all, covert actions).

131. See *Iran-Contra Report, supra* note 3, at 327–74 (describing "The Enterprise").

132. See, generally, S. Segev, *The Iranian Triangle: The Untold Story of Israel's Role in the Iran-Contra Affair* (1988) (describing Israel's involvement in the Iran-contra affair).

133. *Compare Tower Report, supra* note 80, at 98 *with Iran-Contra Report, supra* note 3, at 427 (majority report) ("such consolidation would inevitably erode Congress' ability to perform its oversight function"). See, also, L. Johnson, *America's Secret Power: The CIA in a Democratic Society* 222 (1989) ("The co-optation becomes all the easier when the bureaucrats have to confront only one legislative committee").

134. See W. Cohen & G. Mitchell, *Men of Zeal: A Candid Inside Story of the Iran-Contra Hearings* 65 (1988).

135. See "The Curtain Begins to Fall," *Economist* (Aug. 1, 1987): 19 (describing flow of hearings).

CHAPTER 3: THE NATIONAL SECURITY CONSTITUTION WE INHERITED

1. U.S. Const. art. II, § 2, cl. 2.

2. U.S. Const. art. I, § 8, cl. 11; art. II, § 2, cl. 1.

3. Although Article II, Section 3 of the Constitution, for example, declares that the president "shall receive Ambassadors and other public Ministers," that clause has been read as granting the president the authority not simply to undertake the ceremonial function of admitting ambassadors and examining their credentials, but virtually unfettered power to recognize or not recognize foreign states and governments. T. Franck & M. Glennon, *Foreign Relations and National Security Law* 431 (1987).

4. See Black, "The Working Balance of the American Political Departments," 1 *Hastings Const. L.Q.* 13 (1974).

5. See Dam, "The American Fiscal Constitution," 44 *U. Chi. L. Rev.* 271, 279–90 (1977); Stith, "Rewriting the Fiscal Constitution: The Case of Gramm-Rudman-Hollings," 76 *Calif. L. Rev.* 593 (1988) (describing analogous "fiscal constitution" that guides governmental allocation of taxing and spending authority); Elliott, "INS v. Chadha: The Administrative Constitution, the Constitution, and the Legislative Veto," 1983 *Sup. Ct. Rev.* 125, 169–73 (describing analogous "administrative constitution" that governs operation of American administrative state).

6. C. Black, *Structure and Relationship in Constitutional Law* 15 (1969) (emphasis

added); Black, "Reflections on Teaching and Working in Constitutional Law," 66 *Or. L. Rev.* 1, 11 (1980). See, also, Black, *supra* note 4. For recent applications of the structural method, see Powell, "How Does the Constitution Structure Government?: The Founders' Views," *A Workable Government?* 13 (B. Marshall ed. 1987); Carter, "Constitutional Adjudication and the Indeterminate Text," 94 *Yale L.J.* 821, 853–55 (1985); Amar, "Of Sovereignty and Federalism," 96 *Yale L.J.* 1425, 1426–29 (1987).

7. *The Federalist* No. 75, at 488 (A. Hamilton) (Modern Library ed. 1937) ("It must indeed be clear to a demonstration that the joint possession of the [treaty] power . . . by the President and Senate, would afford a greater prospect of security, than the separate possession of it by either of them"); R. Neustadt, *Presidential Power: The Politics of Leadership* 101 (rev. ed. 1976).

8. See L. Henkin, *Constitutionalism, Democracy and Foreign Affairs* 48 (unpublished manuscript, forthcoming 1990) (reading the Constitution's "[t]ext, context, design, intent and history" to provide the president with "sole and exclusive authority over diplomacy and the diplomatic process, the recognition of states and governments, the maintenance of diplomatic relations, the conduct of negotiations, [and] the gathering of intelligence" through the diplomatic process); see, also, Henkin, "Comment on Testimony of Charles J. Cooper, Assistant Attorney General, before Senate Select Committee on Intelligence, December 11, 1987," *Hearings Before the Subcomm. on Legislation of the House Permanent Select Comm. on Intelligence on H.R. 3822, to Strengthen the System of Congressional Oversight of Intelligence Activities in the United States*, 100th Cong., 2d Sess. 356 (1988) ("some means for gathering intelligence—notably through the diplomatic process—may not be subject to comprehensive regulation by Congress").

9. See Casper, "Constitutional Constraints on the Conduct of Foreign and Defense Policy: A Nonjudicial Model," 43 *U. Chi. L. Rev.* 463, 482 (1976).

10. See Casper, "The Constitutional Organization of the Government," 26 *Wm. & Mary L. Rev.* 177, 187–93 (1985) (including National Emergencies Act of 1976, Congressional Budget and Impoundment and Control Act of 1974, and War Powers Resolution as examples of such framework statutes). See, also, Elliott, *supra* note 5, at 318–19, 361–62 (also including Gramm-Rudman-Hollings Act of 1985 in this category); Dam, *supra* note 5, at 278–82 (1977) (treating the Budget and Accounting Act of 1921 and the Congressional Budget and Impoundment and Control Act of 1974 as quasi-constitutional); Stith, *supra* note 5, at 1363–64 & n.98 (including as appropriations and spending framework statutes the Anti-Deficiency Act of 1905, the Miscellaneous Receipts statute, and other provisions defining terms in appropriations statutes).

11. See *supra* note 8. See, generally, L. Henkin, *Foreign Affairs and the Constitution* 56–65 (1972) (describing presidential "legislation" in zones of exclusive presidential authority); Henkin, "The President and International Law," 80 *Am. J. Int'l L.* 930, 934 (1986) ("Acts within [the president's sole] constitutional authority

may have effect on the law of the United States; they may themselves make law and have effect as law in the United States").

12. I have previously discussed this body of law in Koh, "Introduction: Foreign Affairs under the United States Constitution," 13 *Yale J. Int'l L.* 1, 3 & n.7 (1988). For a thoughtful comparison of customary constitutional law and customary international law, see Glennon, "The Use of Custom in Resolving Separation of Powers Disputes," 64 *B.U.L. Rev.* 109, 128–46 (1984). See, also, Llewellyn, "The Constitution as an Institution," 34 *Colum. L. Rev.* 1, 28–31 (1934) (suggesting requirements for constitutional practice to "be unambiguously a part of the working Constitution"). This body of law also bears some resemblance to what Professor Monaghan has called "constitutional common law": a federal common law "substructure of substantive, procedural, and remedial rules drawing their inspiration and authority from . . . various constitutional provisions," but "subject to amendment, modification, or even reversal by Congress." See Monaghan, "The Supreme Court, 1974 Term—Foreword, Constitutional Common Law," 89 *Harv. L. Rev.* 1, 2–3 (1975); Davis v. Passman, 442 U.S. 228, 241–42 (1979); Bivens v. Six Unknown Named Agents, 403 U.S. 388 (1971).

13. Youngstown Sheet & Tube Co. v. Sawyer, 343 U.S. 579, 610–11 (1952) (Frankfurter, J., concurring).

14. See House Select Comm. to Investigate Covert Arms Transactions with Iran and Senate Select Comm. on Secret Military Assistance to Iran and the Nicaraguan Opposition, *Report of the Congressional Comms. Investigating the Iran-Contra Affair*, 100th Cong., 1st Sess., S. Rept. 216, H. Rept. 433, 387–92, 411–12 (1987) [hereinafter *Iran-Contra Report*] (majority report) (discussing congressional and presidential foreign-affairs powers and Congress's power of the purse); *cf.* Shane, "Legal Disagreement and Negotiation in a Government of Laws: The Case of Executive Privilege Claims against Congress," 71 *Minn. L. Rev.* 462, 477–81 (1987) (describing various nonlegislative means Congress has used to develop customary law of executive privilege).

15. See, *e.g.*, Barnes v. Kline, 759 F.2d 21 (D.C. Cir. 1985) (invalidating pocket veto at intersession adjournment), *vacated as moot sub nom.* Burke v. Barnes, 479 U.S. 361 (1987); Ramirez de Arellano v. Weinberger, 745 F.2d 1500 (D.C. Cir. 1984) (en banc) (enjoining executive action overseas infringing American citizen's enjoyment of private property), *vacated and remanded for reconsideration in light of subsequent legislation*, 471 U.S. 1113 (1985); Goldwater v. Carter, 617 F.2d 697 (D.C. Cir. 1979) (en banc) (upholding presidential termination of treaty in accordance with its terms), *vacated and remanded with directions to dismiss complaint*, 444 U.S. 996 (1979). *Cf. Restatement (Third) of the Foreign Relations Law of the United States* § 339 reporters' note 2, § 444 reporters' note 4 (1987) (treating some of these as rulings with persuasive, although not dispositive, weight).

16. 5 U.S. (1 Cranch) 137 (1803). See, generally, P. Bator, P. Mishkin, D. Meltzer, & D. Shapiro, *Hart and Wechsler's The Federal Courts and the Federal System* 30–

34 (3d ed. 1988) [hereinafter P. Bator] (describing First Judiciary Act); Amar, "*Marbury*, Section 13, and the Original Jurisdiction of the Supreme Court," 56 *U. Chi. L. Rev.* 443 (1989).

17. See INS v. Chadha, 462 U.S. 919 (1983) (invalidating legislative veto in National Emergencies Act); Dames & Moore v. Regan, 453 U.S. 654 (1981) (sustaining president's exercise of IEEPA authorities during the Iranian hostage crisis on statutory and constitutional grounds).

18. Youngstown Sheet & Tube Co. v. Sawyer, 343 U.S. 579, 635 (1952) (Jackson, J., concurring).

19. 299 U.S. 304 (1936). As a United States senator and lecturer, Justice Sutherland had previously set forth his ideas in a lengthy article and book. See Sutherland, "The Internal and External Powers of the National Government," Sen. Doc. No. 417, 61st Cong., 2d Sess. (1910); G. Sutherland, *Constitutional Power and World Affairs* (1919), *criticized in* Levitan, "The Foreign Relations Power: An Analysis of Mr. Justice Sutherland's Theory," 55 *Yale L.J.* 467, 472–78 (1946).

20. See, *e.g.*, J. Smith, *The Constitution and American Foreign Policy* (1989); G. Gunther, *Constitutional Law* 362 (11th ed. 1985); P. Shane & H. Bruff, *The Law of Presidential Power* 507 (1988); G. Stone, L. Seidman, C. Sunstein, & M. Tushnet, *Constitutional Law* 413 (1986); J. Nowak, R. Rotunda, & J. Young *Constitutional Law* 191 (3d ed. 1986).

21. See, *e.g.*, T. Bailey, *A Diplomatic History of the American People* (9th ed. 1974); *Modern American Diplomacy* (J. Carroll & G. Herring eds. 1986); J. Combs, *American Diplomatic History: Two Centuries of Changing Interpretations* (1983); A. DeConde, *A History of American Foreign Policy* (2d ed. 1971); *Guide to American Foreign Relations Since 1700* (R. Burns ed. 1983); *Encyclopedia of American Foreign Policy* (A. DeConde ed. 1978) [hereinafter A. DeConde]; W. LaFeber, *The American Age* (1989); A. Sofaer, *War, Foreign Affairs and Constitutional Power: The Origins* (1976); H. Cox, *War, Foreign Affairs and Constitutional Power: 1829–1901* (1984); A. Schlesinger, *The Imperial Presidency* (1973); W. Goldsmith, *The Growth of Presidential Power: A Documented History* (3 vols.) (1974); L. Henkin, *supra* note 11.

22. Note, "Developments in the Law—The National Security Interest and Civil Liberties," 85 *Harv. L. Rev.* 1130, 1133 (1972).

23. Although the phrase was first used in the National Security Act of 1947, there is no official definition of the term. The only quasi-official definition, prepared for a dictionary used by the Joint Chiefs of Staff, is: "a military or defense advantage over any foreign nation or group of nations, or . . . a favorable foreign relations position, or . . . a defense posture capable of successfully resisting hostile or destructive action from within or without, overt or covert." Barnet, "Rethinking National Strategy," *New Yorker* (Mar. 21, 1988): 107.

24. See *The Federalist*, *supra* note 7, Nos. 3, 4, 14, 23–32, 34, 36 (military and other external weakness); 5–8, 18–20 (fear of foreign intervention and dissolution of the union); 11–12, 22–23 (need to retaliate against foreign restrictions on trade);

22 (treaty enforcement); F. Marks, *Independence on Trial: Foreign Affairs and the Making of the Constitution* 170 (1986) ("Nearly every argument sprang from the concept of a foreign threat"). See, *e.g.*, *The Federalist, supra* note 7, No. 3 at 14 (J. Jay) ("a cordial Union, under an efficient national government, affords them the best security that can be devised against *hostilities* from abroad") (emphasis in original); see, also, *Documents Illustrative of the Formation of the Union of the American States* 115 (C. Tansill ed. 1927) (remarks of Edmund Randolph) (listing protection against foreign invasion as first priority for new government).

25. See Articles of Confederation, arts. VI, IX (1781), *reprinted in* 1 *The Founders' Constitution* 23–24 (P. Kurland & R. Lerner eds. 1987); L. Henkin, *supra* note 11, at 33; see, generally, Amar, *supra* note 6, at 1441–51, 1495–96 (describing problems under the Articles of Confederation).

26. See Articles of Confederation, art. VI (1781), *reprinted in* 1 *The Founders' Constitution* 23–24 (P. Kurland & R. Lerner eds. 1987); Gibbons, "The Eleventh Amendment and State Sovereign Immunity: A Reinterpretation," 83 *Colum. L. Rev.* 1889, 1899–1920 (1983).

27. See, generally, D. Lang, *Foreign Policy in the Early Republic* 67–82 (1985); F. Marks, *supra* note 24, at 3–51; Note, "The Framers' Intent and the Early Years of the Republic," 11 *Hofstra L. Rev.* 413, 416–23 (1982) [hereinafter Hofstra Note].

28. See Schlesinger, "The Constitution and Presidential Leadership," 47 *Md. L. Rev.* 54, 55 (1987). For detailed accounts of the drafting of the provisions of the Constitution regarding foreign affairs, see C. Thach, *The Creation of the Presidency, 1775–1789: A Study in Constitutional History* 55–139 (1922); L. Levy, *Original Intent and the Framers' Constitution* 30–53 (1988); Bestor, "Respective Roles of Senate and President in the Making and Abrogation of Treaties—The Original Intent of the Framers of the Constitution Historically Examined," 55 *Wash. L. Rev.* 1 (1979) [hereinafter Bestor, Respective Roles of Senate and President]; Bestor, "Separation of Powers in the Domain of Foreign Affairs: The Original Intent of the Constitution Historically Examined," 5 *Seton Hall L. Rev.* 529 (1974) [hereinafter Bestor, Separation of Powers]; Hofstra Note, *supra* note 27.

29. F. Marks, *supra* note 24, at 143 ("Some would differ on the question of how these powers should be exercised and where they should be lodged, but on the question of transferring power in the area of foreign relations from the state to the federal level there was virtual unanimity").

30. *The Federalist, supra* note 7, No. 45, at 303 (J. Madison) (emphasis added).

31. L. Henkin, *supra* note 11, at 33; *accord* L. Levy, *supra* note 28, at 30 ("The Framers simply did not intend the President to be an independent and dominating force, let alone the domineering one, in the making of foreign policy"); *The Federalist, supra* note 7, No. 75, at 487 (A. Hamilton) ("The history of human conduct does not warrant that exalted opinion of human virtue which would make it wise in a nation to commit interests of so delicate and momentous a kind as those

which concern its intercourse with the rest of the world to the sole disposal of . . . a President of the United States").

32. U.S. Const. art. I, § 8, cls. 1, 3, 4, 10, 11–16, 18 (emphasis added). For a discussion of the "necessary and proper" clause, see Van Alstyne, "The Role of Congress in Determining Incidental Powers of the President and of the Federal Courts: A Comment on the Horizontal Effect of the Sweeping Clause," 40 *Law & Contemp. Probs.*, Spring 1976, at 102. For a listing of Congress's textual powers in foreign affairs not set forth in Article I, see L. Henkin, *supra* note 11, at 67–69 nn.* & **, 76–86. An early draft of the Constitution gave Congress the exclusive power to "make war," but Madison and Elbridge Gerry jointly moved to substitute the word "declare" for the word "make," in order to allow the president to repel sudden attacks. See L. Levy, *supra* note 28, at 37.

33. U.S. Const. art. II, §§ 2 & 3; *The Federalist, supra* note 7, No. 69, at 488 (A. Hamilton) (clarifying that the commander-in-chief power "would be nominally the same with that of the king of Great Britain, but in substance much inferior to it"). See, also, Casper, "Symposium: Organizing the Government to Conduct Foreign Policy: The Constitutional Questions," 61 *Va. L. Rev.* 777, 778 (1975) (response to Louis Henkin); Amar, *supra* note 6, at 1495–96.

34. *The Federalist, supra* note 7, No. 75, at 448 (A. Hamilton); No. 69, at 488 (A. Hamilton). See, also, 2 *The Debates in the Several State Conventions on the Adoption of the Federal Constitution* 507 (J. Elliot ed. 1896) (statement of James Wilson) ("Neither the President nor the Senate, solely, can complete a treaty; they are checks upon each other, and are so balanced as to produce security to the people").

35. *Compare* Cooper, "What the Constitution Means by Executive Power," 43 *U. Miami L. Rev.* 165 (1988) (broadly construing Art. II, § 1 grant of "executive power") *with* Kurland, "Comment on Schlesinger," 47 *Md. L. Rev.* 75, 78 (1987); Bestor, Respective Roles of Senate and President, *supra* note 28, at 31 ("No serious attempt has ever been made to show that the framers of the Constitution accepted . . . that executive power by its very nature includes control of foreign affairs. As a matter of historical fact, the only utterances made in the Federal Convention of 1787 on the subject were emphatic rejections"); Winterton, "The Concept of Extra-Constitutional Executive Power in Domestic Affairs," 7 *Hastings Const. L.Q.* 1, 24–29 & n. 160 (1979) (rejecting broad view of "executive power" clause); L. Henkin, *supra* note 11, at 43 ("The Supreme Court has not considered [the grant of "executive Power"] as a possible source of constitutional power to conduct foreign relations, and its use to support other Presidential claims has had a mixed reception"); Lobel, "Emergency Power and the Decline of Liberalism," 98 *Yale L.J.* 1385, 1404–05 (1989); P. Shane & H. Bruff, *supra* note 20, at 8–12 (constitutional convention delegates held a wide variety of views on executive power, and therefore "established a Presidency with powers that resist definition").

36. U.S. Const. art. II, § 3; L. Henkin, *supra* note 11, at 54 ("The principal purport of

the clause, no doubt, was that the President should be a loyal agent of Congress to enforce its laws"); *The Federalist, supra* note 7, No. 70, at 459 (A. Hamilton); Youngstown Sheet & Tube Co. v. Sawyer, 343 U.S. 579, 635 (1952) (Jackson, J., concurring) (the "take Care" clause signifies "that ours is a government of laws, not of men"); *Iran-Contra Report, supra* note 14, at 419 (majority report) ("The 'take care' clause embodies the principle of accountability").

37. U.S. Const. art. III, § 2; 1 Stat. 73 (1789). See Bestor, Separation of Powers, *supra* note 28, at 577 (during first few months of convention only resolution that dealt explicitly with foreign affairs was one that called for judicial enforcement of treaties). For a description of the convention's deliberations regarding federal jurisdiction over foreign relations and the enactment of the First Judiciary Act, see P. Bator, *supra* note 16, at 14–16, 30–34. In particular, the First Judiciary Act included the Alien Tort Statute, 1 Stat. 77 (1789), 28 U.S.C. § 1350 (1982), which grants federal district courts "original jurisdiction of any civil action by an alien for a tort only, committed in violation of the law of nations." See, generally, Koh, "Civil Remedies for Uncivil Wrongs: Combatting Terrorism through Transnational Public Law Litigation," 22 *Tex. Int'l L.J.* 169, 198–99 (1987) (describing suits recently brought by aliens under that provision against the U.S. government and its officials challenging the conduct of American foreign policy). The First Judiciary Act did not, however, provide any general "federal question" jurisdiction under which a *U.S. citizen* might sue a U.S. official with regard to similar cases and controversies, but Congress later corrected that discrepancy in the Judiciary Act of 1875. See P. Bator, *supra* note 16, at 37, 995–96.

38. Bestor, Respective Roles of Senate and President, *supra* note 28, at 72 (emphasis added).

39. See *The Federalist, supra* note 7, No. 70, at 454 (A. Hamilton).

40. U.S. Const. art. II, § 2, cl. 1. *Compare* 1 *Records of the Federal Convention of 1787* 292 (M. Farrand ed. 1911) (describing proposed constitutional provisions regarding departments) *with* An Act for Establishing an Executive Department, to Be Denominated the Department of Foreign Affairs, 1 Stat. 28–29 (1789); An Act to Establish an Executive Department, to Be Denominated the Department of War, 1 Stat. 49–50 (1789). See, also, U.S. Const. art. I, § 8, cl. 18 (Congress may make all laws necessary and proper to execute powers vested "in any Department or Officer" of the government); *id.* art. II, § 2, cl. 2 (Congress may vest appointment of inferior officers in "the Heads of Departments"). Significantly, Congress did not designate the Department of the Treasury, the third cabinet department created at this time, as an executive department. See 1 Stat. 65 (1789); Casper, "An Essay in Separation of Powers: Some Early Versions and Practices," 30 *Wm. & Mary L. Rev.* 211, 239–42 (1989). See, generally, Guggenheimer, "The Development of the Executive Departments, 1775–1789," in *Essays in the Constitutional History of the United States in the Formative Period, 1775–1789* 116, 172, 176–83 (J. Jameson ed. 1889).

41. The Declaration of Independence, paras. 2, 14 (U.S. 1776).

42. *Youngstown*, 343 U.S. at 646 (Jackson, J., concurring).

43. U.S. Const. art. I, § 8, cls. 10, 13.

44. *Cf.* L. Hartz, *The Liberal Tradition in America* 284–309 (1955) (America's separatism fostered political tradition of "liberal absolutism").

45. *The Federalist, supra* note 7, No. 41, at 263 (J. Madison); see, also, Lobel, *supra* note 35, at 1397–98 (America's separatism initially fostered constitutional perspective that took narrow view of executive foreign-affairs powers).

46. I. Claude, *American Approaches to World Affairs* 4 (1986). See, also, P. Kennedy, *The Rise and Fall of the Great Powers* 151–58, 178 (1987); R. Keohane, *After Hegemony* 31, 35–37 (1984). For a similar sentiment, expressed by Washington's attorney general, see Letter from Edmund Randolph to James Monroe, *reprinted in* 1 *American State Papers, Foreign Relations* 706 (W. Lawrie & M. Clark eds. 1883): "An infant country, deep in debt; necessitated to borrow in Europe; without a land or naval force; without a competency of arms or ammunition; with . . . a constitution more than four years old; in a state of probation, and not exempt from foes [—] such a country can have no greater curse in store for her than war").

47. W. Wilson, *Congressional Government* 43 (15th ed. 1913) ("The early Presidents were men . . . of such a stamp that they would under any circumstances have made their influence felt"). See, also, T. Lowi, *The Personal President* 32 (1985) ("During that formative period there was inevitably a stronger role for the presidency and a cabinet than that actually called for in the Constitution"); Black, *supra* note 4, at 20 ("Congress is very poorly structured for initiative and leadership; the presidency is very well structured for such things. The result has been a flow of power from Congress to the presidency").

48. See Patterson, "The Rise of Presidential Power before World War II," 40 *Law & Contemp. Probs.* 39 (1976) (identifying 1810–29, 1849–60 as weak periods of presidential power); P. Shane & H. Bruff, *supra* note 20, at 12–16 (describing weak period as 1836–61); Pletcher, "Presidential Powers in Foreign Affairs," in 3 A. DeConde, *supra* note 21, at 805, 807 (period of "slower development" of presidential power from 1815–45); C. Rossiter, *The American Presidency* 83–84 (1960).

49. See P. Shane & H. Bruff, *supra* note 20, at 12.

50. A. Darling, *Our Rising Empire, 1763–1803* 130 (1940) (quoting Washington). For accounts of Washington's acts, see A. Sofaer, *supra* note 21, at 93–129; Hofstra Note, *supra* note 27, at 458–509.

51. Washington did not seek to withhold those documents from the Senate. See A. Schlesinger, *supra* note 21, at 16–17; Casper, *supra* note 40, at 258 (the dispute "had a somewhat 'academic' character because the Senate had received all the papers and the House members apparently could inspect them at the Senate").

52. A. Sofaer, *supra* note 21, at 129 (describing actions against Wabash Indians).

53. *Id.* at 103–16; Sofaer, "The Presidency, War, and Foreign Affairs: Practice under the Framers," 40 *Law & Contemp. Probs.* 12, 18 (1976).

54. A. Sofaer, *supra* note 21, at 129. Washington ultimately concluded that it "rested with the wisdom of Congress to correct, improve, or enforce" neutrality policy. See A. Schlesinger, *supra* note 21, at 18–20 (citing 1 *Messages and Papers of the Presidents* 131 [1897]).

55. Act of June 5, 1794, 1 Stat. 381–84 (codified at 18 U.S.C. §§ 959–61 [1982]). Hamilton and Jefferson took the lead among Washington's cabinet officers in drafting the statute. See C. Thomas, *American Neutrality in 1793: A Study in Cabinet Government* 13–52 (1931). For histories of that statute, see Lobel, "The Rise and Decline of the Neutrality Act: Sovereignty and Congressional War Powers in United States Foreign Policy," 24 *Harv. Int'l L.J.* 1 (1983); Note, "Nonenforcement of the Neutrality Act: International Law and Foreign Policy Powers under the Constitution," 95 *Harv. L. Rev.* 1955 (1982); Note, "The Iran-Contra Affair, the Neutrality Act, and the Statutory Definition of 'At Peace,' " 27 *Va. J. Int'l L.* 343 (1987).

56. Fisher, "The Role of Congress in Foreign Policy," 11 *Geo. Mason U. L. Rev.* 153, 158 (1988).

57. See, generally, Casper, *supra* note 40; *id.* at 261 ("Although the special responsibility of the President for the maintenance of foreign relations was understood, neither the President nor the Congress assumed that the Executive had what John Locke . . . called the 'federative' power, which pertained to foreign relations and was, by him, classified as an executive power"); E. Corwin, *The President: Office and Powers, 1787–1984* 201 (5th ed. 1984).

58. See 1 W. Goldsmith, *supra* note 21, at 410. For accounts of the Pacificus-Helvidius debate, see A. Sofaer, *supra* note 21, at 112–16; L. Levy, *supra* note 28, at 51–52; E. Corwin, *supra* note 57, at 208–12; Berger, "The Presidential Monopoly of Foreign Relations," 71 *Mich. L. Rev.* 1, 17–25 (1972).

59. Sofaer, *supra* note 53, at 36, 37. See, also, *id.* at 37:

Adams avoided a declaration of war, but sought legislative authority at each stage in the nation's movement toward war with France. Jefferson conducted diplomacy with vigor and secrecy, but moved conservatively in military matters, even when he could have claimed that Congress had approved a full-scale military effort to take West Florida. Madison and Monroe defy simplification; but it can be said of their adventures in the Floridas that they were pursuing popular objectives with minimal commitment of material and military resources. Their efforts cannot be equated with the unpopular, massive engagements in Korea and Vietnam.

See, also, *id.* at 15–36; A. Sofaer, *supra* note 21, at 131–379 (providing greater historical detail in support of these themes); A. Schlesinger, *The Cycles of History* 297 (1987) ("Early Presidents, even while they circumvented the Constitution, had a cautious and vigilant concern for consent in a practical if not a formal sense"). See, also, 15 *Annals of Congress* 19 (1805) (remarks of Thomas Jefferson regarding Spanish West Florida) ("Considering that Congress alone is constitutionally invested with the power of changing our condition from peace to war,

I have thought it my duty to await their authority for using force in any degree which could be avoided"); Youngstown Sheet & Tube Co. v. Sawyer, 343 U.S. 579, 638 n.5 (1952) (Jackson, J., concurring) ("The Louisiana Purchase had nothing to do with the separation of powers as between the President and Congress, but only with state and federal power. [The criticism was not] that Mr. Jefferson acted without authority from Congress, but that neither had express authority to expand the boundaries of the United States by purchase or annexation").

60. See Act of Mar. 3, 1799, ch. 48, 1 Stat. 749, 750 (repealed 1802). Professor Detlev Vagts kindly brought this statute to my attention.

61. Marshall was supporting not the president's right to *make* treaties without congressional participation but his right to surrender an American for extradition to Great Britain under an existing treaty. See 10 *Annals of Cong.* 595–618 (Mar. 7, 1800); Berger, *supra* note 58, at 16–17. As Professor Corwin recognized, "[c]learly, what Marshall had foremost in mind was simply the President's role as *instrument of communication* with other governments." E. Corwin, *supra* note 57, at 208 (emphasis in original). *Accord* L. Levy, *supra* note 28, at 52 ("John Marshall's 1800 declaration . . . meant nothing more than that only the President communicates with foreign nations; he is the organ of communication"). For a discussion of congressional acquiescence in these matters, see L. Henkin, *supra* note 11, at 46, 92–94; Kelly, "The Constitution and Foreign Policy," in 1 A. DeConde, *supra* note 21, at 177, 180.

62. See A. Sofaer, *supra* note 21, at 256 n. **.

63. See, generally, H. Cox, *supra* note 21, at 81–83; A. Schlesinger, *supra* note 21, at 28–29; F. Wormuth & E. Firmage, *To Chain the Dog of War* 79–80 (2d ed. 1989).

64. Patterson, *supra* note 48, at 44.

65. Bas v. Tingy, 4 U.S. (4 Dall.) 37 (1800).

66. 5 U.S. (1 Cranch) 1, 28 (1801) (emphasis added). See, also, Note, "Realism, Liberalism and the War Powers Resolution," 102 *Harv. L. Rev.* 637, 643 (1989) (these early decisions "embodie[d] the liberal idea that the executive cannot initiate war or any significant armed conflict without advance congressional approval"); Lofgren, "War-Making under the Constitution: The Original Understanding," 81 *Yale L.J.* 672, 701 (1972).

67. 6 U.S. (2 Cranch) 170, 177–78 (1804). For accounts of the case, see A. Sofaer, *supra* note 21, at 162–63; Glennon, "Two Views of Presidential Foreign Affairs Power: *Little v. Barreme* or *Curtiss-Wright?*" 13 *Yale J. Int'l L.* 5 (1988).

68. 12 U.S. (8 Cranch) 110 (1814).

69. 27 F. Cas. 1192 (C.C.D.N.Y. 1806) (No. 16,342). For colorful accounts of the case, see Reinstein, "An Early View of Executive Powers and Privilege: The Trial of Smith & Ogden," 2 *Hastings Const. L.Q.* 309 (1975); 7 J. Moore, *A Digest of International Law* 917–19 (1906). I am grateful to Professors Walter Dellinger and H. Jefferson Powell for drawing this case to my attention.

70. 27 F. Cas. at 1218, 1230–31. See, also, *id.* at 1231 (declaring that the president

lacked unilateral war-making authority except where necessary to repel a sudden invasion; if authorized to go beyond that, the president could, "contrary to the constitutional will . . . involve the nation . . . in all the calamities of a long and expensive war").

71. *Id.*

72. Suffice it to say that all of Judge Gesell's rulings in the *North* case are consistent with the earlier rulings in *Smith*. Furthermore, in one recent case that was vacated on appeal on other grounds, a district judge relied heavily upon *Smith* to hold that the Neutrality Act prohibited even presidentially authorized paramilitary expeditions that are mounted against a government with whom the United States is at peace. The court rejected claims that the Neutrality Act invaded the president's commander-in-chief power and also concluded that the matter was justiciable. See Dellums v. Smith, 577 F. Supp. 1449, 1452–54 (N.D. Cal. 1983); *id.*, 573 F. Supp. 1489 (N.D. Cal. 1983) (on motion for summary judgment), *vacated on other grounds*, 797 F.2d 817 (9th Cir. 1986).

73. H. Cox, *supra* note 21, at 85.

74. LaFeber, "The Constitution and United States Foreign Policy: An Interpretation," 74 *J. Am. Hist.* 695, 700 (1987); W. LaFeber, *supra* note 21, at 103–18; Patterson, *supra* note 48, at 45; A. Schlesinger, *supra* note 21, at 38–52; H. Cox, *supra* note 21, at 143–54, 167–72; J. Javits, *Who Makes War* 78–103 (1973). Two years after Congress declared war on Mexico, the House disapproved President Polk's actions by resolving that the war had been "unnecessarily and unconstitutionally begun by the President of the United States." See 17 Cong. Globe 95 (1848).

75. H. Cox, *supra* note 21, at 172.

76. 8 F. Cas. 111, 112 (C.C.S.D.N.Y 1860) (No. 4,186). For a complete account of the incident, see 7 J. Moore, *supra* note 69, at 346–54. See, also, Martin v. Mott, 25 U.S. (12 Wheat.) 19, 30 (1827) (Story, J.) (sustaining president's authority to call forth the militia to repel invasion and holding that president's decision as to whether an exigency has arisen "is conclusive upon all other persons"); Fleming v. Page, 50 U.S. (9 How.) 603, 615 (1850) (Taney, C.J.) (reaffirming president's military powers as commander-in-chief "to invade the hostile country, and subject it to the sovereignty and authority of the United States").

77. See P. Kennedy, *supra* note 46, at 179; A. Carr, *The World and William Walker* (1963) (recounting William Walker's use of private army to conquer Nicaragua).

78. *The Political Thought of Abraham Lincoln* 44 (R. Current ed. 1967). In this now-famous letter to his law partner in 1848, Congressman Lincoln wrote: "Allow the President to invade a neighboring nation, whenever *he* shall deem necessary to repel an invasion . . . and you allow him to make war at pleasure. Study to see if you can fix *any limit* to his power in this respect" (emphasis in original). *Id.* at 43.

79. Patterson, *supra* note 48, at 46; M. Cunliffe, *American Presidents and the Presidency* 98–102 (2d ed. 1976); A. Schlesinger, *supra* note 21, at 58–67. See,

generally, J. Randall, *Constitutional Problems under Lincoln* (rev. ed. 1951); W. Whiting, *War Powers under the Constitution of the United States* (43d ed. 1871).

80. See *The Prize Cases,* 67 U.S. (2 Black) 635, 665–71 (1862) (narrowly sustaining Union seizures of ships trading with the Confederacy after Lincoln's blockade of southern ports); *id.* at 670 (president's decisions in suppressing the insurrection were "question[s] to be decided *by him,* and this Court must be governed by the decisions and acts of the political department of the Government to which this power was entrusted") (emphasis in original).

81. *Id.* at 668; Ely, "Suppose Congress Wanted a War Powers Act that Worked," 88 *Colum. L. Rev.* 1379, 1390 n.34 (1988) ("President Lincoln's actions at the outset of the Civil War are sometimes cited as precedent for presidential military ventures. Although Lincoln did engage in a number of unconstitutional acts during this period . . . usurpation of the war power was not among them. . . . For constitutional purposes a domestic rebellion is quite different from a foreign war").

82. Ely, *supra* note 81, at 1389–90 & n.34 (1988); Corwin, "The President's Power," in *The President: Roles and Powers* 360, 361 (D. Haight & L. Johnston eds. 1965) ("the vast majority" of presidential commitments of troops abroad without congressional approval involved fights with pirates, landings on semibarbarous coasts, and dispatches of troops to chase bandits across borders).

83. See Patterson, *supra* note 48, at 47; P. Shane & H. Bruff, *supra* note 20, at 17; Pletcher, *supra* note 48, at 808.

84. Command of the Army Act, § 2, 14 Stat. 485 (Mar. 2, 1867); Tenure of Office Act, § 2, *id.* at 430 (Mar. 2, 1867). See, generally, L. White, *The Republican Era: 1869–1901* 20–44 (1958); M. Benedict, *A Compromise of Principle* 294–314 (1974); B. Ackerman, *Discovering the Constitution,* chapter 10 (1985–86) (unpublished manuscript, forthcoming); Patterson, *supra* note 48, at 46–47 (describing how Johnson's successors in office used their veto and law enforcement powers to "dis[play] moments of comparable assertiveness").

85. W. LaFeber, *supra* note 21, at 157–58; see, also, Pletcher, *supra* note 48, at 808.

86. H. Cox, *supra* note 21, at 312–15.

87. A. Schlesinger, *supra* note 21, at 80; Patterson, *supra* note 48, at 48. See, generally, W. Holt, *Treaties Defeated by the Senate* 121–64 (1933); D. Cheever & H. Haviland, *American Foreign Policy and the Separation of Powers* 48–55 (1952). But see T. Aleinikoff & D. Martin, *Immigration Process and Policy* 3–5 (1985) (describing Chinese immigration treaties concluded during this period).

88. See W. Wilson, *supra* note 47, at 50 (emphasis in original); Lippmann, Introduction to W. Wilson, *Congressional Government* 8 (Meridian ed. 1956).

89. See P. Kennedy, *supra* note 46, at 179 (before demobilization, the United States was briefly "the greatest military nation on earth"); W. LaFeber, *supra* note 21, at 161–73; R. Beisner, *From the Old Diplomacy to the New, 1865–1900* (2d ed. 1986); T. McCormick, *China Market: America's Quest for Informal Empire 1893–1901* (1967). For accounts of this period, see Pletcher, "1861–1898: Eco-

nomic Growth and Diplomatic Adjustments," in *Economics and World Power: An Assessment of American Diplomacy Since 1789* 120 (W. Becker & S. Wells eds. 1984); W. LaFeber, *The New Empire: An Interpretation of American Expansionism 1860–98* (1963).

90. See P. Kennedy, *supra* note 46, at 246; C. Campbell, *The Transformation of American Foreign Relations, 1865–1900* 84–121, 296–318 (1976); S. Skowronek, *Building a New American State* 85–120 (1982) (describing restructuring of the army).

91. W. LaFeber, *supra* note 21, at 158. For accounts of the Brazilian, Chilean, and Venezuelan episodes, see *id.* at 161–67; H. Cox, *supra* note 21, at 274–75 (Congress rose to Cleveland's support in the Venezuelan affair); *id.* at 308–12 (Congress failed to respond with regard to Brazil and Chile).

92. H. Cox, *supra* note 21, at 331.

93. See *id.* at 248–50, 294–95, 326. In *Ex Parte Siebold,* 100 U.S. 371 (1880), decided during this period, the Supreme Court sustained judicial appointment of supervisors of congressional elections pursuant to a statute, but declared in broad dicta that the U.S. government and its agents may exercise on U.S. soil "the power to command obedience to its laws, and hence the power to keep the peace to that extent." *Id.* at 395.

94. 135 U.S. 1 (1890). As Professor LaFeber wryly notes, this was "a question about which [the justices] were hardly disinterested." LaFeber, *supra* note 74, at 702. The facts of this bizarre case are recounted in J. Semonche, *Charting the Future* 23–27 (1978) and C. Swisher, *Steven J. Field: Craftsman of the Law* 321–61 (1930).

95. 135 U.S. at 64 (emphasis added).

96. See *In re Debs,* 158 U.S. 564, 586 (1895) (upholding president's inherent power to obtain injunction against Pullman strike). The Court's broad language in *Debs* was clearly unnecessary to the decision of the case, given that the lower court had already granted the U.S. government injunctive relief against the strike by relying on the Sherman Act. Alternatively, the Court's ruling upholding an implied right of action on behalf of the United States could have been justified as an interstitial judicial remedy supplementing the numerous congressional statutes regulating interstate commerce carried on the railways.

97. See Legal Opinion of Lloyd Cutler, President's Counsel, on War Powers Consultation Relative to the Iran Rescue Mission, para. 2 (May 9, 1980), Subcomm. on Int'l Security and Scientific Affairs of the House Comm. on Foreign Affairs, *War Powers Resolution: Relevant Documents, Correspondence, Reports,* 98th Cong., 1st Sess. 50 (1983).

98. R. Beisner, *Twelve against Empire: The Anti-Imperialists, 1898–1900* xv (1968).

99. A. Schlesinger, *supra* note 21, at 87–89. On the McKinley presidency, see, generally, W. LaFeber, *supra* note 21, at 181–213. On the Boxer Rebellion, see 134 *Cong. Rec.* S17,287 (Oct. 21, 1988) (remarks of Senator Biden) ("McKinley

[dispatched troops to China] without congressional authorization, using as his pretext the protection of American lives and property. His action aroused no congressional objection"). On the Philippines annexation, see H. Cox, *supra* note 21, at 315–16 ("McKinley's action in the Philippines was a victory of executive power"); F. Dulles, *America's Rise to World Power 1898–1954,* at 21–81 (1955); G. Kennan, *American Diplomacy 1900–1950,* at 4–20 (1951). For an argument that the Philippine annexation marked not a new departure, but "the last episode of a nineteenth-century pattern of territorial acquisition and direct political rule of subject peoples" that began with U.S. policy toward native Americans, see Williams, "United States Indian Policy and the Debate over Philippine Annexation: Implications for the Origins of American Imperialism," 66 *J. Am. Hist.* 810, 831 (1980).

100. T. Roosevelt, *An Autobiography* 464 (1929). See, also, R. Hoxie, *Command Decision and the Presidency* 40 (1977).

101. Congress had strongly supported the war against Spain and the Supreme Court broadly deferred to the judgment of the political branches regarding the new American conquests. In Neely v. Henkel, 180 U.S. 109, 124 (1901), the Court declared that "it is not competent for the judiciary to make any declaration upon the question of the length of time during which Cuba may be rightfully occupied and controlled by the United States in order to effect its pacification—it being the function of the political branch of the Government to determine." See, also, De Lima v. Bidwell, 182 U.S. 1 (1901); Dooley v. United States, 182 U.S. 222 (1901); Armstrong v. United States, 182 U.S. 243 (1901); Downes v. Bidwell, 182 U.S. 244 (1901) *(The Insular cases)* (effectively ratifying McKinley's conquests and holding that the newly acquired territories belonged to the United States, but were not "incorporated" into it). See, generally, J. Kerr, *The Insular Cases: The Role of the Judiciary in American Expansionism* 65–97 (1982), Cabranes, "Puerto Rico: Colonialism as Constitutional Doctrine," 100 *Harv. L. Rev.* 450, 453 (1986).

102. Pletcher, *supra* note 48, at 809. Although Roosevelt effectively terminated the Clayton-Bulwer treaty in building the Panama Canal, the Senate rejected the first version of its successor, the Hay-Paunceforte treaty. See W. Holt, *supra* note 87, at 184–96.

103. Moreover, the terms of the Root-Takahira Accord were reaffirmed during World War I by another secret executive agreement, the Lansing-Ishii Agreement of 1917. For discussions of foreign policy during Roosevelt's presidency, see, generally, D. Cheever & H. Haviland, *supra* note 87, at 56–67; L. Margolis, *Executive Agreements and Presidential Power in Foreign Policy* 9–12 (1986); H. Beale, *Theodore Roosevelt and the Rise of America to World Power* (1962); E. May, *Imperial Diplomacy: The Emergence of America as a Great Power* (1961).

104. P. Kennedy, *supra* note 46, at 248.

105. J. Roche & L. Levy, *The Presidency* 23 (1964) (emphasis added).

106. See, generally, W. Scholes & M. Scholes, *The Foreign Policies of the Taft Administration* (1970).

107. W. Wilson, *supra* note 47, at xi-xii.

108. W. LaFeber, *supra* note 21, at 261.

109. Patterson, *supra* note 48, at 51.

110. R. Hoxie, *supra* note 100, at 43; D. Cheever & H. Haviland, *supra* note 87, at 80–81; C. May, *In the Name of War: Judicial Review and the War Powers Since 1918* 197–98, 208 (1989).

111. See D. Cheever & H. Haviland, *supra* note 87, at 68–83.

112. See, generally, Patterson, *supra* note 48, at 52; D. Cheever & H. Haviland, *supra* note 87, at 84–92. On the economic diplomacy of the interwar years, see M. Leffler, *The Elusive Quest: America's Pursuit of European Stability and French Security, 1919–1933* (1979); C. Parrini, *Heir to Empire: United States Economic Diplomacy, 1916–1923* (1969).

113. Ely, *supra* note 81, at 1388–91 (emphasis added).

114. Under United States constitutional law, the president may constitutionally enter into three types of executive agreements: international agreements negotiated to carry out existing treaties ("treaty-related executive agreements"); international agreements negotiated pursuant to specific congressional authorization or approval ("congressional-executive agreements"); and international agreements negotiated pursuant to the president's independent constitutional powers (so-called sole executive agreements). See, generally, *Restatement (Third) of the Foreign Relations Law of the United States* § 303 (1987) ("The prevailing view is that the Congressional-Executive agreement can be used as an alternative to the treaty method in every instance"; *id.* comment e, at 161. See, also, McDougal & Lans, "Treaties and Congressional-Executive or Presidential Agreements: Interchangeable Instruments of National Policy" (pts. 1 & 2), 54 *Yale L.J.* 181, 534 (1945).

115. C. May, *supra* note 110, at 275.

116. Black, *supra* note 4, at 20.

117. Ackerman identifies the signing of the Constitution and the Reconstruction era as two other constitutional moments. See, generally, B. Ackerman, *supra* note 84.

118. 299 U.S. 304 (1936).

119. *Id.* at 318.

120. *Id.* at 319–20 (emphasis added).

121. See, *e.g.*, L. Henkin, *supra* note 11, at 19–26; Levitan, *supra* note 19, at 493; Berger, *supra* note 58, at 26–33; Glennon, *supra* note 67, at 12–17; LaFeber, *supra* note 74, at 710–14; Lofgren, "United States v. Curtiss-Wright Export Corporation: An Historical Reassessment," 83 *Yale L.J.* 1 (1973).

122. See, *e.g.*, Youngstown Sheet & Tube Co. v. Sawyer, 343 U.S. at 635–36 n.2 (Jackson, J., concurring); Glennon, *supra* note 67, at 12–13.

123. See, generally, Berger, *supra* note 58, at 26–33; Levitan, *supra* note 19; Lofgren, *supra* note 121.

124. These congressional powers include Congress's substantive authorities in Article I, §§ 8 & 9 of the Constitution (*e.g.*, Congress's power of the purse and power

to declare war); Congress's procedural powers in Article I, § 7 (*e.g.*, Congress's power to override a presidential veto); and Congress's procedural powers in Article II (*e.g.*, the Senate's right to advise and consent to treaty ratification and ambassadorial appointments).

125. B. Ackerman, *supra* note 84, ch. 12, at 77.

126. See, *e.g.*, Brief for the Federal Respondents, Dames & Moore v. Regan, 453 U.S. 654 (1981), at 30, 40, 44, 52, 53; Brief for the Appellees, American Foreign Service Ass'n v. Garfinkel, No. 87-2127, 109 S. Ct. 1693 (1989), at 18, 19, 22, 24, 25, 44.

127. Levitan, *supra* note 19, at 493.

128. The notion of nonjusticiable political questions dates back to Marbury v. Madison, 5 U.S. (1 Cranch) 137, 170 (1803) ("Questions in their nature political, or which are, by the constitution and laws, submitted to the executive, can never be made in this court"). But in summarizing the history of that doctrine in Baker v. Carr, the Court made clear that "it is error to suppose that every case or controversy that touches foreign relations lies beyond judicial cognizance." 369 U.S. 186, 211 (1962). For further discussion of the political question doctrine, see, generally, *infra* chapter 9.

129. 301 U.S. 324, 330 (1937). For a discussion of the relationship between *Curtiss-Wright* and *Belmont*, see Riesenfeld, "The Power of Congress and the President in International Relations: Three Recent Supreme Court Decisions," 25 *Calif. L. Rev.* 643, 665–75 (1937).

130. 315 U.S. 203, 229 (1942) (quoting *Curtiss-Wright*).

131. See 39 Op. Att'y Gen. 484 (1940). But see Borchard, "The Attorney General's Opinion on the Exchange of Destroyers for Naval Bases," 34 *Am. J. Int'l L.* 690, 690 (1940) (criticizing opinion).

132. See A. Schlesinger, *supra* note 21, at 110–13.

133. See, generally, S. Ambrose, *Rise to Globalism: American Foreign Policy Since 1938* (1971); Huntington, "Coping with the Lippman Gap," 66 *Foreign Aff.* 453 (1987/88); Vasquez, "Domestic Contention on Critical Foreign-Policy Issues: The Case of the United States," 42 *Int'l Org.* 643 (1988).

134. See, generally, F. Kirgis, *International Organizations in Their Legal Setting* (1977).

135. See T. Lowi, *supra* note 47, at 99; Patterson, *supra* note 48, at 39, 56.

136. See, generally, Leuchtenburg, "Franklin D. Roosevelt: The First Modern President," in *Leadership in the Modern Presidency* 7 (F. Greenstein ed. 1988) [hereinafter F. Greenstein].

137. See, generally, S. Hess, *Organizing the Presidency* 1–2 (1976); Staff of House Comm. on Post Office and Civil Service, Subcomm. on Employee Ethics and Utilization, *Presidential Staffing—A Brief Overview*, 95th Cong., 2d Sess. 52–53, 55–61 (1978); Greenstein, "In Search of a Modern Presidency," in F. Greenstein, *supra* note 136, at 347 ("four major changes . . . beginning in 1933, produced the modern presidency—increased unilateral policy-making

capacity, centrality in national agenda setting, far greater visibility, and acquisition of a presidential bureaucracy").

138. See Stout, "Hide and Seek," Wall St. J., Jan. 20, 1989 at R20 (Magazine).
139. 333 U.S. 103, 111 (1948) (emphasis added). In *Waterman,* the Court held unreviewable a presidential decree approving a Civil Aeronautics Board order that had denied an overseas route.
140. See Youngstown Sheet & Tube Co. v. Sawyer, 343 U.S. at 635–36 n.2 (Jackson, J., concurring) (emphasis added).
141. See, *e.g.,* Memorandum in Support of Motion to Dismiss Counts 1 through 3 (Defendant's Pretrial Motion Number 39), United States v. North, No. 88-0080-02, at 32 (D.D.C. filed Oct. 11, 1988) (citing *Waterman*).
142. See J. Jackson & W. Davey, *Legal Problems of International Economic Relations* 293–96 (1986) (describing ITO episode); LeBlanc, "The United Nations Genocide Convention and Political Groups: Should the United States Propose an Amendment?" 13 *Yale J. Int'l L.* 268, 279–82 (1988) (history of U.S. failure to ratify Genocide Convention). The Connally Reservation stipulated that the United States would not subject itself to the World Court's compulsory jurisdiction with respect to "[d]isputes with regard to matters which are essentially within the domestic jurisdiction of the United States of America as determined by the United States." 92 *Cong. Rec.* 10,624 (1946) (remarks of Senator Connally); Wilcox, "The United States Accepts Compulsory Jurisdiction," 40 *Am. J. Int'l L.* 699–736 (1946); Hyde, "Editorial Comment: The United States Accepts the Optional Clause," 40 *Am. J. Int'l L.* 778, 778–80 (1946).
143. See D. Cheever & H. Haviland, *supra* note 87, at 100–42; Winik, "Restoring Bipartisanship," *Wash. Q.* 109, 113–15 (Winter 1989); Felton, "The Man Who Showed Politicians the Water's Edge," 47 *Cong. Q.* 336 (Feb. 18, 1989) (describing bipartisan foreign policy under Vandenberg and Truman).
144. For a brief history of these statutes, from which this discussion derives, see Koh, "Congressional Controls on Presidential Trade Policymaking After *I.N.S.* v. *Chadha,*" 18 *N.Y.U. J. Int'l L. & Pol.* 1191, 1194–1225 (1986).
145. Pub. L. No. 71-361, 46 Stat. 590 (1930). For the classic account of the logrolling that led to Smoot-Hawley, see, generally, E. Schattschneider, *Politics, Pressures and the Tariff: A Study of Free Enterprise in Pressure Politics, as Shown in the 1929–30 Revision of the Tariff* (1935). For a description of the impact of the Smoot-Hawley tariff levels on world trade, see R. Pastor, *Congress and the Politics of U.S. Foreign Economic Policy* 78–79 (1980).
146. Pub. L. No. 73-316, 48 Stat. 943 (1934).
147. See R. Pastor, *supra* note 145, at 93–104; J. Jackson, J.-V. Louis, & M. Matsushita, *Implementing the Tokyo Round: National Constitutions and International Economic Rules* 141 (1984). The concessions obtained by Congress during this period included the first "legislative veto" found in the trade laws. See Trade Expansion Act of 1962, Pub. L. No. 87-794, § 351(a)(2)(B), 76 Stat. 872, 899 (1962).

148. S. Ambrose, *supra* note 133, at 167. *Compare* X, "The Sources of Soviet Conduct," 25 *Foreign Aff.* 566, 576 (1947) *with* W. Lippmann, *The Cold War: A Study in U.S. Foreign Policy* (1947) (criticizing Kennan); G. Kennan, *Memoirs: 1925–1950* 358 (1967) (conceding his own "failure to make clear that what I was talking about when I mentioned the containment of Soviet power was not the containment by military means of a military threat, but the political containment of a political threat").

149. See T. Lowi, *supra* note 47, at 165–66.

CHAPTER 4: THE IRAN-CONTRA AFFAIR

1. Youngstown Sheet & Tube Co. v. Sawyer, 343 U.S. 579, 634 (1952) (Jackson, J., concurring).

2. See, *e.g.*, J. Diggins, *The Proud Decades* (1988); J. & G. Kolko, *The Limits of Power* (1972); S. Landau, *The Dangerous Doctrine: National Security and U.S. Foreign Policy* 33–44 (1988); W. LaFeber, *America, Russia, and the Cold War, 1945–1971* (1972); W. Lippmann, *The Cold War: A Study in U.S. Foreign Policy* (1947).

3. R. Hoxie, *Command Decision and the Presidency* 129–52 (1977); S. Landau, *supra* note 2, at 36–47. The two planks of the Inter-American System, the Inter-American Treaty of Reciprocal Assistance (the Rio Pact) and the Charter of the Organization of American States, were signed in 1947 and 1948, respectively. The North Atlantic Treaty was signed in 1949; the Pact between Australia, New Zealand, and [the] United States (ANZUS) was created in 1952; the South-East Asia Treaty Organization (SEATO) in 1954; and the Central Treaty Organization (Cento) in 1955. See, generally, L. Henkin, R. Pugh, O. Schachter, & H. Smit, *International Law* 792, 801–2 (2d ed. 1987).

4. The umbrella term *covert operations* encompasses both covert military and paramilitary action (*i.e.*, clandestine warfare), as well as a range of nonviolent conduct that is distinct from simple intelligence gathering, for example, spreading propaganda, political action (*e.g.*, bribing foreign officials), and economic covert action (*e.g.*, initiating foreign labor strikes). For taxonomies of covert action, see L. Johnson, *America's Secret Power: The CIA in a Democratic Society* 17–35 (1989); G. Treverton, *Covert Action: The Limits of Intervention in the Postwar World* 13–31 (1987).

5. See Administrative Procedure Act, 5 U.S.C. §§ 551–559, 701–6 (1982); S. Landau, *supra* note 2, at 3–4 ("The National Security Act of 1947 . . . and subsequent amendments and decrees placed the governance of critical foreign and defense policies in the hands of new institutions: a national security apparatus run by national security managers").

6. 50 U.S.C. § 401 (1982). See *supra* chapter 3, (discussing civilian control of the military). Even if the Constitution itself did not oblige the president to prevent the mixing of military and civilian functions within his subordinate agencies, the 1947 act reflects Congress's clear intent to impose such a requirement by

statute. See 50 U.S.C. § 401 (1982) ("each military department shall be separately organized . . . and shall function . . . under civilian control of the Secretary of Defense but [Congress's purpose is] not to merge these departments or services").

7. 10 U.S.C. § 113(a) (1982) ("A person may not be appointed as Secretary of Defense within 10 years after relief from active duty as a commissioned officer of a regular component of an armed force"); *id.* § 134 (deputy secretary); *id.* § 135 (undersecretary).

8. For histories of the executive's intelligence-gathering activities before 1947, see Note, "The Extent of Independent Presidential Authority to Conduct Foreign Intelligence Activities," 72 *Geo. L.J.* 1855, 1856–64 (1984) [hereinafter Georgetown Note]; L. Johnson, *supra* note 4, at 3–16; G. Treverton, *supra* note 4, at 31–43.

9. See 50 U.S.C. § 403(a)–(b) (1982).

10. *Id.* § 403(d)(5) (1982) (emphasis added).

11. See Statement of the Honorable Clark M. Clifford on S. 1721 to the Senate Select Committee on Intelligence 4 (Dec. 16, 1987) (on file with author).

12. See 22 U.S.C. § 2422 (1982) ("No funds appropriated under authority of this chapter or any other Act may be expended by or on behalf of the Central Intelligence Agency for *operations in foreign countries, other than activities intended solely for obtaining necessary intelligence,* unless and until the President finds that each such operation is important to the national security of the United States") (emphasis added).

13. See Senate Select Comm. to Study Governmental Operations with respect to Intelligence Activities, *Foreign and Military Intelligence: Final Report* (Book I), 94th Cong., 2d Sess., S. Rept. 755, 132 (1976); *id.* at 489 (citing first CIA general counsel's concession that Congress had not intended to authorize covert activity).

14. See Testimony of Charles J. Cooper, Assistant Attorney General, Office of Legal Counsel, Before the Senate Select Committee on Intelligence, on S. 1721, at 3–6 (Dec. 11, 1987) (on file with author) (asserting president's exclusive authority "to initiate, direct, and control extremely sensitive national security activities").

15. See Henkin, "Comment on Testimony of Charles J. Cooper, Assistant Attorney General, before Senate Select Committee on Intelligence, December 11, 1987," *Hearings before the Subcomm. on Legislation of the House Permanent Select Comm. on Intelligence on H.R. 3822, to Strengthen the System of Congressional Oversight of Intelligence Activities in the United States,* 100th Cong., 2d Sess. 356–57 (1988); Georgetown Note, *supra* note 8; Note, "Covert Wars and Presidential Power: Judicial Complicity in a Realignment of Constitutional Power," 14 *Hastings Const. L.Q.* 683, 686–97, 710–12 (1987); Note, "Keeping Secrets: The Church Committee, Covert Action, and Nicaragua," 25 *Colum. J. Transnat'l L.* 601, 606–24 (1987) (all suggesting that covert war is subject to concurrent congressional-executive authority). Professor Lobel has argued that covert para-

military action, as a use of force short of declared war, falls within Congress's *exclusive* authority to issue letters of marque and reprisal under Article I, § 8 of the Constitution. See Lobel, "Covert War and Congressional Authority: Hidden War and Forgotten Power," 134 *U. Pa. L. Rev.* 1035 (1986).

16. J. Sundquist, *The Decline and Resurgence of Congress* 107 (1981). See Legislative Reorganization Act of 1946, 60 Stat. 812 (1946). See, also, T. Franck & E. Weisband, *Foreign Policy by Congress* 218–19, 243–44 (1979). The act resulted from recommendations of the Joint Committee on the Organization of Congress, which had argued that these organizational changes were necessary to counter "manifest growing tendencies in recent times toward the shift of policy-making power to the Executive, partly because of the comparative lack of effective instrumentalities and the less adequate facilities of the legislative branch." S. Doc. No. 36, 79th Cong., 1st Sess. 2 (1945).

17. See, generally, J. Sundquist, *supra* note 16, at 238–314; T. Franck & E. Weisband, *supra* note 16, at 61–154 (recounting how Congress legislated a role for itself in virtually every area of foreign policy).

18. See Youngstown Sheet & Tube Co. v. Sawyer, 343 U.S. 579, 635 (1952) (Jackson, J., concurring). "[T]oday it is almost universally believed that the more narrowly framed concurring opinions in [*Youngstown,* not the Court's opinion] capture what it really 'stands for.' " Gewirtz, "Realism in Separation of Powers Thinking," 30 *Wm. & Mary L. Rev.* 343, 352 (1989). Thus, in Dames & Moore v. Regan, 453 U.S. 654 (1981), the entire Court united behind the assertion that Justice Jackson's concurring opinion in *Youngstown* "brings together as much combination of analysis and common sense as there is in this area." See *id.* at 661. In Nixon v. Administrator of General Services, 433 U.S. 425, 443 (1977), the Court noted that in the *Nixon Tapes* case, United States v. Nixon, 418 U.S. 683, 707 (1974), "the unanimous Court essentially embraced Mr. Justice Jackson's view, expressed in his concurrence in *Youngstown.*" For other significant Supreme Court decisions relying upon Jackson's analysis, see, *e.g.*, Mistretta v. United States, 109 S. Ct. 647, 659 (1989) ("Justice Jackson summarized the pragmatic, flexible view of differentiated government power to which we are heir"); Morrison v. Olson, 108 S. Ct. 2597, 2620 (1988); Bowsher v. Synar, 478 U.S. 714, 721 (1986).

19. W. LaFeber, *The American Age* 452–55, 459 (1989).

20. See Lobel, "Emergency Power and the Decline of Liberalism," 98 *Yale L.J.* 1385 (1989); J. Smith & C. Cotter, *Powers of the President During Crises* (1960).

21. W. Lippmann, *supra* note 2, at 15.

22. C. Rossiter, *Constitutional Dictatorship: Crisis Government in the Modern Democracies* 5, 314 (1948) (emphasis omitted). Rossiter recommended that Congress pass a framework legislation giving the president statutory emergency powers to deal with the new crisis state. *Id.* at 310–13.

23. See Waltz, "The Stability of a Bipolar World," *Daedalus* 882 (1964) ("Truman, at the time of the Korean invasion, could not very well . . . claim that the

Koreans were a people far away in the east of Asia of whom Americans knew nothing. We had to know about them or quickly find out").

24. See Schlesinger, "The President's Prerogative as Commander-in-Chief," in *The President: Roles and Powers* 353 (D. Haight & L. Johnson eds. 1965) [hereinafter Haight & Johnson]; H. J. Res. No. 9, 82d Cong., 1st Sess. (1951) (introduced by Rep. Coudert) ("no funds heretofore or hereafter appropriated to the support of the Armed Forces shall be available to pay the cost of sending and maintaining abroad additional military forces without the prior consent of the Congress [except if necessary to facilitate the extrication of United States forces now in Korea]"). On Truman's decision to commit troops, see, generally, G. Paige, *The Korean Decision* (1968); T. Schoenbaum, *Waging Peace and War: Dean Rusk in the Truman, Kennedy, and Johnson Years* 206–28 (1988); Hoyt, "The United States Reaction to the Korean Attack: A Study of the Principles of the United Nations Charter as a Factor in American Policy-making," 55 *Am. J. Int'l L.* 45 (1961); Ely, "Suppose Congress Wanted a War Powers Act That Worked," 88 *Colum. L. Rev.* 1379, 1391 (1988); A. Schlesinger, *The Imperial Presidency* 127–40 (1973).

25. See Commager, "Presidential Power: The Issue Analyzed," in Haight & Johnson, *supra* note 24, at 354 (citing *Martin v. Mott, The Prize Cases, Durand v. Hollins, In re Neagle,* and *Curtiss-Wright,* all discussed in chapter 3, to support the president's inherent power to seize the steel mills).

26. W. Rehnquist, *The Supreme Court: How It Was, How It Is* 64 (1987).

27. See E. Gerhart, *America's Advocate: Robert H. Jackson* 21 (1st ed. 1958); see, also, *Youngstown,* 343 U.S. at 648–49 n.17 (Jackson, J., concurring) (discussing Attorney General Jackson's opinion upholding President Roosevelt's right to seize the North American Aviation Plant during a strike shortly before Pearl Harbor); W. Rehnquist, *supra* note 26, at 62.

28. But see Edgar & Schmidt, "Curtiss-Wright Comes Home: Executive Power and National Security Secrecy," 21 *Harv. C.R.-C.L. L. Rev.* 349, 352 n.7 (1986) (rejecting this view and noting that *Curtiss-Wright* could equally be characterized as addressing government regulation of domestic arms sales). Significantly, in Dames & Moore v. Regan, 453 U.S. 654 (1981), the entire Court later applied Justice Jackson's reasoning in *Youngstown* to analyze the legality of the Iranian hostage accords, a quintessential foreign-affairs question.

29. 343 U.S. at 669, 688, 702 (Vinson, C.J., dissenting).

30. *Id.* at 587–88 (Black, J., for the Court).

31. See *id.* at 589. In INS v. Chadha, 462 U.S. 919 (1983), an equally formalistic opinion issued more than three decades later, the Court applied the opposite reasoning. Rather than invalidate an executive act as unlawful legislation, the Court held unconstitutional a congressional act as an unlawful effort to regulate executive action by nonlegislative means. See *infra* chapter 6.

32. 343 U.S. at 629–30 (Douglas, J., concurring) (citing Myers v. United States, 272 U.S. 52, 293 [1926] [Brandeis, J., dissenting]); 343 U.S. at 610, 613 (Frankfurt-

er, J., concurring). In separate concurring opinions, Justices Clark and Burton both reasoned that the president had impermissibly failed to follow statutory procedures previously required by Congress on a matter falling within the concurrent authority of the two branches. *Id.* at 655 (Burton, J., concurring); *id.* at 660 (Clark, J., concurring in the judgment). Justice Clark expressly likened the case to Little v. Barreme, which is discussed in *supra* chapter 3. See *id.* at 660–62.

33. 343 U.S. at 635–37 (Jackson, J., concurring).

34. *Id.* at 638, 640.

35. *Id.* at 637.

36. *Id.* at 637–38. See, *e.g.,* United States v. Belmont, 301 U.S. 324 (1937) (upholding, pursuant to recognition power in Article II of Constitution, president's authority to make sole executive agreement without congressional approval).

37. See *Youngstown*, 343 U.S. at 637–38 (emphasis added), 635–36 n.2, 646–47 (Jackson, J., concurring).

38. *Id.* at 640–47, 653–54.

39. *Cf. infra* chapter 6 (discussing Burger and Rehnquist Courts' growing acceptance of *Curtiss-Wright's* vision of judicial deference to executive authority).

40. 50 U.S.C. § 401 (1982) (congressional declaration of purpose). See, also, J. Sundquist, *supra* note 16, at 107.

41. *Cf.* Draper, "The Rise of the American Junta," *N.Y. Rev. Books* (Oct. 8, 1987): 47; Draper, "Reagan's Junta," *N.Y. Rev. Books* (Jan. 29, 1987): 5 (characterizing the Iran-contra affair as government by junta).

42. See 50 U.S.C. § 402 (1982); U.S. Const. art. II, § 3. *Cf.* Strauss, "The Place of Agencies in Government: Separation of Powers and the Fourth Branch," 84 *Colum. L. Rev.* 573, 599–604, 662–66 (1984) (discussing constitutional requirement that president be unitary, politically accountable head of government with authority to direct all law administrators); Sunstein, "Constitutionalism After the New Deal," 101 *Harv. L. Rev.* 421, 463 (1987) (suggesting wisdom of centralized presidential supervision of federal bureaucracy).

43. *Cf.* L. Tribe, *American Constitutional Law* § 5–17, at 363 (2d ed. 1988) ("an agency can assert as its objectives only those ends which are connected with the task that Congress created it to perform"); Hampton v. Mow Sun Wong, 426 U.S. 88, 114 (1976) (Civil Service Commission may not assert foreign policy ends to defend its challenged regulation, because "[t]hat agency has no responsibility for foreign affairs"). See, also, Liebmann, "Delegation to Private Parties in American Constitutional Law," 50 *Ind. L.J.* 650 (1975); Jaffe, "Law Making by Private Groups," 51 *Harv. L. Rev.* 201 (1937) (government may not delegate its official functions to private groups).

44. See *Youngstown,* 343 U.S. at 653 (Jackson, J., concurring); A. Bickel, *The Morality of Consent* 18 (1975) (citing Edmund Burke) ("Consent will not long be yielded to faceless officials, or to mere servants of one man, who themselves have no 'connexion with the interest of the people.' . . . [W]e may today oppose excessive White House staff-government by private men whom Congress never

sees. It was not for nothing that the American Constitution provided for 'executive Departments' and for Senate confirmation of the appointments of great officers of state"); Strauss, *supra* note 42, at 600 (president and his subordinates must remain accountable to institutions outside the executive branch).

45. Rostow, "Searching for Kennan's Grand Design," 87 *Yale L.J.* 1527, 1534–35 (1978) (emphasis added).

46. See *Youngstown*, 343 U.S. at 638 (Jackson, J., concurring) (emphasis added); *accord*, T. Lowi, *The Personal President* 175 (1985) ("[W]ithout a constitutional balance the presidency flies apart").

47. See Message from the President Vetoing H.J. Res. 542, A Joint Resolution Concerning the War Powers of Congress and the President, H. Doc. No. 171, 93d Cong., 1st Sess. 3 (1973). See, also, *id.* (praising the "constructive measures [in the resolution] which would . . . enhanc[e] the flow of information from the executive branch to the Congress"). For collections of the president's War Powers reports, see Subcomm. on Int'l Security and Scientific Affairs of the House Comm. on Foreign Affairs, *War Powers Resolution: Relevant Documents, Correspondence, Reports,* 98th Cong., 1st Sess. 50 (1983); Note, "The War Powers Resolution: An Act Facing 'Imminent Hostilities' A Decade Later," 16 *Vand. J. Transnat'l L.* 915, 1040–48 & n.831 (1983) (recounting cases of compliance).

48. See Scheffer, "U.S. Law and the Iran-Contra Affair," 81 *Am. J. Int'l L.* 696, 698–713 (1987) (describing these provisions).

49. See Meyer, "Congressional Control of Foreign Assistance," 13 *Yale J. Int'l L.* 69, 89–94 (1988); sources cited in *supra* note 15 (discussing constitutional allocations of competence in these two areas).

50. President's Special Review Board, *The Tower Commission Report* 79 (N.Y. Times ed. 1987) (by his own account, president then placed "the principal responsibility for policy review and implementation on the shoulders of his advisors"). See House Select Comm. to Investigate Covert Arms Transactions with Iran and Senate Select Comm. On Secret Military Assistance to Iran and the Nicaraguan Opposition, *Report of the Congressional Comms. Investigating the Iran-Contra Affair,* 100th Cong., 1st Sess., S. Rept. 216, H. Rept. 433, 20 (1987) [hereinafter *Iran-Contra Report*] ("At the operational level, the central figure in the Iran-Contra Affair was Lt. Col. North [of the NSC staff], who coordinated all of the activities and was involved in all aspects of the secret operations. . . . [W]e believe that the late Director of Central Intelligence, William Casey, encouraged North, gave him direction, and promoted the concept of an extra-legal covert organization [while] for the most part, insulat[ing] CIA career employees from knowledge of what he and the NSC staff were doing").

51. See Sorenson, "The President and the Secretary of State," 66 *Foreign Aff.* 231 (1987/88) ("the Iran-contra hearings . . . revealed a pattern of White House disdain for the Department of State so pervasive that Secretary George Shultz's own blunt testimony, while preserving his personal reputation, confirmed his department's emasculation").

52. *Iran-Contra Report, supra* note 50, at 11 (majority report). Curiously, the Iran-contra committees made only fleeting mention of *Youngstown*'s role in the constitutional framework of the foreign-policy-making process. See *id.* at 389.

53. See O. North, *Taking the Stand: The Testimony of Lieutenant Colonel Oliver L. North* 741 (1987) (statement of Rep. Lee H. Hamilton).

54. The charges included claims that President Reagan had initialed his approval on a 1985 memo suggesting that the Honduran government be given additional American aid as a quid pro quo for helping the contras based in Honduras and that Vice-President Bush had personally met with the Honduran president to effectuate that quid pro quo arrangement. See, generally, Boyd, "North Trial Reveals a Wider Role for Bush in Aiding Contras in '85," N.Y. Times, Apr. 13, 1989, at A1, col. 4; Engelberg, "North Trial Casts Light on Reagan and Raises New Shadow for Bush," N.Y. Times, Apr. 9, 1989, at A1, col. 1; Engelberg, "Document in North Trial Suggests Stronger Bush Role in Contra Aid," N.Y. Times, Apr. 7, 1989, at A1, col. 1. President Bush vociferously denied the charges. See "Remarks and a Question-and-Answer Session with Reporters following a Luncheon with Prime Minister Brian Mulroney of Canada," 25 *Weekly Comp. Pres. Doc.* 660, 662 (May 4, 1989) ("The word of the President of the United States, George Bush, is there was no quid pro quo").

CHAPTER 5: EXECUTIVE INITIATIVE AND CONGRESSIONAL ACQUIESCENCE

1. Black, "The Working Balance of the American Political Departments," 1 *Hastings Const. L.Q.* 13, 17, 20 (1980).

2. See *The Federalist,* No. 70, at 454 (A. Hamilton) (Modern Library ed. 1937). For a more recent discussion of the same concept, see, generally, R. Neustadt, *Presidential Power: The Politics of Leadership from FDR to Carter* (rev. ed. 1980).

3. *Cf.* Sunstein, "Constitutionalism After the New Deal," 101 *Harv. L. Rev.* 421, 452–53 (1987) (articulating these three reasons as arguments favoring presidential control of the bureaucracy). See, also, Youngstown Sheet & Tube Co. v. Sawyer, 343 U.S. 629, 629 (1952) (Douglas, J., concurring) ("All executive power—from the reign of ancient kings to the rule of modern dictators—has the outward appearance of efficiency. Legislative power, by contrast, is slower to exercise. . . . [T]he ponderous machinery of committees, hearings, and debates is . . . cumbersome, time-consuming, and apparently inefficient").

4. See United States v. Curtiss-Wright Export Corp., 299 U.S. 304, 319 (1936) (quoting U.S. Senate, Reports, Committee on Foreign Relations, vol. 8, at 24 [Feb. 15, 1816]). *Curtiss-Wright*'s language appears to derive from Federalist No. 75 in which Hamilton referred to the treaty process as one requiring "decision, *secrecy* and despatch." But significantly, Hamilton used that reason to justify the *House*'s exclusion from the treaty ratification process, not to justify the president's monopoly over it. See *The Federalist, supra* note 2, No. 75, at 488 (emphasis in original).

5. For a political scientist's recent attempt to untangle the intricate relationship between domestic politics and international relations, see Putnam, "Diplomacy and Domestic Politics: The Logic of Two-Level Games," 42 *Int'l Org.* 427 (1988).

6. See Roskin, "From Pearl Harbor to Vietnam: Shifting Generational Paradigms and Foreign Policy," 89 *Pol. Sci. Q.* 563 (1974).

7. O. Holsti & J. Rosenau, *American Leadership in World Affairs: Vietnam and the Breakdown of Consensus* 29–78 (1984); Russett, "The Americans' Retreat from World Power," 90 *Pol. Sci. Q.* 1, 5 (1975); Vasquez, "Domestic Contention on Critical Foreign-Policy Issues: The Case of the United States," 42 *Int'l Org.* 643, 646 (1988); Vasquez, "A Learning Theory of the American Anti-Vietnam Movement," 13 *J. Peace Res.* 299 (1976); E. May, *"Lessons" of the Past: The Use and Misuse of History in American Foreign Policy* 143–71 (1973).

8. For claims of declining American hegemony, see D. Calleo, *Beyond American Hegemony* (1987); R. Gilpin, *The Political Economy of International Relations* (1987); R. Gilpin, *War and Change in World Politics* (1981); R. Gilpin, *U. S. Power and the Multinational Corporation* (1975); P. Kennedy, *The Rise and Fall of the Great Powers* (1987); M. Olson, *The Rise and Decline of Nations* (1982) (explaining U.S. economic decline as a function of special-interest-group government fostered in part by nation's hegemonic status); Kindleberger, "Systems of International Economic Organization," in *Money and the Coming World Order* 15, 33 (D. Calleo ed. 1976); Krasner, "Transforming International Regimes: What the Third World Wants and Why," 25 *Int'l Stud. Q.* 119 (1981); Gilpin, "American Policy in the Post-Reagan Era," *Daedalus* 33, 42–43 (Summer 1987). See, also, R. Keohane, *After Hegemony* (1984) (recognizing decline of American postwar hegemony but questioning whether hegemony constitutes either necessary or sufficient condition for stable international order).

For academic responses to those claims, see Huntington, "The U.S.—Decline or Renewal?" 68 *Foreign Aff.* 76 (1988); Nye, "Short-Term Folly, not Long-Term Decline," *New Perspectives Q.* (Summer 1988): 33; Nye, "Understating U.S. Strength," 72 *Foreign Pol'y* 105 (1988); Nye, "Before the Fall," *New Republic* (Feb. 13, 1989): 37–39; Russett, "The Mysterious Case of Vanishing Hegemony: Or, Is Mark Twain Really Dead?" 39 *Int'l Org.* 207 (1985); Strange, "The Persistent Myth of Lost Hegemony," 41 *Int'l Org.* 551 (1987) (all questioning notion of America's lost hegemony).

For policy analysis, see, *e.g.*, D. Hendrickson, *The Future of American Strategy* (1989); B. Bosworth & R. Lawrence, "America's Global Role: From Dominance to Interdependence," in *Restructuring American Foreign Policy* 12 (J. Steinbruner ed. 1989) (all making policy recommendations based on lost hegemony assumption).

9. These regimes have been the subject of intensive political science analysis. For general accounts, see R. Keohane, *supra* note 8; *International Regimes* (S. Krasner ed. 1983); Haggard & Simmons, "Theories of International Regimes," 41 *Int'l Org.* 491 (1987). For descriptions of particular political regimes, see, *e.g.*, Keohane & Nye, "Two Cheers for Multilateralism," 60 *Foreign Pol'y* 148 (1986)

(describing debt, peacekeeping, and exchange rate regimes); Donnelly, "International Human Rights: A Regime Analysis," 40 *Int'l Org.* 599 (1986); Bilder, "An Overview of International Dispute Resolution," 1 *Emory J. Int'l Dispute Res.* 1 (1986) (describing international dispute-settlement regime without using regime terminology). For descriptions of particular economic regimes, see, *e.g.,* R. Putnam & N. Bayne, *Hanging Together: Cooperation and Conflict at the Seven-Power Summits* (rev. ed. 1987) (studying cooperation and conflict in the Seven-Power summits); Aeppel, "The Evolution of Multilateral Export Controls: A Critical Study of the CoCom Regime," 9 *Fletcher Forum* 105 (1985); Kahler, "Politics and International Debt: Explaining the Crisis," 39 *Int'l Org.* 357 (1985); Hudes, "Coordination of Paris and London Club Reschedulings," 17 *N.Y.U. J. Int'l L. & Pol.* 553 (1985).

10. For discussion of developments in the trade area, see, *e.g.,* Koh, "Congressional Controls on Presidential Trade Policymaking After *INS* v. *Chadha,*" 18 *N.Y.U. J. Int'l L. & Pol.* 1191, 1227 (1986) [hereinafter Koh, Congressional Controls]; Koh, "The Legal Markets of International Trade: A Perspective on the Proposed United States-Canada Free Trade Agreement," 13 *Yale J. Int'l L.* 193, 240–48 (1987); R. Gilpin, *The Political Economy of International Relations* 171–230 (1987). For a description of the legal structure of the nascent antiterrorism regime, see, *e.g.,* Koh, "Civil Remedies for Uncivil Wrongs: Combatting Terrorism through Transnational Public Law Litigation," 22 *Tex. Int'l L.J.* 169, 170–73 (1987) [hereinafter Koh, Civil Remedies]. For discussion of the international debt problem and regime, see, *e.g.,* H. Lever & C. Huhne, *Debt and Danger* (1986); Kahler, *supra* note 9, Keohane & Nye, *supra* note 9, at 165–66.

11. On the rise of congressional activism, see Koh, Congressional Controls, *supra* note 10, at 1211–21 (discussing enhanced powers of the House Ways and Means and Senate Finance committees under the 1984 Trade and Tariff Act); R. Fenno, *Congressmen in Committees* 26–35 (1973) (discussing power of foreign affairs committees); Hammond, "Congress in Foreign Policy," in *The President, the Congress, and Foreign Policy* 81 (E. Muskie, K. Rush, & K. Thompson eds. 1986) [hereinafter E. Muskie] (listing informal congressional foreign policy caucuses). On the decentralization of the new Congress, see Ornstein, "The Constitution and the Sharing of Foreign Policy Responsibility," in *id.* at 35, 57.

12. On the South African sanctions battle, see Exec. Order No. 12,532, 50 Fed. Reg. 36,861 (1985) (South African sanctions order); R. Lugar, *Letters to the Next President* 208–47 (1988). On the PLO mission controversy, see Designation of Palestine Information Office as a Foreign Mission, 52 Fed. Reg. 37,035 (Oct. 2, 1987) (executive decision to close Palestinian office to forestall enactment of the Anti-Terrorism Act of 1987, Pub. L. No. 100–204, §§ 1001–1005, 101 Stat. 1331, 1406–07); United States Department of State, Statement on the Visa Application of Yassir Arafat, 83 *Am. J. Int'l L.* 253 (1989). On recent presidential preemptive strikes in trade field, see Koh, Congressional Controls, *supra* note 10, at 1225–33; Note, "Defining Unreasonableness in International Trade: Section

301 of the Trade Act of 1974," 96 *Yale L.J.* 1122, 1122–26 (1987) (describing Reagan administration's use of Section 301 of the Trade Act of 1974 to open foreign markets); "Statement on United States Action against Foreign Trade Barriers," 25 *Weekly Comp. Pres. Doc.* 777 (1989) (naming Brazil, India, and Japan as "priority" unfair trading countries under "Super 301" of 1988 Trade Act). On the role of the Kassebaum amendment in the United Nations funding crisis, see Kassebaum Amendment, Pub. L. No. 99–93, § 143, 99 Stat. 405, 424 (1985) (codified at 22 U.S.C. § 287e note [Supp. IV 1985]) (imposing preconditions upon U.S. payment of assessed contributions to United Nations and specialized agencies); Nelson, "International Law and U.S. Withholding of Payments to International Organizations," 80 *Am. J. Int'l L.* 973 (1986).

13. See T. Lowi, *The Personal President* 173 (1985).
14. The political science literature on each of these phenomena is massive. On ideology, see, *e.g.*, M. Hunt, *Ideology and U.S. Foreign Policy* (1987). On the role of political philosophy in international affairs, see Michael Joseph Smith's probing discussion of the role of realism in Kissinger's thought, M. Smith, *Realist Thought from Weber to Kissinger* 192–217 (1986). On groupthink, see I. Janis, *Victims of Groupthink: A Psychological Study of Foreign-Policy Decisions and Fiascoes* (1972). On the role of bureaucratic politics and foreign policy, see G. Allison, *Essence of Decision: Explaining the Cuban Missile Crisis* (1971); M. Halperin, *Bureaucratic Politics and Foreign Policy* (1974); Art, "Bureaucratic Politics and Foreign Policy: A Critique," 4 *Pol'y Sci.* 467 (1973).
15. See T. Lowi, *supra* note 13, at 173. For descriptions of President Carter's actions during the Iranian hostage crisis, see Koh, Congressional Controls, *supra* note 10, at 1229 n.112; 4A *Op. Off. Legal Counsel* 71–333 (1980); G. Smith, *Morality, Reason and Power* 180–207 (1986).
16. See *Newsweek* (Aug. 13, 1987): 16 (Statement of Secretary of State Shultz, quoting President Reagan); O. North, *Taking the Stand: The Testimony of Lieutenant Colonel Oliver L. North* 12, 256 (1987) ("[T]his is a nation at risk in a dangerous world. . . . [W]e all had to weigh . . . the difference between lies and lives").
17. *Cf.* H. Kissinger, *White House Years* 806 (1979) (Because President "Nixon feared leaks . . . he thus encouraged procedures unlikely to be recommended in textbooks on public administration that, crablike, worked privily around existing structures"). When Nixon ordered the Cambodian bombings, for example, he explicitly instructed the NSC that the "State [Department] is to be notified only after the point of no return." *Id.* at 245. When Henry Kissinger returned from his secret mission to China, Nixon instructed him to give the secretary of state only a "sanitized" account of the trip. *Id.* at 756–57.
18. The phenomenon is not restricted to the American legislature. See, *e.g.*, Watson, "Legal Evolution and Legislation," 1987 *B.Y.U. L. Rev.* 353, 375–79 (providing cross-cultural explanation for why legislatures often reject revolutionary proposals).

19. See M. Fiorina, *Retrospective Voting in American National Elections* (1981).
20. For general discussions of the role of interest groups in the legislative process, see Macey, "Promoting Public-Regarding Legislation through Statutory Interpretation: An Interest Group Model," 86 *Colum. L. Rev.* 223 (1986); Sunstein, "Interest Groups in American Public Law," 38 *Stan. L. Rev.* 29 (1985).

On interest-group politics in international trade, see, generally, R. Bauer, I. Pool, & L. Dexter, *American Business and Public Policy: The Politics of Foreign Trade* (1963); S. Cohen, *The Making of United States International Economic Policy* 121–39 (1988); I. Destler, *American Trade Politics: System under Stress* (1986); R. Pastor, *Congress and the Politics of U.S. Foreign Economic Policy* (1980); E. Schattschneider, *Politics, Pressure and the Tariff* (1935); Ray, "Changing Patterns of Protectionism: The Fall in Tariffs and the Rise of Non-Tariff Barriers," 8 *Nw. J. Int'l L. & Bus.* 285 (1987) (arguing that U.S. trade policy results from political equilibrium struck between national-policy and interest-group pressures). The recurring battle between business interests for and against the restriction of textile imports forms a particularly fascinating case study. See, *e.g.,* Felton, "President Vetoes Textile Import-Quota Bill," 46 *Cong. Q.* 2754 (Oct. 1, 1988). For an economic modeling of the role of interest-group politics in the creation of voluntary restraint agreements, see Hillman & Urspring, "Domestic Politics, Foreign Interest, and International Trade Policy," 78 *Am. Econ. Rev.* 729 (1988).

On the role of the defense lobby, see, *e.g.,* Madison, "The Arms Sale Say-So," 19 *Nat'l J.* 667 (1987); H. Smith, *The Power Game* 173–215 (1988) (describing "iron triangle" among the military services, defense contractors, and members of Congress).

On the influence of the Israel lobby, see T. Franck & E. Weisband, *Foreign Policy by Congress* 200–09 (1979); K. Teslik, *Congress, The Executive Branch and Special Interests* (1982) (discussing role of Israel lobby in the enactment of Arab antiboycott legislation); H. Smith, *supra,* at 216–31 (discussing role of American Israel Public Affairs Committee [AIPAC] in opposing Arab arms sales); Madison, "Arms-Sale Armistice," 19 *Nat'l J.* 2606, 2607 (1987); see, generally, *Ethnic Groups and U.S. Policy* (M. Ahrari ed. 1987) (describing influence of pro-Israel, black, Polish-American, Mexican-American, Cuban-American, and Irish-American lobbies on foreign policy).

On interest-group influence on the intelligence committees, see L. Johnson, *America's Secret Power: The CIA in a Democratic Society* 219–20 (1989).

21. On interest-group influence on U.S. human-rights policy, see, generally, D. Forsythe, *Human Rights and U.S. Foreign Policy* (1988); R. Pastor, *supra* note 20, at 301–21. On the Vietnam lobby, see Ornstein, "Interest Groups, Congress and American Policy," in *American Foreign Policy in an Uncertain World* 49, 52–55 (D. Forsythe ed. 1984).
22. D. Mayhew, *Congress: The Electoral Connection* 138 (1974). For Senator Eagleton's proposal, see 119 *Cong. Rec.* 25,079–86 (1973).

23. See, generally, D. Mayhew, *supra* note 22, at 126–40. For examples of legislative "fixes" easily comprehended by the public, see Balanced Budget and Emergency Deficit Control Act of 1985, Pub. L. No. 99-177, 99 Stat. 1037 (1985) (codified as amended in scattered sections of 2, 31, and 42 U.S.C.) (Gramm-Rudman-Hollings budget-balancing act) (numerical approach to domestic deficit reduction); Trade and International Economic Policy Reform Act of 1987, H.R. 3, 100th Cong., 1st Sess. § 126, 133 *Cong. Rec.* 2,755–57 (1987) (Gephardt amendment to 1988 Trade Reform Act, subsequently dropped in conference) (requiring president to retaliate against countries running excessive and unwarranted trade surpluses with U.S. by forcing those countries to reduce their surpluses by 10 percent annually); Madison, "It's Congress's Move," 19 *Nat'l J.* 2014, 2017–18 (1987) (describing "forty-eight-hour notice" intelligence reform bill).

24. I am grateful to Robert J. Kurz of the Brookings Institution (formerly a staff member of the House Subcommittee on Western Hemisphere Affairs during the period when the Boland amendments were enacted) for this observation. On the problems of coalition-formation within committees, see Weingast & Marshall, "The Industrial Organization of Congress; or, Why Legislatures, Like Firms, Are Not Organized As Markets," 96 *J. Pol. Econ.* 132, 146–47 (1988).

25. See *Standing Rules of the Senate Revised to June 1, 1988*, S. Doc. No. 33, 100th Cong., 2d Sess., Rule XXII(2) at 15 (1988); see, also, Molotsky, "A Senator Is Captured, but not His Mind," N.Y. Times, Feb. 25, 1988, at A26, col. 4 (describing Republicans' use of that rule, along with the quorum requirement, to defeat Democrat-supported campaign reform bill).

26. *Compare* 50 U.S.C. § 1542 (1982) *with* J. Carter, *Keeping Faith* 518 (1982) (quoting from President Carter's diary) ("I had planned on calling in a few members of the House and Senate . . . before the rescue team began its move into Tehran. . . . But I never got around to that") (emphasis omitted). As noted in chapter 4, however, most presidents have complied in some form or another with the resolution's consultation requirement. See, generally, Note, "The War Powers Resolution: An Act Facing 'Imminent Hostilities' A Decade Later," 16 *Vand. J. Transnat'l L.* 915 (1983) (citing examples).

27. *Compare* 50 U.S.C. § 1542 (1982) *with* Torricelli, "The War Powers Resolution After the Libya Crisis," 7 *Pace L. Rev.* 661, 666 (1987); R. Lugar, *supra* note 12, at 47–48 ("consultation" of key senators began two hours after planes were in the air and concluded less than thirty minutes before bombing began).

28. See 50 U.S.C. § 1543(a)(1)–(3), 1544(a) (1982).

29. Glennon, "The War Powers Resolution Ten Years Later: More Politics Than Law," 78 *Am. J. Int'l L.* 571, 571 (1984).

30. D. Mayhew, *supra* note 22, at 122.

31. *Compare* the "in every possible instance" phrase in 50 U.S.C. § 1542 (1982) *with* the identical phrase in IEEPA, 50 U.S.C. § 1703(a) (1982). For a cross-cultural discussion of how and why such "legal transplants" occur, see, generally, A. Watson, *Legal Transplants* 21–30 (1974).

32. See Comprehensive Anti-Apartheid Act of 1986, Pub. L. No. 99-440, 100 Stat. 1086 (1986); Remarks of Richard Messick, former counsel to the Senate Foreign Relations Committee, Panel on Sustaining an International Human Rights Campaign in the United States: Passage of the Anti-Apartheid Act in Perspective, Symposium on Human Rights Advocacy and the U.S. Political Process, Yale Law School, April 9, 1988 (on file with author). For a description of the law's loopholes, see, generally, Paretzky, "The United States Arms Embargo against South Africa: An Analysis of the Laws, Regulations, and Loopholes," 12 *Yale J. Int'l L.* 133 (1987).

33. See, *e.g.,* Lowry v. Reagan, 676 F. Supp. 333 (D.D.C. 1987), *appeal dismissed,* No. 87-5426 (D.C. Cir. Oct. 17, 1988) (dismissing suit seeking to compel president to comply with reporting requirement of War Powers Resolution with regard to U.S. military activities in Persian Gulf); Crockett v. Reagan, 720 F.2d 1355 (D.C. Cir. 1983), *cert. denied,* 467 U.S. 1251 (1984) (dismissing similar suit with regard to U.S. military activities in El Salvador).

34. G. Calabresi, *A Common Law for the Age of Statutes* 61, 62 (1982).

35. See Franck & Bob, "The Return of Humpty-Dumpty: Foreign Relations Law After the Chadha Case," 79 *Am. J. Int'l L.* 912, 934 (1985).

36. For accounts of the use or threatened use of the legislative veto in the areas of arms control and transfer of nuclear materials, see Pomerance, "United States Foreign Relations Law After Chadha," 15 *Cal. W. Int'l L.J.* 201, 262–80 (1985). For descriptions of Congress's efforts to use appropriations cutoffs in foreign affairs, see L. Fisher, *Constitutional Conflicts between Congress and the President* 221–51, 318–23 (1985); G. Treverton, *Covert Action* 156–60 (1987) (describing legislative cutoff of funds for covert activities in Angola under Clark amendment); Franck & Bob, *supra* note 35, at 944–48.

37. For a fuller description, see Koh, Congressional Controls, *supra* note 10, at 1196 n.16.

38. 462 U.S. 919 (1983).

39. See Bowsher v. Synar, 478 U.S. 714 (1986); Northern Pipeline Constr. Co. v. Marathon Pipe Line Co., 458 U.S. 50 (1982); Buckley v. Valeo, 424 U.S. 1 (1976). But see Morrison v. Olson, 108 S. Ct. 2597 (1988); Mistretta v. United States, 109 S. Ct. 647 (1989).

40. See C. Rossiter, *The American Presidency* 157 (1956) ("The President often feels compelled to sign bills that are full of dubious grants and subsidies rather than risk a breakdown in the work of whole departments").

41. See Engelberg, "Contra Aid: Loose Law?" N.Y. Times, Jan. 15, 1987, at A12, col. 1 (describing claimed loopholes in Boland amendments).

42. 328 U.S. 303 (1946). For an intriguing account of the decision, see Ely, "*United States v. Lovett:* Litigating the Separation of Powers," 10 *Harv. C.R.-C.L. L.Rev.* 1 (1975).

43. See, *e.g.,* Crovitz, "Crime, the Constitution, and the Iran-Contra Affair," *Com-*

mentary (Oct. 1987): 23, 28; Quade, "The President Is His Only Client," *Barrister* (Winter / Spring 1988): 5, 7 (Interview with A. B. Culvahouse, Jr., counsel to president) ("it was clear in our mind and remains clear that the Boland Amendment could not circumscribe the efforts of the President to speak with foreign leaders about supporting the Nicaraguan freedom fighters").

44. See, *e.g.*, L. Henkin, *Constitutionalism, Democracy and Foreign Affairs* 47 (unpublished manuscript, forthcoming 1990); Stith, "Congress' Power of the Purse," 97 *Yale L.J.* 1343, 1351 & n.32 (1988).

45. See Federal Employees v. United States, 688 F. Supp. 671, 685 (D.D.C. 1988), *vacated and remanded sub nom.* American Foreign Serv. Ass'n v. Garfinkel, 109 S. Ct. 1693 (1989) (per curiam). Shortly before the district court's ruling in this case, another district judge declared that "[w]e are aware of no case striking down federal legislation as an encroachment of the executive's authority to conduct foreign affairs." Mendelsohn v. Meese, 695 F. Supp. 1474, 1483 (S.D.N.Y. 1988) (Palmieri, J.).

46. See Ameron, Inc. v. United States Army Corps of Eng'rs, Inc., 809 F.2d 979 (3d Cir. 1986), *cert. dismissed,* 109 S. Ct. 297 (1988); Stith, *supra* note 44, at 1390–92 & nn.232–47 (describing constitutional difficulties of using comptroller general to enforce appropriations requirements against the executive); Note, "The Role of the Comptroller General in light of *Bowsher v. Synar,*" 87 *Colum. L. Rev.* 1539 (1987). Two more recent separation-of-powers rulings suggest, however, that the comptroller general's authority would be sustained. See *infra* chapter 6 (discussing Morrison v. Olson and Mistretta v. United States).

47. See House Select Comm. to Investigate Covert Arms Transactions with Iran and Senate Select Comm. On Secret Military Assistance to Iran and the Nicaraguan Opposition, *Report of the Congressional Comms. Investigating the Iran-Contra Affair,* 100th Cong., 1st Sess., S. Rept. 216, H. Rept. 433, 16 (1987) [hereinafter *Iran-Contra Report*] (emphasis added); Stith, *supra* note 44, at 1358 (only monies receivable by the U.S. government *and* subject to its control and expenditure are subject to Congress's appropriations power). Congress recently sought to redress this problem by passing an appropriations rider (which the President later vetoed) that would punish U.S. officials who solicit funds from foreign countries to carry out activities for which Congress has cut off aid. See S. Amend. 268, S. 1160, 101st Cong., 1st Sess., 135 *Cong. Rec.* S8107–09 (daily ed. July 18, 1989) (Moynihan amendment to the FY 1990 State Department Authorization Act); H.R. 2939, 101st Cong., 1st Sess. § 577, 135 *Cong. Rec.* H4071-72 (daily ed. July 21, 1989) (parallel provision in House foreign-aid bill), *infra* chapter 8, note 10.

48. O. North, *supra* note 16, at 473 (1987) (emphasis added).

49. For descriptions of presidential devices to control spending, see L. Fisher, *President and Congress: Power and Policy* 110–32 (1972); L. Fisher, *Presidential Spending Power* (1975); Meyer, "Congressional Control of Foreign Assistance," 13 *Yale J. Int'l L.* 69, 74–75 (1988).

50. Sharpe, "The Real Cause of Irangate," 68 *Foreign Pol'y* 33–34 (1987).

51. See *infra* chapter 6 (demonstrating how Dames & Moore v. Regan, 453 U.S. 654 [1981] permits courts to construe any congressional action short of these two measures as de facto acquiescence in president's initiative).

52. See U.S. Gov't Printing Office, *Presidential Vetoes, 1977–1984* ix (1985); 43 *Cong. Q. Almanac* 6 (1987) (103 of 1,417 have been overridden). See, generally, R. Spitzer, *The Presidential Veto: Touchstone of the American Presidency* (1988).

53. See Fulbright, "Congress and Foreign Policy," in 5 Appendices to *U.S. Commission on the Organization of the Government for the Conduct of Foreign Policy* 58, 59 (1975) [hereinafter *Murphy Commission Report*].

54. See 133 *Cong. Rec.* S15,011 (daily ed. Oct. 23, 1987) (Bork vote); Seib & Fialka, "Advise and Reject: Tower Fiasco Hurts Bush, But It Also Puts Congress on Defensive," Wall St. J., Mar. 10, 1989, at A1, col. 1 (Tower vote); "Trade Policy: New Trade Legislation Expected in Congress As Senate Sustains Reagan's Veto of HR 3," 5 *Int'l Trade Rep.* (BNA) 879 (June 15, 1988) [hereinafter New Trade Legislation]. The president defeated an override of his trade bill veto because the Senate failed to gain the unanimous consent necessary to bring to a vote a concurrent resolution stripping an Alaskan oil export limitation from the bill. By retaining that single provision in its one-thousand-page bill, Congress lost the critical override votes of both Alaskan senators. See "Trade Policy: Trade Bill Goes to Reagan This Week for Certain Veto; Override Unlikely," 5 *Int'l Trade Rep.* (BNA) 678 (May 11, 1988).

55. See Black, "Some Thoughts on the Veto," 40 *Law & Contemp. Probs.*, Spring 1976, at 87, 93; *House of Representatives 1989–90, Cong. Index* (CCH) 24, 151 (Feb. 24, 1989) (House currently has only 257 Democrats versus 176 Republicans).

56. *Cf.* B. Eckhardt & C. Black, *The Tides of Power* 62–65 (1976) (statement of Professor Black) (proposing that Congress simply follow convention of overriding all presidential vetoes, regardless of substance).

57. See Spann, "Spinning the Legislative Veto," 72 *Geo. L.J.* 813 (1984).

58. See Note, *supra* note 26, at 1008–14.

59. See, *e.g.*, Feuerbringer, "Senate Defers Vote on Gulf Escort Policy," N.Y. Times, Oct. 22, 1987, at A3, col. 4.

60. New Trade Legislation, *supra* note 54, at 880 (describing such an action by Senate majority leader, who led drive to override president's veto of trade bill). It would be highly unlikely, however, that a congressional leader would cast such a vote if it would be decisive in securing an override.

61. Henkin, "'A More Effective System' for Foreign Relations: The Constitutional Framework," in Appendices to Murphy Commission Report, *supra* note 53, at 9, 16. *Accord,* T. Eagleton, *War and Presidential Power* 146 (1974).

62. See Vance, "Striking the Balance: Congress and the President under the War Powers Resolution," 133 *U. Pa. L. Rev.* 79, 94–95 (1984) (describing events

leading to enactment of Multinational Force in Lebanon Resolution, Pub. L. No. 98-119, 97 Stat. 805 [1983]).

CHAPTER 6: THE PROBLEM OF JUDICIAL TOLERANCE

1. See *Youngstown*, 343 U.S. at 585 (Black, J., for the Court) ("The President's power, if any, to issue the order [under challenge] must stem either from an act of Congress or from the Constitution itself"); *id.* at 635–36 n.2 (Jackson, J., concurring) (*Curtiss-Wright* involved not "the question of the President's power to act without congressional authorization, but the question of his right to act under and in accord with an Act of Congress").

2. See, *e.g.*, United States v. Robel, 389 U.S. 258, 263 (1967) (refusing to accept executive invocation of congressional war power as "talismanic incantation" to support violation of constitutional rights). During the Warren era, President Eisenhower generally acted on the philosophy "that the Constitution assumes that our two branches of government should get along together," as illustrated by his decision to seek authorizing joint resolutions before he dispatched troops to the Formosa Straits in 1955 and to the Middle East in 1957. See D. Eisenhower, *Waging Peace 1956–1961* 179 (1965). Although President Kennedy clashed with Congress over international trade matters, he conducted his blockade of Cuba during the Cuban missile crisis with the blessing of a congressional resolution. See Koh, "Congressional Controls on Presidential Trade Policymaking After *I.N.S. v. Chadha*," 18 *N.Y.U. J. Int'l L. & Pol.* 1191, 1197–99 (describing congressional-executive clashes during the Kennedy round of international trade talks); *Public Papers of the Presidents, John F. Kennedy,* 806–11 (1962) (Cuban missile crisis).

3. 357 U.S. 116 (1958); *accord,* Greene v. McElroy, 360 U.S. 474, 507–08 (1959). Fourteen years earlier, Justice Douglas had presaged the "clear statement" principle. See *Ex Parte Endo,* 323 U.S. 283, 300 (1944) (Douglas, J., for the Court) (judges "must assume, when asked to find implied powers in a grant of legislative or executive authority, that the law makers intended to place no greater restraint on the citizen than was clearly and unmistakably indicated by the language [that the chief executive and Congress] used"). The "clear statement" method of statutory construction exemplifies what I have elsewhere called the "liberal constitutional internationalism" of Justice Douglas: the philosophy that both presidential and American overreaching in international affairs should be checked both by congressional restraints and judicial protection of individual rights. See Koh, "The Liberal Constitutional Internationalism of Justice Douglas," in *"He Shall Not Pass This Way Again": The Legacy of Justice William O. Douglas* (S. Wasby ed. forthcoming U. of Pittsburgh Press 1991).

4. Edgar & Schmidt, "*Curtiss-Wright* Comes Home: Executive Power and National Security Secrecy," 21 *Harv. C.R.-C.L. L. Rev.* 349, 355–56 (1986).

5. New York Times Co. v. United States, 403 U.S. 713 (1971) (*Pentagon Papers* case).

6. See *id.* at 753, 756 (Harlan, J., joined by Burger, C.J., and Blackmun, J., dissenting); *id.* at 718–19 (Black, J., joined by Douglas, J., concurring); *id.* at 726–27 (Brennan, J., concurring). See, generally, Edgar & Schmidt, *supra* note 4, at 360–65 (discussing concurring and dissenting opinions).

7. See *id.* at 728–29 (Stewart, J., joined by White, J., concurring).

8. See United States v. Progressive, Inc., 467 F. Supp. 990 (W.D. Wis. 1979), *dismissed summarily,* 610 F.2d 819 (7th Cir. 1979) (effort to enjoin publication in article dropped after similar information appeared elsewhere). One year after the *Pentagon Papers* case, in United States v. United States District Court (*Keith*), 407 U.S. 297 (1972), the Court similarly ruled against the president by invalidating warrantless wiretaps for domestic intelligence gathering that had been authorized only by the attorney general. Like the *Pentagon Papers* case, however, the *Keith* decision did not represent an unmitigated defeat for the executive. The *Keith* Court carefully declined "judgment on the scope of the President's surveillance power with respect to the activities of foreign powers, within or without this country." *Id.* at 308; see, also, *id.* at 322 (reiterating that case did not involve issues "with respect to activities of foreign powers or their agents").

9. *Curtiss-Wright,* 299 U.S. 304, 320 (1936) (emphasis added).

10. For a recent statement of this view by the former assistant attorney general in charge of the Office of Legal Counsel, see Cooper, "Comment on Schlesinger," 47 *Md. L. Rev.* 84, 91 (1987) (*Curtiss-Wright* "emphatically declared . . . that congressional efforts to act in this area must be evaluated in the light of the President's constitutional ascendancy").

11. During the Carter administration, the Court decided three significant cases concerning the foreign-affairs power and declined to hear two others. See Christopher, "Ceasefire between the Branches: A Compact in Foreign Affairs," 60 *Foreign Aff.* 989 (1982) (discussing Edwards v. Carter, Dole v. Carter, Goldwater v. Carter, Haig v. Agee, and Dames & Moore v. Regan). As even President Carter's former deputy secretary of state conceded, the only unifying feature of these cases was that "the outcome in all instances was to let the President have his way." *Id.* at 995.

12. See 444 U.S. 507, 510 n.3 (1980) (citing director's authority under 50 U.S.C. § 403(d)(3), which makes him "responsible for protecting intelligence sources and methods from unauthorized disclosure" but specifies no remedies for such disclosure). For criticisms of *Snepp,* see Edgar & Schmidt, *supra* note 4, at 371–76; Lewis, "Limits on Presidential Power," 49 *U. Pitt. L. Rev.* 745, 750 (1988).

13. 453 U.S. 654 (1981). Justice Rehnquist declined to hold that either IEEPA or the Hostage Act of 1868 specifically authorized the president to suspend claims, but found both statutes "highly relevant in the looser sense of indicating congressional acceptance of a broad scope for executive action." *Id.* at 677.

14. *Compare* 453 U.S. at 674 n.6 & 688–90 *with id.* at 690–91 (Powell, J., concur-

ring in part and dissenting in part) (dissenting from Court's decision with respect to attachments).

15. *Id.* at 661. See, also, *id.* at 660 (we are "acutely aware of the necessity to rest decision on the narrowest possible ground capable of deciding the case"); *id.* at 661 (we "attempt to confine the opinion only to the very questions necessary to decision of the case"); *id.* at 688 ("we re-emphasize the narrowness of our decision").

16. *Compare Dames & Moore,* 453 U.S. at 675–79 *with Youngstown,* 343 U.S. at 669, 683–700 (1936) (Vinson, C.J., dissenting). For other critiques of the Court's technique of statutory construction in *Dames & Moore,* see W. Eskridge & P. Frickey, *Legislation: Statutes and the Creation of Public Policy* 317–21 (1987); L. Tribe, *Constitutional Choices* 38–39 (1985).

17. See W. Rehnquist, *The Supreme Court: How It Was, How It Is* 45–60 (1987) (recalling national mood during *Youngstown*).

18. See, *e.g.,* Mikva & Neuman, "The Hostage Crisis and the 'Hostage Act' " 49 *U. Chi. L. Rev.* 292 (1982) (arguing that President Carter sought to use the so-called Hostage Act of 1868, 22 U.S.C. § 1732 (1982), as a blank check authorizing the president to use any means to rescue hostages). See O. North, *Taking the Stand: The Testimony of Lieutenant Colonel Oliver L. North* 503–04 (1987); *id.* at 606 (remarks of Rep. Henry Hyde) (claiming that Hostage Act provided the executive branch with "the authority to do whatever [was] necessary" during the Iran-contra affair).

19. Haig v. Agee, 453 U.S. 280, 291 (1981). *Compare id.* at 309 (upholding secretary's act as " 'an inhibition of *action,*' rather than of speech") (emphasis in original) (citation omitted) *with id.* at 318 (Brennan, J., dissenting) ("The point . . . today's opinion should make, is that the Executive's authority to revoke passports touches an area fraught with important constitutional rights, and that the Court should therefore 'construe narrowly all delegated powers that curtail or dilute them' ") (citing *Kent v. Dulles*).

20. 468 U.S. 222 (1984). See *id.* at 255 (Blackmun, J., dissenting) (the Court's construction "loses all sight of the general legislative purpose of the IEEPA and the clear legislative intent behind the grandfather clause. . . . Ironically, the very pieces of legislative history that the Court cites to justify its result clearly support the contrary view").

21. *Compare* 468 U.S. at 243 (citation omitted) *with* Wald v. Regan, 708 F.2d 794, 800 (1st Cir. 1983) (Breyer, J.).

22. See Boudin, "Economic Sanctions and Individual Rights," 19 *N.Y.U. J. Int'l L. & Pol.* 803, 809 (1987).

23. 462 U.S. 919, 952 (1983).

24. *Compare* Carter, "The Constitutionality of the War Powers Resolution," 70 *Va. L. Rev.* 101, 129–33 (1984) (arguing that § 5(c) of War Powers Resolution survives *Chadha*) *with* Koh, *supra* note 2, at 1209 n.53 (arguing that it does not). However, Congress has gone on to enact more than 140 legislative vetoes even

after *Chadha,* most of them in appropriations bills. See Tolchin, "The Legislative Veto: An Accommodation That Goes On and On," N.Y. Times, Mar. 31, 1989, at A11, col. 1. President Reagan usually signed those bills into law, but with an express declaration that he was not legally bound by their legislative veto provisions. See, *e.g.,* "Department of Housing and Urban Development—Independent Agencies Appropriation Act, 1985," 20 *Weekly Comp. Pres. Doc.* 1040 (July 18, 1984).

25. See, generally, Pomerance, "United States Foreign Relations Law After *Chadha,*" 15 *Cal. W. Int'l L.J.* 201, 262–80 (1985).

26. See, *e.g.,* United States v. Guy W. Capps, Inc., 204 F.2d 655 (4th Cir. 1953), *aff'd on other grounds,* 348 U.S. 296 (1955) (refusing to give effect to sole executive agreement regulating trade because agreement was inconsistent with statute regulating same subject matter enacted under Congress's foreign-commerce power).

27. 453 U.S. at 686–87 (relying upon "history of acquiescence in executive claims settlement" and the fact that "Congress has not enacted legislation, or even passed a resolution, indicating its displeasure with the [Hostage] Agreement").

28. 462 U.S. at 952.

29. See Bowsher v. Synar, 478 U.S. 714 (1986). For criticism of *Chadha* and *Bowsher*'s formalistic approach, see, generally, Sunstein, "Constitutionalism After the New Deal," 101 *Harv. L. Rev.* 421, 493–500 (1987); Strauss, "Formal and Functional Approaches to Separation-of-Powers Questions—A Foolish Inconsistency?" 72 *Cornell L. Rev.* 488 (1987).

30. See Morrison v. Olson, 108 S. Ct. 2597 (1988); Mistretta v. United States, 109 S. Ct. 647 (1989). Shortly after these two decisions, the solicitor general moved to dismiss a third pending separation-of-powers case, which would have evaluated the comptroller general's authority to implement Congress's appropriations control. See Ameron, Inc. v. United States Army Corps of Eng'rs, 809 F.2d 979 (3d Cir. 1986), *cert. dismissed,* 109 S. Ct. 297 (1988) (challenging constitutionality of Competition in Contracting Act). The Court also vacated, without passing on the merits of, a district court judgment that had invalidated a duly enacted appropriations statute as an unconstitutional interference with "the President's power to fulfill obligations imposed upon him by his express constitutional powers and the role of the Executive in foreign relations." American Foreign Serv. Ass'n v. Garfinkel, 109 S. Ct. 1693 (1989) (per curiam), *vacating and remanding* Federal Employees v. United States, 688 F. Supp. 671, 685 (D.D.C. 1988).

31. *Morrison,* 108 S. Ct. at 2619; *Mistretta,* 109 S. Ct. at 659 ("It is this concern of encroachment and aggrandizement that has animated our separation-of-powers jurisprudence"). But see *Morrison,* 108 S. Ct. at 2622 (Scalia, J., dissenting); *Mistretta,* 109 S. Ct. at 675 (Scalia, J., dissenting) (continuing to apply formalistic approach to argue for invalidation of statute and guidelines).

32. See Franck & Bob, "The Return of Humpty-Dumpty: Foreign Relations Law After the Chadha Case," 79 *Am. J. Int'l L.* 912, 951 n.274 (1985).

33. See "Bipartisan Accord on Central America," 25 *Weekly Comp. Pres. Doc.* 420 (Mar. 24, 1989); Pear, "Baker Plan: A New Deal," N.Y. Times, Mar. 25, 1989, at A1, col. 5. This accord, which chapter 7 describes in greater detail, simply illustrates Louis Fisher's observation that *Chadha* did not so much kill the legislative veto as it "drove underground a set of legislative and committee vetoes that used to operate in plain sight." L. Fisher, *Constitutional Dialogues: Interpretation as Political Process* 228 (1988).

34. See, *e.g.,* Koh, *supra* note 2, at 1200–1203, 1216–17 (describing fast-track regulatory device used in international trade statutes). See, also, *infra* chapter 7.

35. *Compare* 454 U.S. 139 (1981) *with* 5 U.S.C. § 552(a)(4)(B) (1982). See, also, Halperin, "The National Security State: Never Question the President," in *The Burger Years: Rights and Wrongs in the Supreme Court 1969–1986* 50, 54 (H. Schwartz ed. 1987).

36. 478 U.S. 221 (1986).

37. See Pelly Amendment to the Fishermen's Protective Act of 1967, 22 U.S.C. § 1978(a)(1) (1982), and the Packwood Amendment to the Magnuson Fishery Conservation and Management Act, 16 U.S.C. § 1821(e)(2) (1982).

38. *Compare* 478 U.S. at 227–29 (opinion of the Court) *with id.* at 241, 246 (Marshall, J., dissenting).

39. In Reagan v. Abourezk, 785 F.2d 1043 (D.C. Cir. 1986), *aff'd by an equally divided Court,* 108 S. Ct. 252 (1987), an equally divided six-justice Court affirmed without opinion a decision remanding for clarification the INS's construction of § 212(a)(27) of the Immigration and Nationality Act, 8 U.S.C. § 1182(a)(27) (1982). In Webster v. Doe, 108 S. Ct. 2047 (1988), the Court read the National Security Act of 1947 to permit judicial review of a CIA decision to terminate an employee but did not pass on the merits of the employee's constitutional claim. *Id.* at 2054 n.9. Two justices dissented from *Webster*'s modest finding of reviewability, not surprisingly citing *Curtiss-Wright.* See 108 S. Ct. at 2055 (O'Connor, J., dissenting in part); *id.* at 2060 (Scalia, J., dissenting).

40. 108 S. Ct. 818, 824 (1988) (emphasis added).

41. 108 S. Ct. at 829 (White, J., dissenting). The dissent cited the Warren Court's decision in Greene v. McElroy, 360 U.S. 474 (1959), which had held that the executive branch could not deprive a person of a security clearance, without full hearing, without express congressional authorization. See 108 S. Ct. at 828 (White, J. dissenting) (citing 360 U.S. at 507) ("Such [congressional] decisions cannot be assumed by acquiescence or non-action. They must be made explicitly . . . to assure that individuals are not deprived of cherished rights under procedures not actually authorized").

42. See, *e.g.,* Zemel v. Rusk, 381 U.S. 1, 17 (1965) ("Congress—in giving the President authority over matters of foreign affairs—must of necessity paint with a brush broader than that it customarily wields in domestic affairs").

43. See *Dames & Moore,* 453 U.S. at 684–86. In *Youngstown,* Justice Jackson had taken the opposite position on this issue. *Cf. supra* chapter 4 at notes 36–37 and accompanying text.

44. See Regan v. Wald, 468 U.S. 222, 240–42 (1984); Haig v. Agee, 453 U.S. 280 (1981); Snepp v. United States, 444 U.S. 507 (1980).
45. INS v. Chadha, 462 U.S. 919 (1983); Bowsher v. Synar, 478 U.S. 714 (1986).
46. See O. North, *supra* note 18, at 523–25, 527.
47. 444 U.S. 996 (1979). The justices voted to reject Senator Goldwater's challenge to the president's treaty termination on a variety of grounds: ripeness, *id.* at 997–98 (Powell, J., concurring in the judgment); the political question doctrine, *id.* at 1002–1003 (Rehnquist, J., concurring in the judgment); and the merits, *id.* at 1006–1007 (Brennan, J., dissenting). Had the case been heard today, Justice Scalia would almost certainly have voted to deny Goldwater's claim for lack of congressional standing. See Moore v. United States House of Representatives, 733 F.2d 946, 960–61 (D.C. Cir. 1984) (Scalia, J., concurring in the result), *cert. denied,* 469 U.S. 1106 (1985).
48. 479 U.S. 361 (1987).
49. The Vietnam cases include: Schlesinger v. Reservists Comm. to Stop the War, 418 U.S. 208 (1974); Holtzman v. Schlesinger, 414 U.S. 1316 (1973) (Douglas, J.) (Opinion in Chambers); Laird v. Tatum, 408 U.S. 1 (1972); Sarnoff v. Shultz, 409 U.S. 929 (1972); DaCosta v. Laird, 448 F.2d 1368 (2d Cir. 1971), *cert. denied,* 405 U.S. 979 (1972); Orlando v. Laird, 443 F.2d 1039 (2d Cir.), *cert. denied,* 404 U.S. 869 (1971); Massachusetts v. Laird, 400 U.S. 886 (1970); Holmes v. United States, 391 U.S. 936 (1968); Hart v. United States, 391 U.S. 956 (1968); Shiffman v. Selective Service Board, 391 U.S. 930 (1968); Epton v. New York, 390 U.S. 29 (1968); Zwicker v. Boll, 391 U.S. 353 (1968); Luftig v. McNamara, 387 U.S. 945 (1967); Mora v. McNamara, 389 U.S. 934, 935 (1967); Mitchell v. United States, 386 U.S. 972 (1967). See, generally, Sugarman, "Judicial Decisions concerning the Constitutionality of United States Military Activity in Indo-China: A Bibliography of Court Decisions," 13 *Colum. J. Transnat'l L.* 470 (1974) (collecting cases).

Cases arising out of the Central American conflict include: Dellums v. Smith, 797 F.2d 817 (9th Cir. 1986); Sanchez-Espinoza v. Reagan, 770 F.2d 202 (D.C. Cir. 1985); Ramirez de Arellano v. Weinberger, 745 F.2d 1500 (D.C. Cir. 1984) (en banc), *vacated and remanded for reconsideration in light of subsequent legislation,* 471 U.S. 1113 (1985); Crockett v. Reagan, 720 F.2d 1355 (D.C. Cir. 1983). See, generally, Cole, "Challenging Covert War: The Politics of the Political Question Doctrine," 26 *Harv. Int'l L.J.* 155 (1985); Note, "Covert Wars and Presidential Power: Judicial Complicity in a Realignment of Constitutional Power," 14 *Hastings Const. L.Q.* 683 (1987) (reviewing decisions).
50. In Kleindienst v. Mandel, 408 U.S. 753, 762 (1972), the Supreme Court ruled that because an excluded foreigner seeking entry into the United States has no right to enter, he or she lacks standing to challenge the exclusion. Consequently, challenges to ideological exclusions of aliens have generally been raised not by the excluded foreigners, but by American citizens who want to hear their message. See, *e.g.,* Abourezk v. Reagan, 785 F.2d 1043, 1050–51 (D.C. Cir. 1986), *aff'd*

by an equally divided Court, 108 S. Ct. 252 (1987); Harvard Law School Forum v. Shultz, 633 F. Supp. 525 (D. Mass.), *vacated,* No. 86-1371 (1st Cir. June 18, 1986). Decisions denying standing based on citizenship include: Schlesinger v. Reservists Comm. to Stop the War, 418 U.S. 208 (1974); United States v. Richardson, 418 U.S. 166 (1974); Laird v. Tatum, 408 U.S. 1 (1972); Velvel v. Nixon, 415 F.2d 236 (10th Cir.), *cert. denied,* 396 U.S. 1042 (1969). The courts have rejected taxpayer standing in United States v. Richardson, 418 U.S. 166 (1974); Phelps v. Reagan, 812 F.2d 1293 (10th Cir. 1987). The lower courts have rejected congressional standing in: United Presbyterian Church in the U.S.A. v. Reagan, 738 F.2d 1375 (D.C. Cir. 1984); Harrington v. Bush, 553 F.2d 190 (D.C. Cir. 1977); Holtzman v. Schlesinger, 484 F.2d 1307 (2d Cir. 1973), *cert. denied,* 416 U.S. 936 (1974). The Supreme Court considered, but did not decide, the constitutionality of congressional standing in Burke v. Barnes, 479 U.S. 361 (1987). See, generally, Note, "The Justiciability of Congressional-Plaintiff Suits," 82 *Colum. L. Rev.* 526 (1982) (reviewing cases).

51. For decisions recognizing official immunity, see Anderson v. Creighton, 107 S. Ct. 3034 (1987); Mitchell v. Forsyth, 472 U.S. 511 (1985); Harlow v. Fitzgerald, 457 U.S. 800 (1982); Nixon v. Fitzgerald, 457 U.S. 731 (1982).

52. For decisions barring suits by members of the armed forces, see, *e.g.,* United States v. Johnson, 107 S. Ct. 2063 (1987); Feres v. United States, 340 U.S. 135 (1950); see, also, Note, "From Feres to Stencel: Should Military Personnel Have Access to FTCA [Federal Tort Claims Act] Recovery?" 77 *Mich. L. Rev.* 1099 (1979). On government contractor immunity, see Boyle v. United Technologies Corp., 108 S. Ct. 2510 (1988) (creating federal common-law immunity barring a serviceman's estate from suing an independent contractor who had allegedly supplied a defective military helicopter to United States).

53. See, *e.g.,* Smith v. Reagan, 844 F.2d 195 (4th Cir. 1988); Sanchez-Espinoza v. Reagan, 770 F.2d 202 (D.C. Cir. 1985); United States v. Stanley, 107 S. Ct. 3054 (1987) (barring a former serviceman from maintaining *Bivens* constitutional tort action against military officers and civilians who administered experimental drug to him without his consent).

54. See, *e.g.,* Sanchez-Espinoza v. Reagan, 770 F.2d 202, 207–09 (D.C. Cir. 1985); Crockett v. Reagan, 558 F. Supp. 893, 902–03 (D.D.C. 1982), *aff'd,* 720 F. 2d 1355 (D.C. Cir. 1983) (per curiam), *cert. denied,* 467 U.S. 1251 (1984). See, generally, T. Franck & M. Glennon, *Foreign Relations and National Security Law* 824–27 (1987) (discussing equitable discretion doctrine).

55. See, *e.g.,* Johnson v. Weinberger, 851 F.2d 233 (9th Cir. 1988) (dismissing for lack of standing suit challenging U.S. "Launch on Warning" policy, which district court had dismissed under political question doctrine); Smith v. Reagan, 844 F.2d 195 (4th Cir. 1988) (dismissing suit under Hostage Act as political question and for want of cause of action); Americans United for Separation of Church & State v. Reagan, 786 F.2d 194 (3d Cir.) (dismissing establishment clause challenge to dispatch of ambassador to Vatican on mixed standing and political ques-

tion grounds), *cert. denied,* 107 S. Ct. 314 (1986); Sanchez-Espinoza v. Reagan, 770 F.2d. 202 (D.C. Cir. 1985) (dismissing suit on grounds of sovereign immunity, equitable discretion, absence of *Bivens* constitutional tort remedy, and implied statutory causes of action, mootness, and as nonjusticiable political question); Crockett v. Reagan, 720 F.2d 1355 (D.C. Cir. 1983) (rejecting congressional suit for declaratory judgment requiring president to remove U.S. armed forces from El Salvador, reasoning that whether War Powers Resolution's sixty-day cutoff provision had been triggered was political question), *cert. denied,* 467 U.S. 1251 (1984); Lowry v. Reagan, 676 F. Supp. 333 (D.D.C. 1987) (dismissing suit brought by members of Congress to compel president to report on U.S. military activities in Persian Gulf on mixed political question and equitable discretion grounds), *appeal dismissed,* No. 87-5426 (D.C. Cir. Oct. 17, 1988) (dismissed on political question grounds); Chaser Shipping Corp. v. United States, 649 F. Supp. 736 (S.D.N.Y. 1986), *aff'd mem.,* 819 F.2d 1129 (2d Cir. 1987), *cert. denied,* 108 S. Ct. 695 (1988) (dismissing as political question suit by shipowner whose vessels were damaged by U.S. mines in Nicaraguan port); Cranston v. Reagan, 611 F. Supp. 247 (D.D.C. 1985) (dismissing suit brought by members of Congress seeking determination that bilateral treaties violate Atomic Energy Act as nonjusticiable political question and, alternatively, on grounds of remedial discretion).

56. See, *e.g.,* INS v. Chadha, 462 U.S. 919 (1983) (ruling for president on merits after rejecting intervenor House and Senate's claim that president's challenge to constitutionality of legislative veto raised political question).

57. See Chemerinsky, "A Paradox without a Principle: A Comment on the Burger Court's Jurisprudence in Separation of Powers Cases," 60 *S. Cal. L. Rev.* 1083, 1084 (1987).

58. See, *e.g.,* Narenji v. Civiletti, 617 F.2d 745, 748 (D.C. Cir. 1979) (Robb, J.), *cert. denied,* 446 U.S. 957 (1980) ("it is not the business of courts to pass judgment on the decisions of the President in the field of foreign policy").

59. See, *e.g.,* Department of Navy v. Egan, 108 S. Ct. 818 (1988); Haig v. Agee, 453 U.S. 280 (1981); Snepp v. United States, 444 U.S. 507 (1980) (citing considerations of "national security"); Korematsu v. United States, 323 U.S. 214 (1944) ("military necessity"); United States v. Johnson, 107 S. Ct. 2063, 2069 (1987); Chappell v. Wallace, 462 U.S. 296, 301–02 (1983); Brown v. Glines, 444 U.S. 348, 354–57 (1980); Schlesinger v. Councilman, 420 U.S. 738, 757 (1975) ("military discipline"); Orloff v. Willoughby, 345 U.S. 83, 93–94 (1955); Burns v. Wilson, 346 U.S. 137, 142, 144 (1953); Gilligan v. Morgan, 413 U.S. 1 (1973); Goldman v. Weinberger, 475 U.S. 503, 507–8 (1986); Rostker v. Goldberg, 453 U.S. 57, 64–68 & n.6 (1981); Parker v. Levy, 417 U.S. 733, 743, 756–57 (1974) (citing need to defer to executive discretion in "military affairs").

60. See, *e.g.,* Chicago & S. Air Lines v. Waterman S.S. Corp., 333 U.S. 103 (1948); Phelps v. Reagan, 812 F.2d 1293 (10th Cir. 1987); Crockett v. Reagan, 720 F.2d 1355 (D.C. Cir. 1983), *cert. denied,* 467 U.S. 1251 (1984); Lowry v. Reagan,

676 F. Supp. 333 (D.D.C. 1987), *appeal dismissed*, No. 87-5426 (D.C. Cir. Oct. 17, 1988) (per curiam); Chaser Shipping v. United States, 649 F. Supp. 736 (S.D.N.Y. 1986), *aff'd mem.*, 819 F.2d 1129 (2d Cir. 1987), *cert. denied*, 108 S. Ct. 695 (1988); Dole v. Carter, 569 F.2d 1109 (10th Cir. 1977).

61. See Japan Whaling Ass'n v. American Cetacean Soc'y, 478 U.S. 221, 230 (1986) ("Under the Constitution, one of the judiciary's characteristic roles is to interpret statutes, and we cannot shirk this responsibility merely because our decision may have significant political overtones").

62. See O. North, *supra* note 18, at 555 (remarks of Rep. Fascell); *id.* at 358–62 (remarks of Arthur Liman).

63. *Testimony of Fawn Hall: Joint Hearings before the Senate Select Comm. on Secret Military Assistance to Iran and the Nicaraguan Opposition and the House Select Comm. to Investigate Covert Arms Transactions with Iran*, 100th Cong., 1st Sess. 5, 552 (1987).

64. Interview with David Frost (May 19, 1977), *quoted in* Glennon, "Can the President Do No Wrong?" 80 *Am. J. Int'l L.* 923, 923 (1986).

CHAPTER 7: SOME GUIDING PRINCIPLES

1. See Birnbaum, "President Reagan Signs Big Trade Bill, But Signals He May Ignore Parts of It," Wall St. J., Aug. 24, 1988, at 40, col. 1; Roberts, "President Decides Not to Veto Bill Requiring Notice of Plant Closings," N.Y. Times, Aug. 3, 1988, at A1, col. 2; "Nothing Was Gained by Administration Veto of Original Omnibus Trade Bill, Yeutter Says," 5 *Int'l Trade Rep.* (BNA) 1161, 1161 (Aug. 17, 1988) (remarks of U.S. Trade Representative Clayton Yeutter).

2. See Koplow, "Constitutional Bait and Switch: Executive Reinterpretation of Arms Control Treaties," 137 *U. Pa. L. Rev.* 1353, 1372 (1989).

3. See S. Res. 167, 100th Cong., 1st Sess., 133 *Cong. Rec.* S12,498 (daily ed. Sept. 22, 1987); Senate Comm. on Foreign Relations, *The ABM Treaty Interpretation Resolution*, 100th Cong., 1st Sess., S. Rept. 164 (1987); "Message to the Senate on the Soviet-United States Intermediate-Range Nuclear Force Treaty," 24 *Weekly Comp. Pres. Doc.* 779, 780 (June 10, 1988) (president's statement challenging Byrd amendment to INF Treaty as infringing upon his constitutional powers to interpret treaties). See, generally, Koh, "The Treaty Power," 43 *U. Miami L. Rev.* 106, 113–14 (1988).

4. For the progression of events in the Nicaragua case, see Letter from Secretary of State George P. Shultz to Secretary-General of the United Nations Javier Perez de Cuellar (Apr. 6, 1984), *reprinted in* 23 I.L.M. 670 (1984) (immediately and temporarily "modifying" United States' 1946 acceptance of International Court of Justice's compulsory jurisdiction, three days before Nicaragua filed suit); Case concerning Military and Paramilitary Activities in and against Nicaragua (Nicaragua v. U.S.), 1984 I.C.J. 392 (Judgment of Nov. 26, 1984) (ruling against the United States on the jurisdictional issue); Letter from Secretary of State George P. Shultz to Secretary-General of the United Nations Javier Perez de Cuellar (Oct. 7,

1985), *reprinted in* 24 I.L.M. 1742 (1985) (terminating U.S. acceptance of compulsory jurisdiction of International Court of Justice after the U.S. had withdrawn from the suit); Case concerning Military and Paramilitary Activities in and against Nicaragua (Nicaragua v. United States), 1986 I.C.J. 14 (Judgment of June 27, 1986) (ruling against the U.S. on the merits); Committee of United States Citizens Living in Nicaragua v. Reagan, 859 F.2d 929 (D.C. Cir. 1988) (suing executive officials for refusing to comply with World Court judgment). For an account of the litigation, see, generally, Chayes, "Nicaragua, the United States, and the World Court," 85 *Colum. L. Rev.* 1445 (1985).

5. See, generally, Henkin, "International Law and National Interest," 25 *Colum. J. Transnat'l L.* 1 (1986); A. Schlesinger, *The Cycles of American History* 83–86 (1986); Malawer, "Reagan's Law and Foreign Policy, 1981–1987: The 'Reagan Corollary' of International Law," 29 *Harv. Int'l L.J.* 85 (1988) (enumerating Reagan administration foreign policy decisions that have modified or deviated from preexisting international legal rules).

6. Frye, "Congress and President: The Balance Wheels of American Foreign Policy," 49 *Yale Rev.* 1, 2 (1979).

7. See O. North, *Taking the Stand: The Testimony of Lieutenant Colonel Oliver L. North* 745 (1987).

8. *Cf.* Elliott, "Regulating the Deficit After *Bowsher v. Synar,*" 4 *Yale J. on Reg.* 317, 353–61 (1987) (describing how our political organization creates strong incentives for politicians to behave irresponsibly on fiscal matters).

9. The 100th Congress enacted only one piece of legislation directly related to the Iran-contra affair: a rider attached to the fiscal year 1989 foreign-aid appropriations bill that increases the involvement of Congress in sales or transfers by one foreign country to another of U.S.-made weapons. See Pub. L. No. 461, 100th Cong., 2d Sess. (1988). See, generally, Felton, "Legislative Impact of Iran-Contra Affair Fades," 46 *Cong. Q.* 2981, 2983 (Oct. 15, 1988); Kurkjian, "Iran-Contra Lesson on Covert Action Lost, Some Say," Boston Globe, Oct. 9, 1988, at 30, col. 1.

10. My colleague Susan Rose-Ackerman has proposed a similar framework statute to govern judicial review of legislative consistency in the domestic arena. See Rose-Ackerman, "Progressive Law and Economics—and the New Administrative Law," 98 *Yale L.J.* 341, 349–68 (1988).

11. For specific proposals to modify these statutes, applying the general principles offered in this chapter, see *infra* chapter 8.

12. See House Select Comm. to Investigate Covert Arms Transactions with Iran and Senate Select Comm. on Secret Military Assistance to Iran and the Nicaraguan Opposition, *Report of the Congressional Comms. Investigating the Iran-Contra Affair,* 100th Cong., 1st Sess., S. Rept. 216, H. Rept. 433, 423–27 (1987) (majority report) (listing recommendations) [hereinafter *Iran-Contra Report*]. In this chapter and the next, I suggest how some of those recommendations might be incorporated into the legislative package that I would propose.

13. See L. Fisher, *Constitutional Dialogues: Interpretation As Political Process* 3 (1988) (arguing that "constitutional law is not a monopoly of the judiciary" but "a process in which all three branches converge and interact with their separate interpretations").

14. Korematsu v. United States, 323 U.S. 214, 246 (1944) (Jackson, J., dissenting).

15. E. Corwin, *The President: Office and Powers 1787–1984* 179 (5th rev. ed. 1984).

16. See, *e.g.*, P. Odeen, *National Security Policy Integration: Report of a Study Requested by the President under the Auspices of the President's Reorganization Project* (September 1979); G. Allison & P. Szanton, *Remaking Foreign Policy* (1976); *U.S. Commission on the Organization of the Government for the Conduct of Foreign Policy* (1975) [hereinafter *Murphy Commission Report*]; C. Crabb & K. Mulcahy, *Presidents and Foreign Policy Making: From FDR to Reagan* (1986). See, also, Gelb, "Why Not the State Department?" in *Decisions of the Highest Order: Perspectives on the National Security Council* 229, 240–41 nn.1 & 16 (K. Inderfurth & L. Johnson eds. 1988) (listing twelve other studies dating back to 1949 Hoover Commission Report on Foreign Affairs).

17. See *supra* chapter 4. See, also, Brest, "Congress As Constitutional Decision-maker and Its Power to Counter Judicial Doctrine," 21 *Ga. L. Rev.* 57, 61–65 (1986); Sager, "Fair Measure: The Legal Status of Underenforced Constitutional Norms," 91 *Harv. L. Rev.* 1212 (1978); Ross, "Legislative Enforcement of Equal Protection," 72 *Minn. L. Rev.* 311 (1987) (arguing that Congress has both the power and the responsibility to interpret and enforce underenforced constitutional norms).

18. Duffy, "Mr. Consensus," *Time* (Aug. 21, 1989): 16, 18 ("On domestic matters . . . Bush relies on a highly structured decisionmaking process . . . [k]nown to government-school types as multiple advocacy"); *compare* George, "The Case for Multiple Advocacy in Making Foreign Policy," 66 *Am. Pol. Sci. Rev.* 751 (1972).

19. See Quade, "The President Is His Only Client," *Barrister* (Winter / Spring 1988): 7 (Interview with A. B. Culvahouse, Jr., counsel to president) (emphasis added); see, also, *id.* ("White House office lawyers were not consulted about the reach or the extent of the Boland Amendment"). For descriptions of these controversial findings, see Butterfield, "Key Contra Ruling Claimed by Novice," N.Y. Times, June 9, 1987, at A1, col. 2, A15, col. 4 (the only executive branch legal analysis of applicability of Boland amendments was based on cursory review of facts by attorney who had failed bar examination four times); *Iran-Contra Report, supra* note 12, at 185–86; Victor, "CIA Counsel's Role Questioned," *Nat'l L.J.*, Feb. 2, 1987, at 3, col. 1 (both describing CIA general counsel's retroactive finding in Iran-contra affair).

20. *Cf.* Sunstein, "Constitutionalism After the New Deal," 101 *Harv. L. Rev.* 421, 454–60 (1987) (enumerating advantages of such centralized review); Diver, "Presidential Powers," 36 *Am. U.L. Rev.* 519 (1987) (such centralized review does not create imbalance in constitutional order).

21. See, *e.g.*, Ehrlich, "Remarks," in 5 Appendices to *Murphy Commission Report, supra* note 16, at 26–27 (urging that legal adviser to State Department conduct such review).

22. See 28 U.S.C. §§ 510, 512–13 (1982); 28 C.F.R. § 0.25(a) (1987).

23. For examples of Office of Legal Counsel opinions that restrained presidential conduct during the Reagan administration, see Frankel, "Ted Olson's Five Years in Purgatory," *Am. Law.* (Dec. 1988): 68, 70 (describing opinions of Assistant Attorney General Theodore B. Olson). For a fascinating account of the role of the Office of Legal Counsel during the Iranian hostage crisis, see "Introduction and Summary: Opinions of the Attorney General of the United States and of the Office of Legal Counsel relating to the Iranian Hostage Crisis, November 7, 1979 through February 5, 1981," 4A Op. Off. Legal Counsel 69–333 (1980).

24. Willard, "Law and the National Security Decision-making Process in the Reagan Administration," 11 *Hous. J. Int'l L.* 129, 132 (1988).

25. See *Iran-Contra Report, supra* note 12, at 424.

26. See Exec. Order No. 11,030, § 2(b), 3 C.F.R. 610 (1959–1963).

27. See Chayes & Chayes, "Testing and Development of 'Exotic' Systems under the ABM Treaty: The Great Reinterpretation Caper," 99 *Harv. L. Rev.* 1956, 1971 (1986).

28. See *The ABM Treaty and the Constitution: Joint Hearings before the Senate Comm. on Foreign Relations and the Senate Comm. on the Judiciary,* 100th Cong., 1st Sess. (1987).

29. See, *e.g.*, *Iran-Contra Report, supra* note 12, at 408 n.15, 421 n.37, 542 n. ** (discussing various executive branch legal opinions).

30. See, generally, J. Grabow, *Congressional Investigations: Law and Practice* 167–92 (1988) (describing house rules for demanding executive branch information); Standing Rule of the Senate 36.4, *reprinted in* F. Cumming, *Capitol Hill Manual* 180 (1976) ("Any Senator or officer of the Senate who shall disclose the secret or confidential business or proceedings of the Senate shall be liable, if a Senator, to suffer expulsion from the body; and if an officer, to dismissal from the service of the Senate, and to punishment for contempt"); S. Res. 23, 100th Cong., 1st Sess. § 6, 133 *Cong. Rec.* S89, 91 (daily ed. Jan. 6, 1987) (resolution establishing Senate Iran-Contra Committee) (requiring all committee staff members and consultants, as condition of employment, to obtain security clearances and sign nondisclosure agreements, with immediate removal as sanction for disclosure, and providing that any senator who violates security procedures of committee may be referred to Senate Select Committee on Ethics for imposition of sanctions in accordance with Senate rules).

31. See Pear, "Clash of Experts Blurs Policy on Central America," N.Y. Times, Aug. 24, 1989, at B10, col. 1 (describing NSC-State clashes during the Bush administration); Sorensen, "The President and the Secretary of State," 66 *Foreign Affairs* 231, 232 (1987/1988) (recounting recent history of such clashes).

32. See I. Destler, *Presidents, Bureaucrats and Foreign Policy* (1972); Gelb, *supra*

note 16, at 230 ("For the last twenty years or so most public commissions, organization experts and foreign policy commentators . . . have consistently recommended that the authority to make policy should be clearly and firmly lodged in the Department of State"). But see D. Warwick, *A Theory of Public Bureaucracy* (1975); Clarke, "Why State Can't Lead," 66 *Foreign Pol'y* 128 (1987); Gelb, *supra*, at 231–34; Rockman, "America's Departments of State: Irregular and Regular Syndromes of Policy Making," 75 *Am. Pol. Sci. Rev.* 911 (1981) (noting problems in State Department decision making).

33. See, *e.g.*, D. Warwick, *supra* note 32, at 205–15 (proposing institutional reforms to debureaucratize State Department).

34. See, *e.g.*, G. Allison & P. Szanton, *supra* note 16, at 78–80 (urging that NSC be abolished and its functions assumed by executive committee of cabinet); Clarke, *supra* note 32, at 137–40 (urging that national security assistant be reduced from policy adviser to neutral policy broker); Destler, "A Job That Doesn't Work," 38 *Foreign Pol'y* 80 (1980) (proposing abolition of position of national security assistant). For description of the Tower commission and Iran-contra committees' recommendations, see *supra* chapter 2.

35. See *Iran-Contra Report, supra* note 12, at 423–24.

36. See *id.* at 425 (making similar recommendation).

37. See Bamford, "Carlucci and the N.S.C.," N.Y. Times, Jan. 18, 1987, § 6 (Magazine), at 26; Kirschten, "White House Notebook," 19 *Nat'l J.* 2808, 2808 (1987).

38. See S. 715, 100th Cong., 1st Sess., *described in* 133 *Cong. Rec.* S15,620 (daily ed. Nov. 3, 1987) (legislation introduced by Sen. Tom Harkin); see, also, *id.* (quoting Adm. William J. Crowe, chairman of the Joint Chiefs of Staff) ("I don't think an active military man should lead the NSC. I just don't really believe that").

39. *Iran-Contra Report, supra* note 12, at 426.

40. See Hertzberg, "Bar Nunn," *New Republic* (May 23, 1988): 16.

41. See J. Goldstein, *The Modern American Vice Presidency: The Transformation of a Political Institution* 159–75 (1982) (describing foreign policy roles as special envoy and presidential adviser played by vice presidents from Nixon to Mondale); B. Patterson, *The Ring of Power: The White House Staff and Its Expanding Role in Government* 287 (1988) (during Eisenhower's presidency, Vice President Nixon chaired some twenty-six NSC meetings); *id.* at 293 (quoting Gerald Ford) ("I personally feel that the Vice President could, very properly, be the Chief of Staff in the White House itself"). For a similar proposal to make the vice president "more of an executive vice president," offered by President Reagan's special counselor on the Iran-contra affair, see D. Abshire, *Preventing World War III: A Realistic Grand Strategy* 280 (1988).

42. Nine vice presidents—Tyler, Fillmore, Andrew Johnson, Arthur, Theodore Roosevelt, Coolidge, Truman, Lyndon Johnson, and Ford—have succeeded to the presidency either by the death or resignation of the incumbent. J. Goldstein, *supra* note 41, at 10. Five others—John Adams, Jefferson, John Quincy Adams, Van

Buren, and Bush—have gone on to win the presidency after serving as vice president. See Goldstein, "Van Buren's 'Jinx,' " N.Y. Times, May 28, 1988, at 27, col. 7. For a thoughtful refutation of the various constitutional and policy objections to such a proposal, see, generally, Friedman, "Some Modest Proposals on the Vice-Presidency," 86 *Mich. L. Rev.* 1703, 1714–24, 1731–34 (1988).

43. See Fitts, "The Vices of Virtue: A Political Party Perspective on Civic Virtue Reforms of the Legislative Process," 136 *U. Pa. L. Rev.* 1567, 1628–33 (1988) (tracing history of power diffusion in Congress); Ornstein, "The Constitution and the Sharing of Foreign Policy Responsibility," in *The President, the Congress, and Foreign Policy* 35, 57 (E. Muskie, K. Rush, & K. Thompson eds. 1986) (to the extent that Congress has been able to reassert itself in foreign affairs, it has done so in a decentralized manner, which has given too much power to the congressional rank and file and insufficient power to the leadership); T. Franck & E. Weisband, *Foreign Policy by Congress* 210–26, 228 (1979).

44. See S.J. Res. 323, 100th Cong., 2d Sess., 134 *Cong. Rec.* S6,239 (daily ed. May 19, 1988) (text on file with author). Congressman Hamilton introduced the same bill on the House side. See H.R. J. Res. 601, 100th Cong., 2d Sess. (1988); Hamilton, "War Powers: Revise Resolution to Make It Work," Wall St. J., Mar. 20, 1989, at 14, col. 3. This bill has been reintroduced in the 101st Congress. See S.J. Res. 2, 101st Cong., 1st Sess., 135 *Cong. Rec.* S167, S184–85 (daily ed. Jan. 25, 1989). See, also Halperin, "Lawful Wars," 72 *Foreign Pol'y* 173, 176 (1988) (endorsing creation of a special leadership committee).

45. See Felton, "Will Bush-Hill Honeymoon Bring Bipartisanship?" 47 *Cong. Q.* 332, 335 (Feb. 18, 1989) (describing proposal of six senators, led by Senators Boren and Danforth); see, also, D. Abshire, *supra* note 41, at 287 (endorsing similar idea).

46. Frye, *supra* note 6, at 15.

47. See, *e.g.*, G. Ford, *A Time To Heal* 252 (1979) (president could not consult with key congressional leaders about 1975 Da Nang evacuation, because ten were abroad and twelve were scattered throughout U.S.).

48. *Cf.* the Boren-Danforth proposal described in *supra* note 45 and accompanying text; C. Vance, *Hard Choices* 14 (1983) (pointing out that during Iranian hostage crisis, secretary of state or his deputy spent up to two hours each day in meetings or briefing sessions with members of Congress).

49. See Frye, *supra* note 6, at 13, 11–15.

50. See Falk, "Remarks," in 5 Appendices to *Murphy Commission Report*, *supra* note 16, at 29 (urging the creation of a similar congressional unit).

51. See T. Franck & E. Weisband, *supra* note 43, at 245.

52. See Continuing Appropriations for Fiscal Year 1987, Pub. L. No. 99-500, § 213, 1986 *U.S. Code Cong. & Admin. News* (100 Stat.) 1783, 1783-305 to -306; see, also, Meyer, "Congressional Control of Foreign Assistance," 13 *Yale J. Int'l L.* 69, 88 (1988).

53. Henkin, " 'A More Effective System' for Foreign Relations: A Constitutional Framework," 5 Appendices to *Murphy Commission Report*, *supra* note 16, at 19.

54. See Act of Aug. 18, 1856, § 22, 11 Stat. 52, 60 (1856); 1 Stat. 28, 49, 65, 68, 553. These authorities are currently codified in 5 U.S.C. § 301 (1982).

55. Department of Navy v. Egan, 108 S. Ct. 818, 824 (1988).

56. 433 U.S. 425, 445 (1977). As chapter 6 noted, *Egan*'s narrow holding rested upon a construction of the peculiar statute creating the Merit Systems Protection Board, thus rendering much of its broad language obiter dicta. See, also, *Egan,* 108 S. Ct. at 825 (*"unless Congress specifically has provided otherwise,* courts traditionally have been reluctant to intrude upon the authority of the Executive in . . . national security affairs") (emphasis added); Sofaer, "Executive Power and the Control of Information: Practice under the Framers," 1977 *Duke L.J.* 1, 48 ("The claim that the President has unlimited power to withhold material sought by Congress or the courts is as untenable as the assertion that he has no power to do so. Practice indicates that the division of authority between the branches is somewhere between these extremes, and is worked out anew in each instance of controversy").

57. See Act of Mar. 3, 1911, ch. 226, 36 Stat. 1084 (repealed 1917); Espionage Act, 18 U.S.C. §§ 793–794 (1982); Atomic Energy Act, 42 U.S.C. §§ 2161–2163, 2165, 2274 (1982); Internal Security Act of 1950, 64 Stat. 987, 991, 50 U.S.C. § 783 (1982); Classified Information Procedures Act, 18 U.S.C. app. §§ 1–16 (1982).

58. See Exec. Order No. 10,290, 3 C.F.R. 789 (1949–1953); Exec. Order No. 10,501, 3 C.F.R. 979 (1949–1953); Exec. Order No. 11,652, 3 C.F.R. 678 (1971–1975); Exec. Order No. 12,065, 3 C.F.R. 190 (1978); Exec. Order No. 12,356, 3 C.F.R. 166 (1982), 50 U.S.C. § 401 note. For a history of these orders, see Ehlke & Relyea, "The Reagan Administration Order on Security Classification: A Critical Assessment," 30 *Fed. Bar News & J.* 91 (Feb. 1983); Note, "Developments in the Law—The National Security Interest and Civil Liberties," 85 *Harv. L. Rev.* 1130, 1190–1207 (1972).

59. Ehlke & Relyea, *supra* note 58, at 96.

60. See Frye, *supra* note 6, at 10 ("The exclusion of Congress from access to classified products of . . . the National Security Council system is a virtual guarantee of inadequately informed legislative participation in foreign policy decisions"); Casper, "Response to Professor Henkin," 61 *Va. L. Rev.* 777, 779 (1975) ("With the acquiescence of a Congress until recently shying away from its constitutional responsibilities, the President . . . invoked executive privilege to deny access to foreign relations information, and then in turn argued that Congress lacks a proper understanding of foreign affairs. This circular pattern is as unbearable as the remedy is easy. Congress must resist . . . the blanket invocation of executive privilege").

61. 18 U.S.C. § 798(c) (1982).

62. *Cf.* 26 U.S.C. § 6103(f) (1982) (restricting congressional access to tax return information to identified committees).

63. Henkin, *supra* note 53, at 14 n.32; United States v. Nixon, 418 U.S. 683, 706 (1974).

64. See *Iran-Contra Report, supra* note 12, at 689 (describing waiver of privilege

during Iran-contra investigation); Koh, *supra* note 3, at 113–14 (describing waiver during ABM Treaty reinterpretation debate); Gelb, "Overseeing of C.I.A. by Congress Has Produced Decade of Support," N.Y. Times, July 7, 1986, at A1, col. 1 (describing largely cooperative atmosphere between intelligence committees and executive branch).

65. Christopher, "Ceasefire between the Branches: A Compact in Foreign Affairs," 60 *Foreign Aff.* 989, 1001 (1982); see, also, Goodman, "Reforming U.S. Intelligence," 67 *Foreign Pol'y* 121, 132 (1987). Former House Speaker Jim Wright's September 1988 disclosure regarding CIA "testimony" received by Congress does not disprove this rule. As chapter 2 pointed out, it remains unclear whether Wright's remark derived from a CIA official's classified testimony to Congress (which the former Speaker, who did not sit on the House Intelligence Committee, would not likely have heard) or from a former CIA official's public testimony before the International Court of Justice.

66. See, *e.g.,* Morrison, "Blabbermouths," 19 *Nat'l J.* 2002, 2002 (1987) (only 9 percent of leaked national security news stories published during the first five months of 1986 originated in Congress); L. Johnson, *America's Secret Power: The CIA in a Democratic Society* 122, 295 n.63 (1989) (in the 1970s, as many as five hundred thousand executive branch officials had top-secret clearance, many times the number in Congress).

67. See Standing Rule of the Senate 36.4-.5, *reprinted in* F. Cummings, *Capitol Hill Manual* 180 (1976). Standing Rule of the Senate 36.5 states that confidential documents communicated to the Senate by the president or a department head "shall not be disclosed *without leave of the Senate*" (emphasis added). The House and Senate intelligence committee rules authorize the committees to disclose publicly information in their possession if they determine that "the public interest would be served by such disclosure." S. Res. 400, 94th Cong. § 8(a); Rule of House of Representatives 48.7(a). If such action is taken, a majority of the committee must agree and notify the president so that he or she may state any opposition to such disclosure. If the president opposes the disclosure, the committee can refer the matter to a secret session of the full house, which can by majority vote reject or modify the president's objections. See Stern, "Disclosing Secrets the (W)Right Way," *First Principles* (Dec. 1988): 11 (describing this procedure).

68. *Hearings before the Subcomm. on Legislation of the House Permanent Select Comm. on Intelligence on H.R. 3822, to Strengthen the System of Congressional Oversight of Intelligence Activities in the United States,* 100th Cong., 2d Sess. 99 (1988) (testimony of Rep. Lee Hamilton) [hereinafter Hamilton Testimony].

69. *Cf.* Christopher, *supra* note 65, at 1001 ("In my own experiences, I recall very few instances in which the added risk of a leak on Capitol Hill outweighed the potential damage that excessive secrecy would cause"); Hamilton Testimony, *supra* note 68, at 99 ("We must balance the harm that may result from the disclosure of a secret against the value of consultation and independent advice for the President prior to the initiation of a covert action").

70. See Fitts, *supra* note 43, at 1603–7 (because centralized institutions tend to represent broad constituencies and experience fewer collective action problems, they are more likely to promote public-regarding action). Another way the charter could discourage interest-group bargains from controlling the substance of particular provisions would be to incorporate a statutory provision directing judges to review action under the statute and to demand internal consistency between the charter's specific language and its stated purposes. See Rose-Ackerman, *supra* note 10, at 352–53.

71. *Compare* Davidson, "Congress and the Dispersion of Powers," *Mr. Madison's Constitution and the Twenty-first Century: A Report from the Williamsburg Conference 1988* 25, 28 (1988) ("The average tenure of senators and representatives is about 10.5 years," with some members serving several times that length) *with* Frye, *supra* note 6, at 3–4 (cabinet officers currently average only two years' consecutive service and assistant secretaries serve an average of only eighteen months).

72. See R. Lugar, *Letters to the Next President* 51 (1988) (six future presidents, nine vice presidents, and nineteen secretaries of state have served on the Senate Foreign Relations Committee).

73. See, generally, W. Eskridge & P. Frickey, *Cases and Materials on Legislation: Statutes and the Creation of Public Policy* 829–43 (1988) (presenting nine drafting commandments).

74. See § 8 of the War Powers Resolution, 50 U.S.C. § 1547 (1982).

75. The recent Boren-Danforth proposal for an informal consultative group apparently incorporates such an agreement. See Felton, *supra* note 45, at 335.

76. Henkin, *supra* note 53, at 19.

77. See *supra* chapter 6 (discussing *INS v. Chadha*).

78. See, generally, Breyer, "The Legislative Veto After Chadha," 72 *Geo. L.J.* 785, 794 (1984); Bruff & Gellhorn, "Congressional Control of Administrative Regulation: A Study of Legislative Vetoes," 90 *Harv. L. Rev.* 1309 (1977) (recounting inefficiencies and constitutional defects of the legislative veto).

79. See Trade Act of 1974, 19 U.S.C. §§ 2191–93 (1982); Koh, "Congressional Controls on Presidential Trade Policymaking After *I.N.S. v. Chadha*," 18 *N.Y.U. J. Int'l L. & Pol.* 1191, 1211–21 (1986); *The Legislative Fast Track: Its Illustrative Use for the U.S.-Canada Free Trade Agreement* (A. Holmer & J. Bello eds. forthcoming 1990) (describing how this technique has been used in trade area). The fast-track procedure has also been included in several other foreign affairs statutes, including the foreign assistance and war powers legislation. See Meyer, *supra* note 52, at 78–79 & n.38, 86–88 (citing statutes). For recent proposals to incorporate fast-track provisions into other foreign affairs statutes, see, *e.g.*, Note, "Reinterpreting Advice and Consent: A Congressional Fast Track for Arms Control Treaties," 98 *Yale L.J.* 885 (1989); Note, "Congress and Arms Sales: Tapping the Potential of the Fast-Track Guarantee Procedure," 97 *Yale L. J.* 1439, 1448, 1453–57 (1988).

80. See U.S. Const. art. I, § 5, cl. 3 ("the Yeas and Nays of the Members of either House on any question shall, at the Desire of one fifth of those Present, be entered on the Journal"); Breyer, *supra* note 78, at 794.

81. For an example of how this might work in the war powers context, see *infra* chapter 8. As a congressional control device, the fast-track procedure admittedly has two disadvantages that the legislative veto lacked. First, in cases where the president's action will take effect unless Congress expresses fast-track disapproval, both houses must disapprove that act by supermajorities in order to override a presidential veto (as opposed to the one- or two-house majority sufficient to sustain a legislative veto). Second, because fast-track procedures are simply statutory modifications in internal house rules and Article I, § 5, cl. 2, of the Constitution authorizes "[e]ach House [to] determine the Rules of its Proceedings," each house theoretically retains discretion to change those rules at any time. See Koh, *supra* note 79, at 1217 n.79; Meyer, *supra* note 52, at 98–99.

82. See 19 U.S.C. § 2112(b)(4)(A) (1982). For a description of the role played by the procedure in negotiating the U.S.-Canada Free Trade Agreement, see Koh, *supra* note 79, at 1211–21; Koh, "The Legal Markets of International Trade: A Perspective on the Proposed United States-Canada Free Trade Agreement," 12 *Yale J. Int'l L.* 193, 208–18 (1987).

83. See *Procedure in the U.S. House of Representatives,* ch. 31, § 1, at 697 (looseleaf ed. 1982) (describing point-of-order procedure); Franck & Bob, "The Return of Humpty-Dumpty: Foreign Relations Law After the Chadha Case," 79 *Am. J. Int'l L.* 912, 942–43 (1985) (suggesting that each chamber could adopt rules triggering point of order against such a bill). For descriptions and illustrations of how point-of-order procedures have been used in each of the houses, see Ross, *supra* note 17, at 359–62.

84. The Byrd-Nunn-Warner-Mitchell war powers proposal provides, for example, that money to pay troops that the president had committed abroad would be automatically cut off (except to remove them from hostilities) once Congress had voted to withdraw them pursuant to a concurrent resolution introduced under fast-track procedures. See § 6, S.J. Res. 323, 100th Cong., 2d Sess., 134 *Cong. Rec.* S6,239 (daily ed. May 19, 1988) (text on file with author).

85. See *Hearings on the Separation of Powers before the Subcomm. on Separation of Powers of the Senate Comm. on the Judiciary,* 90th Cong., 1st Sess. 43 (1967). Appropriations authorizations are statutes enacted pursuant to internal House and Senate rules which permit Congress to appropriate certain sums or monies for certain activities, but bar Congress from appropriating larger sums or monies for any activities that have not been authorized. Stith, "Congress' Power of the Purse," 97 *Yale L.J.* 1343, 1370 n.135 (1988); F. Cummings, *supra* note 67, at 97–99.

86. Professor Casper was the first to make this suggestion. See Casper, "Remarks," in 5 Appendices to *Murphy Commission Report, supra* note 16, at 24–25. Such a rethinking of the role of the authorization process would be particularly timely

during the current Congress, in light of a recent House Foreign Affairs Committee task force report recommending large-scale revisions in the foreign-aid authorization process. See Felton, "Foreign Aid System Criticized As Cumbersome, Ineffective," 47 *Cong. Q.* 272 (Feb. 11, 1989).

87. For descriptions of the accords, see Pear, "Baker Plan: A New Deal," N.Y. Times, Mar. 25, 1989, at A1, col. 5; Glennon, "The Good Friday Accords: Legislative Veto by Another Name?" 83 *Am. J. Int'l L.* 544 (1989).

88. See Foreign Assistance Act of 1961, § 634A, 22 U.S.C. § 2394-1 (1982). On reprogramming generally, see L. Fisher, *President and Congress: Power and Policy* 118–19 (1972); L. Fisher, *Presidential Spending Power* 75–98 (1975).

89. I am grateful to Robert J. Kurz of the Brookings Institution for elaborating the details of this process for me.

90. See Glennon, *supra* note 87. For descriptions of a similar informal arrangement reached in 1984 between the appropriations committees and the National Aeronautics and Space Administration, see L. Fisher, *supra* note 13, at 226–27. As Louis Fisher notes, however, more than 140 legislative vetoes have actually been signed into law since *Chadha,* and many of them have been honored on an informal basis. See Tolchin, "The Legislative Veto, An Accommodation That Goes On and On," N.Y. Times, Mar. 31, 1989, at A11, col. 1 (quoting Louis Fisher).

91. Thus, although the White House counsel subsequently challenged the pact as an encroachment on the president's constitutional powers, Secretary of State Baker was on stronger ground when he defended the accord as one that would enhance the president's power in foreign affairs. *Compare* Pear, "Pact Challenged by Bush Counsel," N.Y. Times, Mar. 26, 1989, at A1, col. 5 *with* Friedman, "Baker Says Accord on Contra Aid Enhances Powers of the President," N.Y. Times, Mar. 27, 1989, at A10, col. 1; Wicker, "Baker's 'Nice Try,' " N.Y. Times, Mar. 29, 1989, at A21, col. 1. Although I applaud the bipartisan result of the Good Friday accords, I question the president's decision to implement the accords without obtaining the approval of the attorney general or the White House counsel's office (although the legal adviser to the National Security Council was said to have seen them). See Pear, *supra*; Solomon, "Sometimes, Being Right on the Merits . . . Won't Undo Being Wrong Politically," 21 *Nat'l J.* 874 (1989). The absence of constitutional ratification by the president's legal counsel left the door open for a future executive claim resembling that recently made about the Boland amendments: that the accord—although both sought after and accepted by the president—violates the president's constitutional prerogatives and thus need not be respected. See *supra* chapter 5.

92. See Statement of the Honorable Clark M. Clifford, *Hearings before the Subcomm. on Legislation of the House Permanent Select Comm. on Intelligence on H.R. 3822, to Strengthen the System of Congressional Oversight of Intelligence Activities in the United States,* 100th Cong., 2d Sess. 56–57 (1988).

93. Stith, *supra* note 85, at 1361.

94. See H.R. 2522, 100th Cong., 1st Sess., 133 *Cong. Rec.* E2987-88 (daily ed. July 22, 1987) (remarks of Rep. Mel Levine) (proposing to amend Neutrality Act, 18 U.S.C. §§ 959, 960–61 (1982) [criminalizing organization or initiation of hostile expeditions on U.S. territory against a foreign country with which U.S. is "at peace"]). Even without this statutory modification, six individuals, including a former U.S. military officer, were recently indicted under the act on charges of recruiting, training, and arming mercenaries to fight in Nicaragua. See Volsky, "Six in Florida Indicted on Charges of Training Anti-Nicaragua Force," N.Y. Times, Aug. 23, 1988, at A10, col. 1. But see United States v. Terrell, No. 88-6097 (S.D. Fla. July 13, 1989) (Roettger, J.) (dismissing indictment because U.S. was not "at peace" with Nicaragua).

95. See Official Accountability Act of 1987, H.R. 3665, 100th Cong., 1st Sess., 133 *Cong. Rec.* H10,723 (daily ed. Nov. 20, 1987) (introduced by Rep. Conyers) (authorizing independent counsel to indict and convict U.S. government officials who "order or engage in the planning of, preparation for, initiation or conduct of intelligence activity which violates any statute or Executive Order in force or international agreements to which the United States is a party"); *cf.* Dellums v. Smith, 573 F. Supp. 1489 (N.D. Cal. 1983), motion to alter judgment denied, 577 F. Supp. 1449 (N.D. Cal. 1984) (holding Neutrality Act applicable to actions of government officials and enforceable by independent counsel), *vacated on other grounds,* 797 F.2d 817 (9th Cir. 1986).

96. The Iran-contra committees made the related recommendation that an independent CIA inspector general be created to conduct internal intelligence agency investigations. See *Iran-Contra Report, supra* note 12, at 425.

97. U.S. Const. art. II, § 4 (emphasis added); *id.* art. I, §§ 2–3; *id.* art. II, § 2. For historical and constitutional analysis of the impeachment remedy, see, generally, C. Black, *Impeachment: A Handbook* (1974); R. Berger, *Impeachment: The Constitutional Problems* (1973). I am grateful to Akhil Amar and Stephen F. Ross for discussing this remedy with me.

98. See House Comm. on the Judiciary, *Impeachment of Richard Nixon, President of the United States,* 93d Cong., 2d Sess., H. Rept. 1305, 217–19 (1974).

99. U.S. Const. art. I, § 3, cls.6–7. Dean Choper, for example, argues against the need for judicial review of presidential action in foreign affairs in part because Congress retains the political remedy of impeachment. See J. Choper, *Judicial Review and the National Political Process: A Functional Reconsideration of the Role of the Supreme Court* 286 (1980).

100. See Koh, *supra* note 79, at 1216–17 & n.77.

101. See *Chadha,* 462 U.S. at 955 n.20; U.S. Const. art. I, § 5, cl. 2 ("Each House may determine the Rules of its Proceedings").

102. See *Chadha,* 462 U.S. at 955.

103. See Meltzer, "Deterring Constitutional Violations by Law Enforcement Officials: Plaintiffs and Defendants as Private Attorney Generals," 88 *Colum. L. Rev.* 247, 295–327 (1988) (describing utility of such provisions in deterring constitutional violations by government officials).

104. See Synar v. United States, 626 F. Supp. 1374, 1378, 1381 (D.D.C. 1986) (per curiam) (citing Pub. L. No. 99-177, § 274, 99 Stat. 1037, 1098). But see Bowsher v. Synar, 478 U.S. 714 (1986) (avoiding congressional standing issue by relying upon standing of coplaintiff).

105. See, *e.g.*, Barnes v. Kline, 759 F.2d 21, 25–30 (D.C. Cir. 1985), *vacated as moot sub nom.* Burke v. Barnes, 479 U.S. 361 (1987); Kennedy v. Sampson, 511 F.2d 430 (D.C. Cir. 1974).

106. See United States v. Johnson, 107 S. Ct. 2063, 2071 (1987) (Scalia, J., dissenting). See, also, Note, "Making Intramilitary Tort Law More Civil: A Proposed Reform of the *Feres* Doctrine," 95 *Yale L.J.* 992 (1986). Although the *Feres* doctrine was originally predicated on the existence of a statutory compensation scheme and concerns about military discipline, it could also be applied to bar suits by members of the armed forces against superiors who order them to participate in illegal wars. This barrier to adjudication is particularly significant because members of the armed forces under orders to report to a war zone for battle are the individuals who most clearly have standing to sue their superiors under current doctrine. See, *e.g.*, Massachusetts v. Laird, 451 F.2d 26 (1st Cir. 1971); Berk v. Laird, 429 F.2d 302 (2d Cir. 1970).

107. See Nixon v. Fitzgerald, 457 U.S. 731, 748–49 (1982); Harlow v. Fitzgerald, 457 U.S. 800, 818 n.31 (1982). See, generally, P. Schuck, *Suing Government: Citizen Remedies for Official Wrongs* (1983); Kinports, "Qualified Immunity in Section 1983 Cases: The Unanswered Questions," 23 *Ga. L. Rev.* 597 (1989) (arguing that confused *Harlow* standards require clarification).

108. See 5 U.S.C. § 553(a)(1) (1982) (foreign affairs exception); *id.* § 702 (right of review); *id.* § 706 (scope of review). *Cf.* Sanchez-Espinoza v. Reagan, 770 F.2d 202, 207, 209 (D.C. Cir. 1985) (Scalia, J.) (finding discretionary nonmonetary relief "arguably available" under the APA against federal officials for unlawful actions in foreign affairs).

109. See INS v. Cardoza-Fonseca, 107 S. Ct. 1207, 1221 (1987) (judiciary is final authority on issues of statutory construction); Japan Whaling Ass'n v. American Cetacean Soc'y, 478 U.S. 221, 230 (1986) ("Under the Constitution, one of the judiciary's characteristic roles is to interpret statutes, and we cannot shirk this responsibility merely because our decision may have significant political overtones").

110. See, *e.g.*, Ramirez de Arellano v. Weinberger, 745 F.2d 1500 (D.C. Cir. 1984) (en banc), *vacated and remanded for reconsideration in light of subsequent legislation*, 471 U.S. 1113 (1985).

111. See U.S. Const. amend. V ("nor shall private property be taken for public use, without just compensation"); Dames & Moore v. Regan, 453 U.S. 654, 691 (1981) (Powell, J., concurring and dissenting in part) ("The Government must pay just compensation when it furthers the Nation's foreign policy goals by using as 'bargaining chips' claims lawfully held by a relatively few persons and subject to the jurisdiction of our courts. The extraordinary powers of the President and Congress . . . cannot . . . displace the Just Compensation Clause of the Con-

stitution") (footnote omitted). See, generally, Cohen & Ravitch, "Economic Sanctions, Domestic Deprivations, and the Just Compensation Clause: Enforcing the Fifth Amendment in the Foreign Affairs Context," 13 *Yale J. Int'l L.* 146 (1988).

112. *Cf.* Foreign Sovereign Immunities Act of 1976, 28 U.S.C. § 1391(f)(4) (1982) (laying venue in the district courts of the D.C. Circuit for suits against foreign sovereigns).

113. See, *e.g.*, Ramirez de Arellano v. Weinberger, 745 F.2d 1500, 1511, 1512–15 (D.C. Cir. 1984) (en banc) (both D.C. Circuit majority and Judge Scalia's dissent reject U.S. officials' political question defense); Tel-Oren v. Libyan Arab Republic, 726 F.2d 774, 803 n.8 (D.C. Cir. 1984) (Bork, J., concurring), *cert. denied*, 470 U.S. 1003 (1985) (same). See *infra* chapter 9.

114. Cover, "The Supreme Court, 1982 Term—Foreword: Nomos and Narrative," 97 *Harv. L. Rev.* 4, 57 (1983). The social consequences of judicial complicity in executive acts formed a recurrent focus of Cover's work. See R. Cover, *Justice Accused* 226–38 (1975); Cover, Violence and the Word, 95 *Yale L.J.* 1601, 1622 n.48 (1986) [hereinafter Cover, Violence] (A judge "may or may not be able to bring a good prison into being, but she can refrain from sentencing anyone to a constitutionally inadequate one"); Cover, "Book Review," 68 *Colum L. Rev.* 1003, 1005–08 (1968) (reviewing R. Hildreth, *Atrocious Judges: Lives of Judges Infamous as Tools of Tyrants and Instruments of Oppression* [1856]) [hereinafter Cover, Book Review].

115. *Accord*, Cover, Book Review, *supra* note 114, at 1008 n.31 ("[T]he judiciary as enforcers of [the selective service] law cannot help but be accomplices in that which the Executive perpetrates"). Although Cover's outrage at what he viewed as "judicial complicity in the crimes of Vietnam" sparked his research about slavery and the judicial process (see R. Cover, *supra* note 114, at xi), he did not live long enough to conduct a systematic assessment of the role of judges in evaluating executive conduct in foreign affairs. But see Cover, Violence, *supra* note 114, at 1619–21 (describing judicial role in restraining executive action abroad in United States v. Tiede, 86 F.R.D. 227 [U.S. Ct. for Berlin 1979]).

CHAPTER 8: SOME SPECIFIC PROPOSALS

1. See, *e.g.*, J. Birnbaum & A. Murray, *Showdown at Gucci Gulch: Lawmakers, Lobbyists, and the Unlikely Triumph of Tax Reform* 285–88 (1987) (describing how similar factors converged to enact the 1986 Tax Reform Act in defiance of "all the lessons of political science, logic, and history"); J. Kingdon, *Agendas, Alternatives, and Public Policies* (1984) (describing how policy entrepreneurs, key elected public officials, and public receptivity all combined to bring about deregulation movement of late 1970s); Cohen, March, & Olsen, "A Garbage Can Model of Organizational Choice," 17 *Admin. Sci. Q.* 1 (1972) (characterizing organizations such as Congress as a garbage can, or organized anarchy, in

which important policy problems can be solved when shifting combinations of problems, solutions, and decision makers coalesce to make action possible).

2. See, *e.g.*, J. Birnbaum & A. Murray, *supra* note 1 (describing enactment of Tax Reform Act of 1986); W. Eskridge & P. Frickey, *Legislation: Statutes and the Creation of Public Policy* 2–28 (1987) (Civil Rights Act of 1964); J. Kingdon, *supra* note 1, at 9–13 (describing deregulation movement of late 1970s); Koh, "Congressional Controls on Presidential Trade Policymaking After *I.N.S. v. Chadha*," 18 *N.Y.U. J. Int'l L. & Pol.* 1191, 1200–1208 (1986) (Trade Act of 1974); Elliott, Ackerman, & Millian, "Toward a Theory of Statutory Evolution: The Federalization of Environmental Law," 1 *J.L. Econ. & Org.* 313 (1985) (describing environmental movement of the late 1960s and 1970s).

3. See, *e.g.*, Felton, "Will Bush-Hill Honeymoon Bring Bipartisanship?" 47 *Cong. Q.* 332 (Feb. 18, 1989); Felton, "Baker Woos Hill with Call for Bipartisanship," 47 *Cong. Q.* 125 (Jan. 21, 1989); Rasky, "Mitchell Details Democratic Goals," N.Y. Times, Jan. 26, 1989, at D23, col. 1.

4. Elliott, Ackerman, & Millian, *supra* note 2 (arguing that competition between Nixon and Muskie to take credit for strict environmental laws contributed to their enactment).

5. See 132 *Cong. Rec.* S14,629 (daily ed. Oct. 2, 1986). For Lugar's account of this battle, see R. Lugar, *Letters to the Next President* 208–47 (1988).

6. See Elliott, Ackerman, & Millian, *supra* note 2, at 324–26 (using concept of "politician's dilemma" to help explain congressionally led environmental reform movement of late 1960s and early 1970s).

7. Senator Specter proposed bills that would have created a politically appointed director of national intelligence (with a fixed seven-year term); reformed the congressional intelligence committees; and installed an independent inspector general at the CIA. See S. 1818, 100th Cong., 1st Sess., 133 *Cong. Rec.* S15, 190 (daily ed. Oct. 27, 1987); S. 1820, 100th Cong., 1st Sess., 133 *Cong. Rec.* S15,193 (daily ed. Oct. 27, 1987). The intelligence committees did not adopt any of those proposals but did modify the fiscal 1989 intelligence authorization bill to require that the CIA director report to Congress more regularly about the activities of the CIA inspector general. See Felton, "Intelligence Bill Endorses New Spy Satellite," 46 *Cong. Q.* 2344, 2345 (1988). Senator Specter has reintroduced each of his bills in the 101st Congress. See S. 145, S. 175, S. 199, 101st Cong., 1st Sess., 135 *Cong. Rec.* S122–29, S171 (daily ed. Jan. 25, 1989). See *infra* note 41 (subsequent history).

8. See Hamilton, "War Powers: Revise Resolution to Make It Work," Wall St. J., Mar. 20, 1989, at 14, col. 3 (urging enactment of the Byrd-Nunn-Warner-Mitchell proposal by the 101st Congress as S.J. Res. 2, 101st Cong., 1st Sess., 135 *Cong. Rec.* S167, S184–85 [daily ed. Jan. 25, 1989]). See, also, *supra* chapter 7 (discussing Danforth-Boren proposal regarding core consultative group).

9. See S. 347, 101st Cong., 1st Sess., 135 *Cong. Rec.* S1,106-08 (daily ed. Feb. 2, 1989) (introduced by Senators Kerry, Lugar, and Lautenberg); H.R. 91,

101st Cong., 1st Sess., 135 *Cong. Rec.* H48 (daily ed. Jan. 4, 1989) (introduced by Representatives Berman, Fascell, Hamilton, and Hyde). See, generally, Section Note, "Congress Making New Try on Arms-Sale Curbs," 47 *Cong. Q.* 473 (Mar. 4, 1989).

10. See Rogers, Wall St. J., Nov. 22, 1989, at A14, col. 1; *supra* chapter 5, note 47 (describing Moynihan amendment); *supra* chapter 7, notes 38, 94–95 (describing Conyers, Levine, and Harkin proposals).

11. See "The Presidential Pen, The Congressional Eraser," N.Y. Times, Mar. 23, 1988, at D26, cols. 5–6; Alston, "Reagan's Support Index Up—But Not Much," 46 *Cong. Q.* 3323 (Nov. 19, 1988). See the overrides of the presidential vetoes of the Water Act of 1987, 133 *Cong. Rec.* H515 (daily ed. Feb. 3, 1987) (House override), 133 *Cong. Rec.* S1,691 (daily ed. Feb. 4, 1987) (Senate override); the Federal-Aid Highway Act of 1987, 133 *Cong. Rec.* H1,635 (daily ed. Mar. 31, 1987) (House override), 133 *Cong. Rec.* S4,408 (daily ed. Apr. 2, 1987) (Senate override); and the Civil Rights Restoration Act of 1988, 134 *Cong. Rec.* H1,037 (daily ed. Mar. 22, 1988) (House override), 134 *Cong. Rec.* S2,730 (daily ed. Mar. 22, 1988) (Senate override). As we saw in chapter 7, despite its narrow failure to override a fourth veto—of the omnibus trade bill—Congress later ultimately secured nearly identical trade legislation. Indeed, Congress overrode nine of President Reagan's thirty-nine regular vetoes (roughly 23 percent), a ratio that compares favorably with the less than 3 percent override percentage of Dwight Eisenhower, the last two-term Republican president facing a largely Democratic Congress. See "Presidential Vetoes, 1789–1988," 47 *Cong. Q.* 7 (Jan. 7, 1989). In the first ten months of the Bush presidency, Congress failed to override the president's only regular vetoes, of a proposed minimum-wage bill, a bill prohibiting the export of defense articles to coproduce the FS-X fighter aircraft with Japan, the 1990 foreign-operations and State Department authorization bills, and two abortion-funding bills.

12. See, *e.g.*, Ely, "Suppose Congress Wanted a War Powers Act That Worked," 88 *Colum. L. Rev.* 1379 (1988) (discussing, *inter alia*, Byrd-Nunn-Warner-Mitchell proposal); Symposium, "Legal and Policy Issues in the Iran-Contra Affair: Intelligence Oversight in a Democracy," 11 *Hous. J. Int'l L.* 1 (1988) (surveying intelligence oversight reform proposals).

13. I have set forth my proposals for reform of the National Security Council in *supra* chapter 7.

    With regard to arms sales, the one other foreign policy realm discussed in chapter 2, the 100th Congress made a modest advance by attaching a rider to the fiscal year 1989 foreign-aid appropriations bill that stiffens presidential notification requirements and increases the involvement of Congress in sales or transfers of various U.S.-made weapons. See Pub. L. No. 461, 100th Cong., 2d Sess. (1988). In the current Congress, both the Senate and the House have introduced useful legislation to amend the Arms Export Control Act and other export laws to prohibit arms transactions with countries supporting terrorism. See S. 347, 101st Cong., 1st Sess., 135 *Cong. Rec.* S1,106-08 (daily ed. Feb. 2, 1989) (introduced by Senators Kerry, Lugar, and Lautenberg); H.R. 91, 101st Cong., 1st Sess., 135 *Cong. Rec.* H48 (daily ed. Jan. 4, 1989) (introduced by Representatives Berman, Fascell, Hamilton, and Hyde). A House Foreign Affairs Committee task force has recently recommended further amendments to the Arms Export Control Act of 1968, which are currently before the committee. See Felton, "Foreign Aid System Criticized as Cumbersome, Ineffective," 47 *Cong. Q.* 272 (Feb. 11, 1989). For a sensible discussion of reform proposals in the area of arms sales, including the Biden-Levine proposal, see, generally, Note, "Congress and Arms Sales: Tapping the Potential of the Fast-Track Guarantee Procedure," 97 *Yale L.J.* 1439, 1448, 1453–57 (1988).

14. In a typically penetrating article, Professor Ely has articulated many of my agreements and objections to that proposal. See Ely, *supra* note 12. See, also, Halperin & Stern, "Lawful Wars," 72 *Foreign Pol'y* 173 (1988); Committee on Federal Legislation, "The War Powers Resolution," 44 *Rec. of Ass'n of the Bar of the City of New York* 106 (1989); Bennett et al., "The President's Powers as Commander-in-Chief Versus Congress' War Power and Appropriations Power," 43 *U. Miami L. Rev.* 17–59 (1988); "Cheney on Congress: Vacillation, Blame Avoidance," Wall St. J., Mar. 17, 1989, at A14, cols. 4, 6 (statement of Secretary of Defense Richard Cheney) ("The War Powers Act should be repealed"). For samples of earlier commentary, see Berger, "Warmaking by the President," 121 *U. Pa. L. Rev.* 29 (1972); Carter, "The Constitutionality of the War Powers Resolution," 70 *Va. L. Rev.* 101 (1984); Rostow, "Great Cases Make Bad Law: The War Powers Act," 50 *Tex. L. Rev.* 833 (1972); Turner, "The War Powers Resolution: Unconstitutional, Unnecessary and Unhelpful," 17 *Loyola L.A. L. Rev.* 683 (1984); Van Alstyne, "Congress, The President, and the Power to Declare War: A Requiem for Vietnam," 121 *U. Pa. L. Rev.* 1 (1972).

15. Firestone, "The War Powers Resolution," paper presented to the November 1987 Hofstra University Presidential Conference on "Richard Nixon: A Retrospective on His Presidency" (conference proceedings forthcoming from Greenwood Press).

16. See 50 U.S.C. § 1544(c) (1982).

17. As Professor Geoffrey Miller has noted, the resolution "significantly limits the President's power [to retain troops abroad] in general terms that are not directed at any particular controversy." Miller, "The President's Powers as Commander-in-Chief Versus Congress' War Power and Appropriations Power," 43 *U. Miami L. Rev.* 31, 35 (1988).

18. S.J. Res. 323, 100th Cong., 2d Sess., 134 *Cong. Rec.* S6,239 (daily ed. May 19, 1988) (reintroduced in 101st Congress as S.J. Res. 2, 135 *Cong. Rec.* S167, S184–85 [daily ed. Jan. 25, 1989]). Former Secretary of State Cyrus Vance had earlier proposed that Congress amend the War Powers Resolution to declare that "no funds made available under any law may be obligated or expended for any presidential use of force not authorized by Congress" under the terms of the amended act. See Vance, "Striking the Balance: Congress and the President under the War Powers Resolution," 133 *U. Pa. L. Rev.* 79, 93–94 (1984).

19. As currently written, the War Powers Resolution provides expedited fast-track procedures for considering certain joint resolutions introduced after a presidential report on "hostilities" is submitted or "required to be submitted" to Congress. See 50 U.S.C. §§ 1544(b), 1545 (1982). Reasoning that a presidential report was required to be submitted after U.S. forces had destroyed an Iranian oil platform, Senator Brock Adams attempted in 1988 to invoke this procedure to force a vote on the president's compliance with the War Powers Resolution in the Persian Gulf. See Adler, "Senator Adams' Gambit Paves the Way for Vote on Tanker-Escort in the Persian Gulf," *First Principles* (Feb.–Mar. 1988): 4.

20. See S.J. Res. 323, § 4, 100th Cong., 2d Sess., 134 *Cong. Rec.* S6,239 (daily ed. May 19, 1988).

21. Black, "The Working Balance of the American Political Departments," 1 *Hastings Const. L.Q.* 13, 18 (1980). The wisdom of this observation was recently illustrated by the controversial commitment of United States troops to Lebanon, which went on for eighteen months without any clear articulation of the purpose that the American military presence was to serve. See *supra* chapter 2.

22. See S. 440, 93rd Cong., 1st Sess. (1973), *reprinted in* T. Franck & M. Glennon, *Foreign Relations and National Security Law* 590 (1987); S. 2956, 92d Cong., 1st Sess., 117 *Cong. Rec.* 44,794–95 (1971) (similar bill proposed by Sen. Javits). For a history of S. 440 and its removal from the final War Powers Resolution, see *Prepared Testimony and Statement for the Record of Morton H. Halperin, Director, and Gary M. Stern, Research Associate, Washington Office, American Civil Liberties Union, on the War Powers Resolution before the Subcomm. on Investigations, House Armed Services Comm.* 2–5 (May 24, 1989) (copy on file with author).

23. *Cf.* § 3(3), S. 440, 93d Cong., 1st Sess. (1973), *reprinted in* T. Franck & M. Glennon, *supra* note 22, at 591 (authorizing the president to commit U.S. troops to protect threatened U.S. citizens while evacuating them from a foreign country). President Reagan eventually signed the 1988 omnibus trade bill, which contained numerous provisions restricting his discretion, primarily to secure similar congressional authorization to engage in future multilateral trade talks. See Silk, "Looking Ahead in World Trade," N.Y. Times, Aug. 26, 1988, at D2, col. 1. The National Security Agency supported the 1980 Intelligence Oversight Act, which restricted its discretion, in part because that statute was the first congressional enactment to recognize and endorse that agency's existence. See Remarks of Daniel Silver, former general counsel to the National Security Agency, American Society of International Law Annual Meeting, Washington, D.C. (Apr. 20, 1988) (on file with author).

24. Ely, *supra* note 12, at 1409.

25. For rulings in the human rights area, see, *e.g.*, Filartiga v. Pena-Irala, 630 F.2d 876 (2d Cir. 1980); Forti v. Suarez-Mason, 672 F. Supp. 1531 (N.D. Cal. 1987); Von Dardel v. U.S.S.R., 623 F. Supp. 246 (D.D.C. 1985). For commercial rulings under the Act of State Doctrine and the Foreign Sovereign Immunities Act, see G. Born & D. Westin, *International Civil Litigation in United States*

Courts: Commentary and Materials 335–404, 493–566 (1989) (collecting cases).

26. See, generally, Eisenberg & Yeazell, "The Ordinary and the Extraordinary in Institutional Litigation," 93 *Harv. L. Rev.* 465 (1980); Note, "Complex Enforcement: Unconstitutional Prison Conditions," 94 *Harv. L. Rev.* 626 (1981); Special Project, "The Remedial Process in Institutional Reform Litigation," 78 *Colum. L. Rev.* 784 (1978) (collecting cases). See, also, Chayes, "The Role of the Judge in Public Law Litigation," 89 *Harv. L. Rev.* 1281 (1976); Fiss, "The Supreme Court, 1978 Term—Foreword, The Forms of Justice," 93 *Harv. L. Rev.* 1 (1979) (approving this domestic trend).

27. *Cf.* Ramirez de Arellano v. Weinberger, 745 F.2d 1500, 1543 (D.C. Cir. 1984) (en banc) (restraining unauthorized military action in Honduras on the ground that "[t]he Judiciary is fully empowered to vindicate individual rights overridden by specific, unconstitutional military actions"). I have elsewhere addressed the relationship between "domestic public law litigation" (also called "institutional reform litigation") and the burgeoning international litigation in U.S. domestic courts, which I call "transnational public law litigation." See, generally, Koh, "Civil Remedies for Uncivil Wrongs: Combatting Terrorism through Transnational Public Law Litigation," 22 *Tex. Int'l L.J.* 169, 193–201 (1987). In transnational public law litigation, private individuals, government officials, and nations sue one another in domestic courts, making "transnational" legal claims that blend private and public, domestic and international law. For a brief description of the origins of the phenomenon, see *id.* at 200 n.104.

28. See, *e.g.*, Clark Resolution, S. Res. 536, 95th Cong., 2d Sess., 124 *Cong. Rec.* S27,851 (daily ed. Aug. 25, 1978) (requiring executive branch to consult with the Senate regarding the method to be used in concluding a particular type of agreement); Rehm, "Making Foreign Policy through International Agreement," in *The Constitution and the Conduct of Foreign Policy* 126, 133–37 (F. Wilcox & R. Frank eds. 1976).

29. See 617 F.2d 697 (D.C. Cir. 1979) (en banc) (upholding presidential termination authority), *vacated on other grounds*, 444 U.S. 996 (1979); *Restatement (Third) of the Foreign Relations Law of the United States* § 339 (1987). See, generally, Henkin, "Treaties in a Constitutional Democracy," 10 *Mich. J. Int'l L.* 406 (1989) (providing examples of each of these interbranch accommodations).

30. "Senate's Condition to Treaty," N.Y. Times, May 28, 1988, at A4, cols. 5–6; 134 *Cong. Rec.* S6,937 (daily ed. May 27, 1988), *reprinted in* 82 *Am. J. Int'l L.* 810–15 (1988).

31. See Department of State, *Foreign Affairs Manual,* chapter 700, Treaties and Other International Agreements (June 6, 1969); Department of State, *Foreign Affairs Manual,* chapter 700, Treaties and Other International Agreements (Oct. 25, 1974) (describing State Department's "Circular No. 175" procedure).

32. *Compare* Sumitomo Shoji America, Inc. v. Avagliano, 457 U.S. 176 (1982); United States v. Decker, 600 F.2d 733 (9th Cir. 1979), *cert. denied*, 444 U.S. 855

(1979) (deferring to executive interpretation) *with* United States v. Stuart, 109 S. Ct. 1183, 1192 n. 7 (1989); Rainbow Navigation, Inc. v. Dep't of the Navy, 699 F. Supp. 339, 343 (D.D.C. 1988) (Greene, J.) (looking to record of Senate preratification materials as a guide to interpreting a particular treaty). See, also, Vagts, "Senate Materials and Treaty Interpretation: Some Research Hints for the Supreme Court," 83 *Am. J. Int'l L.* 546 (1989). But see United States v. Stuart, 109 S. Ct. at 1195–97 (Scalia, J., concurring in the judgment) (challenging relevance of preratification materials).

33. See Henkin, "'A More Effective System' for Foreign Relations: The Constitutional Framework," in 5 *Appendices to U.S. Commission on the Organization of the Government for the Conduct of Foreign Policy* 19 (1975) [hereinafter Appendices to *Murphy Commission Report*]; Henkin, *supra* note 29, at 428. In important respects, Professor Henkin's proposal resembles the Clark Resolution cited in *supra* note 28.

34. See S. Res. 86, 99th Cong., 1st Sess., *reprinted in* 131 *Cong. Rec.* S2,437–38 (daily ed. Feb. 28, 1985); Muskie, "Congress and National Security," 28 *Va. J. Int'l L.* 949, 958–59 (1988) (describing Senate observer group's activities).

35. The extent of information sharing between the House Ways and Means and Senate Finance committees and the executive branch was so extensive that an interbranch memorandum of understanding was even signed whereby the president's trade representative agreed to provide the committees with classified cables relating to the negotiations. See Koh, *supra* note 2, at 1214 n.65.

36. For a recent comprehensive recommendation for restructuring the current U.S. statutory regime governing international economic sanctions, see B. Carter, *International Economic Sanctions: Improving the Haphazard U.S. Legal Regime* (1988).

37. See Japan Whaling Ass'n v. American Cetacean Soc'y, 478 U.S. 221, 230 (1986) ("Under the Constitution, one of the judiciary's characteristic roles is to interpret statutes, and we cannot shirk this responsibility merely because our decision may have significant political overtones"). Because of the exigencies of the Iranian hostage crisis, a de facto expedited judicial review of the president's IEEPA authority occurred in Dames & Moore v. Regan, 453 U.S. 654 (1981).

38. 22 U.S.C. § 1732 (1982). See O. North, *Taking the Stand: The Testimony of Lieutenant Colonel Oliver L. North* 503–4 (1987); *id.* at 606 (remarks of Rep. Henry Hyde). See, also, House Select Comm. to Investigate Covert Arms Transactions With Iran and Senate Select Comm. on Secret Military Assistance to Iran and the Nicaraguan Opposition, *Report of the Congressional Comms. Investigating the Iran-Contra Affair,* 100th Cong., 1st Sess., S. Rept. 216, H. Rept. 433, 426 (1987) [hereinafter *Iran-Contra Report*] (recommending repeal of Hostage Act). The arms export control amendments currently pending before the House and Senate would narrow the president's delegated authority under the Hostage Act but not repeal it altogether. See § 9, S. 347, 101st Cong., 1st Sess., 135 *Cong. Rec.* S1,106-08 (daily ed. Feb. 2, 1989) (introduced by Senators Kerry, Lugar,

and Lautenberg); § 9, H.R. 91, 101st Cong., 1st Sess., 135 *Cong. Rec.* H48 (daily ed. Jan. 4, 1989) (introduced by Representatives Berman, Fascell, Hamilton, and Hyde). See, generally, Section Note, *supra* note 9.

39. Dames & Moore v. Regan, 453 U.S. 654, 677 (1981). For a thorough historical examination of the narrow legislative intent underlying the statute, see Mikva & Neuman, "The Hostage Crisis and the 'Hostage Act,' " 49 *U. Chi. L. Rev.* 292 (1982). For executive branch legal opinions invoking the act, see "Opinions of the Attorney General of the United States and of the Office of Legal Counsel relating to The Iranian Hostage Crisis, November 7, 1979 through February 5, 1981," 4A *Op. Off. Legal Counsel* 155–56, 227 (1980).

40. Silver, "The Uses and Misuses of Intelligence Oversight," 11 *Hous. J. Int'l L.* 7, 16 (1988).

41. See *Iran-Contra Report, supra* note 38, at 425. Although the 1990 intelligence authorization bill recently created a statutory CIA inspector general, President Bush signed that bill subject to certain "understandings" that may ultimately undercut that officer's independence. See "Statement on Signing the Intelligence Authorization Act, Fiscal Year 1990", 25 *Weekly Comp. Pres. Doc.* 1851, 1853 (Nov. 30, 1989).

42. See *Iran-Contra Report, supra* note 38, at 426.

43. See ABA Standing Comm. on Law and National Security, *Oversight and Accountability of the U.S. Intelligence Agencies* 107–9 (1985).

44. See Silver, *supra* note 40, at 15. For many years, the CIA general counsel reported questions of impropriety and illegality to the Intelligence Oversight Board, not the attorney general, leaving little effective external oversight of the legality of agency action. See Fagelson, "The Constitution and National Security: Covert Action in the Age of Intelligence Oversight," 5 *J.L. & Pol.* 275, 303 (1989).

45. See *supra* note 7; Fisher, "Lessons From the Iran/Contra Affair," 40 *Int'l Practitioner's Notebook* 7, 8 (Sept. 1988) ("I doubt if [William] Casey's name would have been put forth [for reconfirmation in President Reagan's second term], given his record over the first 4 years").

46. See L. Johnson, *America's Secret Power: The CIA in a Democratic Society* 223, 263 (1989) (noting that division of intelligence committees has proved to be a source of strength to the Congress in the performance of its oversight duties); O'Neil, "Remarks of Michael O'Neil," 11 *Hous. J. Int'l L.* 211, 217 (1988).

47. See "Statement of the Honorable Clark M. Clifford," *Hearings before the Subcomm. on Legislation of the House Permanent Select Comm. on Intelligence on H.R. 3822, to Strengthen the System of Congressional Oversight of Intelligence Activities in the United States,* 100th Cong., 2d Sess. 56 (1988).

48. See Stith, "Congress' Power of the Purse," 97 *Yale L.J.* 1343, 1387 n.213 (1988) (collecting cases in which courts have determined whether the executive has exceeded specified appropriations limitations). See, also, *supra* chapter 7, notes 94–95 (discussing Conyers and Levine bills to impose criminal penalties on government officials who violate the Neutrality Act and other statutes); § 3, S.

1818, 100th Cong., 1st Sess., 133 *Cong. Rec.* S15,190 (daily ed. Oct. 27, 1987) (introduced by Sen. Specter) (imposing similar criminal penalties).

49. See 50 U.S.C. §§ 1801–11 (1982). Under the Foreign Intelligence Surveillance Act (FISA), the executive branch may not engage in certain forms of electronic surveillance for national security purposes unless it has received advance approval from the attorney general and presented in camera, ex parte applications for warrants to a Foreign Intelligence Surveillance Court, comprised of seven federal district judges appointed by the chief justice, in proceedings conducted under strictest security. The chief justice also designates three federal appeals court judges to review government appeals in cases where initial warrants have been denied. Over four thousand surveillance requests were brought before this court in its first ten years. For descriptions of how the FISA judicial process has operated, see, generally, Cinquegrana, "The Walls (and Wires) Have Ears: The Background and First Ten Years of the Foreign Intelligence Surveillance Act of 1978," 137 *U. Pa. L. Rev.* 793 (1989); Saltzburg, "National Security and Privacy: Of Governments and Individuals under the Constitution and the Foreign Intelligence Surveillance Act," 28 *Va. J. Int'l L.* 129 (1987).

50. Note, "Developments in the Law—The National Security Interest and Civil Liberties," 85 *Harv. L. Rev.* 1130, 1190 (1972).

51. *U.S. Government Information Policies and Practices—The Pentagon Papers: Hearings before a Subcomm. of the House Comm. on Gov't Operations,* 92d Cong., 1st Sess., pt. 1, at 12 (1971). See, also, *id.* at 97 (statement of William Florence, retired civilian security classification policy expert) (estimating that 99.5 percent of all Defense Department classified information could be released without prejudicing defense interests); *id.,* pt. 3, at 791 (statement of then–Assistant Attorney General William Rehnquist) (agreeing that government officials have persistent tendency to overclassify).

52. See, *e.g.,* Abourezk v. Reagan, 785 F.2d 1043 (D.C. Cir. 1986), *aff'd by an equally divided Court,* 108 S. Ct. 252 (1987); Allende v. Shultz, 845 F.2d 1111 (1st Cir. 1988); Randall v. Thornburgh, 854 F.2d 472 (D.C. Cir. 1988), *cert. denied,* 109 S. Ct. 3186 (1989); Shapiro, "Ideological Exclusions: Closing the Border to Political Dissidents," 100 *Harv. L. Rev.* 930 (1987).

53. See Regan v. Wald, 468 U.S. 222 (1984); Haig v. Agee, 453 U.S. 280 (1981); Walsh v. Brady, Civ. No. 89-1112-GAG (D.D.C. filed Apr. 25, 1989) (charging that the Treasury's Cuban Assets Control Regulations inhibit plaintiff's right to travel to Cuba for the purpose of importing Cuban posters to the U.S.).

54. See Meese v. Keene, 107 S. Ct. 1862 (1987); Bullfrog Films, Inc. v. Wick, 646 F. Supp. 492 (C.D. Cal. 1986), *aff'd,* 847 F.2d 502 (9th Cir. 1988) (invalidating under First and Fifth Amendments U.S. Information Agency regulations regarding exemptions of certified material from customs duties and licensing requirements); Palestine Information Office v. Shultz, 853 F.2d 932 (D.C. Cir. 1988) (closing Palestine Information Office in Washington, D.C. pursuant to the Foreign Missions Act).

55. See Comment, "The Press and the Invasion of Grenada: Does the First Amendment Guarantee the Press a Right of Access to Wartime News?" 58 *Temp. L.Q.* 873 (1985).

56. See United States v. Morison, 844 F.2d 1057 (4th Cir.) (upholding conviction under espionage and theft statutes of government employee who leaked classified information to press), *cert. denied,* 109 S. Ct. 259 (1988); American Foreign Service Ass'n v. Garfinkel, 109 S. Ct. 1693 (1989), *vacating and remanding* 688 F. Supp. 671 (D.D.C. 1988) (government employees' constitutional challenge to administration's use of secrecy pledge forms). See, also, Willard, "Law and the National Security Decision-making Process in the Reagan Administration," 11 *Hous. J. Int'l L.* 129, 132–37 (1988) (describing government's "anti-leak" efforts). These efforts have continued under the Bush administration. See, *e.g.,* Wines, "U.S. Intensifies Drive on Source of Press Leak," N.Y. Times, Aug. 24, 1989, at A21, col. 6; Noah, "Shhhhhh!" *New Republic* (Oct. 30, 1989): 8.

57. See "Mega-Spin Don," *New Republic* (Dec. 8, 1986): 11. See, generally, Abrams, "The New Effort to Control Information," N.Y. Times, Sept. 25, 1983, § 6 (Magazine), at 22.

58. See, *e.g.,* H.R. 1767, 101st Cong., 1st Sess., 134 *Cong. Rec.* H1028 (daily ed. April 11, 1989) (introduced by Representatives Berman, Miller, Frank, and Kastenmeier).

59. See 5 U.S.C. §§ 552(a)(3), 552(b)(1) (1982). See, also, *Litigation under the Federal Freedom of Information Act and Privacy Act* 21–36 (A. Adler ed.) (13th ed. 1988).

60. See *id.* § 552(a)(4)(B) (1982). See, also, S. Rep. No. 1200, 93d Cong., 2d Sess. 11–12 (1974) (articulating standards of judicial deference to agency affidavits under national-security exemption).

61. See Exec. Order No. 12,356, 3 C.F.R. 166 (1986), *revoking and superseding* Exec. Order No. 12,065, 3 C.F.R. 190 (1979).

62. See, *e.g.,* Miller v. Casey, 730 F.2d 773 (D.C. Cir. 1984); Taylor v. Dep't of the Army, 684 F.2d 99 (D.C. Cir. 1982).

63. Rostow, "Searching for Kennan's Grand Design," 87 *Yale L.J.* 1527, 1536 n.35 (1978).

64. A similar amendment was introduced in 1982 by Senator Durenberger. See S. 2452, 97th Cong., 2d Sess., 128 *Cong. Rec.* 8058–64 (1982).

65. See Exec. Order No. 12,065, § 3-303, 3 C.F.R. 190 (1979), *revoked and superseded by* Exec. Order No. 12,356, 3 C.F.R. 166 (1986); Ehlke & Relyea, "The Reagan Administration Order on Security Classification: A Critical Assessment," 30 *Fed. Bar J.* 91, 97 n.42 (1983).

66. *Cf.* Goldberg v. U.S. Dep't of State, 818 F.2d 71, 77 (D.C. Cir. 1987) (under FOIA courts should accord "substantial weight" to agency affidavits "without relinquishing their independent responsibility" to determine the propriety of classification decisions) (emphasis omitted).

67. Sharpe, "The Real Cause of Irangate," 68 *Foreign Pol'y* 19 (1987); Lobel,

"Emergency Power and the Decline of Liberalism," 98 *Yale L.J.* 1385, 1423–30 (1989).

68. Sharpe, *supra* note 67, at 38. Professor Lobel similarly suggests: "The answer to abuse of executive power [does not lie in] the reform of insufficient laws, but rather . . . [in] the dissipation of the 'forces, motives and fears which underlie the exercise and the rationale of excessive presidential power.' " Lobel, *supra* note 67, at 1425 (citation omitted).

69. Bork, Foreword to *The Fettered Presidency, Legal Constraints on the Executive Branch* i, xi, xii (L. Crovitz & J. Rabkin eds. 1989) (citation omitted) [hereinafter *The Fettered Presidency*]. Accord, Bator, "Legalistic Constitutionalism and Our Ineffective Government," in *The Fettered Presidency, supra,* at 265, 271 ("We are witnessing an expansion of the hegemony of our highly legalistic system of formal constitutionalism over an ever-widening domain of government policy making").

70. Nor could any conscientious lawyer do so, mindful of Grant Gilmore's wonderful caveat that "[i]n Hell there will be nothing but law, and due process will be meticulously observed." G. Gilmore, *The Ages of American Law* 111 (1977).

71. I am grateful to Professor Burt Neuborne for this "Berraism."

72. As former Senate Foreign Relations Committee Chairman J. William Fulbright recalled:

> The trouble with the resurgent legislature of the late 1970s is that it went in the wrong directions too often, carping and meddling, in the service of special interests, not engaging in reflective deliberation on basic issues of national interest. This tendency, once again, is tied to the general weakening of the party and leadership system in the Congress, which in turn has made Congress more susceptible to the pressures of special interests than previously. The executive thus with some justification complains about congressional incursions on its flexibility and its ability to make important decisions, or about Congress locking it in with legislative prohibitions. What executive branch officials choose to ignore is that Congress has been driven to this from the years of ignored advice.

J. Fulbright, *The Price of Empire* 72 (1989).

73. Asking who should safeguard the Republic from future Iran-contra affairs, Justice Hans Linde put the point eloquently:

> We are looking . . . for something with these characteristics: (1) It must be a permanent institution, with authority beyond that of its changing members; (2) it must be nonpartisan and independent of Congress and the President, and seen to be so; (3) it must explain its conclusions publicly, not advise in secret; (4) it must have some factfinding procedures if facts are decisive; (5) it must maintain a long view, beyond the exigencies of the immediate case; and (6) it must have enough other work so that a constitutional case is the exception rather than its *raison d'être.* . . .
> We do not have to search far for a body that meets these criteria. It is a court.

Linde, "A Republic . . . If You Can Keep It," 16 *Hastings Const. L.Q.* 295, 307–8 (1989).

74. See, *e.g.*, Chevron U.S.A., v. Natural Resources Defense Council, 467 U.S. 837, 865–66 (1984) (deferring to agency discretion). See, generally, Starr, "Judicial Review in the Post-*Chevron* Era," 3 *Yale J. on Reg.* 283 (1986).

75. See Schuck, "The Transformation of Immigration Law," 84 *Colum. L. Rev.* 1, 17 (1984).

76. No fewer than four members of the current Supreme Court—Chief Justice Rehnquist and Justices White, Marshall, and Scalia—previously held high executive branch positions.

77. See Koh, *supra* note 27, at 185–89. For a recent statement of this view, see Abourezk v. Reagan, 785 F.2d 1043, 1063–64 (D.C. Cir. 1986) (Bork, J., dissenting); see, also, Mathews v. Diaz, 426 U.S. 67 (1976); Kleindienst v. Mandel, 408 U.S. 753 (1972).

78. Amar, "Of Sovereignty and Federalism," 96 *Yale L.J.* 1425, 1495 (1987).

79. Myers v. United States, 272 U.S. 52, 293 (1926) (Brandeis, J., dissenting).

80. See, *e.g.*, Crovitz & Rabkin, Introduction to *The Fettered Presidency, supra* note 69, at 1, 3 (criticizing "excessive reliance on legal standards in the formulation or control of public policy").

81. See, generally, Franck, "Improving the Performance of Congress in Foreign Policy," 11 *Geo. Mason U. L. Rev.* 183, 188–89 (1988).

CHAPTER 9: A NATIONAL SECURITY CONSTITUTION FOR THE POSTHEGEMONIC AGE

1. Krauthammer, "Divided Superpower," *New Republic* (Dec. 22, 1986): 14, 16, 17 [hereinafter "Divided Superpower"]; *accord,* Krauthammer, "The Price of Power," *New Republic* (Feb. 9, 1987): 23 ("Imperial responsibility demands imperial government, which naturally encourages an imperial presidency, the executive being (in principle) a more coherent and decisive instrument than its legislative rival"); Sharpe, "The Real Cause of Irangate," 68 *Foreign Pol'y* 41 (1987) ("It is not national security but pursuit of empire that clashes with constitutional democracy"); see, also, Lobel, "Emergency Power and the Decline of Liberalism," 98 *Yale L.J.* 1385, 1426–27 (1989).

2. P. Kennedy, *The Rise and Fall of the Great Powers* 524–25 (1987); see, also, Strange, "The Persistent Myth of Lost Hegemony," 41 *Int'l Org.* 551, 572 (1987) ("The United States is ill-suited to sustaining . . . consistency in policymaking, partly by reason of its constitutional provisions").

3. See Sharpe, *supra* note 1; Lobel, *supra* note 1; see, also, Krauthammer, "Divided Superpower," *supra* note 1, at 17 ("Confronted with the choice [between fulfilling his obligations as leader of a superpower and as leader of a democracy] a president must choose the latter").

4. See, *e.g.*, Bork, Foreword to *The Fettered Presidency, Legal Constraints on the Executive Branch* i, ix (L. Crovitz & J. Rabkin eds. 1989) [hereinafter *The Fettered Presidency*] ("America has usually prospered most in eras of strong presidents, and the state of today's world makes the capacity for strong executive action more important than ever").

5. See, *e.g.*, Cutler, "To Form a Government," 59 *Foreign Aff.* 126, 139 (1980); Committee on the Constitutional System, *A Bicentennial Analysis of the American Constitutional Structure* 12 (1987); J. Sundquist, *Constitutional Reform and Effective Government* 224–38 (1986).

6. See O. North, *Taking the Stand: The Testimony of Lieutenant Colonel Oliver North* 12, 256, 525–27 (1987).

7. See *Newsweek* (Aug. 13, 1987): 16 (statement of Secretary of State Shultz, quoting President Reagan).

8. C. Rossiter, *Constitutional Dictatorship: Crisis Government in the Modern Democracies* (1948).

9. See Schlesinger, "The President's Prerogative As Commander-in-Chief," in *The President: Roles and Powers* 353 (D. Haight & L. Johnson eds. 1965); A. Schlesinger, *The Imperial Presidency* viii–ix (1973) ("Especially in the twentieth century, the circumstances of an increasingly perilous world as well as of an increasingly interdependent economy and society seemed to compel a larger concentration of authority in the Presidency").

10. Fulbright, "American Foreign Policy in the Twentieth Century under an Eighteenth-Century Constitution," 47 *Cornell L.Q.* 1, 2 (1961) (issue is "whether in the face of the harsh necessities of the 1960s we can afford the luxury of 18th century procedures of measured deliberation").

11. For symbolic confirmation of the waning of the cold war, see the article by George Kennan, the author of the famous 1947 "X" article on containment, entitled "After the Cold War," N.Y. Times, § 6 (Magazine) Feb. 5, 1989, at 32. See, also, Schlesinger, "Somebody Tell Bush We've Won the Cold War," Wall St. J., May 17, 1989, at A18, col. 3; "The Cold War Is Over," N.Y. Times, Apr. 2, 1989, at 30, col. 1 (editorial); Allison, "Success Is within Reach," N.Y. Times, § 4, Feb. 19, 1989 at 19, col. 2; Krauthammer, "Beyond the Cold War," *New Republic* (Dec. 19, 1988): 14; Mandelbaum, "Ending Where It Began," N.Y. Times, Feb. 27, 1989, at A19, col. 1; "After the Cold War," *Newsweek* (May 15, 1989): 20.

12. See, *e.g.*, Trimble, "The Constitutional Common Law of Treaty Interpretation: A Reply to the Formalists," 137 *U. Pa. L. Rev.* 1461, 1477 (1989) ("diminution of presidential power . . . would undermine important elements of the prevailing ideology of United States foreign policy. . . . [T]he critics of presidential power are implicitly attacking the vision of American world leadership that is fundamental to the national self-image. That leadership would be significantly less effective in a world of formal congressional co-determination of specific decisions in foreign policy").

13. See, *e.g.*, G. Allison & P. Szanton, *Remaking Foreign Policy* (1976); Clarke, "Why State Can't Lead," 66 *Foreign Pol'y* 128 (1987); Gelb, "Why Not the State Department?" in *Decisions of the Highest Order: Perspectives on the National Security Council* 229, 240–41 nn.1 & 16 (K. Inderfurth & L. Johnson eds. 1988); Rockman, "America's *Departments* of State: Irregular and Regular Syndromes of Policy Making," 75 *Am. Pol. Sci. Rev.* 911 (1981) (all noting problems in State Department decision making).

14. Youngstown Sheet & Tube Co. v. Sawyer, 343 U.S. 579, 585 (1952) ("The President's power, if any . . . must stem either from an act of Congress or from the Constitution").

15. *Cf.* George, "The Case for Multiple Advocacy in Making Foreign Policy," 66 *Am. Pol. Sci. Rev.* 751 (1972) (urging similar adversarial review with regard to policy initiatives); Sunstein, "Constitutionalism After the New Deal," 101 *Harv. L. Rev.* 421, 452–500 (1987) (urging replication of constitutional checks and balances in the executive structure of domestic regulatory administration).

16. See, generally, A. Chayes, *The Cuban Missile Crisis: International Crises and the Role of Law* (1974); "Introduction and Summary, Opinions of the Attorney General and of the Office of Legal Counsel relating to the Iranian Hostage Crisis, November 7, 1979, through February 5, 1981," 4A *Op. Off. Legal Counsel* 71–114 (1980) (describing role of legal opinions in Iranian hostage crisis).

17. See, *e.g.*, Trimble, *supra* note 12, at 1477.

18. Youngstown Sheet & Tube Co. v. Sawyer, 343 U.S. 579, 637 (1952) (Jackson, J., concurring).

19. A. Schlesinger, *supra* note 9, at x (emphasis in original).

20. See, *e.g.*, Oreskes, "Senate Rejects Tower, 53–47," N.Y. Times, Mar. 10, 1989, at A1, col. 6; "The Iran-Copter Affair," N.Y. Times, May 22, 1989, at A16, col. 1 (editorial) (describing confirmation battles over appointments of John Tower, Donald Gregg, and John Negroponte); Engelberg & Rasky, "White House, Noriega, and Battle in Congress," N.Y. Times, Oct. 25, 1989, at A10, col. 1.

21. "Message to the Senate Returning Without Approval the Bill Prohibiting the Export of Technology, Defense Articles, and Defense Services to Codevelop or Produce FS-X Aircraft With Japan," 25 *Weekly Comp. Pres. Doc.* 1191, 1192 (July 31, 1989); Scally, "Bush Vetoes Sanctions Bill Because of 'Iran-Contra' Provision," Reuters, Nov. 21, 1989 (vetoes of 1990 foreign-aid and State Department authorization bills).

22. See, *e.g.*, Kissinger & Vance, *Bipartisan Objectives for American Foreign Policy*, 67 *Foreign Aff.* 899, 901 (1988) ("A relationship of trust between the Congress and the White House is essential, even with policy differences").

23. Although historical examples date back to well before the Senate's 1919 rejection of the Versailles Treaty, the most recent example has been the Senate's imposition of the Byrd amendment upon its advice and consent to ratification of the Intermediate Nuclear Forces Treaty. See *supra* chapters 2 and 7; "Message to the

Senate on the Soviet-United States Intermediate-Range Nuclear Force Treaty," 24 *Weekly Comp. Pres. Doc.* 779, 780 (June 10, 1988). See, also, Oreskes, "An 'Imperial Congress' in Conservatives' Sights," N.Y. Times, Mar. 27, 1989, at B13, col. 5.

24. *Hearings before the Subcomm. on Legislation of the House Permanent Select Comm. on Intelligence on H.R. 3822, to Strengthen the System of Congressional Oversight of Intelligence Activities in the United States,* 100th Cong., 2d Sess. 99 (1988) (testimony of Rep. Lee Hamilton) ("Congress cannot, without seriously eroding its powers, accept the notion that some secrets can be held only by the Executive Branch, and not by the leadership of the Congress").

25. As shown in chapter 6, the Supreme Court rejected the former decision in *Youngstown* and tolerated the latter in *Goldwater* v. *Carter.*

26. *Cf.* Friedman, "Baker Says Accord on Contra Aid Enhances Powers of the President," N.Y. Times, Mar. 27, 1989, at A10, col. 1.

27. See, generally, A. Bickel, *The Least Dangerous Branch* 183–98 (1962); J. Choper, *Judicial Review and the National Political Process: A Functional Reconsideration of the Role of the Supreme Court* 217–315 (1980); Scharpf, "Judicial Review and the Political Question: A Functional Analysis," 75 *Yale L.J.* 517 (1966) (offering another "functional" approach); Wechsler, "Toward Neutral Principles of Constitutional Law," 73 *Harv. L. Rev.* 1, 7–8 (1959); see, also, *Marbury* v. *Madison,* 5 U.S. (1 Cranch) 137 (1803) ("Questions in their nature political, or which are, by the constitution and laws, submitted to the executive, can never be made in this court."). For a similar categorization of approaches to the political question doctrine, see L. Tribe, *American Constitutional Law* 96–107 (2d ed. 1988).

28. Ramirez de Arellano v. Weinberger, 745 F.2d 1500, 1514 (D.C. Cir. 1984) (en banc), *vacated on other grounds,* 471 U.S. 1113 (1985).

29. See Henkin, "Is There a 'Political Question' Doctrine?" 85 *Yale L.J.* 597, 606 (1976) (in most cases, the Court "does not refuse judicial review; it exercises it"). *Accord,* Henkin, "Viet-Nam in the Courts of the United States: 'Political Questions,' " 63 *Am. J. Int'l L.* 284, 286 (1969) ("In regard to foreign affairs, I believe, the Supreme Court has never found a true 'political question' "). *Cf.* Ely, "Suppose Congress Wanted a War Powers Act That Worked," 88 *Colum. L.Rev.* 1379, 1407 (1988) ("it's not even clear that it is a 'doctrine': even in its heyday it was never more than a congeries of excuses for not deciding issues otherwise properly before the court. Most have been eliminated by the Supreme Court").

30. See, *e.g.,* Redish, "Judicial Review and the 'Political Question,' " 75 *Nw. U.L. Rev.* 1031, 1033 (1985); Tigar, "Judicial Power, the 'Political Question Doctrine' and Foreign Relations," 17 *UCLA L. Rev.* 1135, 1141–52 (1970); Tigar, "What the Constitution Means by Executive Power," 43 *U. Miami L. Rev.* 177 (1988).

31. As I argue below, Professor Bickel's view favoring broader application of the doctrine, based on prudential factors, fades away upon closer examination. Simi-

larly, Dean Choper's "functional" claim could not support judicial refusal to decide cases brought to enforce a national security charter. For the major political weapon that Congress has to protect itself from the president is the passage of a statute. If Congress were to enact such a statute to reassert its national security role, it would be bizarre to cite Choper's rationale to justify judicial refusal to enforce that quintessential form of congressional self-protection. For other critiques of the Choper approach, see Redish, *supra* note 30, at 1057–59; Ely, *supra* note 29, at 1411 ("I doubt that Choper would apply [his own rationale] when a statute directed otherwise"); Tribe, "On Reading the Constitution," 1988 *Utah L. Rev.* 747, 768–69.

32. See Henkin, *supra* note 29, 85 *Yale L.J.* at 612 ("None of the [foreign affairs cases] . . . involved abstention from judicial review, or other extraordinary deference to the President. *In none of them did the Court refuse to consider whether the President had exceeded his constitutional authority; rather, it concluded that the President's decision was within his authority and therefore law for the courts*") (emphasis added).

33. Baker v. Carr, 369 U.S. 186, 211–13 (1962) (finding that courts had historically construed treaties and statutes that conflicted with treaties, applied statutes to recognized territories, construed proclamations of belligerency abroad and executive determinations of foreign diplomatic status, and evaluated claims of foreign sovereign immunity). Significantly, the Court in *Baker* also declined to apply the political question doctrine to the particular facts before it. *Id.* at 226–37.

34. See, *e.g.*, United States v. Belmont, 301 U.S. 324 (1937) (construing executive agreement); Sumitomo Shoji America v. Avagliano, 457 U.S. 176 (1982) (construing treaty); The Paquete Habana, 175 U.S. 677 (1900) (ruling on matter of customary international law).

35. See, *e.g.*, INS v. Chadha, 462 U.S. 919, 942 (1983) ("Resolution of litigation challenging the constitutional authority of one of the three branches cannot be evaded by courts because the issues have political implications"). Although greater judicial deference to the executive may be warranted in cases where no interbranch dispute exists, such a rationale would not apply when a constitutional impasse arose between two political branches. See Barnes v. Kline, 759 F.2d 21 (D.C. Cir. 1985), *vacated as moot sub nom.* Burke v. Barnes, 479 U.S. 361 (1987).

36. See, *e.g.*, New York Times Co. v. United States, 403 U.S. 713 (1971); Kent v. Dulles, 357 U.S. 116 (1958); Faruki v. Rogers, 349 F. Supp. 723, 732 (D.D.C. 1972) (Wright, J.) ("Where constitutionally protected rights are at stake . . . notions of automatic deference disappear"). See, also, J. Choper, *supra* note 27, at 127–28, 169–70.

37. 478 U.S. 221, 230 (1986). *Accord,* INS v. Cardoza-Fonseca, 107 S. Ct. 1207, 1221 (1987) (quoting Chevron U.S.A. v. Natural Resources Defense Council, 467 U.S. 837, 843 n.9 [1984]) (reiterating that even in the immigration context

the "judiciary is final authority on issues of statutory construction"); Trans World Airlines, Inc. v. Franklin Mint Corp., 466 U.S. 243 (1984) (adjudicating challenge based on federal regulations to liability limitations in a treaty); Romer v. Carlucci, 847 F.2d 445, 461–63 (8th Cir. 1988) (en banc) (whether Air Force deployment of MX missiles violates National Environmental Policy Act of 1969 involves statutory interpretation and thus is not a political question); Committee of U.S. Citizens Living in Nicaragua v. Reagan, 859 F.2d 929, 932 (D.C. Cir. 1988) (deeming "reliance on the political question doctrine . . . misplaced" in case where individuals claimed deprivations stemming from war in Nicaragua).

38. *Webster v. Doe,* 108 S. Ct. 2047 (1988) (1947 act did not intend to preclude judicial review of a constitutional challenge to CIA employment termination decision).

39. *Cf.* Abourezk v. Reagan, 785 F.2d 1043 (D.C. Cir. 1986), *aff'd by equally divided Court,* 108 S. Ct. 252 (1987) (remanding case for further evidence that INS had previously construed statute to deny visas to aliens on ground that their entry would prejudice foreign policy); see, also, Abourezk v. Reagan, Civ. No. 83-3739, 1988 U.S. Dist. LEXIS 5203 (D.D.C. June 7, 1988), 1988 W. L. 59,640 (decision on remand ordering INS to issue visas).

40. On Congress's power to pass "statutes creating legal rights, the invasion of which creates standing, even though no injury would exist without the statute," see, *e.g.,* Linda R.S. v. Richard D., 410 U.S. 614, 617 n.3 (1973); Warth v. Seldin, 422 U.S. 490, 500 (1975); TVA v. Hill, 437 U.S. 153, 164 & n.15 (1978); Fallon, "Of Justiciability, Remedies, and Public Law Litigation: Notes on the Jurisprudence of *Lyons,*" 59 *N.Y.U. L. Rev.* 1, 48–56 (1984); Monaghan, "Third Party Standing," 84 *Colum. L. Rev.* 277, 313 (1984). On Congress's power to override official immunities, see, *e.g.,* Nixon v. Fitzgerald, 457 U.S. 731, 748–49 (1982); Harlow v. Fitzgerald, 457 U.S. 800, 818 n.31 (1982); Little v. Barreme, 6 U.S. (2 Cranch) 170, 178–79 (1804) (president's order to naval officer to seize foreign vessel did not immunize officer from action for damages arising under the statute). On Congress's power to override doctrine of equitable discretion, see, *e.g.,* Synar v. United States, 626 F. Supp. 1374, 1382 (D.D.C. 1986) (per curiam), *aff'd sub nom.* Bowsher v. Synar, 478 U.S. 714 (1986).

41. For the best-known elaboration of these prudential concerns, see, generally, A. Bickel, *supra* note 27, at 183–98. See, also, Scharpf, *supra* note 27, at 577. For convincing refutations of the same, see Redish, *supra* note 30, at 1045–55; Ely, *supra* note 29, at 1407–12.

42. Ramirez de Arellano v. Weinberger, 745 F.2d 1500, 1531 (D.C. Cir. 1984) (en banc), *vacated on other grounds,* 471 U.S. 1113 (1985). For a discussion of the rule in *Marbury,* see, generally, Amar, "*Marbury,* Section 13, and the Original Jurisdiction of the Supreme Court," 56 *U. Chi. L. Rev.* 443, 448 (1989).

43. Redish, *supra* note 30, at 1052.

44. See, *e.g.,* Buckley v. Valeo, 424 U.S. 1 (1976) (per curiam) (declaring unconstitutional portions of Federal Election Campaign Act); Bowsher v. Synar, 478

U.S. 714 (1986) (invalidating portions of Gramm-Rudman-Hollings budget-balancing act).

45. See Northern Pipeline Constr. Co. v. Marathon Pipe Line Co., 458 U.S. 50 (1982) (declaring bankruptcy statute unconstitutional, but staying judgment until Congress could repair constitutional defects).

46. See Koh, "Civil Remedies for Uncivil Wrongs: Combatting Terrorism through Transnational Public Law Litigation," 22 *Tex. Int'l L.J.* 169, 202–08 (1987) (discussing these doctrines).

47. *Cf.* Henkin, "The Supreme Court, 1967 Term—Foreword: On Drawing Lines," 82 *Harv. L. Rev.* 63, 91 (1968) (questioning Supreme Court's refusal to hear cases challenging constitutionality of the Vietnam War) ("I should be happier . . . if the Court would demonstrate that the decision to hear or not to hear a constitutional claim is based on something sturdier than caprice").

48. Narenji v. Civiletti, 617 F.2d 745, 748 (D.C. Cir. 1979) (Robb, J.), *cert. denied,* 446 U.S. 957 (1980).

49. Ramirez de Arellano v. Weinberger, 745 F.2d 1500, 1566 (D.C. Cir. 1984) (en banc) (Scalia, J., dissenting).

50. *Id.* at 1543–44 (Wilkey, J.) (emphasis in original) (footnote omitted). Judge Wilkey, formerly the assistant attorney general for the Office of Legal Counsel of the Department of Justice, is currently the U.S. ambassador to Uruguay.

51. See Lobel, *supra* note 1, at 1426–27 (arguing that the U.S. should discard "pervasive anti-communism . . . relinquish the prevailing assumption that our national security requires the prevention or overthrow of leftist revolutionary governments throughout the world . . . move to end the cold war" with the Soviet Union, and increase "reliance on multilateral political, economic, and judicial institutions to resolve international problems"); see, also, Sharpe, *supra* note 1; Krauthammer, "Divided Superpower," *supra* note 1.

52. See, *e.g.,* Turner, "Separation of Powers in Foreign Policy: The Theoretical Underpinnings," 11 *Geo. Mason U.L. Rev.* 114, 116 (1988) ("We live in a dangerous world. . . . [Congress's] botched efforts to tie the president's hands and seize control of the nation's foreign policy have produced many tragic consequences [which] should make all of us realize how wise our Founding Fathers really were in vesting primary responsibility for foreign intercourse to the president"). See, also, Trimble, *supra* note 12; Block, Casey, & Rivkin, "The Senate's Pie-in-the-Sky Treaty Interpretation: Power and the Quest for Legislative Supremacy," 137 *U. Pa. L. Rev.* 1481 (1989); Fein & Reynolds, "Don't Constrain Presidential Diplomacy," Legal Times, July 31, 1989, at 18, col. 1; Cooper, "What the Constitution Means by Executive Power," 43 *U. Miami L. Rev.* 165 (1988); Rostow, "What the Constitution Means by Executive Power," 43 *U. Miami L. Rev.* 188 (1988); J. Moore, *Government under Law and Covert Operations* (1980), *reprinted in* House Select Comm. to Investigate Covert Arms Transactions with Iran and Senate Select Comm. on Secret Military Assistance to Iran and the Nicaraguan Opposition, *Report of the Congressional Comms. Investigat-*

ing the Iran-Contra Affair, 100th Cong., 1st Sess., S. Rept. 216, H. Rept. 433, 614 (1987) (minority report). *Cf.* Trimble, "The President's Foreign Affairs Powers," 83 *Am. J. Int'l L.* 750 (1989) (more moderate statement of this position).

53. *Compare* Cooper, *supra* note 52, at 177 ("the understanding of article II displayed by Washington, Madison, Hamilton, and Jefferson indicates that the conduct of foreign relations is an aspect of the executive power entrusted to the President, subject only to narrowly defined exceptions") *with* L. Levy, *Original Intent and the Framers' Constitution* 53 (1988) ("Nowadays, leading supporters of a constitutional jurisprudence of original intent are advocates of inherent presidential powers in the field of foreign relations, a stance that sheds light on either their ignorance or their hypocrisy").

54. See, *e.g.,* Kristol, "The Virtues and Vices of Democracy in Conducting Foreign Affairs," 43 *U. Miami L. Rev.* 211, 220 (1988) ("I hope we will soon have a President who understands that the dynamics of American foreign policy are between the President and the American people, and that [Congress and the State Department] do not matter when these dynamics are correct").

55. For a compelling explication of this point and its relevance to foreign affairs, see L. Henkin, *Constitutionalism, Democracy and Foreign Affairs* 12–23 (unpublished manuscript, forthcoming 1990).

56. Myers v. United States, 272 U.S. 52, 293 (1926) (Brandeis, J., dissenting).

57. See R. Dworkin, *Taking Rights Seriously* 134–49 (1977) (drawing distinction between concept and conception).

58. See, *e.g.,* Cutler, *supra* note 5, at 139; Committee on the Constitutional System, *supra* note 5, at 12; J. Sundquist, *supra* note 5, at 224–38.

59. Perpich v. United States Department of Defense, 1988 U.S. App. LEXIS 16,494 (8th Cir. Dec. 6, 1988); *vacated,* 1989 U.S. App. LEXIS 2,104 (8th Cir. Jan. 11, 1989), *dist. ct. judgment aff'd,* 1989 U.S. App. LEXIS 9,385 (en banc) (8th Cir. June 28, 1989).

60. Youngstown Sheet & Tube Co. v. Sawyer, 343 U.S. 579, 654 (Jackson, J., concurring).

Index